REVEALING THE SACRED IN ASIAN AND PACIFIC AMERICA

REVEALING THE SACRED
IN ASIAN AND PACIFIC AMERICA

EDITED BY JANE NAOMI IWAMURA AND PAUL SPICKARD

ROUTLEDGE • NEW YORK AND LONDON

Published in 2003 by
Routledge
29 West 35th Street
New York, NY 10001
www.routledge-ny.com

Published in Great Britain by
Routledge
11 New Fetter Lane
London EC4P 4EE
www.routledge.co.uk

Routledge is an imprint of the Taylor & Francis Group.

Cataloging-in-Publication Data is available from the Library of Congress.
ISBN 0-415-93807-4 (hb)
ISBN 0-415-93808-2 (pb)

To

Mitsuko Iwamura

and

Henry and Dilling Yang

CONTENTS

ACKNOWLEDGMENTS

The editors wish to thank our colleagues in the Asian and Pacific American Religions Research Initiative (APARRI) and in the Asian North American Religions, Culture, and Society group (ANARCS) of the American Academy of Religion for the road they have traveled with us. Some of them are authors of chapters in this book. Others contributed to APARRI conferences and ANARCS sessions. All of them have helped shape our thinking and indeed the field of Asian and Pacific American religious studies.

We are grateful to our home institutions, the University of Southern California and the University of California, Santa Barbara, for supporting our work as well as providing congenial environments for scholarly and spiritual reflection. We are also indebted to the sharp and insightful minds of our students and teaching assistants, who read through many of these chapters and provided invaluable comments and criticisms. Jane especially would like to thank Shivana Khanna and her students in Religion 336 (Fall 2001) and Paul would like to thank Kathleen Garces-Foley. Karen Yonemoto and Dianna Truong have provided invaluable assistance during the indexing and proofing stages of the manuscript, and we would like to thank them for their conscientious work and cheerful support.

We acknowledge with gratitude the financial support that several offices and agencies of the University of California provided for APARRI conferences that contributed to this volume: the UCSB Office of the Chancellor, the UCSB College of Letters and Science (in particular Dean Ed Donnerstein and Provost Everett Zimmerman), the UCSB Departments of Religion and Asian American Studies, the UCSB Center for the Study of Religion, the UCSB Interdisciplinary Humanities Center, the UC Berkeley Townsend Center for the Humanities, the UC Office of the President's Office of Research, and the UC Pacific Rim Research Program. We also appreciate grant support from the James Irvine Foundation, administered through the Program in American Studies and Ethnicity at the University of Southern California.

A number of individuals deserve special acknowledgment for the part they have played in supporting our work. We are grateful for the comradeship and encouragement of David Yoo, whose book *New Spiritual Homes* pioneered this field, and of Pyong Gap Min and Jung Ha Kim, who continued the work so ably with *Religions in Asian America.*[1] Both editors offer thanks to Wade Clark Roof, who has been a scholarly model and a steady supporter of the study of Asian and Pacific American religions; and to Fumitaka Matsuoka (and Chris Chua and Debbie Lee) for their visionary efforts at the Institute for Leadership Development and Study of Pacific and Asian North American Religion (PANA). We also offer our appreciation to Nick Street, our editor, who has provided critical feedback and unflagging support, and Damian Treffs and Henry Bashwiner for seeing the project through to completion. Jane Iwamura thanks Desmond Smith, and her parents, Seishi and Mitsuko Iwamura; Paul Spickard thanks Naomi Spickard and Daniel Spickard. Without them in our lives, most of this probably would not mean very much.

NOTES

1. David K. Yoo, ed., *New Spiritual Homes: Religion and Asian Americans* (Honolulu: University of Hawai'i Press, 1999); Pyong Gap Min and Jung Ha Kim, eds., *Religions in Asian America: Building Faith Communities* (Walnut Creek, CA: Altamira, 2002).

ENVISIONING ASIAN AND PACIFIC AMERICAN RELIGIONS

JANE NAOMI IWAMURA

Revelation is a tricky business. One can be struck with a vision or one can nurture one's insight through ritual contemplation and spiritual exercise. In the Buddhist tradition, enlightenment can be gradual or sudden. If one is Hindu, insight may be a life-long pursuit or it may come upon one in a dream. While distinctive in their particular cultural features, each of these experiential modes of transmission entails an utmost respect for the sacred and leads the devoted subject to a new way of seeing the world, a new way of being.

It is with this same reverence and respect that we approach the phenomena of Asian and Pacific American religions and seek to bring new perspective from the heart of an emerging field of scholarly enquiry. The sheer diversity of ethnic communities and religious traditions that fall under the rubric of Asian and Pacific America can make things feel and appear quite chaotic. Given the heterogeneous nature of Asian and Pacific American religions, it is not surprising for one to ask: what do Pacific Islander Mormons in Hawai'i have to do with Keralite Orthodox Christians in the Midwest or with Chinese Buddhists in California? Indeed, it seems difficult to make coherent sense of these various ways of life that—on the surface—seem to have little in common.

Scholars in the field of Asian and Pacific American religious studies have proceeded on a hunch, an intuition, that there is something worthwhile in presenting these different ethno-religious communities under the same rubric. At the most basic level, "Asian American/Pacific Islander" (API) serves as a salient marker of identity in the U.S. This racial category creates a space at the multicultural table for previously ignored, underrepresented points of view. The inclusion of the religious experience of Asian American communities and individuals thus broadens and enriches our general understanding of American religious life. The contributors to this volume also recognize the way in which racialization affects and influences the creation of religious community, as well as personal faith. Even within the seemingly protected spaces of Asian ethnic enclaves and mono-ethnic religious institutions, race has multiple effects on how APIs craft their religious identity, even if those effects are not readily apparent.

Once the dimension of race is squarely in focus, a more difficult set of questions begins to emerge: How does one begin to *reveal* the sacred in Asian and Pacific America given this context? Broadly speaking, how does one present a balanced portrait of the spiritual and the material, or (in Durkheim's classic phrase) the sacred and the profane? And again more specifically, how does one represent the complex, unique, and diverse ways in which religion is lived and practiced within a racialized arena? Each of the contributors to this collection negotiates these questions in distinctive and fruitful ways.

We, the editors, offer our own response in the way we have decided to organize the volume. In searching for an appropriate structure, we recognized several options available to us. The first would be to organize the readings according to religious tradition (Buddhism, Christianity, Hinduism, etc.). The second would have divided the contents according to ethnic group affiliation (Korean American, Filipino American, Indian American, etc). A third structure would have highlighted a particular theoretical concept or angle (e.g., congregations, acculturation). And finally, a fourth option would have led us to simply present the articles with a minimum level of formal organization to highlight the religious and ethnic diversity that exists in Asian and Pacific America.

Each of these delineations provides valuable perspective. However, in our minds, there is more to be realized and seen. In addition to conscientiously considering the process of racialization, we also wanted to represent Asian and Pacific American religions as *lived religions*. In many ways, the conventional categories of religious tradition and ethnic affiliation seem to artificially divide the religious experience of Asian American and Pacific Islanders into static arenas (e.g., Buddhist or Korean American) that do not capture the situational nature of API religious life (for example, how religious actors enact their faith commitments in creative response to their social environment). Furthermore, concentrating on a single theoretical aspect to interpret and understand an API ethno-religious community tends to say more about the theory at stake, than about the group at hand.

We are also not content simply to throw together articles in piecemeal fashion as a show of diversity. Although we have been careful to provide a range of perspectives, we feel obligated to offer some type of interpretive angle on lived religion in the Asian American/Pacific Islander context. On a practical level, we also seek to encourage a comparative perspective that highlights commonalities, but that at the same time is respectful of differences and tensions.

Our own attempt to envision Asian and Pacific American religions imaginatively is embedded in the way the contents of the volume are presented and structured. Each section is meant to highlight a particular aspect of API religious life:

> Orientation
> Spirit
> Context
> Practice
> Identity
> Community
> Reflection
> Legacy
> Texts
> Direction

However, in order to understand the overall logic of the volume, one needs to consider the linear presentation of the sections and essays in a more holistic sense. The multi-leveled schema below is more reflective of our approach:

The collection is framed by two pieces—*orientation* and *direction*. These

⟶ Orientation

Spirit   Context

Practice   Identity   Community

Reflection

Legacy   Texts

Direction ⟶

sections are meant to mark the academic location from which the contributors to this volume write. Although some of the authors are actively involved in the everyday life of the church, temple, mandir, or gurdwara, or at one time have had some type of personal experience as practitioners within Asian American religious communities, our discussion and analysis of API religious life is equally informed by our training as scholars in universities and theological seminaries. We bring critical tools from our academic backgrounds and disciplines to shed new light on the complex spiritual lives of APIs. Our work proceeds from a firm belief that the study of Asian and Pacific American religions represents a necessary component to both religious studies and Asian American Studies. We also hope that our efforts here will serve as a useful point of reflection for the communities and individuals about which we research and write.

The volume begins with Rudy V. Busto's introductory essay, "DisOrienting Subjects: Reclaiming Pacific Islander/Asian American Religions." Busto, through a mixture of story and analysis, offers *orientation* to the critical debates in the study of Asian and Pacific American religions and makes a compelling case for the need to see religion and race as inextricably linked within the API context. Although, as the title suggests, the piece is meant to "disorient" the reader— to unmoor the reader and lead her away from "orientalized" notions she might have about Asian and Pacific American religions—it also prepares new ground for us to think about and to reconceptualize API religions. As such, Busto's essay provides an indispensable entrée into the volume.

The sections, *spirit* and *context* immediately follow. Spirit and context— or, alternatively, spirituality and race—represent two defining elements of API religious life and experience that have not been given full consideration. The articles in the *spirit* section attest to the creative ways in which Asian and Pacific Americans understand, interact, are inspired, and offer unique expression to the sacred. For instance, William Kauaiwiulaokalani Wallace's personal narrative demonstrates a delicate negotiation between the folk religious beliefs of his Hawaiian ancestors and his faith in God as a Mormon. In the face of personal trial, Wallace invokes the powers of both religious systems in a strategic way. However, the significance of his story is not simply in the fact that it highlights the multiplex nature of his response, but also the way in which he is spiritually *moved* to address the situation. Similarly, Peter Yuichi Clark offers an in-depth look into the ethic of compassion among aging second-generation Japanese Americans (Nisei)—both Christians and Buddhists. While Japanese Americans—especially Buddhists—have been criticized for their unreflective devotion, Clark demonstrates that quite the opposite is the case. As a result his study challenges our conventional notions of faith and practice when it comes to understanding the religious lives of Asian and Pacific Americans, and suggests that there is much for our discernment and appreciation.

While "spirit" bespeaks the life-giving force and ethical impulse that sustains APIs, the essays in the following section highlight the *context* in which API religious lives are publicly carried out. Carolyn Chen's piece on the Dharma Light Temple—a Taiwanese American Buddhist temple in Southern California—serves to bridge spirit and context. It demonstrates the ways in which the institution's spiritual mission—its "transhistorical, transracial, indeed, universal ideals about the way that the world ought to be"—is both "constrained and inspired" by the contemporary discourse of multiculturalism in the U.S. Jaideep Singh and Paul Spickard offer a grimmer yet essential profile of Asian and Pacific American religious life. Their disturbing accounts not only shed light on the racist attitudes and actions that APIs must still confront, but also help us to see the not-so-obvious and insidious ways these attitudes are now expressed, even as they also highlight ways that APIs resist racial domination that comes in religious guise.

From here, the volume moves towards more in-depth analyses of everyday aspects of API religious life—*practice, identity,* and *community.* These sections, like others in the volume, are not meant to offer any sort of comprehensive picture (an impossible task), but rather to draw the reader's attention to contemporary issues that characterize our understanding of Asian and Pacific American religions. The articles in the section on *practice* by Pyong Gap Min, and Shampa Mazumdar and Sanjoy Mazumdar, can be productively read together and lead us to question the primacy of the church or temple as a necessary means of cultural survival. Min examines two mechanisms that allow Asian immigrants to maintain their ethnicity through religion: the ethnic congregation (e.g., Korean American Christians) and religious faith and rituals that are inextricable from ethnic culture (e.g., Indian American Hindus). Mazumdar and Mazumdar further demonstrate the way in which home altars and non-institutional practice play an important role in transmitting a sense of ethno-religious identity to second-generation Hindu Americans. Both articles represent preliminary research, but offer important points of discussion regarding the role and nature of religious practice and its relationship to Asian American ethnic identity.

In the section on *identity,* Thomas J. Douglas's piece highlights the tactical manner in which Cambodian Americans craft their religious identity so that is often not beholden to a single religious affiliation. Indeed, as the stories included in Douglas's article testify, Cambodian immigrants often criss-cross different religious institutions and employ identity markers from both the Christian and Buddhist traditions. As the author further argues, it is important to recognize this dimension of personal agency, especially among Cambodian Americans who live under the shadow of their refugee status and are stereotypically seen by the dominant culture as tragic victims and "impoverished dropouts". In the following essay, Sharon Suh demonstrates an alternative dynamic at work in Los Angeles Koreatown, where lines of religious affiliation, faith, and practice are more strictly drawn. As she explains, Korean American Buddhists at the Sa Chal temple lay claim to Koreanness through an essentialized notion of religious identity and gain a sense of mission from this identity.

The pieces in the *community* section investigate the social dynamics of religious group formation within Asian and Pacific America. Sheba George offers a complex portrait of the schisms within the Keralite Orthodox Christian church in the U.S. Gender, racialization, and changes in institutional structure are dimensions that contribute to the crisis the church suffers in its new context. George's analysis is significant in that it links internal division to something more than theological conflicts and disagreements. Russell Jeung's article documents the emergence of a new form of API religious community: the Asian American pan-ethnic church. While Asian mono-ethnic religious groups (e.g., Chinese American Baptists) rely upon a keen sense of their ethnic identity as the basis for community (Chinese-ness or Chinese American-ness), the isolation of a similar singular bond is more elusive when it comes to pan-ethnically defined religious institutions. Jeung demonstrates how these Christian organizations and their members have transformed a "political racial category"—Asian American—into a "symbolic racial identity" that is able to sustain religious community. The author also illuminates the different ways evangelical and mainline churches invoke this new racial identity and highlights how such a communal identity is fundamentally hybrid and fluid.

The sections on practice, identity, and community form one tier of understanding Asian and Pacific American religions. *Reflection* constitutes the next level of approach. Himanee Gupta, in her exploration of Hindu temple building and the politics of Indian American identity, recognizes the ways in which these architectural projects provide a means for Hindus in the U.S. to resist religious and cultural assimilation. However, she also highlights a contradictory effect of this trend, i.e., the way in which Hindu Americans lay claim to Indian American-ness (at the expense of Sikhs, Jains, and South Asian American Christians) through these spectacular and most public expressions. Controversial in nature, perspectives such as Gupta's demonstrate the contested nature of religious practice and therefore, serve as a valuable flashpoint for ongoing discussion.

From reflection, we move on to the penultimate tier of analysis—*legacy* and *texts*. In recent times, research on Asian and Pacific American religions has focused primarily on API immigrant groups—those peoples who have come to the U.S. since the passage of the 1965 Immigration Act. While such research is necessary and important, it overshadows careful consideration of APIs who have been here since before the dawn of the 20th century, and are still in existence today. Although these communities have their own unique sets of experiences, and although attitudes towards racial-ethnic minorities and non-Christian religious traditions have changed over the past century, these early communities are still worthy of serious consideration. Indeed, an understanding of Asian and Pacific American religions is incomplete without their representation. Their inclusion helps us realize that API religions have a long history in the U.S. And the struggles of these groups still have much to add to our understanding of the persistence of racialized meaning and of the ways API religious communities and individuals have responded to the challenges of racism.

Hence, we dedicate a section to the *legacy* of API religious forebears. Timothy Tseng in his essay on Chinese North American Protestants traces the historical shift from Chinese Americans' strong affiliation with mainline denominations to their involvement with independent, evangelical churches in the past half a century. What accounts for this religious and cultural "transposition" is complex. The historical perspective Tseng brings to our understanding of this shift sweeps back in time and across national boundaries. As a result, his piece displays the interconnectedness of historical moments and religious actors and reflects deep respect for the Chinese American religious congregational life about which he writes. In Joanne Doi's essay, Japanese Americans themselves enact this sense of interconnectedness with the past and with one another through participation in the annual pilgrimage to Tule Lake—one of the ten concentration camps where Japanese Americans were interned during World War II. Although the pilgrimage is a secular event, the elements of the journey and the meaning and experiences it creates for Japanese Americans take on a sacred quality. Doi's piece suggests how the spiritual can exceed the boundaries of what we recognize as "religious" (the temple, prayer, etc.), as well as the intricate ways that suffering and oppression can galvanize the soul of an ethnic community and give birth to new rituals of meaning.

In the following section, *texts*, Madeline Duntley and Sandra Oh bring attention to spiritual autobiographies that give voice to Asian American subjects. Duntley—by prominently highlighting the commemorative works published by Japanese American Protestant congregations in Seattle—helps us to appreciate these public expressions of faith and to reevaluate them as important resources for the historical understanding of these ethno-religious communities. Sandra Oh's look at Mary Paik Lee's autobiography, *Quiet Odyssey,* unveils the politics of scholarly interpretation of the primary text. Lee's work has become a staple in Asian American studies classrooms, as it is one of the few self-accounts that give witness to the experience of early Asian American immigrants, and specifically Korean American women of the period. Oh reframes Lee's autobiography to highlight the intricate nature of the protagonist's expression of religious belief that is complicated by gender, class, and nationalism.

Finally, we end with David Kyuman Kim's philosophical reflection on diaspora, race, and religion. Racial-ethnic identity for certain Asian and Pacific Americans, Kim argues, has become something more than a political category or a bio-cultural marker. In the contemporary environment of the U.S. in which "race matters" and where institutions informed by ethnic consciousness—such as Asian American and postcolonial studies—have gained a toehold, Asian American-ness itself takes on an almost sacred quality. Concepts that are meant to theoretically capture Asian American experience —for example, diaspora—become infused with religious and spiritual significance. In Kim's provocative essay, Asian American theory is in fact theology, as it seizes and gives formative expression to a new type of group consciousness.

In the above ways, the sacred in Asian and Pacific America is revealed at home and at church. It is also revealed in other, less likely, spaces as well. Yet there is still much to be recognized, studied, and learned from these vital ethno-religious communities and the stories that they tell. Like any revelation, the insight achieved in this volume is but a partial glimpse of things to come.

ORIENTATION

DISORIENTING SUBJECTS: RECLAIMING PACIFIC ISLANDER/ASIAN AMERICAN RELIGIONS

RUDIGER V. BUSTO

"What would be the implications for their unholy, double-freak souls were one to remain a disciple of the Great Buddha and the other half should be converted to the true gospel?"

BOSTON DAILY COURIER, SEPTEMBER 18, 1829

CONJOINED DISCIPLINES: GREAT BUDDHA OR TRUE GOSPEL? ASIAN AMERICAN STUDIES OR AMERICAN RELIGIONS?

According to the *Boston Daily Courier*, the religious lives of Asians and Pacific Islanders in the United States are an either/or proposition.[1] Either they are "other" and as such "disciples of the Great Buddha" or they desire to be like "us" and are to be "converted to the true gospel." Before the large scale arrival of Chinese in the 1840s, individual Asians and Pacific Islanders were unusual sights for most Americans. With the rare exception of individuals like Henry Obookiah, the Owyhee (Hawai'i) "pagan boy," whose 1809 Christian conversion in New England inspired Protestant missionary work in the Pacific, religion among Asians and Pacific Islanders in the United states has been of secondary interest in American religion and in the study of Asian American history.[2] Mostly, the early presence of Asians among the

American public occasioned simple curiosity. This is certainly true for the famous "Siamese Twins," Chang and Eng; the "double-freak souls" who occasioned the theological puzzle posed by a *Boston Daily Courier* journalist.

Recent interest in the conjoined Asian twins has hardly moved us away from the Asian-as-spectacle pattern set two centuries ago. Made famous by their association with P.T. Barnum's ongoing display of "freaks" and human oddities, Chang and Eng have been reintroduced to a new audience through the fictionalization of even the most intimate details of their lives. They have even appeared on billboards advertising an Internet service provider ("get linked"). While the Oriental-as-sideshow theme lives on, what remains hidden in the lives of Chang and Eng Bunker is an opportunity to disorient and disrupt assumptions and expectations that they be either disciples of the Great Buddha, or converts to the true gospel. After years of traveling the globe as living exhibits, Chang and Eng, like many Asians after them, decided to settle in the United States. For the most part the famous Asian immigrant brothers led spectacularly mundane lives. Eventually marrying a pair of rather doughty sisters they built twin residences in rural North Carolina and spent a good deal of their lives farming (with the assistance of slaves), and raising large families. By all accounts the Siamese Twins had the respect of their neighbors and managed their existence as well as could reasonably be expected given their physical abnormality. Ironically, when they did face discrimination it was because they were Chinese.[3] As it happened, Chang and Eng were also Baptists. In fact they donated property for the White Plains Baptist Church which they themselves in large part built; cutting and hauling wood, constructing the roof, and fashioning a special two-seater pew for themselves. Maybe they chose to be Baptist as a way to lessen their singularity, as sources indicate "they seem to have embodied a personal blend of Buddhist and Christian fundamentals" (which I suppose is appropriate for conjoined Asian twins in the United States). In the biographies of Chang and Eng, it is this last fact—their religious lives—that is somehow disorienting (disappointing?) and reveals the challenge and unexpected rewards of reclaiming Asian American and Pacific Islander religious history. For unlike the Protestant conversion of Henry Obookiah, whose tragic, "martyrlike death" from typhus seems tragically fitting, there is something unsettling yet tantalizing about the triple combination of Asianness, physical enfreakment, and the Baptist faith. [4]

The study of Pacific Islander and Asian American religions is still in its infancy. The effort grows at the nexus of Asian American studies and religious studies. And although there is much to be reclaimed by disorienting paradigms in these twin disciplines, the study of Asian American and Pacific

Islander religious traditions cannot survive without both of them. This essay ponders the study of Pacific Islander and Asian American religions and suggests how and why they cannot be contained or informed solely by either of the uncomfortably conjoined disciplines of religious/Asian American studies. The *Courier* recommended "separation of the unholy double-freak by surgical operation" as a solution to the Siamese Twin enigma. I am not so sure such a separation is useful for our task. After all, the twins survived intact and parented twenty-one children. We begin with three stories about Asian American/Pacific Islander religions, and conclude with some observations about the politics of knowledge.

THE SACRED STONES OF WAHIAWA

Story number one.
In the fall of 1927, word was out that a religious "cult" had organized around two sacred stones at Kukaniloko, "the birthplace of the ancient [Hawaiian] chiefs of highest rank" in the Oahu uplands. Two years prior the Daughters of Hawai'i (an organization devoted to the preservation of historic sites, started by the daughters of Protestant missionaries) "enclosed the ancient 'birthing' stone and another . . . within a wire fence and conducted appropriate dedication services." Local folklore attributing healing properties to the stones soon spread beyond the island attracting pilgrims from the diverse ethnic groups comprising Hawai'i's plantation workforce. According to one account: "People of all races began coming to the stones—Japanese, Chinese, Filipinos, Koreans, Hawaiians, Portuguese, Puerto-Ricans, Haoles, seeking relief from all kinds of ailments. Chinese, Japanese, and Filipinos were the most faithful devotees, some of them ascribing such power to the stones that it was thought dangerous to point their fingers at either stone, to take pictures of them, or to show disrespect in any way." [5]

Filipino laborers reported miraculous cures; a Korean woman who prayed there claims to have seen six angels hovering above the stones. An enterprising "self appointed Chinese priest received fees for his 'services' and from the sale of eucalyptus leaves from neighboring trees which were supposed to have certain curative values when used in the bath." A Korean "lay priest . . . went almost daily . . . and offered his prayers; drawing water from a nearby source, placing it before the shrine, pray[ing] over it and then drinking the 'holy water.' He claimed it gave him "strength and health." "One girl had a kodak picture . . . in which one could see an indistinct white form . . . slightly resembling a madonna and her child." A colorful pageant of pilgrims brought offerings of flowers, leis, and jewelry to adorn the stones.

Fruit and money were lovingly set at the base of the stones, and the curlicues rising from a forest of incense sticks added to the mystery of that sacred spot. One unlucky Filipino pilgrim "died instantly because he had sacrilegiously pushed aside the stones. . . . " Hot dog booths, lei stands, candle and joss-stick peddlers, refreshment dealers and concessions of all sorts appeared almost overnight. Weekends found crowds of believers and gawkers jockeying for a place at the fence's perimeter; the stones "literally buried in leis."[6]

Local residents, however, began to complain to the Board of Health about the unsanitary practices of the devotees who kissed and rubbed the stones. They also worried about the potential health hazard of decaying food, flowers, and other ritual detritus left behind by visitors. The president of the Board of Health called for calm, reassuring the residents that any pollution "would be taken care of by the elements . . . the sun and rain . . . act[ing] as sterilizing agents." A local doctor dismissed wholesale the "the Lourdes-like miracles of healing" as nothing more than "psychological auto-suggestion."[7] Still, thousands gathered each day to witness the healing powers of the stones or partake of their benefits. Eventually, as quickly and as impromptu as it had all started, and for no apparent cause, the crowds of worshippers disappeared.

Although short lived, the ritual practices and beliefs surrounding these stones seventy-five years ago remain an obscure event, a curious footnote buried in the history of Asian American/Pacific Islander history. The event is nevertheless oddly contemporary because it "reads" well through the theories and propositions favored in the current academic study of Asian American and Pacific Islanders. The themes of cultural hybridity and pan-ethnicity are immediately apparent. Indeed, one is tempted to see a veritable postmodern assemblage of practices, worldviews, and subject perspectives in the multiple readings of all those who approached the stones. And when framed from within the political-economy of Hawai'i's plantation capitalism, the account of this religious "cult" becomes fertile soil for academic models of social movements under situations of colonialism, and even demonstrates how religion does indeed serve up an opiate for the toiling, exploited masses.

However, before we get caught up in the rush to audition new academic interpretations, what occurred at Wahiawa reveals two indisputable facts. First, for the supplicants involved in the "cult" of the sacred healing stones, religious belief and practices "happened." That is, matters of health, life, happiness, and death were literally laid before the stones. Second, even in the scant and confusing sources about the uproar over the sacred healing stones, current theory and the cumulative knowledge about Asian American and Pacific Islander history and experience (hybridity, pan-ethnicity, transnational labor, assemblage, etc.) are already present. The "cult" also predates the current fashion in religious studies for transnational, multicultural, vernacular, lived, and hybrid expressions of religion.

Until very recently Asian American studies would have preferred to focus on the theoretical and methodological issues at the expense of the religious power and meaning contained in that nameless Korean woman's supplications that rewarded her with a vision of angels. Why this is so has much to do with the genealogy of theory in Asian American studies and particularly the debt to Marxian labor history and sociology. In addition to the negative bias (or at best a benign neglect) towards religion as a category of analysis in Asian American studies, praxis in Asian American activism has traditionally revolved around the urgent issues of community empowerment, racial discrimination, education reform, and poverty. Curiously, the community and activist praxis of Asian American and Pacific Islander religious organizations is rarely if ever acknowledged. Although the topic of religion has not been completely absent in Asian American studies, it continues to appear primarily as a sociological category (as an institution), as a part of a cultural inventory, or, as in Jan Nattier's provocative term about Asian American Buddhism nuances, "baggage." Only within the past decade has there been a focused and sustained effort at foregrounding religion in Asian American studies .[8]

Religious studies, however, has hardly fared any better with regard to Pacific Islanders and Asian Americans, especially with regards to Hawai'i. In his magisterial *A Religious History of the American People,* Sydney Ahlstrom considers Hawai'i's religious history in an ominously titled chapter, "Crusading Protestantism." Under the subheading "Missions and Empire," Hawai'i is his example of how Protestant foreign missions organizations successfully domesticated a foreign mission field. Ignoring the complex social processes that created Hawai'i, Ahlstrom sweeps aside the native Hawaiians and their feudal monarchy, applauding the "introduc[tion] of viable modern forms of government and lawmaking." Connecting Protestantism to modernity and civilization, he effectively dismisses Hawai'i's independent nation status prior to annexation. Nodding towards the importance of the economic engine driving Hawaiian society and the key role that immigrants play, Ahlstrom's erasure of native Hawai'i is complete as he divides religion in the Islands into Christians (read: Europeans) and "non-Christian elements" (read: Asians). He exults: "Nowhere else under the American flag, or any other flag, have the Orient and the Occident met and blended with such good will and amity."[9]

Edwin Gaustad's classic, *A Religious History of America,* plays off popular notions of "Oriental Religions" and ignores indigenous Hawaiians altogether. He laments the exclusionary immigration policies at the turn of the century which "led to sharp restrictions of those who would introduce Buddhism and

Shinto (i.e. the Japanese), even as the Chinese had brought with them Confucianism and Taoism." Note here the simple "world religions" enumeration of the traditions Asians are purported to represent in the West. Later, again describing the dramatic religious pluralism occasioned by Hawai'i's annexation by the U.S. in 1898, Gaustad sees Hawai'i as only a stepping stone, the "port of embarkation" for Buddhism, Confucianism, and Shinto to the mainland.[10]

More recently, Laurie Maffly-Kipp's valuable exploration of U.S. religion from a "Pacific Rim" perspective sees the study of religion in the Pacific arranged around colonialism and exchanges with Asia and Latin America. Indigenous religion in the Pacific is of no interest here despite three pages devoted to the idea of the Pacific Rim and Hawai'i's centrality in the traffic of religious movements across the Pacific. As an historian of the American West, Maffly-Kipp is predisposed to refer to the Pacific as "a vast liquid desert" rather than take into account the diversity of religious traditions and histories throughout the immense region.[11]

The treatment of Hawai'i, and the Pacific Islands in general, in Asian American studies has hardly fared any better than the narratives in American religious history. For Asian American scholars Hawai'i too often serves merely as a stage for the struggle between Yankee Puritan plantation owners and the toiling multiethnic proletariat. The geological accident that created the Hawaiian islands between Asia and California has meant, unfortunately, that in the formula: Asian American/Pacific Islander, "Pacific Islander" usually means the history of nonnatives in that virgin space between Asia and North America rather than Native Hawaiians, Samoans, Tongans, or Chamorros. Ronald Takaki's book, *Pau Hana: Plantation Life and Labor in Hawaii*, for example, avoids the distinctiveness of diverse Pacific cultures in favor of the collective proletariat and their common struggle against the plantation owners.[12]

The only substantive account of the 1927 events surrounding the Sacred Stones of Wahiawa similarly transfers our attention away from indigenous Hawai'i and towards non-Native religious beliefs and practices. Yet underneath the multicultural bricolage of prayers, gifts, and ritual actions directed at the stones, it is the ancient Hawaiian connection to the stones that lures the pilgrims. It is the spiritual aroma of Kukaniloko, the ancient, sacred Chief's birthing place that invites the miraculous cures. As recently as 1994, legend held that the larger of the two stones embodied "the white Hawaiian god Lono, the priest healer of ancient times," or that the pair entombed "two Hawaiian sisters from the island of Kauai, who were turned into stone."[13] Or so it would seem. Initial library research on the stones, however, revealed a confusion between the ancient royal birthing site of Kukaniloko and the sacred stones of Wahiawa. A long digression in J. Gilbert McAllister's study of archaeological sites on Oahu suggests that the large sacred healing stone is not original to the Kukaniloko sacred site, but that it had been dredged up from a nearby gulch by one Mr. George Galbraith who placed it among the Kukaniloko birthing stones. Because this stone stood higher than the others it naturally attracted attention. The stone was later moved by the Daughters of Hawai'i to another location in front of the California Avenue cemetery where it then became the object of veneration. McAllister offers another possible origin for the stone, quoting an earlier opinion that the stone originally served as a milestone marker "at the side of the old Hawaiian pathway" on the eastern side of the island.[14] We do not know the history of the second, smaller stone.

Further research turned up Vasudha Narayanan's 1992 description of Hindu temples in the United States and mention of the "birthing stone." Narayanan records that an India-based organization, the Lord of the Universe Society (acronym L.O.T.U.S.), intended to erect a permanent temple structure around the miraculous Sacred Healing Stone venerated now as a Shiva *linga*. Today, if you make your way through the streets of Wahiawa, you will find tucked along a side street a whitewashed concrete shrine with the healing stone firmly cemented in the center; adorned once again with garlands and swathed in incense. An online posting to Hindunet.org informs us that "through sunshine, rain and wind a cheerful group of worshippers has been gathering at the quaint open-air temple to partake in the ancient Pooja that is conducted regularly on a pre-appointed day of every month."[15]

"WHAT HAVE I DONE IN THIS STRANGE LAND?"

Story number two.
In 1905 a 29 year old man—let's call him "N.S."—traveled over the Pacific between Yokohama and San Francisco in the cargo hold of a steamer ship. Pulled by the promise of work and other opportunities in the United States, N.S. was among the 4,000 other Japanese immigrants making the long boat journey to California that year. Although drawn to the possibilities of economic success in the United States, in N.S.'s case an additional reason for leaving Japan was fear of retribution over his public condemnation of Japanese nationalism. Upon arrival he sought out an old friend among the 90,000 Issei (first generation Japanese immigrants) already living and working on the West Coast. After facing the gruff scrutiny of the immigration

inspectors, N.S. managed to avoid the labor contractors waiting to recruit new arrivals. With the assistance of his friend he landed his first job as a houseboy for a wealthy family along the windswept coast south of the city. However, unable to overcome the language barrier adequately and quickly enough to do his job, N.S. was soon dismissed and handed a five-dollar gold piece for his troubles. Thinking he would find consolation from his friend, he was abruptly abandoned by his companion in the middle of Golden Gate Park with the parting words, "Just face the great city and see whether it conquers you or you conquer it."[16]

Following the labor patterns of the Japanese "schoolboy" N.S. worked again as an "Oriental" houseboy, a job he may have landed through advertising in the "Situations Wanted" columns popular at the time. As he struggled to eke out a modest living, N.S. regularly took the ferry across the bay to Oakland to teach Japanese. When he could, he sat in the San Franscisco Public Library and read Thomas Paine, Ralph Waldo Emerson, and William James. With rising antagonism growing against the Japanese in San Francisco, and especially after the 1908 "Gentleman's Agreement" that ended Japanese immigration and capped anti-Japanese agitation, N.S. soon found himself unemployed. Like thousands of other out of work Japanese "boys" N.S. headed out of the city to look for work, joining the flood of 40,000 Japanese labor contract workers dislocated by the hostile situation in California.[17]

N.S. tried his hand at farm labor, becoming one of the faceless immigrant farm workers required to support California's corporate agricultural miracle. However, unlike many of his companions he was unaccustomed to backbreaking agricultural labor and resolved to find his way back into the city. By 1910 N.S. had returned to San Francisco and was lucky to find a job as a porter in a San Francisco hotel. He moved up to the position of clerk, and eventually manager. Six years later, perhaps through joining a rotating credit association with his friends, he was able to purchase half interest in a hotel, a common business enterprise among the Issei. Unfortunately, by then the Japanese population, his clientele, had dwindled to less than 1,000 in San Francisco. With Japanese immigration restriction laws in place his prospects for hosting new arrivals and transient laborers were dim. Many of the Issei had moved south or settled into homes with their families in the fertile Sacramento delta, or further inland throughout the San Joaquin Valley. After enduring the hardships of immigrant life and scraping by to make ends meet, N.S.'s attempt at success in a small business endeavor ended in dismal failure. He was forced to earn his living as a short order cook.[18]

Undefeated by years of anti-Asian caste and exclusion policies that marked the opening decades of this century, N.S. survived the dispiritedness and anger found in much of the immigrant Japanese community. "Like the carp, which they admired for its inner strength and intrepid spirit," Takaki writes, "the immigrants had swum against the currents of adversity; still, struggling upstream and climbing waterfalls in search of a calm pool where Japanese might live peacefully in America, they found themselves driven backward."[19]

Following the Japanese exodus south and unhampered by family life, N.S. moved to Los Angeles in 1929 or 1931. There anti-Japanese agitation was less intense and economic opportunities were relatively plentiful during the Depression. He rented a room in a residence hotel on Turner Street, comforted by the routines and sounds of the Japanese community around him and the familiar aromas of the Little Tokyo open air markets. No doubt lonely at times, N.S. managed, however, to avoid the "magic-three": the gambling dens of the Tokyo Club and Chinatown, drinking, and prostitution. He occasionally visited the Jodo Shin temple which was not, however, his chosen affiliation. By taking the odd job and teaching Japanese culture in his apartment, he usually managed to raise the $25 required for rent and utilities.[20]

In February, 1942, when President Roosevelt issued Executive Order 9066 that interned over 100,000 Japanese Americans, there is good reason to believe that N.S. had already been detained and later temporarily housed at the Pomona "Assembly Center." On September 5, he found time to write, "this morning, the winding train, like a big black snake, takes us away as far as Wyoming." N.S. was assigned to the Heart Mountain internment camp in northern Wyoming and spent three days traveling over the Rockies in a train heavily guarded by armed soldiers. There he endured the tedium of harsh winters and desolate windswept days in a small 20 x 20-foot wooden room he shared with a family of three. Having hastily packed his belongings, he relied upon his white friends to send him books that he could not bear to be without. "From the window of this cell," he wrote in November 1944, "I saw the stars strewn in the heavens, each twinkling its eternal loneliness. I lit the lamp til dawn and mused alone. What have I done in this strange land?"[21]

After his release from the internment camp in 1945, N.S. returned to Los Angeles—as rootless as he had been forty years earlier when he had been abandoned by his friend in Golden Gate Park. Too poor to afford decent housing, he returned to what was left of Little Tokyo and took a small apartment in a residence hotel. The tiny kitchen and the apartment's main room crowded with his books became his refuge from the hotel's other clients—whores, pimps, and numbers runners. One chilly evening in late October, standing alone on the street in the rain, N.S. remembered his friend, now dead, and composed a poem for him:

> *The cold rain purifies everything on the earth*
> *In the great city of Los Angeles, today.*
> *I open my fist and spread the fingers*
> *At the street corner in the evening rush hour.*[22]

The context for this poem, purposely omitted for this account, is in fact a religious one. The poem begins, "For forty years I have not seen / My teacher, So-yen Shaku, in person. / I have carried his Zen in my empty fist, / Wandering ever since in this strange land. . . . " Our Issei wanderer, it is now clear, opens his fist in order to spread the Buddhist dharma in the United States.

Although there is some acknowledgment of Buddhism's arrival in the United States with the Chinese in the 1840s, and with Shinshu Buddhist teachers in the 1870s, most of the academic attention to Buddhism's arrival in the United States has been drawn to the 1893 World's Parliament of Religions. There in Chicago, a drama unfolded that featured the Asian representatives of "Oriental" religions—men like Vivekananda, Dharmapala, and the Zen master, Shaku Soen (the "friend" to whom N.S.'s poem is dedicated). These articulate representatives explained and defended their traditions in front of large curious American audiences and at times found it necessary to criticize the triumphalist Protestantism of the Parliament's organizers.[23]

The well known narratives of Soen Shaku, his most famous student, D.T. Suzuki, and the establishment of Zen Buddhism in the U.S., however, are not the ones I recounted here. Rather, my story is a reconstructed Asian American version of the early years of the Zen teacher, Nyogen Senzaki, retold through the fragmented and scattered biographical remnants in the Zen in America literature. This body of scholarship/hagiography of the earliest Japanese Zen teachers is understandably focused on the transmission of the dharma in the West and is rarely concerned with the economic, political, or sociological contexts natural to Asian American studies.

Reading the Zen details back into our story, it is his teacher, Soen Shaku, whom Senzaki seeks out when he arrives in San Francisco. And it is his teacher who abandons him in Golden Gate Park, challenging him to take the Buddhist teachings into the world. In the Zen in America accounts, we are led to believe that the material basis for Senzaki's life is merely colorful details in the otherwise exceptional life of a Zen master. In this literature,

Senzaki's jobs as houseboy, cook, and migrant laborer are not essential for meeting the basic necessities of life so much as they are ways to earn money for renting public spaces for his lectures on Buddhism. To quote Rick Fields, from *How the Swans Came to the Lake*:

> . . . he would *simply* hire a hall whenever he had the money. Sometimes he would simply speak on Buddhism in a friend's parlor. He called the various meeting places "the floating zendo."[24]

Senzaki's famous innovative "floating Zendo" in San Francisco, and eventually in his Los Angeles home, may have "floated" more out of economic necessity than innovation if we consider the details of his economic life. Putting aside the established forms and rules of Japanese Zen Buddhism, Senzaki persevered in his adaptation of the Zen tradition in the United States even during his internment, gathering around him students that were also interned there. Curiously, the Zen in America narratives tend to depict him as merely waiting out the war, completely detached from the turmoil and racism of the internment experience and the internal factionalism rife among the Japanese internees.[24]

In the Buddhism in America accounts, Asian Buddhist teachers have set the pattern for other Asian masters who are remembered primarily for their influence on their *non*-Asian disciples and followers. As the first Zen teacher to take up permanent residence in the United States (so far as the Zen in America literature claims) Senzaki remains an important but lesser figure in the American Buddhism story, perhaps because he rejected the traditions of what he called "cathedral Zen" which was what most interested non-Asians. Unlike his more famous dharma brother, D. T. Suzuki, who attracted intellectuals and the "avant garde underground," and whose emphasis on the mysteries of "emptiness" and enlightenment were lapped up by the Beats, Senzaki was, according to Helen Tworkov, too "square" for the Beats. "I have neither an aggressive spirit of propaganda," he confessed, "nor an attractive personality to draw crowds." Whereas his teacher Soen Shaku, and D.T. Suzuki eagerly sought out the American public, Senzaki remained relatively isolated, always on the edge of poverty, working quietly but steadily to spread the Zen tradition.[25]

What is fascinating is the *absence* of these Zen teacher stories in Asian American histories even as they figure centrally in the Zen in America narratives. Similar to the function of Hawai'i in Asian American studies, Japanese Zen masters are "middle" locations between Asia and North America. The integral role that celebrity followers of Buddhism (Allen Ginsburg, Jack Kerouac, Richard Gere, and the Beastie Boys, for example) play in drawing attention to their teachers may explain why the lives and careers of Asian religious teachers remain beyond the interest of Asian American scholars. Yet other Asian religious leaders nowhere near the bright lights of Hollywood or on the university lecture tour remain obscure in both Asian American studies and the "Asian religions in America" literature. Who remembers, for example, Yoshiaki Fukuda, the founder of the Konko-Kyo Shinto tradition in the United States, who offered to care for the Japanese Peruvian internees when Peru refused to allow them to return after internment? Where in Asian American history, or in the Buddhism in America literature, is an account of the Diluv Khutagt, the Mongol "living Buddha," whose arrival in the U.S. predates by seven years the more famous Lamas, Geshes, Tulkus, and Rimpoches in bringing Tibetan Buddhism to the West? Or the names of the earliest Chinese religious teachers, Japanese Jodo Shin missionaries, Filipino Catholic priests, or the first Vietnamese Buddhist missionaries and teachers?[26]

Although my retelling of his biography has been strategically "de-religioned," Nyogen Senzaki and other Buddhist teachers do not easily fit into normative Asian American histories even though the material conditions for their daily existence in the United States were, for the most part, the same as for other Asians. Their religious status did not protect them from racial discrimination, stereotyping, violence or harassment. Senzaki, for example, grew his hair after "having once watched mischievous boys sneak up to rub Soyen Shaku's shaved head" on a San Francisco streetcar. Tworkov, however, interprets Senzaki's decision to grow his hair as a strategy to protect the dharma from ridicule rather than as a pragmatic way to protect himself from ruffians. On at least one occasion, Senzaki was too poor to pay his laundry bill and resorted to watching the laundry owner's disabled son in exchange. Shimano Eido, Senzaki's disciple, prefers however to see this reciprocity as "skillful means" for cultivating the assistance of the laundry owner's wife who later became Senzaki's caretaker. Admitting to the mutual benefit of the babysitting-for-laundry arrangement, Shimano finds, "the real significance of this encounter lies in a realm much deeper than that of mere exchange of labor. . . . "[27]

It is necessary, however, to note that bias against religious teachers like Senzaki in Asian American studies has also to do with the earliest primary sources for Asian American history. Yamato Ichihashi's authoritative *Japanese in the United States*, for instance, explains Japanese labor emigration as "impelled by desire for improvement rather than by the necessity of escaping the misery at home" as the "fundamental, positive cause of Japanese emigration." Sadly, he ignores the steady trickle of religious specialists, like Senzaki, whose main reason for emigration was in fact religion. "Neither religion nor politics constituted a cause for Japanese emigration," Ichihashi emphatically asserts.[28]

In general, Asian American history seems to have adopted two responses to religion in the early immigration period: religion is uninteresting, or it is about Christianity. Note, for instance, Ichihashi's transition to the topic of Buddhism after three pages devoted to Christianity: "While we are considering the subject of religion *a brief comment* may be made on Buddhism. . . . " He gives the dharma only three paragraphs, ending his comment with

> But while the good work of the successful [Jodo Shinshu] Buddhist missionaries is to be appreciated from a broad social standpoint, we must also recognize that since the net influence of the non-Christian institutions is to retard Americanization, the Buddhist enterprise may be considered unfortunate, particularly if it affects education of children.[29]

Thus, given Ichihashi's importance as a primary source for Japanesee American history, it is no wonder Senzaki's experience has been overlooked in the ethnic histories.

As "bridges" between the mysteries of Asian religions and philosophies and European Americans, the role of Asian "import/export" teachers now instructs us in their potential to transgress a formidable boundary between two distinct parallel histories. Asian American history does its work separately on one side, and the history of Asian religions in America on the other. What, for example, would it require to include the biographies of Nyogen Senzaki, Yoshiaki Fukuda, the Diluv Khutagt, or even Thich Nhat Hanh, alongside the lives of those presented by Takaki in *Strangers from a Different Shore*, or Sucheng Chan's narration of the devout Mary Paik Lee in *Quiet Odyssey*?[30] What is lost or gained by including the philosophical writings of Zen, Jodo Shin, Sikh, Hindu, or Japanese American Methodist teachers in America to the canon of Asian American writing? Is it justifiable to ignore Asian "gurus" simply because they cater largely to a non-Asian clientele? Is it defensible to ignore the early Zen teachers because an estimated 75 to 90 percent of Japanese American Buddhists in America at the time were in the Pure Land tradition? What are the shibboleths required for inclusion in Asian American studies, American religion, or the study of Pacific Islander and Asian American religions? And what is at stake?

WRITING SELF WRITING NATION: REWRITING THERESA HAK KYUNG CHA'S RELIGIOUS HISTORY

Story number three.

At the end of *Writing Self Writing Nation: Essays on Theresa Hak Kyung Cha's* Dictée, there is a narrative chronology of the life and artistic accomplishments of Korean American *artiste* Theresa Cha. Cha upset the canonicity of Asian American studies in the 1990s because of her book, *Dictée*. This slim volume contained a disjointed text interspersed with photographs, calligraphy and other illustrations traversing the worlds of high aesthetic culture and the material histories of her Korean American identity. Cha is known in Asian American studies primarily for *Dictée,* and through the *Writing Self Writing Nation* collection of critical essays by leading Asian American literary critics. Her mystique is enhanced by the tragedy of her untimely death at age thirty-one in 1982. The rescue of her text and her installation as an Asian American writer came about as an act of intervention. Elaine Kim explains that "we wished to intervene in the published conversations about *Dictée* just beginning among a number of contemporary critics who largely ignored or sidelined Korea and Korean America in their discussions of the book." Worried that Cha's text was becoming the playground of post-modern critics, Kim writes that "when post-structuralist critics ignore Cha's Korean heritage, thus denying Korean American identity and gender, it is a case of meaningful omission: they are practicing a kind of reverse Orientalism, according to which we are all the same (white) people."[31] As a result, Cha's complicated, fragmented, multilingual and visually stunning *Dictée* has "come home" to Asian American studies.

The narrative chronology of Cha's life appended to the *Writing Self Writing Nation* collection struck me in an odd way when I first saw it. It reminded me of the annotated timelines that inevitably appear at the end of Asian American history texts cataloging the important events in Asian America's long and excruciating history: 1882, 1908, 1917, 1924, 1934, etc. Indeed, Cha's chronology is a recapitulation of Asian American history in microcosm: leaving Asia as a child as a result of political turmoil; temporary residence in Hawai'i followed by a move to California; the influence of Christian education; academic successes—University of San Francisco, Berkeley, graduate study; naturalization, work, a return trip to Korea; outmarriage, awards, autobiography. After her death, a career in the scholars' interpretations. Intended as Asian American literary criticism, *Writing Self Writing Nation* is also an Asian American history text, Cha's life and career as an Asian American history homunculus.

I do not mean to trivialize Cha's life. Cha's life and the interpretation of *Dictée*, as forms of Asian American history, repeat a cautious and distasteful view of religion, as something to be overcome, or at least neutralized through interpretation. In *Writing Self Writing Nation* the religious content and quality of the text is interrogated and found wanting. Thus Cha's playful rendition of the Catholic catechumen's responses to the basic questions about the faith in *Dictée* is read by her critics as the struggle by the narrator to articulate her escape from religion's grasp. Catholicism for the *Writing Self Writing Nation* critics represents a woeful reminder of Cha's " 'sins'—of female otherness, racial and ethnic Korean alterity, [and] colonial difference. . . . " or as an indictment of what is seen as "male-identified religion."[32]

But what are the possibilities for other readings of Cha's text if we set aside the Asian American cultural studies bias against religion and employ a charitable hermeneutic? Placing religion at least near the center of analysis yields a more textured interpretation of Cha that invigorates the narrator's subject. It may even move us toward solving rather than aggravating the riddle of her fragmented and shifting subjectivities that so concerns her critics. The potential benefits gained through a critical assessment of religion alongside the Asian American concern for material history, inequality, and politics could result, for instance, in reading Cha through Mark Taylor's postmodern theological method (as proposed by David Kyuman Kim) and exploring "how Cha's and Taylor's portraits of the subject affect our understanding of religious and theological ideals such as reconciliation, and wholeness, and so on, on the one hand, and, on the other, Asian American political and cultural agency." Or, by acknowledging the Korean religious history that precedes Cha's Catholicism, one might see the shamanistic polyphony of ancestral voices woven through her text—not as disembodied reflections of her postmodern identity, but as Cha's real family—her Korean ancestors erupting through her art and writing.[33]

As an enigmatic text that continues to trouble the waters of Asian American literature, Teresa Cha's text represents an opportunity for scholars of Asian American and Pacific Islander religion. Cha's life is impoverished by the dismissal of her religious identity even if it grates against the critics' belief that religion, gender and racial identity cannot occupy the same space. By reading *Dictée* as an Asian American religious text, students of Asian American/Pacific Islander religions insist on recognizing religion as an intrinsic value in understanding self and community. Literary criticism and history textbooks are only guides; returning to the original texts in Asian American literature with an openness to the possibility that religion is not always a bad thing improves the field.

Lisa Lowe has argued that the study and content of Asian American literature disrupts the assumptions of what constitutes a literary canon, and by its very existence resists appropriation by traditional academic disciplines. Because Asian American literature is inextricably bound to its material contexts of labor, racism, stereotyping and social history, Lowe concludes that it "resists the formal abstraction of aestheticization and canonization."[34] That is, as Asian American literature functions to critique the ideology of liberal "multiculturalism" and academic abstraction, it refuses to be subsumed under the usually instituted methods and approaches to literary study. Substituting the word "religion" for "literature," Lowe's argument is helpful. The study of Asian American and Pacific Islander religions, like Asian American and Pacific Islander literature, is also inextricably bound to the material contexts of labor, racism, stereotyping, and social history. And like the indicting function of Asian American literature, the study of Asian American/Pacific Islander religions must also function to critique a liberal "multiculturalism" that flattens out the differences among groups, ignores history, and hides inequality. Along with Asian American literature, Asian American and Pacific Islander religions refuse to be subsumed under the dominant methods and approaches of either Religious or Asian American studies as they have developed. This is why it is essential to acknowledge the constellation of relationships among colonialism, the plantation political economy, and the religious experiences of Hawai'i's transnational labor force; or why it is necessary to know that Nyogen Senzaki worked as a short order cook; and why Theresa Cha's Catholic identity does not have to threaten her Korean American and gendered identities.

Buddhist scholar Bernard Faure observes that attending too rigorously to disciplinary paradigms and methods is limiting, and that eventually "all religious, ideological, or scholarly standpoints are eventually reinscribed in new, complex, and at times conflicting strategies." Proposing what he terms "performative" scholarship, Faure argues for allowing the object of study "to project its structures onto the theoretical approach" as a way to avoid closing off other, new ways of viewing religion. His caution here is that the scholar's interpretation is always limited. "Ultimately, revealing is always hiding; any insight generates its own blindness; any deconstruction is always already a reconstruction."[35] What, we must ask, is hidden/revealed in favoring particular disciplines or regimes of scholarship in the study of Pacific Islander and Asian American religions? How can we apply Faure's paradoxical dynamic to insure a "better," more comprehensive and open approach to our work? In the end, Faure's point about the contextual nature of scholarship is about taking seriously the prayers and requests of workers directed at stones and remembering why and how they—the workers and the stones—got there, and what happened to them later. To do so brings us one step closer to a fuller understanding and appreciation for each expression of Asian American and Pacific Islander religion; at least for the time being.

NOTES

1. This talk originated as a plenary paper for the Asian Pacific American Religions Initiative (APARRI), University of California-Santa Barbara, 4 March 1999, and was revised for the Pacific Asian North American (PANA) Religion Institute's Senior Fellow public lecture, Berkeley, California, October 16, 2001. I would like to thank Jane Iwamura, Paul Spickard, Fumitaka Matsuoka, David Kyuman Kim, Rita Nakashima Brock, Jennifer Michael, Jan Nattier, Carl Bielefeldt, Chris Chua and Debbie Lee for assisting this essay in a variety of ways; and acknowledge the students in my Asian American/Pacific Islander Religious Traditions course at the Pacific School of Religion. I have tried to preserve the spoken character of the public presentation throughout.

2. Laurie Maffly-Kipp describes the place of Henry Obookiah (Opukahaia) in American religious history in "Eastward Ho! American Religion from the Perspective of the Pacific Rim," in *Retelling U.S. Religious History*, ed. Thomas Tweed (Berkeley: University of California Press, 1997), 127.

3. Their future in-laws initially rebuffed the twins proposal to marry their daughters not because they were conjoined, but because they were Asian. Irving Wallace and Amy Wallace, *The Two: A Biography* (New York: Simon and Schuster, 1978), 173, 221–226. Opening quote is from the *Boston Daily Courier*, 1829, as quoted in Darin Strauss, *Chang and Eng: A Novel* (New York: Plume, 2000), 198. The twins appeared on Bay Area billboards in 2001 advertising Earthlink.com's internet service. Folklorist Jenny Michael first drew my attention the reinterest in Chang and Eng.

4. Wallace and Wallace, *The Two*, 185, 186, 221–226. The phrase "martyrlike death" is Maffly-Kipp's, "Eastward Ho!," 127.

5. Henry Lum and M. Miyazawa, "An Abortive Religious Cult," *Social Process in Hawaii* 7 (November 1941):20-23. All quotes taken from this source. Other sources on the healing stones include Edward B. Scott, *The Saga of the Sandwich Islands: A Complete Documentation of Honolulu's and Oahu's Development over One Hundred and Seventy Five Years*" (Crystal Bay/Lake Tahoe, CA: Sierra-Tahoe Publication Co., 1968), 780; J. Gilbert McAllister, *Archaelogy of Oahu*, Bulletin 104 (Honolulu: Bernice P. Bishop Museum, 1993), 134–137. "Founded in 1903 by seven women who were daughters of American Protestant missionaries, the Daughters of Hawaii was one of the first organizations in Hawai'i to recognize the importance of historical preservation." Online: http://www.daughtersofhawaii.org/daughters/about.shtml. Downloaded 2001 8 October. McAllister notes that the the larger stone measures "almost 6 feet long, 2 feet wide and less than 1 foot thick," *Archaelogy of Oahu*, 136.

6. Scott, *The Saga of the Sandwich Islands*, 780.

7. Ibid.

8. Jan Nattier, "Visible and Invisible: The Politics of Representation in Buddhist America," *Trycycle: The Buddhist Review* 5 (Fall 1995): 42–49. The current effort has its origins in the 1993 Association for Asian American Studies conference panel "Asian American Religious Identity/Critical Reflections" organized by students from the Harvard Divinity School.

9. Sydney E. Ahlstrom, *A Religious History of the American People* (New Haven: Yale University Press, 1972), 862, 863.

10. Edwin Scott Gaustad, *A Religious History of America*, 2nd ed. (San Francisco: HarperSanFrancisco, 1990), 162–163, 221.

11. Maffly Kipp, "Eastward Ho!," 132.

12. Ronald Takaki, *Pau Hana: Plantation Life and Labor in Hawaii, 1835-1920* (Honolulu: University of Hawaii Press, 1983).

13. Jai Maharaj, "Subject: The Historic Healing Stone," posting on the Hindunet.org; alt.hindu listserve, May, 19 1994. Online: http://www.hindunet.org/alt_hindu/1994/msg00262.htm.

14. McAllister, *Archaelogy of Oahu*, 136.

15. Vasudha Narayanan, "Creating the South Indian 'Hindu' Experience in the United States," in *A Sacred Thread: Modern Transmissions of Hindu Traditions in India and Abroad*, ed. Raymond Brady Williams (Chambersburg, PA: Anima Publications, 1992), 156–57. In 1989, a concrete traffic bollard that had been dumped in San Francisco's Golden Gate Park attracted Hindu devotees who venerated it as a Shiva linga. See Cybelle Shattuck, *Dharma in the Golden State: South Asian Religious Traditions in California* (Santa Barbara: Fithian Press, 1996), 49; Maharaj, "Historic Healing Stone." The current status of the stone is confirmed in a site visit and photographs taken in July 2000 by folklorist Jennifer Michael.

16. This general account of Nyogen Senzaki's life is taken from Rick Fields, *How the Swans Came to the Lake: A Narrative History of Buddhism in America* (Boston: Shambhala, 1981). Other details of Issei immigration come from H. Brett Melendy, *Chinese & Japanese Americans* (New York: Hippocrene, 1984), 104; and Yoshisada Kawai's oral history in *Issei Christians: Selected Interviews from the Issei Oral History Project* (Sacramento: Issei Oral History Project, 1977), 7; and Yamato Ichihashi, *Japanese in the United States: A Critical Study of the Problems of the Japanese and Their Children* (Stanford: Stanford University Press, 1932), 58. See also the biographical material in Nyogen Senzaki, Soen Nakagawa, Eido Shimano, and Louis Nordstrom, eds., *Namu Dai Bosu: A Transmission of Zen Buddhism to America* (New York: Bhaisajaguru Series/The Zen Studies Society/ Theatre Arts Books, 1976); Ichihashi, *Japanese in the United States*, 87–88.

17. Senzaki, *Namu Dai Bosa*, 58, 59; Roger Daniels, "The Issei Generation," in *Roots: An Asian American Reader*, eds. Amy Tachiki, et al. (Los Angeles: UCLA Asian American Studies Center/Regents of the University of California, 1971), 144; Ichihashi, *Japanese in the United States*, 161ff.

18. Ichihashi, *Japanese in the United States*, 129–136.

19. Ronald Takaki, *Strangers from a Different Shore: A History of Asian Americans* (New York: Penguin Books, 1989), 212.

20. Daniels, "The Issei Generation," 146; Ichihashi, *Japanese in the United States*, 109ff; *Issei Christians*, Riichi Satow oral history, 80; Senzaki, *Namu Dai Bosa*, 169.

21. He was most likely held at the Pomona Assembly Center due to its proximity to his home at the time and because those held at the Pomona Center were all sent to Heart Mountain. Lester E. Suzuki, *Ministry in the Assembly and Relocation Centers of World War II* (Berkeley: Yardbird Publishing Co., 1979), 96; Senzaki, *Namu Dai Bosa*, 14; Isao Fujimoto, "The Failure of Democracy in a Time of Crisis: The War-Time Internment of the Japanese Americans and Its Relevance Today," in Tachiki, *Roots*, 207. Fujimoto was also interned at Heart Mountain. Senzaki may have been the only representative of the Zen tradition at Heart Mountain. Williams reports that most of the Buddhist priests interned there were either in the Shin, or Nichiren traditions. Duncan Ryuken Williams, "Camp Dharma: Buddhist History and the Japanese American Internment," Panel presentation, Buddhism Section/Asian North American Religion Culture and Society Group, American Academy of Religion Conference, Orlando, Florida, 23 November 1998; Senzaki, *Namu Dai Bosa*, 11; the poem is dated 5 November 1944.

22. This paragraph follows Fields, *How the Swans Came to the Lake*, 199, 194.

23. Alfred Bloom, "Shin Buddhism in America: A Social Perspective," in *The Faces of Buddhism in America*, eds. Charles S. Prebish and Kenneth K. Tanaka (Berkeley: University of California Press, 1998), 34; See Richard Hughes Seager, *The World's Parliament of Religions: The East/West Encounter, Chicago, 1893* (Bloomington: Indiana University Press, 1995), 94–120.

24. Fields, *How the Swans Came to the Lake*, 179; Helen Tworkov, *Zen in America: Five Teachers and the Search for an American Buddhism* (New York/Tokyo: Kodansha, 1994), 11–12.

25. See Jane Naomi Iwamura's demonstration of how the Oriental Monk functions as a therapeutic figure in the West in "The Oriental Monk in American Popular Culture," in *Religion and Popular Culture in America*, eds. Bruce David Forbes and Jeffrey H. Mahan (Berkeley: University of California Press, 2000), 25–43; Tworkov, *Zen in America*, 7-8.

26. Yoshiaki Fukuda, *My Six Years of Internment: An Issei's Struggle for Justice* (San Francisco: Konko Church, 1990), 64-68; Tibetan Buddhism's arrival in the United States has been attributed to Geshe Wangyal, a Mongol priest who came to serve the immigrant/refugee Kalmyk Mongol community in New Jersey and Pennsylvania. See Fields, *How the Swans Came to the Lake*, 290–294; Donald S. Lopez, Jr., *Prisoners of Shangri-La: Tibetan Buddhism and the West* (Chicago: University of Chicago Press, 1998), 42, 163–164, 172–173, 175; Joshua W. C. Cutler, "Introduction" in Geshe Wangyal, *The Jewelled Staircase* (Ithaca, NY: Snow Lion Publications, 1986). Owen Lattimore, "Introduction," in *The Diluv Khutagt: Memoirs and Autobiography of a Mongol Buddhist Reincarnation in Religion and Revolution*, eds. Owen Lattimore and Fujiko Isono (Wiesbaden, Germany: Otto Harrassowitz, 1982).

27. Helen Tworkov, *Zen in America*, 32; Shimano Eido Roshi, "The Way to Dai Bosatsu," in Senzaki, *Namu Dai Bosa*, 218–219.

28. Ichihashi, *Japanese in the United States*, 90.

29. Ichihashi, *Japanese in the United States*, 222, 224.

30. Ronald Takaki, *Strangers from a Different Shore*. Mary Paik Lee, *Quiet Oddysey: A Pioneer Korean Woman in America* (Seattle: University of Washington Press, 1990).

31. Theresa Hak Kyung Cha, *Dictée* (Berkeley: Third Woman Press, 1995; orig. New York: Tanam Press, 1982). Moira Roth, "Theresa Hak Kyung Cha 1951–1982: A Narrative Chronology" in *Writing Self Writing Nation: Essays on Theresa Hak Kyung Cha's* Dictée, eds. Elaine H. Kim and Norma Alarcón (Berkeley: Third Woman Press, 1994), 151–160; Elaine H. Kim, "Preface," in *Writing Self Writing Nation*, ix; Elaine H. Kim, "Poised on the In-between: A Korean American's Reflections on Theresa Hak Kyung Cha's *Dictée*" in *Writing Self Writing Nation*, 22.

32. Lisa Lowe, "Unfaithful to the Original: The Subject of Dictée" in *Writing Self Writing Nation*, 58, see also her explanation in 64fn3; Shelley Sunn Wong, "Unnaming the Same: Theresa Hak Kyung Cha's Dictée" in *Writing Self Writing Nation*, 122–3.

33. David Kyuman Kim, "Agency Unbound: An A/theological Reading of Theresa Hak Kyung Cha's *Dictée*," paper proposal for Association for Asian American Studies Conference, Philadelphia, PA, April 1999. Kyuman Kim also fruitfully reads Cha through the idea of redemptive nihilism and alongside Kristeva's notion of melancholy in his paper, "The Melancholy of Authenticity: Agency, and the Spiritual Struggle in *Dictée*," (unpublished ms); Rudiger V. Busto, "The Religious Subject as *Tertium Quid* in Theresa Hak Kyung Cha's *Dictée*," panel presentation, Association for Asian American Studies Conference, Philadelphia, PA, April 1999.

34. Lisa Lowe, "Canon, Institutionalization, Identity: Contradictions for Asian American Studies," in *The Ethnic Canon: Histories, Institutions and Interventions,* ed. David Palumbo-Liu (Minneapolis: University of Minnesota Press, 1995), 54.

35. Bernard Faure, *Chan Insights and Oversights: An Epistemological Critique of the Chan Tradition* (Princeton: Princeton University Press, 1993), 151.

SPIRIT

PROTECTING THE "SACRED *IPU*": CONNECTING THE SACRED IN BEING HAWAIIAN-CHRISTIAN IN HAWAI'I— A PERSONAL JOURNEY

WILLIAM KAUAIWIULAOKALANI WALLACE III

Noho ana ke akua i ka nāhelehele
The gods dwell in the forest
I ʻālaiʻia o ke kīʻohuʻohu,
Hidden away in the mists
E ka ua koko.
In the low lying rainbow
E nā kino malu i ka lani
O beings sheltered under the heavens
Malu e hoe.
Clear our paths (of all that may trouble us).
E hoʻoulu mai ana ʻo ke Akua i kona mau kahu,
Akua or God inspires me (us), his devotee(s)
ʻO wau (mākou), ʻo wau (mākou)nō a (la e).
Me (us), ay, me (us) indeed.[1]

This *ʻoli pale* (chant of protection) is one of many *oli* (chant) used by *kupuna* (ancestors)[2] to ask *Akua* (God)[3] for protection. An *ʻoli* such as this would be used prior to going into the forests to gather ferns, flowers, and timber for making canoes, building houses, or other essentials. This *oli* is also used when people come together for conferences or a *hui* (gathering). Using this *ʻoli pale* to start my essay is the Hawaiian way of asking *Akua* (God) to help us on our journey through this essay so that what is found will be useful to us as scholars, and as human beings living on Sacred Mother Earth. Through common experiences we are joined by the same *piko* or life force known as *Na Kānaka*[4] or the Human Race.

I'm Hawaiian, Samoan, Tongan, Tahitian, Scottish, Irish, French, Danish, English, German and Chinese. I'm married to a *wahine* (woman) from *Aotearoa* (New Zealand) who is Maori, Scottish, German, Jewish, and Spanish. Together we have four children. Three daughters and a son. We have five grandsons. One daughter married a young man from Newbury Park, California, who is part Cherokee. They have one of our grandsons who, in addition to all the above ethnicities, is also Cherokee. Our family is a rich background of multi-ethnic people who over time, came together, lived together, married, had families, and left family stories filled with successes, failures, heartaches, and triumphs. Most people today are made up of more than one ethnic identity. We are held together by a tapestry of *piko* I call "our central life force connections."[5] This *piko* comprises thousands of ancestors who came before, gave their *aka* (essence),[6] and their *mana* (power)[7] to solidify our central life force connections. Their information is stored on what my friend Dr. Cleve Barlow from Auckland University in New Zealand calls our *wairua* (spirit), or "spiritual computer disc."[8] Dr. Barlow describes this "central life force connection" as not only a cultural one but a scientific one which teaches that we are made up of the genes of all of our ancestors. We know that as human beings we have both our mother's and our father's genes giving us their hereditary genetic information. Our connection to our parents and our ancestors clearly shows that our *piko* or life connected force had a beginning, is present within us, is ongoing, nurturing, hereditary, and real.[9] This *makana* (gift) left by my Hawaiian ancestors is the gift of knowing who we are, where we came from, and our connection with *Ke Akua* (God), *Ka 'Aina* (the Land), *'Ohana* (the Family), and *Na Kānaka* (the Human Race). Each constitute a venue for the sacred *ipu* and the challenge of "Protecting the Sacred *Ipu*" is ongoing.

To the *kanaka maoli*, an *ipu* is defined and described as a bottle gourd used as a vessel, container, dish, mug, calabash, pot, cup, utensil, urn, bowl, basin, pipe, and a drum consisting of a single gourd or made of two large gourds of unequal size joined together.[10] My essay focuses on the definition of *ipu* as a container or a holding vessel. I use this description as a metaphor for those vessels which are sacred and highly protected and cherished by our *Kupūna* (Ancestors). I write about three customary *ipu* practices that are sacred to our people. These three practices are not to be construed as the only "sacred *ipu*" of our people. They only constitute a starting point from which our discussion about sharing sacred things can begin. The first is the *'ohe hano ihu* or the Hawaiian bamboo nose flute. The second, the *umeke* or *ipu poi* (poi bowl). The third, the *ipu heke* or double gourd drum used for chanting and hula.

'OHE HANO IHU AS A SACRED IPU

The *'Ohe hano ihu* is the bamboo nose flute. *'Ohe* is the Hawaiian name for bamboo. *Hano* refers to the kind of breath or sound used to show that there is life. *Ihu* means nose and refers to the source from which the breath of life comes. The *'Ohe hano ihu* was never played by mouth. Hawaiians believed that the air from the mouth was not life giving but was impure and defiled. They were always careful in speaking. They knew that words could give life or they could give death. *Kahuna* (Priests) and *Ali'i* (Chiefs) were cautious with spoken words. There were many *kapu* (laws) associated with speaking in the presence of an *Ali'i* (Chief). Proper Hawaiian protocol was followed otherwise chiefdoms went to war if insulting words were used, even if unintentional. Because of this, the *'ohe hano ihu* is given high regard in Hawaiian culture. As a cultural metaphor it represents a life-giving entity. When the sound of the *'ohe hano ihu* is heard, everyone listens. The voice of the *'ohe hano ihu* provides the foundation for peaceful exchange of gifts which included different food items such as *kalo* (taro), *uala* (sweet potato), *mai'a* (banana), *kō* (sugar cane), and *awa* (root plant). Hawaiians believe that the bamboo or the *'ohe* is the *kinolau* (other life form) of the Hawaiian God *Lono*, especially during the period known as the *Mākahiki*. *Lono* symbolizes life, harvest, fertility, bounty, and peace. All of these aspects of life gave hope to the Hawaiian people allowing them to deal with life's pressures in a more acceptable way.

Hawaiians believed that many natural objects, geological formations, rocks, plants, and animals were *kinolau* (different body forms) of the gods. Each of the four major gods had more than one *kinolau* (body form), in which they dwelled simultaneously. *Kalo* (taro), *Kō* (sugarcane), and *'ohe* (bamboo) were known as bodies of *Kane*, the great life-giver.[11] *Kanaloa*, who among the four principal deities was most closely associated with the sea, was held to be present in *mai'a* (banana), *he'e* (octopus), and many of the marine mammals and large fish.[12] The god *Ku*, who was referred to as the god of war and of building temples and large important structures for the chiefs and priests, also had many *kinolau* such as the *niu* (the coconut), some marine animals, and many forest trees.[13] The god *Lono* was known as the Hawaiian god of peace, planting, fertility, and *mākahiki* and was embodied in rain clouds, *ʻuala* (sweet potato), *ʻipu* (gourds), and *puaʻa* (the Polynesian pig).[14]

Of the four principal gods, those uppermost in the minds of the *makaʻainana* (labor force or commoners) and the *mahiʻai* (farmers) were the gods *Kāne* and *Lono* who were both associated with the source and the deliverer of water respectively and the god *Kū* who was known in numerous aspects such as *Kūikahaʻawi* (*Kū* the giver), *Kūmauna* (*Kū* of the mountain), and *Kūkeaohoʻoihamihaikalani* (*Kū* of the clouds that dot the sky).[15] The god *Kū* is closely associated with the forest as protector of its plants, and his approval was asked before removing any forest vegetation, whether it be a huge tree for woodworking or tiny herbs for medicinal use. Permission to remove certain plants was also sought from the forest goddesses *Hina* and *Laka,* and the volcano goddess *Pele.*[16]

More importantly, to the Hawaiian people these gods or deities were not looked upon as distant strange unfamiliar beings, but instead, they were *ʻohana,* or family, who could be called upon for help, and often several of them together were invoked.[17] Every family and some individuals could also look for assistance to *ʻaumākua,*[18] personal gods or deified ancestors or protector spirits, that took the form of animals. Among the common *ʻaumakua* were *manō* (shark), *puʻeo* (owl), *honu* (turtle), and *ʻalae* (mudhen).[19] Even after the infrastructure of the Hawaiian religion was dismantled in 1819 and Christianity was introduced in 1820, many accepted the new god but also continued to honor their *ʻaumākua* and some members of the traditional pantheon, deities like *Pele* and her cousin *Kamapuaʻa,* who did not demand sacrifices. To many Hawaiians, the new god of Christianity did not conflict with their gods, especially a god who sacrificed his only son for the sins of the world. Hawaiians had personal ties with their gods. Their gods were not mysterious but real beings responsible for taking care of the people: to provide rain for the crops; to give signs of impending disasters. Many Hawaiians did not see Christianity as a threat to their old religious practices. To many the story of Jesus Christ was very similar to the story of *Maui* and other heroes who died while engaged in doing something good for *Na Kānaka,* the human race.

The symbolism and connection of the cross and the *ʻohe hano ihu* as being vessels or sacred *ipu* with similar purposes raises interesting questions to ponder. It was from the cross that the Lord Jesus Christ gave his last breath of life, not so that man might die, but on the contrary so that humankind might live and have eternal life. His last breath gave life to *Na Kānaka,* the human race. The *'ohe hano ihu* symbolizes the breath of life which is shared by all and can therefore become interrelated and connected to the symbolism of the cross on Calgary. The *'ohe hano ihu* is the Hawaiian people's way of sharing the same kind of life-giving message as is found in singing the sacred hymns of the crucifixion.

UMEKE/IPU POI (THE POI BOWL) AS A SACRED *IPU*

There are multiple *piko*[20] at work when we look at the *umeke* or *ipu poi* (poi bowl) as a sacred ipu to the Hawaiian people. First, the *umeke* (calabash) or *ipu* container holding the poi. Second, the *poi* and its relationship to the Hawaiian people. Third, the *Na Po'e* (the people) who sit around the poi bowl to eat and partake of the *poi*. Each of these components are able to stand by themselves within Hawaiian culture but they become more significant to the culture when they are brought together at one place, namely the dinner table or any place where a meal will be served. Let's examine each of the above parts more carefully in order to understand their importance.

First, the *umeke* (calabash) or *ipu* container that holds the *poi* was always made of the finest wood or *ipu* (gourd). The Hawaiians preferred using *umeke* (bowls) made of *koa*, *kou*, or *milo* wood.[21] All were sacred to *Kāne*, god of the forests and god of living or life-giving waters. Great work and time went into making the *umeke* (bowls) used to hold the *poi* that would be eaten by the people. The *umeke* (bowl) or *ipu poi* is symbolic because it connects the world of man with nature and with the world of the gods. *Kāne's Kinolau* (other life form) is the *umeke* (calabash) which holds the *poi*. The *umeke* (calabash) is another metaphor showing the great power of *Kāne* to give life to *Na Kānaka*, humanity. It reminds us of *kuleana* (responsibility) we have in caring for *Papa Hanau Moku* (Sacred Mother Earth). While the *umeke* (calabash) *ipu poi* remained on the table and as long as *poi* was in it, the *umeke* would be covered and not left open to be defiled by the careless actions of people moving around it. However, once the people sat around the table to partake of a meal, the *umeke* (calabash) *ipu poi* would be uncovered and people would eat the *poi* from the *umeke* (calabash) *ipu poi*.

Our *Kūpuna* (Ancestors) taught that when the *umeke* (calabash) *ipu poi* was uncovered and open and people were sitting around to eat the *poi* that the conversation around the *umeke* (calabash) *ipu poi* had to be of a positive nature. This meant that no negative conversations were to be conducted while the *poi* bowl was open.[22] Everyone sitting around the *poi* bowl had to speak with kind voices and be respectful of each other, and no gossiping or use of foul language was to be tolerated.

There were also procedures for eating the *poi* properly and not being wasteful and disrespectful. You could eat the *poi* with your finger or with your spoon. Either way, you ate the *poi* from the center of the bowl and not from the sides. You could not splash or whip your *poi* and cause it to move outside or across the *poi* bowl. If you did, this was considered *kāpulu*[23] or showed that you did not have proper manners or that you were raised by uncaring parents. Your conduct around the *poi* bowl showed in many ways the quality of person you were in the eyes of the Hawaiian people.

The second part or the *poi* is of equal importance to the Hawaiian people. The *poi* is made from the *kalo* or taro plant. To Hawaiians the *kalo* plant has a very important place in our society. It is believed that the *kalo* represents the senior line or genealogy of the Hawaiian people. The first born child of *Wakea* was named *Hāloa*.[24] He was born prematurely and died. He did not have any real human form and his body was buried in the corner of the house of *Wakea*. In a short time a plant grew from the place *Hāloa* was buried. This plant was the *kalo*. The *kalo* is a special gift from our older brother *Hāloa* and is the most favored life food source of the Hawaiian people. Like the *umeke* (calabash), the *kalo* symbolizes life and family. It stands for our senior line between the gods and the human race. The *kalo* is the food source from the gods and our older brother *Hāloa*. The *lo'i kalo* or taro patches and fish ponds or *loko kuapā*[25] of *Hawai'i* took care of all the food and nutritional needs of the people. The *kalo* and fish was sufficient to feed a million people living in *Hawai'i* prior to Western contact in 1789.[26]

Making *poi* from the *kalo* was hard work. The land for planting *kalo* had to be prepared. *Mālama 'aina* (caring for the land) was an important part of raising *kalo*. The *mahi'ai* (farmer) took long hours to clear and prepare the *'āina* for planting.[27] He would bless his work with *pule* (prayers), chants, and songs he had learned from his *kupuna* about the land and about the planting of *kalo*.[28] I recall as a young child my mother and father leaving me in the care of my paternal grandfather on *Moloka'i*. *Tutu Kane* would wrap me in a blanket and take me out into the fields during the early morning hours as he prepared to plant his *kalo*. I will never forget the devotion my *tutu kane* showed to each of his *kalo* plants. He treated them as though they were his own children. He would take each one of them rub some dirt on the bottom of the *huli* (plant cuttings) hold each one up to the sky and cry out *"kokua, kokua, ke Akua,"* which means " give your help, give your care, O God," to these plants. This ritual went on all day until *tutu kane* completed planting all of his *kalo*. After the *kalo* were planted, *tutu kane* would go out to visit and sing and talk to his *kalo* every day. He told me that talking to your plants gave them life because you were sharing your own breath of life. That your *hā* which you exhaled from your nose was being taken in by the *kalo* and used to give each of them strength and life. What was amazing was that my *tutu kane* did not graduate from high school and never received any kind of formal education. Yet, he understood in his own simple way the importance of exchange and interchange between man and plants. We take in oxygen and breath out carbon dioxide while plants take in carbon dioxide and release oxygen back into the air. A simple lesson learned from *tutu kane* I still practice today.

Once planted the *kalo* grows quickly if well cared for. Each individual taro plant will give five to ten *keiki* or baby *huli* (plant cuttings) which can be taken from the mother plant and planted on its own. The number of *keiki* from the *makua* (parent) plants would allow a Hawaiian farmer to increase his taro farm from just a few *huli* (plant cuttings) in the beginning to five or ten times more *huli* every ten to twelve month period. The *kalo* could reach heights of seven to eight feet tall within six to seven months. At about its eight-or nine-month period, the *kalo* reduces its height as most of its nourishment is transferred to the corm of the *kalo* root. When the leaves and the stems of the *kalo* plants are two to three feet tall, the *kalo* is ready to harvest. The family or *'ohana* would come together to help harvest and pull the taro. It was hard work and required practice and skill. Your feet and your hands had to work together in order to harvest *kalo* in the proper way. Once the *kalo* was pulled, cleaned, and cooked (preferably by steaming), it was then pounded into a sticky paste-like matter called *poi*.[29] The Hawaiian people believed that the *poi* was the best way to prepare the *kalo* because when pounded correctly, the *poi kalo* (*pa'i 'ai poi* or firm/hard *poi*)[30] could last a very long time in a dried or semi-dried state and be taken on long voyages. The dried *kalo*, when water was added, became a starchy food eaten with fish or other sources of protein. The *kalo*, now *poi*, in the *umeke* (calabash) is an extension of the sacred connection between gods, man, and nature.

The final element, that of *na kānaka*, (humankind) adds support to the above. We are caretakers, planters, harvesters, custodians, users, and beneficiaries of all which *ke Akua* (God) have placed upon *Papa Hanau Moku* (Mother Earth). We are the sacred *ipu*; when the *kalo* is harvested; the *poi* is made and placed into the *poi* bowl, we take into our bodies that nourishment given to us by our eldest brother *Hāloa Naka*. We must control our senses so that we will not be ungrateful in his presence. The magic of the *poi* bowl is found in the mixing and bringing together of plants, water, food, and people in a moment of sharing life.

IPU HEKE OR DOUBLE GOURD DRUM AS A SACRED *IPU*

The *ipu heke* or double gourd drum of the Hawaiian chanters and *kumu hula* is a sacred instrument used to accompany the *hula kahiko* (ancient Hawaiian dance). Oral traditions say that the *ipu heke* was a traditional drum used by master teachers of chant and dance dedicated to *Laka* the patron goddess of the *hula*. The *ipu heke* has great *mana* or spiritual power, for it holds sound and voices of *kumu hula* and chanters of the past. Each *ipu heke* has its own genealogy tracing its lineage from one *kumu hula* to the next. It is a sacred *ipu* of knowledge which stores vital information for all *ho'opa'a* (chanters) and *'olapa* (dancers) of the *hula kahiko* (ancient dance).

As a *Kumu Hula* (Dance Master) I believe in the *mana* (strength) of the *ipu heke*. Three experiences in my life helped me see the *ipu heke* as a sacred container of knowledge. The first happened during my years as a student of *kumu hula* auntie, Harriet Ne, on the island of *Moloka'i*. The second happened while attending law school at Brigham Young University in Provo, Utah. The third occurred on March 26, 2000, as I traveled from *Hawai'i* to Albuquerque, New Mexico.

After I graduated from Church College of *Hawai'i* in 1972, there were no jobs in secondary school teaching, especially in history or social sciences. I was lucky that a family friend told me about the need for training teachers in Hawaiiana or Hawaiian studies on *Moloka'i*. I put a proposal together and with the support of the community, the Kamehameha Schools/Bishop Estate, and the Queen Lili'uokalani Children's Center, the Department of Education (Maui School District), State of *Hawai'i* accepted my proposal and the program "*Moloka'i Ana*" was born.

Moloka'i Ana was designed to teach students and teachers basic core information about Hawaiian culture, language, and history through music, song, dance, games, and learning-by-doing activities. It was during this time that Auntie Harriet Ne became my *kumu hula*. My life changed when she took me under her wings and tutored me in the chants and *hula* of my *'āina hanau* or my birth land. I can hear her calm and patient voice telling me, "Bill, don't rush, take your time, it will come to you when you are ready to receive it." These very powerful words have stuck in my mind throughout my lifelong pursuit of higher learning and education. I recall learning a very special *mele hula* (hula song) entitled *"Aia Moloka'i ku'u iwa."* This was a love story about two sweethearts who lived on *Moloka'i*. I was having difficulty with the rhythm and words of this *mele hula* (hula song). I was asked to do the chanting of this *hula* for a special event on *Moloka'i*. I recall going outside of our house and sitting under our garage, practicing for hours to learn the proper rhythm and words. As I stopped chanting, I closed my eyes and simply said *"kokua, kokua, ke Akua!"*. . . the words of my grandfather, which simply meant "help me, O please help me my god!" After a few moments of silence, I was startled when, in the distance, coming from a place called *Na'iwa* where the old traditional *makahiki* (athletic) fields and *hula* plat- forms are located over the hill from my home, I heard the distant sounds of ancient Hawaiian *pahu* drums and *ipu heke* beats.

Their rhythms were so distinct and clear. It was as though my *kupuna* wanted to make sure that I heard them and would never forget them. My hands began to follow their beat and I began chanting the words to the *mele hula*. Within a few moments the beats became stronger and stronger and my chanting voice became stronger and stronger and the words of the chant became clearer and clearer. Within a short time, my wife called out from the house and asked if everything was all right because it sounded as though many people were there chanting along with me. Needless to say, I had a very special spiritual experience with my *ipu heke* and with the *ipu heke* of my *kupuna*. The container of knowledge was poured over into my heart and soul or *na'au* (internal spiritual center) and I would never be the same.

The next day at the program, my *kumu hula*, Auntie Harriet Ne, looked at me and asked if everything was all right and if I was ready to perform. I told her that I was ready and that I would try my best. After the performance was completed Auntie Harriet came to me and simply said, "our *kupuna* visited you last night, didn't they?" All I could say was "yes Auntie, they did" . . . and I cried. Years later, as we were leaving *Moloka'i* so that I could pursue a law degree, Auntie Harriet told me that my experience with my *kupuna* on *Moloka'i* would not be my last but was only the beginning. Auntie Harriet was right; my *kupuna* never abandoned me and my family.

That first experience of the sacredness of the *ipu heke* as a source of knowl- edge and a symbol of collective knowledge in my Hawaiian culture is a living and ongoing metaphor which continues to thrive among my people. The sacredness of the *ipu heke* continued into law school for me and for my fam- ily even while I struggled through my training at Brigham Young University in Utah nearly ten years later.

I can recall starting law school with only one thought in mind and that was to survive the first year. My first semester was a real struggle and I was in tears when I received my grades on Christmas Eve 1981. They were low and I was placed on academic probation. I had one semester to improve or I would be dismissed from school. As I sat in my bedroom by myself, in tears, depressed, and believing that I had made a mistake for myself and for my family, my hands reached over to the corner of the room and I picked up my *ipu heke.* I held the *ipu heke* for a moment. A warm feeling came over me as I began to *pai* (beat) my *ipu heke* and I began to chant *"Aia Moloka'i ku'u iwa."* Tears filled my eyes and I cried out to my *kupuna*. I asked them to help me finish law school so I could return home to help my people. Shortly after completing *"Aia Moloka'i ku'u iwa,"* I began beating my *ipu heke*, but instead of chanting another Hawaiian *mele* I began doing something which I did not plan . . . I began chanting in Hawaiian *mele* form *". . . ea la, ea la, e 'ia . . .* Burglary is the unlawful breaking and entering of the dwelling of another without consent with intent to take property . . . *ea la, ea la, e 'ia . . .* Murder is the unlawful killing of a human being with malice afore-thought . . . *ea la, ea la, e 'ia . . .* "All of a sudden, my entire first semester of law school became relevant and alive to me. I remembered everything I had learned that first semester.

I was so excited! Unfortunately, I had already taken all my final exams and I had failed nearly all of them. On the positive side, the law school gave me one more semester to prove myself. With my *ipu heke* by my side and with the voices of my *kupuna* in my heart, I was eager to implement my new method of studying and learning the law. I believed, for the very first time, that I was no longer alone in my pursuit of my law degree. I felt that the use of the sacred *ipu heke* would not only make it much easier for me to learn and process the information I needed in order to understand the law, but the concept of traditional and cultural learning had not been taken away. It had simply been forgotten by many of us as we have become highly influenced by Western society and Western systems of education.

Further, I realized for the first time that learning was a lot more fun and I could retain a lot more. Law school would no longer be laborious but become somewhat enjoyable. And I was correct. My *kupuna* were there with me and they made law school more fun for me and my family. I never had any problems memorizing "black letter law" and other important things as long as I put them together *(haku mele)* in a chant format. This experience in law school gave me a new way to take, sort, and commit to memory impor-tant pieces of information for school and for life. I have continued to use this method to assist with major projects currently under way at our Hawaiian Studies Program at BYU-Hawai'i. Traditional and cultural methods of learn-ing are as important as any Western method imposed on us over the last one hundred years. The test for us is to build bridges which peacefully link these methods and enable us to share and benefit from one another.

The lessons of the *ipu heke* are many. For me, the most profound is found in my final story. On March 26, 2000, students, administrators and I from BYU-Hawai'i left Honolulu for a networking conference sponsored by the

W.K. Kellogg Foundation in Albuquerque, New Mexico. We went from Honolulu to Los Angeles on Hawaiian Airlines. I checked in all my luggage and boarded our flight with my *ipu heke* as my only carry on item. I traveled all over the world taking my *ipu heke* as a carry on and had never run into any problems. The flight from Honolulu to Los Angeles was excellent and my *ipu heke* was right above me in the overhead bin. Our flight was late leaving Honolulu and we had to run to make our connection from Los Angeles to Phoenix.

With three minutes to spare, with excitement and anticipation for the conference I got to the gate to board our flight to Phoenix. I gave a big smile and a kind "Aloha" to the gate attendant. She looked at me and said, "Sorry sir, but you're gonna have to check that thing in at the counter. You can't carry it on the plane." I told her that I wanted to hand carry it as it was a very important cultural artifact. She said it would not fit into the overhead bins. I responded that it was a lot smaller than some of the bags carried on by the other passengers boarding the flight. By this time she was getting quite upset and so was I. She said that if I did not check it in that I would not be allowed on the flight. I paused, took several deep breaths, and under protest, checked in my *ipu heke*. I told her that I would hold her and her airline responsible for any damage to my *ipu heke*. She assured me that they would take care of it and someone would hand deliver it to me upon my arrival in Phoenix. My mind and heart was on my *ipu heke*. I had never traveled anywhere without my *ipu heke* close to me.

Upon arriving in Phoenix, a strange feeling came over me. As I stood up from my seat, a pain hit deep in my *na'au* (internal center) and tears streamed from my eyes. I knew, even before seeing my *ipu heke*, that something had gone terribly wrong on this flight. As I approached the area where I was told I could pick up my *ipu heke*, one of the flight attendants came up to me and said, "Mr. Wallace, you're not going to like what you're going to see." I grabbed onto the wall, braced myself and started sobbing. The entire top piece of my *ipu heke* was smashed. Some of the pieces were stuck into it by the baggage man who brought it to the door. I was deeply wounded and I could feel that my *ipu heke* had been violated.

As I met the other members of our party they were all very upset about the damage to the *ipu heke*. As we were driving from the airport to the hotel and I held my *ipu heke*, tears were streaming from my eyes, I felt a calmness come over me. I told the members of our group that there was a reason for this happening and that everything would be all right.

I participated in the dedication of the new cultural center at the Institute for American Indian Arts in Santa Fe. This was a very spiritual experience for me. I remember that the first stop was at the old museum site in Santa Fe. As I entered the museum I was struck by the architectural centerpiece in their orientation center. It resembled chiefly images that were important to the Hawaiian people. I felt a strong kinship with these people and I felt at home in their presence. I was allowed to share my *hā* (breath of life) by playing my *'ohe hano ihu*. This set the stage for things that were to come. This allowed for the healing process to begin. The ceremonial dedication of the new cultural center lifted my spirit and clarified in my mind as to why I had traveled so far to share in this ritual of spiritual encounter. With our participation in the fashion show and in sharing the dances of Hawai'i with our Native American Indian family, my heart had become one with my newfound family in Albuquerque, New Mexico. At the close of our program, I held my *ipu heke* in the air and I presented it as a gift *(makana)* to Dr. Della Warrior, the President of the Institute for American Indian Arts in Santa Fe. In presenting the *ipu heke* to her I shared my story of my journey from Hawai'i, with my *ipu heke*. I told them what happened on the airplane and how my *ipu heke* had been cracked and damaged. To our people, this cracked *ipu heke* could be seen in several different ways. The way I saw it was that our ancestors were reminding us that like this *ipu heke*, our people have been cracked, damaged, displaced, and dismantled. We are still suffering as we continue to feel the pains of victimhood. However, even though my *ipu heke* was cracked on the top, the bottom or the base was still intact, solid, and secure. The foundation had not been destroyed. It was still the repository of knowledge handed down to us from our ancestors. The *ipu heke* still sounded good, still played its song, and still fulfilled its purpose. This *ipu heke* symbolizes all of us: though we are cracked in many different places, we still survive. Like the *ipu heke* there are still a lot of good songs, a lot of good stories, and a lot of good deeds yet to be discovered and shared.

Holo i ke kula, holo, holo, e . . . Let us journey to the source of knowledge together, let us go, let us go. *A'ohe pau ka ike i kau Hālau ho'okahi.* Think not that all wisdom resides in one school or one place of learning. *Mahalo nui loa kākou, e mālama pono kākou.* . . . *e* . . . Thank you all very much and may peace be with you all. *Aloha a hui hou kākou.* Until we meet again.

NOTES

1. *'Oli pale* or a chant of protection taught to me by several Kumu Hula in different forms. The form chosen comes from my Kumu Hula Auntie Harriet Ne from the island of Moloka'i and was learned by me in her presence at Kalama'ula Moloka'i in August 1975.

2. Mary Kawena Pukui and Samuel H. Elbert, *Hawaiian Dictionary,* Hawaiian-English-Hawaiian (Honolulu: University Press of Hawaii, 1971), 171.
3. Michael Kioni Dudley, *Man, Gods, and Nature* (Honolulu: Nā Kāne O Ka Malo Press, 1990), 31–37.
4. Pukui and Elbert, *Hawaiian Dictionary,* 118.
5. Pukui and Elbert (*Hawaiian Dictionary,* 302) define the *piko* as being the umbilical cord, the navel string. I have been taught to interpret this to mean the connection between mother and child, life and death, and the source of life. Because the number of ancestors for each of us are numerous, I believe that we are connected by what I call the unified *piko* or that *piko* which joins all of the past to the present, which I believe is our genetic makeup.
6. Dudley, *Man, Gods, and Nature,* 31–32.
7. Ibid., 67–74.
8. Cleve Barlow, from talk given at Kanaka Maoli Educators Conference at Brigham Young University-Hawai'i, August 1998. His talk is on file and a transcript of the conference proceedings is being edited at the present time. Concepts of *wairua,* or spirit, and *wheiao* or worlds of transition, is also discussed in Dr. Barlow's book entitled *Tikanga Whakaaro: Key Concepts in Maori Culture* (Auckland, New Zealand: Oxford University Press, 1991).
9. Pukui, Haertig, and Lee, *Nana I Ke Kumu,* Queen Lili'uokalani Children's Center Publication, 182–188. These pages give examples of the different aspects of *piko* and tell in more detail why this word was important to the Hawaiian people.
10. Mary Kawena Pukui and Samuel H. Elbert, *Hawaiian Dictionary,* revised and enlarged edition (Honolulu: University of Hawai'i Press, 1986), 103.
11. Isabella Aiona Abbott, *La'au Hawai'i: Traditional Hawaiian Uses of Plants,* 15.
12. Ibid., 15.
13. Ibid., 16.
14. Ibid., 16.
15. Ibid., 16.
16. Ibid., 16.
17. Pukui, Haertig, and Lee, 23–24.
18. Ibid., 35–43.
19. Ibid., 16.
20. Pukui, Haertig, and Lee, 182-188.
21. Pukui and Elbert. *New Pocket Hawaiian Dictionary.* The simple definitions and explanation for each are found 62, 65, 99.
22. This footnote is to simply remind the reader that there are many stories and personal experiences used in this paper that come directly from my own recollection and experiences with my *kupuna* while growing up on the island of Moloka'i. This story of the *poi* bowl is one of many versions that I have heard over the years. It comes from my recollection of time I spent with my paternal grandmother, Ellen Wahinehelelaokaiona Makaiwi Wallace, at our family homestead in Ho'olehua. My recollection takes me back to the period during the summer of 1954 when I was about six years old.

23. Pukui and Elbert (1986), 133.
24. Handy, Handy, and Pukui. *Native Planters in Old Hawaii: Their Life, Lore, and Environment* (Honolulu: Bishop Museum Press, 1972), 80.
25. Ibid., 171.
26. David E. Stannard, *Before the Horror, The Population of Hawai'i on the Eve of Western Contact*, (Honolulu: Social Science Research Institute, University of Hawai'i, 1989), 25–31. Stannard believes, and I support his view, the pre-contact and contact population of Hawai'i to be between 800,000 and one million people.
27. Handy, Handy, and Pukui, 83–94.
28. Ibid., 97–100.
29. Handy, Emory, Bryan, Buck, Wise, et.al., *Ancient Hawaiian Civilization*, Revised Edition, (Rutland VT.: Charles E. Tuttle, 1970), 100–103.
30. Malo, *Hawaiian Antiquities*, 42–44. Also, please read through the Notes on Chapter 14 at the bottom of the page. It gives more information on the Hawaiian "Hard poi."

COMPASSION AMONG AGING NISEI JAPANESE AMERICANS[1]

PETER YUICHI CLARK

This chapter will explore the spiritualities of aging second-generation (Nisei) Japanese American men and women as they grow older, with my key source of data being a series of ethnographic group interviews I conducted with seventy elders in the San Francisco Bay Area and in Chicago in 1997 and 1998. Specifically, we will hear how these Nisei respondents negotiate their aging lives through a religious dynamic of compassion.

"Compassion" is commonly represented in the Japanese language with the word *dojoshin*. The first character, *do*, represents many speaking with a common voice; its reading is "the same." The next is *jo*, which indicates emotion; the last is *shin* or *kokoro*, which means, "heart." The combination conveys that compassion involves sharing the same feelings in one's heart as the other. This understanding correlates with my definition of compassion, which entails five aspects. First, it animates people's capacity to reconstruct others' situations imaginatively and to respond emotionally in ways shaped by the meanings and values of their cultures. Hence it engages the cognitive, imaginative, affective, and sociocultural dimensions of human personality. Second, it inclines people toward informed, beneficent action. This inclination toward action is a power energized by love, as theologian Wendy Farley asserts: "Compassion is love as it encounters suffering. . . . [It] is primordially a power; its knowledge of creatures and their suffering serves as an entrée through which to mediate the power of love."[2] Third, it resists viewing situations as absolutely irremediable. In this sense, it is an enduring disposition—a persistent, characteristic way of interpreting and responding to the world that compares favorably with the Buddhist bodhisattva vow.[3]

Fourth, compassionate people demonstrate a willingness to risk and give of themselves to alleviate another's suffering because of a concern for the other's good. They combine a cognitive distance that allows them not to confuse their reactions for others' with an emotional intimacy that maintains a sense of their shared vulnerability to suffering and their common humanity. Fifth, compassion conveys a respect for the other, which distinguishes it from the condescension of pity. As Farley states, "To receive compassion is to receive respect. Compassion as a form of love includes a recognition of the value and beauty of others. Far from insulting the sufferer with gratuitous pity, it mediates to the other a sense of her [or his] own integrity."[4] This respect implies that compassion is empowering. It seeks justice and mutuality, as well as to alleviate the immediate cause of pain and suffering.

Having offered this definition, however, I recognize the inherent irony of defining compassion abstractly, since it is fully known only as it is lived out. Therefore we will hear the responses of Nisei interview participants who describe compassion as they have lived it and understood it, using five interpretive themes: namely, (1) the conditions that evoke their compassionate action; (2) the utility of acting compassionately; (3) the "homeward" focus of compassion; (4) the competition between compassion and materialism; and (5) how compassion is (and perhaps is not) a quality of the soul. Along the way, we will delineate Buddhist and Christian religious worldviews that support compassionate action. On the Buddhist side, we will see how the Pure Land school's emphasis on Amida Buddha's primal vow particularizes and nourishes the bodhisattva ideal for Japanese American Buddhists.[5] On the Christian side, we will address the value of compassion by describing the connection between divine and human compassion, especially stressing the links between community and compassion.

1. CONDITIONS THAT EVOKE COMPASSIONATE ACTION

My conversations with older second-generation Japanese Americans revealed five clusters of observations that these Nisei had about the value of compassion in their lives. The first cluster involves what conditions might evoke compassionate feelings and actions. The Nisei pinpointed three such conditions: their own awareness of aging, diversity, and their experiences of discrimination.

Being aware of one's own aging was a gateway toward an awareness of others' needs and how they could meet those needs. For example, two Chicago women spoke of their volunteer efforts with age-cohort peers. Shigeko[6] said that "one of the things that I've found as I age... is concern for my friends who are getting older and weaker, especially weaker. And wishing to be with them and support them, help them, and that has sort of been my focus more recently. I want to be there for them. Because you can almost feel for how it would be for your own self if you were in that stage. And that's not volunteering—it's a compassion that comes out as you get older. It's part of the maturing process, I guess. You become a little bit more compassionate, a little bit more caring." Shigeko felt her compassion arise as she saw her peers become physically weaker. She made it clear that she saw a distinction between volunteering—which for her connoted a form of condescension— and compassion, which implied the knowledge that a human being gains by sharing the situation of being older.

In response to Shigeko, Hiroko focused on how she helped people who had recently lost a spouse: "There are so few of us that are still mated. . . . And you—then you realize how fortunate you are if you still have a spouse; you have children nearby you can turn to; you have grandchildren to enjoy. And you realize how many people don't have that. Because of how much you have, you become more compassionate and caring about those who have that lack. . . . When we have someone in our church that becomes widowed, I try if I can to follow through and take food periodically. . . . But those are things that I never thought of as a younger person." Hiroko's awareness of her own aging process—and of the inevitability of losing a spouse—sensitized her to the needs of grieving Nisei who needed concrete assistance. Now that she was aware in a way that she could not imagine when she was younger, she acted upon it by ensuring that recently widowed Nisei had enough to eat, along with the companionship of another human face. Intriguingly, when both women described their own compassionate dispositions, they used second-person pronouns, thus distancing themselves from their own charitable impulses. When they described their actions, however, they claimed them by using first-person language. Regardless of their modesty, which I assume has a cultural component, it is clear that their own aging and anticipatory grief (over the potential of losing one's abilities or losing a spouse) had activated their inclinations toward compassionate outreach.

But reaching out to others carries a cost. For one Chicago Buddhist participant, knowing about his own aging helped him to be more compassionate, but it also taught him about his limitations: "I don't think I could work in a nursing home. . . . I have a lot of empathy for people. And I really enjoy it. But I don't think I could do it on a daily basis." This man gained a great deal of fulfillment from his volunteer work; it was a practice that gave him a sense of purpose, not to mention sheer joy. Intuitively he connected "empathy" with "enjoyment" as interrelated, mutually reinforcing forces. At the same time, however, he had to count the costs of compassion to ensure that he did not overextend himself. The realization that he could overreach his energy in serving others was related to a differentiating awareness tied to his own aging process. While he felt a joyful compassion that drew him toward volunteer service, in that moment he also had to differentiate himself from those for whom he cared. Because he was more able-bodied and able to live without nursing assistance, he was *not* like them in a crucial respect. Couched within that vital distinction, however, was the implicit recognition that he could very well *become* like them in the near future, and in the present he had to pace his compassion so as not to deplete it.

Another condition that seemed to evoke compassion for these Nisei was their growing awareness of the diversity that is permeating their communities. Unlike their Issei parents, the Nisei are facing an increasing intermarriage rate among their children—which prompts a fear in some that their Japanese heritage is being diluted—as well as a growing diversification of ethnic and cultural groups in the larger American context. For several interview respondents, the challenge that this diversity poses was a rich one, prompting leanings toward compassion in them. One San Jose participant spoke of this in terms of how one can nurture healthy relationships between individuals and groups:

> I see that the idea of diversity among us has taken hold. And people are saying, 'Yes, you are different. And I like, I don't like, but at least we can accept you as being diversity. . . . But the next step—if I'm talking about church even—is not only to understand that people are different but how are those different people going to relate to each other in a way that is constructive and productive in our own society. . . . I mean we have racism. We have all kinds of problems there that can be traced back to diversity. But our challenge is how are we going to ameliorate that so that we aren't killing each other off.

One Chicago Christian woman took an even stronger, more proactive approach. She sought out diversity because she desired the spiritual nourishment that came from facing it consciously: "One of the ways that I nurture myself is to actually be with groups of people who, to me, evidence a deep sense of their own spirituality as well as spirituality that comes in the midst of groups. . . . And I'm finding that for me it is a place of nurture, because there is a sense of discernment that there is the possibility that there may be a Spirit, an entity outside one's individual self that's active in groups. . . . I find that it's very freeing for me to try to experience [there] what it must have been like from the Christian perspective when they say, 'Where two or three are gathered.'"7

For this woman, working in an ethnically diverse environment facilitated her calling as a social advocate. Knowing others in their particularity helped her to connect to a deep sense of her own spirituality, which in turn activated and animated her compassionate service. While one could argue (and rightly so) that accepting our common humanness is central to the cultivation of compassion, these Nisei were also noting how one must acknowledge the uniqueness of the other in order not to stereotype others or project paternalistic wishes upon them.[8]

Related to the issue of diversity is another condition that calls forth compassion in these Nisei: their experience of discrimination, especially as represented by the Internment and the years after World War II. As one Chicago participant said, the Internment prompted a sensitivity that makes some Japanese Americans more aware of systemic injustices, including those that occur beyond the boundaries of the Japanese American community:

> I guess I hark back to our concentration camp experiences. I think it had a profound impact on my life and the way I look at groups and whether it's in the workplace or in church or in the public arena, I think that it's important to really look at situations and systems and it's not sufficient that we received redress out of our efforts. . . . And that there are now people coming after you who need your attention and awareness and challenge and advocacy. So I think, I see us there... that's the kind of mantle I would pass on to the next generation. . . . You have to look without being so naïve.

The years following the Internment, when Japanese Americans were seeking to resettle and reestablish themselves, were difficult because of a great deal of residual discrimination. Often they found that they were restricted to marginal housing environments and lower-paying occupations. Even today, several Japanese American participants have experienced themselves as victims of racial discrimination or harassment because of generalized anti-Asian sentiments in some economic or political contexts. Yet in these circumstances, they have discovered that some groups were willing to assist them (including religious groups like the Quakers), and that discovery also helped them to perceive compassion in others. As one participant observed about housing in Chicago following the war,

> I think we all noticed that Jewish people were very, very tolerant of Japanese. For some, don't ask me why. Maybe they had gone through enough prejudice themselves that they felt more compassionate. But we always seemed to be following where the Jewish people were living, and we were accepted there.

Thus discrimination sharpened the Nisei's awareness of the compassion that was surrounding them. It also has helped some Nisei to live more compassionately, too, because their experience of discrimination has made them more sensitive to the discriminatory situations of others—leading certain Nisei toward advocacy and compassionate actions for other minorities, especially other Asian Pacific American populations.

2. THE UTILITY OF COMPASSION

The second group of observations could be summarized as the utilitarian argument for compassion, in both senses of that word. Collectively, these comments argue that compassionate action contains a measure of self-interest because it helps people to feel purposeful and "useful"; it keeps people from feeling and being "useless." Its utility is that it prevents atrophy. These thoughts seemed pervasive among the interview participants, such as this San Jose elder:

> For me enjoying life involves a lot of trying to be useful, you know, because that's one of the things when you retire. . . . You're a has-been, and so you have to cautiously look for things to continue to then be useful. Just 'cause you are retired doesn't mean that you have suddenly lost whatever experience you gain over the years. You like to find some sort of outlet, you know, to use that to help others.

A peer in the same interview group echoed the same sentiment:

> I recently retired, and I think that's the trouble I'm having now is to find purpose in something where I can really feel useful. . . . I had hoped to do some traveling and have time for grandchildren and all that. But I think there has to be a little more, for me anyway, to feel that I'm living a really fulfilling, satisfying life.

It was as if retirement left them directionless. Their experience and energy were unconcentrated, unfocused, and therefore unutilized. "How can I help others and therein give my life meaning and purpose?" seemed to be the underlying question for these Nisei.

This East Bay Christian man made the same connection from the other side of the fence—that is, he saw a similar dynamic, yet as someone who found an outlet for his compassionate activity:

> I retired in 1979. And at that time my nephew was delivering lunches [to] shut-ins. . . . And so, when my nephew quit, I happened to take

over. And I did it for about twelve or thirteen years. And to me it felt like I was giving back to the community. And it really gave me a good feeling. It was something—a purpose in my life. I had to quit about five years ago because it was getting to be too much when you deliver and the person dies. . . . So I finally gave it up. But while I was doing it, I was real happy and energetic in doing it.

Significantly, he referred to compassion as "giving back to the community," which we will soon discuss. What was also telling is that, for him, the costs of compassion (the stress of meeting people and then knowing that they have died) eventually outweighed the benefits of compassion (the happiness and energy he felt while volunteering). As with the Chicago man we heard earlier, this man seems to tell us that compassion is not an inexhaustible quality. It can get "worn out."

The tension between usefulness and uselessness is highlighted more strongly in the words of this East Bay Buddhist grandmother:

You have a certain feeling, especially from the children. They call you and say, "What do you think, Mom?". . . So I'm grateful that you are needed. Even my grandchildren—they will call me up and say, "*Obachan* ['Grandmama,' a term of endearment] I'm thinking of this or that. And what do you think? Do you think I'm doing the right thing?", you know. And that makes me not so useless, you know.

She wavered between knowing that she was a "valued elder" in the eyes of her children and grandchildren—and feeling gratitude for being needed—and the implied confession that without this need she would feel useless. Being of some use and purpose to one's family or the larger Japanese American community seemed to be a strong value among the Nisei I interviewed— so much so that becoming "useless" is greatly feared.

In a clear statement of the "utilitarian" argument for compassion, one Bay Area Christian woman urged her husband to continue his volunteer service:

I don't think you should ever lose sight of something purposeful in your life. Like my husband has done a lot of volunteer work. . . . But he's getting [to be] eighty-three. And for the first time he says, 'Gee, I don't know if I can do this much longer. . . . ' And I said, 'You must stay with it. It's good for you. It keeps you mentally alert.' And it really has helped him.

In other words, his compassion was good for his health. The note of obligation in this woman's admonishment to her husband—"You must stay with it"—underscores for me not only an awareness that being compassionate keeps one alive and involved, but also an underlying fear that I believe may be fed by the dual cultural heritages that the Nisei share. On the one hand, many Americans live with the perceptions that aging is synonymous with decrepitude and that one's value rests in what one does—one's work—so retired elders are more "useless" than "useful." On the other hand, in the Nisei's Japanese heritage is a tradition that elders are honored in their old age—and yet one must continuously prove that one is worthy of such esteem. This complex of cultural messages thus points to a need to recover and reframe images of vitally involved elders from the Nisei's religious traditions.[9]

3. COMPASSION BEGINS AT HOME

The third cluster of observations involved how the Nisei sought to act with compassion in their daily lives. One East Bay participant spoke about striving for excellence in every aspect of his life because doing so would contribute to the improvement of the world: "I said to myself, 'I'd like to make this world a little better place because you pass[ed] through it. . . .' Ever since my college days, I decided to be of some use to the community." He described how his efforts contributed to the success of his company, and how that in turn gave him the will and energy to pour himself into work to assist the Japanese American churches.

Notably, among the Nisei men whom I interviewed, there were several comments that lead to the perception that compassion is an obligation that one assumes because of one's community. Compassion was not just something that they sought to do, but in a way something for which they were sought out. In some cases, the obligation can be very subtle, as I heard when speaking with a Nisei woman about a Chicago Christian man while he was present:

> One of the things I heard about Atsushi, she said, from a younger person observing him teaching the kite-making was how he is so patient in relationship to young children. So, I think that that's really a wonderful role model. . . . Well, he's a role model for us, too, to see him going like sixty [mph] every day. It makes us feel like we can't be or do any less.

I asked Atsushi, "How do you feel about that?", and he replied, "The more encouragement I have, I have to do a little bit more." Atsushi's comment implies that his compassionate action, while an avocation he enjoyed, was also a response to the affirming social pressure that he felt from his peers. The encouragement of others spurred him on; it was an obligation he sought to fulfill in his daily life. What was also significant is how his action had a reciprocal effect on the woman. She felt that she "can't be or do any less" in her own life. Compassion thus has a mutually reinforcing obligatory effect on these Nisei respondents.

Yet tied to this insight—that one must begin living compassionately where one is, with emphasis on both aspects—I heard an uncertainty among some Nisei elders about whether their actions have much impact on the larger world. One of the Buddhist interview groups, in fact, debated whether they were "handing off the reins" to their children and grandchildren and whether one was "never too old to participate" in political issues and religious institutions. The group did not reach a consensus on that matter; some thought that they can and should remain involved all their lives, while others thought it more important to "step aside" (in the words of one Chicago Buddhist). This debate reflects intergenerational concerns quite clearly, but it also speaks to whether older Nisei feel empowered to stay involved and live out their compassionate impulses. The solution that some have found is in moving from more global toward more localized concerns, such as this Christian man in San Francisco expressed:

> I used to worry about, you know, peace in the Middle East and the process there, what was going on, about Bosnia, about these things, but now there's too much to worry about and too little I see that I can do. . . . To me faith has become more here and now and what is it that I can do, what is it that needs to be done, and [then] do it. The more physical, the better. The less thinking, the better.

Another participant in the same group discovered, though, that when he did not possess the energy or resources to directly intervene in a situation, prayer itself could be a compassionate act:

> We always pray, we pray a lot. We're all growing old. . . . The Sisters always tell us that we can never solve all the problems of the world, even in society, you know. So you pray inside, you know, and pray every night. Always pray and there is soon some solution.

There is a resonance between this man's focus on prayer, as something that he can do in the present, and this East Bay Buddhist's way of expressing his compassion, which was by being a secretary-receptionist for his temple:

So he [the Buddhist minister] wanted somebody who had been at the church for a while to help him get adjusted back to our church situation. So, I've been there almost two years. It's supposed to be a two-day-a-week job. . . . [But] I work about four-and-a-half days. It's not a job. I feel it's an opportunity to help the church. Also gives me a chance to get out of the house. . . . But, being retired, that's one of the pleasures I have now.

There is a resonance in how these two men approached their service. The Christian man's prayer and the Buddhist man's office work were both ingrained parts of their lives and expressions of their compassion, which became—to use Tocqueville's now-famous phrase—a "habit of the heart" or an embedded, enacted moral norm.[10] Stated another way, these elders were embodying and expressing what Robert Coles describes as a "modest moral stand," meaning the ways in which an older idealism finds expression in small daily acts of compassionate service motivated by "a long-standing sifting and sorting of interests and preferences."[11] The key to this modest moral stand lies in their intentionality. Compassion is not simply something that arises, but it is something that is practiced, and practiced consciously over a lifetime, in order to become an ingrained part of one's character. Being a person of compassion, in the opinion of some Nisei participants, is as much about choice as it is about circumstance. As one San Jose respondent described it,

> I spent most of my life after college in Southern California and all my business contacts and social contacts were there. And when I moved up here to the Bay Area, I had no business contacts and not a lot of friends. I've made a lot of friends since, but the difference there is in the opportunity for service. Because if I'd stayed in Southern California I would have been drawn into a lot of different activities and service projects that I was into, because my contact with people in [a particular city]. But when I came up here, I didn't have any of that. So if I want to go out and do service, I have to go out and intentionally seek it out.

The fact that this participant was active in volunteer service demonstrates that compassion emerges wherever one is—and happens as one embodies compassion with conscious, persistent intention. Rather than simply "falling into" compassion because of location or circumstance, this elder chose to live a compassionate existence by seeking occasions to make the "opportunities for service" happen. This speaks to the empowering character of compassion, a theme we will revisit later.

4. COMPASSION IN COMPETITION WITH MATERIALISM

In line with the Nisei's observation above that one must be intentional about compassionate action in one's daily life, there seemed to be some consensus (at least among the Japanese American Christians who spoke with me) that compassion's voice competes with the siren call of materialism. These elders were most intent on emphasizing how one's spirituality relies on one's willingness to serve. As one San Jose man stated,

> I guess I would like to leave with my children the fact that although making a living is important, it's not the only thing. And that developing the spiritual dimension in their lives is significant and important. And also that they should, you know, should return to the community. You know, help serve the community a little bit in addition to taking from it. That's what I would like to leave them with. Hopefully my wife and I have lived our lives in a way that serves. I hope that they will see us as good examples.

This man's hope that his children would return something to the larger community is not only an example of how he wants them to be compassionate, but also of how he connects compassion with gratitude. To him, serving the community is a way of repaying the indebtedness one has toward the larger human family.

Further, while I heard these elders advising their children and grandchildren not to be overwhelmed by the quest for material goods, I also heard them acknowledge the tension of doing so, especially in one's "householder" years when one must provide for one's family. Yet these elders were encouraging their descendants to strike a balance between what is needed and what is desired and yet unnecessary. In the words of one Chicago participant,

> What I would like to tell young people is not to get so caught up—and this is very difficult in today's world—not to get so caught up in material goods. And to really think about the real values and the real priorities that we ought to be focused on. Because life is... a gift and when it's your time to go it's not how much money you've accumulated but how much good you've done in the world when you were here.

This sounds like an exegesis on Jesus' counsel about not worrying: "Strive first for the kingdom of God and its righteousness, and all these things will be given to you as well" (Matt. 6:33 NRSV). From a Buddhist perspective, this could be heard as a call to free oneself from attachments and to focus on what is central—an invitation to alleviate suffering and strive toward being a bodhisattva. Yet these Nisei continue to acknowledge that such a stance is one that few people possess all their lives; for many of them, it is something that "grows on them" as they get older, as this Chicago participant expressed:

> And I also feel, as these other people have said, that I have. . . I feel more compassion for people that I didn't really know too well. . . . You know, my concern is for their wellbeing now. I think I'm not quite as selfish as I used to be.

In this respondent's words, I hear a sense that compassion can increase and mature as one ages, that the experience of aging can facilitate a broadening of one's vision and consequently the scope of one's compassionate action. This widening compassionate lens is not an automatic transition or an inherent part of the aging process. However, for those who are so attuned, an awareness of one's own aging and transience can nourish a compassionate response that moves toward what Buddhists would term "equanimity."[12] Thus aging is not only a condition that can evoke compassionate action, as I asserted earlier, but it can bear the potential to expand one's compassionate capacity.

Yet this respondent also voiced a self-acceptance that includes a willingness to admit one's own flaws—in this case, selfishness. In speaking about her compassion, though, this respondent's awareness of herself as a flawed, selfish being contributed to a seeming reluctance to attribute compassion to her self. She felt compassion, but her language implies that this quality was not inherently hers; it is not "I am more compassionate," but rather "I feel more compassion." This distancing from compassion raises several issues. First, is this something that is prevalent among several Nisei participants, or is it her idiom alone? Second, is compassion perceived as a characteristic of one's own soul or is it a gift that one is given through the power of God's grace or Amida Buddha's vow? Third, if it is a gift, is it received once and definitively, or must it be continually provided and exercised? With these issues in mind, we move to the fifth cluster.

5. COMPASSION AS A RELIGIOUS QUALITY OF THE SOUL?

Given what we have just heard, the question mark is obviously intentional. The Nisei's fifth cluster of observations connects compassion to the key metaphors of their religious traditions. For several of these Japanese American elders, compassion is part of the foundation of their lives, as exemplified by their personal life creeds. One Nisei participant expressed this creedal focus by talking about a high school motto and an intriguing image of life:

We had a motto for the high school, and it's stayed with me all these years, so I want to share it with you. It was printed across the top of the auditorium in assembly because—on top of the stage, you know. . . . The first thing was obedience to law. And I interpreted that as God's laws. . . . Respect for others is the second. . . . Number three is mastery of self, and that's a biggie. And the [fourth] one is joy in service — those are the four. . . . And the final word that he [the principal] gave us was, 'These constitute life'—just these four lifted up. And the way I see it is that as your life is like it's on a wheel and as you are going up, you are acquiring knowledge and all the rest of it and help from everybody or education. . . . And you are developing strengths and resources and abilities so that when you start on the down side of that curve, you are on the giving side. You know, you have been accepting all this time, now you are going to be able to share it.

For this man, respect for others and joy in service are major pillars in a healthy, meaningful existence. What is intriguing is how this elder employed the image of a wheel to symbolize life and aging. When I initially heard it, I thought of a Ferris wheel, with the "down side of the curve" being one's aging years. But now I wonder if this Japanese American Christian was not borrowing from the Buddhist image of the wheel of samsaric (transitory) existence to illustrate his view.

These comments do, however, illustrate how compassion can be motivated by deeply held religious convictions. The Nisei with whom I spoke expressed much modesty about speaking authoritatively from their faith traditions; some participants, indeed, initially were concerned about whether they were "qualified" for the interview research. Yet it became obvious as they spoke that a good number had thought quite profoundly about their lives and faith. As it relates to compassion, Eiko, an East Bay woman, spoke about her motivation in becoming a registered nurse: "When I entered nursing school, we were asked to write an essay of why we chose nursing as a career. . . . I said I would want to serve mankind, my fellow human beings. And that's why I chose the nursing career as a way to serve. And the paper came back and all she [the professor] had marked underneath was, 'Why not serve God instead?' And that really made an impression on me because the dean of the school at the time was our teacher. . . . And over and over again it was brought out that no matter how deplorable the situation may be, remember the godliness and Christ-likeness in a person."

For Eiko, finding the Christ in the other was a key to serving dying patients with empathy and care. This awareness guided her toward claiming her vocational purpose, which prompted her to feel empowered in her compassion. For example, she recalled an incident with a terminally ill, unconscious patient and his wife. Hearing from the wife about the virtue of the patient, Eiko encouraged the wife to express her feelings to her husband: "Gradually more and more she kept telling him, 'Thank you for the wonderful family you have helped me with. And thank you for the loving things you did.'" Eiko continued, "The more I thought of it, it made such an impression on me that I thought, 'My purpose is to help with the living and the dying, in the sense that they can accept it to help them help their families cope with their impending death.'" This woman tied her empowering awareness of compassion to her theological affirmation that she could find God in all the humans she meets. Because she could see the divine image in the patients she served, she could respond compassionately to them.

Like many of the Christians I interviewed, Eiko's understanding of human compassion was grounded in her belief in divine love and compassion. Judeo-Christian traditions affirm that God loves the beings whom God has created and endowed with the divine image, and that God desires to be in relationship with humanity; according to the prophet Jeremiah, God declares, "Is Ephraim a dear son to me, a darling child? For every time I speak of him, in fact remember him again, that is when my very heart trembles for him, when in fact I show compassion on him" (31:20).[13] God's stance toward the world is described as a yearning for relationality, which moves God toward compassion.[14] In Christian doctrine, God demonstrates (or embodies, with the pun fully intended) the depth of God's love through the incarnation—that "God was in Christ" and so Jesus' life and ministry yields definitive evidence of God's caring.[15] Consequently, many Christian theologians —including many Nisei Christians I met—ground their understanding of compassion in the healing ministry and teachings of Jesus. In his sermon on the plain, Jesus commands his listeners to "Be merciful [or be compassionate], just as your Father is merciful" (Luke 6:36 NRSV); his saying on the two great commandments marries love of God with love of one's neighbor (Mark 12:28–34); and he clearly states that loving one's enemies yields a benefit—"that you may be children of your Father in heaven" (Matt. 5:45). Jesus' recorded teaching thus calls his followers to model themselves in accord with and emulate the emergent Hebrew picture of God, an ultimate reality whose compassion is always related to justice for the poor and oppressed, and who commands devout followers to do likewise (cf. Exod. 34:6–7; Isa. 61:1–3; Micah 6:6–8). There is a distinct biblical imperative for Jesus' disciples to live in an awareness of compassion, because ultimately they are related to all others, including the stranger, the widow, the poor, the imprisoned, the orphaned, and even their own enemies.

One is empowered toward this compassion because of Christ's presence in one's life, as Paul asserts: "I have been crucified with Christ; it is no longer I who live, but Christ who lives in me; and the life I now live in the flesh I live by faith in the Son of God, who loved me and gave himself for me" (Gal. 2:20). Thus this Nisei woman saw Christ in the other, and her faith in Christ told her that she could embody Christ's compassion to the other because of Christ's presence in her soul. She saw Christ, she acted as Christ, and in a Pauline sense she was Christ. Thus there arises a call and response in Eiko's (and in other Nisei Christians') compassionate actions. Their action is a response to God's inviting action in their lives, inviting them to live compassionately, which is prompted by God's own compassion toward the world, which arises in response to the world's actions. Like several other Nisei Christians with whom I spoke, Eiko felt called to live compassionately through her nursing, and she felt empowered—which she would attribute as God's gift—to answer that call in her life.

By so doing, this woman and other Nisei Christians who spoke about compassion affirm that compassion does not happen *in vacuo*, but in relation, and that their actions can contribute to the development of the body of Christ in the world.[16] Thus compassionate action addresses both the proleptic and the teleologic sides of the Christian understanding of existence—the "now" and the "not yet" of life. Even with the Nisei who earlier spoke of focusing on local concerns, there is a strong chord of amelioration in this present existence as one is reaching toward the future peaceful and just reign of God. For this reason, Japanese social reformer and evangelist Toyohiko Kagawa (1888–1960) and American Baptist minister Jitsuo Morikawa (1912–1987) have been esteemed as modern examples of Christians who answered that call to embody compassion.

The comments of several Nisei Buddhists whom I interviewed show the connection with the Christians' realization that compassion happens within a community context as a call and response. For these Nisei, compassion seemed animated by a dual emphasis on interconnectedness and causality:

> My response to your question is—you know, the Buddhists like to say
> that all mankind are [*sic*] on this big net.[17] Every intersection of the net
> is a person. And any failure at that one knot affects all the ones right
> around them immediately. But in the end it affects the furthest reaches
> out. Any strength, it strengthens all the ones around them and strength-
> ens the entire net. And so one should really live to—it's your responsi-

bility to try and strengthen the net. If everybody strengthens the net, then everybody will be uplifted by this,

one respondent said. Another stated,

> I try to live the Buddhist way daily. And I think if you are helpful to other people, they'll be helpful to you. I mean this is karma. And also I visit my *butsudan* [a Buddhist home altar] every evening and say the sutra. And I've been doing this for many, many years—ever since I was a little kid. I mean this is the way I grew up.

The first statement is a fairly straightforward presentation of *pratitya-samutpada*. We arise and perish together, and our actions affect all others. If I live compassionately, my action enhances the lives of all others on the net, and if everyone did likewise, the "net" itself would be stronger and healthier. Hence, as we noticed earlier, this elder Nisei saw compassionate action as a way of benefiting the larger community as well as one's own existence—a hint of obligation ("it's your responsibility") blended with a taste of mixed motives ("if everybody strengthens the net, then everybody [including oneself] will be uplifted"). This leads into the second comment which, intriguingly, is an argument from both causal and communal grounds. Compassion is a way of perpetuating good karma. Yet it is also, as Robert Wuthnow points out, a sociologically beneficial act. It affects an entire society because it symbolizes "a commitment to those who may not be able to reciprocate, an acknowledgment of our essential identities as human beings, and a devotion to the value of caring itself." Furthermore, it is beneficial because "compassion gives us hope—both that the good society we envision is possible and that the very act of helping each other gives us strength and a common destiny."[18]

We will return to Wuthnow's statement later, but for the moment I would note that, for these older Nisei Buddhists, an argument from sociological benefit only partially explicates their compassionate activity. Just as Nisei Christians draw inspiration and impetus for their compassion from their understanding of the character of divine love, so Nisei Buddhists also find a rationale for their compassion through their faith affirmations. To get a better sense, some groundwork must be laid by the Chinese Pure Land master T'an-luan (476–542 C.E.) and by Shinran, the founder of the Jodo Shin Buddhist tradition to which the majority of Japanese Americans belong.

According to T'an-luan, "[A]ll Buddhas and bodhisattvas have dharma-bodies[19] of two dimensions: dharma-body as suchness and dharma-body as compassionate means. Dharma-body as compassionate means arises from dharma-body as suchness, and dharma-body as suchness emerges out of dharma-body as compassionate means."[20] This distinction between dharma-body as *suchness* (in Japanese, *hossho hosshin*) and dharma-body as compassionate *means* (*hoben hosshin*) is the Pure Land way of expressing an important Buddhist awareness. The former is ultimate reality in its formlessness, openness, and namelessness—what Buddhists also call nirvana. The latter is its manifestation or embodiment, so to speak, in the appearance of the Bodhisattva Dharmakara (*Hozo Bosatsu*) in this transitory, samsaric existence. This bodhisattva, according to the Larger Sutra,[21] made a series of forty-eight vows while beginning the quest to become enlightened, of which the eighteenth is the most important for Shin practice: "If, when I attain Buddhahood, sentient beings in the lands of the ten directions who sincerely and joyfully entrust themselves to me, desire to be born in my land, and call my Name even ten times, should not be born there, may I not attain perfect Enlightenment."[22] Following many aeons of accumulating good karma, Dharmakara was able to fulfill all of his vows and became Amida Buddha. Amida, whose name combines the notions of immeasurable life (Amitayus) and light (Amitabha), now presides over the Pure Land (*jodo*) where sentient beings are purified of suffering and attachment and can attain enlightenment. Essentially, one enters the Pure Land because Amida's good karma works in our behalf, transferring merit (*eko*) and directing virtue to us.[23] The implication is that not even Amida is exempt from the law of karma and thus also participates in *pratitya-samutpada*.

How Amida's practice becomes one's own—how one is born in the Pure Land—has involved extensive doctrinal development, which we will not address here. What we should notice, though, is that Shinran represents a sea change in understanding this process of birth. He applies a revisionist understanding to a passage in the Larger Sutra that reiterates the crucial eighteenth vow. While the traditional reading places the stress on how sentient beings can transfer merit through the recitation of the *nembutsu* (the phrase *Namu Amida Butsu*, "I take refuge in Amida Buddha"), Shinran focuses on Amida's activity in us independent of our own actions.

Herein lies the foundation of the Jodo Shinshu school as shaped by Shinran's religious vision: Enlightenment rests in the salvific efficacy of Amida's compassionate vow, not in our own efforts. Shinran's term for the former is "Other-power" (*tariki*) and "self-power" for the latter (*jiriki*), and according to Shinran all depends on Other-power, including our response of *shinjin* (awareness based on sincere trust in Amida's vow). Thus Shinran can say in his most famous aphorism: "Even the good person attains birth in the Pure Land, how much more so the evil person."[24] In Shinran's mind and in later Pure Land doctrine, Amida Buddha's compassion toward all sentient beings is so complete that it transforms all karmic evil.[25] In opposition to other Buddhist traditions that stress extensive and strenuous effort by practitioners to gain merit and attain enlightenment, the Pure Land school emphasizes the availability of enlightenment to all sentient beings, regardless of their current circumstances—including women, the poor, the uneducated, and even those who violate the Buddhist precepts.[26]

What is important here is that Shinran grounds human compassion in the compassion manifested in Amida's vow. The *eko* of Amida's primal vow working in the lives of Jodo Shinshu practitioners allows them to act in *eko* toward all beings, and it allows them to transcend their normally limited capacities for compassion. Amida's compassion also moves Buddhists beyond the dichotomy of self and other and toward a profound recognition of the interdependence of all beings. In a characteristically confessional passage Shinran is recorded as saying, "I, Shinran, have never even once uttered the *nembutsu* for the sake of my father and mother. The reason is that all beings have been fathers and mothers, brothers and sisters, in the timeless process of birth-and-death. When I attain buddhahood in the next birth, each and every one will be saved."[27] This assurance that all beings are destined for enlightenment reinforces the pervasiveness of Amida Buddha's compassionate nature. The working of the Primal Vow awakens us to our Buddha-nature and facilitates one's entry into the Pure Land and nirvana; and since, in Shinran's view, this movement begins at the immediate moment when one realizes *shinjin*, compassion therefore lives and should be manifested in the here-and-now of *samsara*. For a person of *shinjin*, compassion should arise naturally and spontaneously in the fabric of her or his life due to the operation of Amida's primal vow.

Given this logic, how do Buddhist affirmations influence the shape of compassionate action in the lives of these Nisei elders? In some ways, compassion is a "null curriculum" in their lives because it can be actively practiced by, while not attributed to, the people who count themselves as Pure Land practitioners. Compassion is not their possession, but is rather the gift or mind of Amida Buddha in their lives, in a process that Dennis Hirota terms "mature engagement."[28] It is an awareness of themselves as flawed beings with mixed motives and what Shinran calls "blind passions," and yet it is also the simultaneous awareness and acceptance of Amida's primal vow as a compassionate means by which all beings shall enter the Pure Land. Thus, insofar as they act compassionately, they are participating in a process that is not inherently theirs, and yet is occurring and situated within their own experience. It is easier and more realistic for these respondents to be aware of their failings than to speak of their qualities. Hence, these Nisei

Jodo Shinshu Buddhists are reticent to attribute compassion as a quality of their souls because Buddhist teaching does not presuppose a soul that survives death and because, while compassion is a great virtue, it is not one that resides in the non-substantial, samsaric, karmically blind self. Instead, compassion is grounded in ultimate reality, which at its base is the complete and utter interdependence of all entities. Rather than speak about themselves and their own compassion (as if it were a possession), then, these Buddhists are inclined instead to talk about compassion by speaking about how they are linked with others. Because it is based in interdependence, compassion is not a static quality, but is characterized and affected by the dynamics of relation.

To answer the three questions posed at the end of the previous section, then, we can affirm that, for both Nisei Buddhists and Christians, it seems common for them to speak about compassion without applying self-attribution to it as a quality within oneself, though Buddhists demonstrated more reluctance than Christians on this point. It appears that there is an operative *enryo* or reserve about this spiritual dimension in the lives of these Nisei. In addition, it seems clear that both Christians and Buddhists consider compassion to be a gift, but that there is a difference in emphasis about where compassion is located and how a human being participates in it as a quality of ultimate reality. While Christians are inclined to speak of compassion as God's gift in their lives, located within them because of Christ's presence in the soul, Buddhists tend to conceive of compassion as a gift because of Amida Buddha's vow, which makes itself manifest through them. Furthermore, both Christians and Buddhists seem in agreement that while compassion is a gift that is received definitively (whether through the Christian process of salvation by grace through faith or the Jodo Shinshu process of receiving *shinjin*), the exercise of that gift is a continual process because it only exists through relational action. Compassion without a relational context is meaningless. Therefore, compassion is indeed seen by these Nisei respondents—Buddhists and Christians alike—as a religious quality, but it is situated within the soul *of a community* rather than that *of an individual*: "I *feel* more compassion" and "*We* live out compassion as we engage with one another."

CONCLUSION

Hence we have reached a stopping point for this discussion of compassion. Yet I do so knowing that provocative matters still exist around this topic. I will mention three in passing.

First, I hypothesized that compassion is a key interreligious value for Nisei elders. What I have learned is that it indeed is an important quality, but it is not often discussed explicitly as such. Rather, it is subsumed under categories of relatedness for many, particularly the Jodo Shinshu Buddhists. Thus, while I was searching for compassion, I heard it in muted tones.

Second, many of my respondents felt more comfort in discussing how they could be the givers or conduits of compassion than in being recipients of compassion. I hear this as a reluctance on the part of several Nisei to think about what it means to be aged, with the possible connotations of frailty and dependency that often accompany advanced age. What is significant, however, is that in both Jodo Shinshu Buddhism and Christianity, we can find themes of interdependence that can address this issue powerfully. Yet for many of these Nisei, it is easier to see themselves as independent and capable of acting compassionately than it is to contemplate their fates if they were dependent. The challenge for these Nisei may be in reconceptualizing compassion through the affirmation of interdependence, and thereby being able to see how being an occasion for the exercise of compassion is itself a compassionate act. An example cited by Minor Rogers yields a clue to how this might happen in a Nisei's life. It involves the renowned Zen and Jodo Shinshu teacher D. T. Suzuki's terminal illness in 1966. Rogers reports how Suzuki often simply said "Thank you" to those who were caring for him.[29] He was at a point where he could not do anything else, and yet in his grateful acceptance of care, he was becoming the occasion for others' compassion to flourish. To revise Jesus' reported words in the *Acts of the Apostles*, compassion suggests that it may be as blessed to receive as it is to give (20:35).

Third, previously we heard Robert Wuthnow's comment that compassion provides hope because it reminds people that a good social framework is possible and that it is possible to build a good common future. Based on what I have heard these elders say, I would suggest a corollary to Wuthnow's assertion that reverses the terms. Compassion may give hope, but compassion also relies upon hope, for there is little point in acting compassionately unless one can hope that fruitful, life-enhancing change can occur. Therefore, compassion must be understood within a constellation of several religious values in the lives of these aging Nisei men and women. As crucial as compassion is in their lives, their religious self-understanding is multivalent and therefore cannot be reduced to one dimension. This preliminary exploration of Japanese Americans' spiritualities thus points toward the rich potential for religious expression within the human aging process, particularly among Asian and Pacific Islander Americans who recognize and commit themselves to a transformative vision of ultimate reality.

NOTES

1. This essay is derived from "Japanese Americans and Aging: Toward an Interreligious Spirituality" (Ph.D. diss., Emory University, 2001), which was funded in part by the Civil Liberties Public Education Fund and by the Louisville Institute, a program for the study of American religion underwritten by the Lilly Endowment, Inc.
2. Wendy Farley, *Tragic Vision and Divine Compassion* (Louisville, KY: Westminster John Knox Press, 1990), 79.
3. By arguing that compassion demands an enduring disposition, I am foreshadowing the conclusion of this chapter—that compassionate action requires hope as its foundation.
4. Farley, *Tragic Vision*, 79.
5. The form of Pure Land Buddhism addressed in this chapter is the Jodo Shinshu school represented on the U.S. mainland by the Buddhist Churches of America, founded in 1899 and based in San Francisco. The BCA and its Japanese "mother" temple trace their origins back to Shinran Shonin (1173–1262), a Tendai monk who studied with the Pure Land teacher Honen (1133–1212) and expanded his mentor's teaching.
6. Out of respect for interview participants' privacy, pseudonyms will be used.
7. She is alluding to a saying of Jesus recorded in Matt. 18:20.
8. Or to avoid what Erik Erikson has called pseudospeciation, which in this instance can cause compassion to deteriorate into contempt or, as with the Japanese Americans during World War II, internment due to race; see *Identity: Youth and Crisis* (New York: W. W. Norton, 1968), passim. The Internment was justified, among other "reasons," by stating that separation and relocation protected the West Coast from sabotage but also protected the Japanese Americans from anti-Japanese racial backlash vigilantism. In other words, the U.S. government utilized arguments of national security and (ironically) of compassion toward the very people who were being imprisoned. These attempts at justification are documented by the U.S. Commission on Wartime Relocation and Internment of Civilians in *Personal Justice Denied* (Washington, DC, and Seattle: Civil Liberties Public Education Fund and the University of Washington Press, 1997).
9. For instance, a Jodo Shinshu Buddhist could look at the life of that school's founder, Shinran, and see how he continued to teach and write well into his late eighties, as well as to the life of Shakyamuni Buddha, who entered *parinirvana* at age eighty after forty-five years of teaching. More familiar to most Western readers would be the biblical stories of such elders as Anna and Simeon in the Gospel of Luke, who greet the infant Jesus and prophesy about his ministry. Less familiar, but still in the Christian tradition, is the fascinating suggestion of the early Christian bishop Irenaeus of Lyons (120–202 C.E.) that Jesus of Nazareth died as an old man because, as God incarnate, he had to experience every stage of the life cycle in order to redeem all people, no matter what their age. See *Against Heresies* II.xxii.4.
10. The phrase is from Alexis de Tocqueville's *Democracy in America* and was made popular by Robert N. Bellah and colleagues with their book *Habits of the Heart* (Berkeley: University of California Press, 1985). In speaking of compassion as a habit, I am also indebted to William James in *The Principles of Psychology* (Chicago: Encyclopædia

Britannica, 1952). With James, I do believe that compassion can become a habituated act if initiated with enough frequency within a context of caring relation.

11. Robert Coles, *The Call of Service* (Boston: Houghton Mifflin, 1993), 232.

12. From a Mahayana Buddhist perspective, equanimity serves as a precondition for the emergence of compassion. The virtues of compassion and wisdom are both realized as we become fully conscious of the realization that all phenomena—including ultimate reality—are empty of inherent, self-sustaining existence. When we can negate a reified objective self and live with all things and beings in dependent co-arising, then compassion becomes possible because we can experience the giving and receiving of compassion as part of who we are as interdependent beings. Furthermore, this compassion is one that does not differentiate in matters of good and evil, because they are transcended in an awareness of interdependence and the emptiness of all reality. Thus we can work toward helping both humans and nature most effectively when we are unattached to human self-interest, permitting emptiness to surmount all self-other distinctions. Hence a Buddhist perspective would take issue with my emphasis on affective response in compassion because of the attachments that emotions reinforce in us. This does not mean denying our emotions, but it does mean, again, emphasizing equanimity toward all.

13. William L. Holladay, *Jeremiah 2: A Commentary on the Book of the Prophet Jeremiah, Chapters 26–52*, ed. Paul D. Hanson (Minneapolis: Fortress Press, 1989), 154.

14. This has been asserted most clearly by feminist theologians such as Sallie McFague in *Models of God* (Philadelphia: Fortress Press, 1987) and Rita Nakashima Brock in *Journeys by Heart* (New York: Crossroad, 1988), but it is also an essential part of the larger Christian theological tradition.

15. The quotation is drawn from 2 Cor. 5:18–19. The meaning of this affirmation has been persistently and heatedly debated throughout the history of Christian thought. The debate has not been about whether God acts compassionately, but rather about how deeply involved God is with the world (that is, how completely God feels with the world, and the degree of influence that the world has upon God) and in what way(s) Christ's compassion embodies God's compassion and informs ours. In theological terms, the debate has focused on divine impassibility and the nature of Christ's mediating activity, but evaluating those claims moves us beyond the scope of this chapter.

16. Cf. Paula M. Cooey, "The Redemption of the Body: Post-Patriarchal Reconstruction of Inherited Christian Doctrine," in *After Patriarchy: Feminist Transformations of the World Religions*, ed. Paula M. Cooey, William R. Eakin, and Jay B. McDaniel (Maryknoll, NY: Orbis Books, 1991); Brock, *Journeys by Heart*; and Donald P. McNeill, Douglas A. Morrison, and Henri J. M. Nouwen, *Compassion: A Reflection on the Christian Life* (Garden City, NY: Doubleday, 1982).

17. This participant is referring to the metaphor of Indra's net, in which each knot contains a jewel, and each jewel reflects all the other jewels on the net. When one junction is touched, the whole net vibrates because of its interconnectedness. The metaphor comes from the Avatamsaka Sutra, a lengthy Buddhist scripture composed in India during the first or second centuries C.E.

18. Robert Wuthnow, *Acts of Compassion* (Princeton, NJ: Princeton University Press, 1991), 301, 304.

19. Dharma-body (Jpn., *hosshin*) is one of the "three bodies of the Buddha." According to Taitetsu Unno in *River of Fire, River of Water* (New York: Doubleday, 1998), it is the "fundamental reality that is beyond human conception and linguistic description" (p. 232).

20. Hisao Inagaki, *Ojoronchu: T'an-luan's Commentary on Vasubandhu's Discourse on the Pure Land* (Kyoto: Nagata Bunshodo, 1998), 265.

21. The Larger Sutra (Jpn., *Daimuryoju kyo*), also known as the Sutra on the Buddha of Infinite Life (Amitayus) or Larger Sukhavativyuha Sutra, is one of three Buddhist scriptures that the Jodo Shinshu tradition accepts as its primary authoritative texts.

22. Hisao Inagaki, *The Three Pure Land Sutras* (Kyoto: Nagata Bunshodo, 1995), 243.

23. Dennis Hirota et al., eds., *The Collected Works of Shinran,* vol. 1 (Kyoto: Jodo Shinshu Hongwanji-ha, 1997), 93.

24. Taitetsu Unno, trans., *Tannisho* (Honolulu: Buddhist Study Center Press, 1996), 6.

25. Hirota et al., eds., *Collected Works,* 453.

26. Ibid., 456–458.

27. Ibid., 8.

28. Dennis Hirota, ed., *Toward a Contemporary Understanding of Pure Land Buddhism* (Albany: State University of New York Press, 2000).

29. Minor L. Rogers, "Shin Buddhist Piety as Gratitude," in *Spoken and Unspoken Thanks: Some Comparative Soundings,* ed. John B. Carman and Frederick J. Streng (Cambridge and Dallas: Harvard University Center for the Study of World Religions and the Center for World Thanksgiving, 1989), 108–109.

CONTEXT

CULTIVATING ACCEPTANCE BY CULTIVATING MERIT: THE PUBLIC ENGAGEMENT OF A CHINESE BUDDHIST TEMPLE IN AMERICAN SOCIETY

CAROLYN CHEN

To inaugurate the beginning of the twenty-first century, Dharma Light Temple,[1] a Chinese Buddhist temple in Southern California, hosted a "World Peace Day," inviting groups of different religious faiths from the community to share in a ceremony of prayer and blessing. Following the opening welcome delivered by the abbess in Mandarin and translated into English, the American national anthem was played, and the American flag was ceremoniously presented by six Taiwanese men in dark suits and white gloves, and with proper protocol, raised up on the flagpole. With their hands upon their hearts and their amber robes flapping in the wind, three rows of Buddhist monks arose to sing the American national anthem. The crowd, mostly Taiwanese devotees, followed along, humming with the melody, not quite certain of the lyrics. Peppered among the crowd were whites, Latinos, blacks and other Asians, who had been invited from the local community to come to celebrate and pray for world peace. Facing the crowd on a raised platform were the distinguished guests, religious leaders who represented the diverse religious and racial mosaic of the local community: a white Baha'i minister, a Chinese Roman Catholic priest, an Indian Hindu priest, a Japanese Buddhist Church of America bishop, and an African American Methodist Episcopal minister, a Chinese Mormon minister, as well as a Latino school board representative, and a white judge.

The event of "World Peace Day" at Dharma Light Temple challenges popular stereotypes of the way that immigrant religious institutions interact with American society on two fronts. First, Dharma Light is hardly the withdrawn sanctuary that most people associate with a Buddhist temple. Hosting a day of prayer for community leaders is only one of many ways that it attempts to reach out into the community. Second, most immigrant institutions are perceived to be inward-focused and ethnically exclusive because of the cultural and social barriers they encounter in entering mainstream society. In its invitation to various community leaders and in its display of American patriotism, Dharma Light sheds the image of immigrant insularity and instead reveals the face of an engaged and civic Chinese Buddhism in America. In the vicinity of Dharma Light are a few Christian churches that are similarly composed of Taiwanese immigrants. Where one might expect these to fit into American society more easily because they are Christians, instead they are withdrawn and maintain their interactions within the immigrant community. As a Buddhist temple, Dharma Light is a religious outsider to American society. On top of that, being Chinese, it is also a racial outsider, and yet it makes every attempt to be engaged in American society. Using the case study of Dharma Light Temple, I attempt to explain this seeming paradox by examining not only how particular religious ideals guide public engagement, but also how representations of religious and racial difference shape an immigrant religious institution's interactions with the wider society.

RELIGIOUS INSTITUTIONS AND THE NEW POST-1965 IMMIGRATION

With an increasing number of non-European immigrants to the United States since the liberalization of immigration laws in 1965, a growing body of scholarly attention has been given to the religion of these new immigrants.[2] The focus of much of the literature on new immigrant religion, however, has been on the happenings within the religious institutions and little attention has been given to the public presence and relationship of immigrants to those outside their institutional walls. For example, it has been well documented that beyond being merely a religious and spiritual resource, immigrant religious institutions often offer a wide array of formal and informal social services facilitating the material, social, and psychological adjustment of their members to the United States.[3]

Much of the literature also speaks to the theme of the immigrant religious institution as an ethnic fortress where immigrants can communally practice, preserve, and pass down their ethnic traditions.[4] Pervasive in all this literature is the recognition that immigrant religious institutions undergo changes and develop new congregational forms as they adapt towards American religious life.[5] This literature describes shifts within the institutional walls, such as the development of professionalized clergy, Sunday Schools, and weekly meetings, as "natural" adaptive responses to the American environment, rather than analyzing how these immigrant religions connect to the larger society.[6]

This lacuna in the literature misses two important aspects of new immigrant religious institutions that my study brings to light. The first is a consideration of how the unique characteristics of post-1965 immigrants as well as the contemporary racial climate of multiculturalism shape the public interactions of immigrant religious congregations. Reflected in much of the pre-1965 immigrant-religion literature is the model of the immigrant church as a withdrawn, sheltered enclave that is disengaged from mainstream American society.[7] While this characterization may be appropriate for the historically specific, class-bound experiences of most immigrants in pre-1965 America, it does not capture the diversity of experiences of post-1965 immigrants, especially those of the new, highly skilled, and professional class of immigrants coming largely from Asia.[8] No longer residing in urban ethnic ghettos, these new immigrants settle in affluent suburbs and come prepared with higher levels of education, income, and English skills to make a speedier climb up the American ladder of mobility.[9]

Not only distinct both class-wise and educationally from earlier immigrant cohorts, they arrive at a period in America where the racial ethnic ideal of multiculturalism, rather than the "melting pot," reigns supreme.[10] Where ethnic and racial differences were to be suppressed and "melted" in the earlier melting pot era, multiculturalism, at least rhetorically, calls for the celebration of difference. Without neglecting the continuing persistence of racism that immigrants face in American society, it must also be recognized that the climate of multiculturalism minimizes some of the obstacles that difference—racial, ethnic and religious—presents to participation in mainstream America, while perhaps simultaneously presenting different obstacles.[11] Specifically regarding the case of post-1965 skilled Asian immigrants, their class and educational advantages, along with the current multicultural climate of the United States, undoubtedly challenge some of the assumptions of immigrant life based upon immigration during different historical eras. Do their religious institutions continue to play the role of the protective ethnic sanctuary disengaged from the concerns of those outside? Or do they make efforts to reach out?

The second issue to which this chapter draws attention is how religious ideals shape the public mission of an immigrant religious institution. Like other associations and institutions within the immigrant community, the religious organization provides a space for communal solidarity through the sharing of resources, symbols, and traditions. What differentiates religious institutions from other immigrant institutions is that they consider themselves to be the living embodiment of universal and timeless truths. They are, to use Robert Wuthnow's term, the "public expression of the sacred."[12] As such, they carry a certain weight, a gravity of responsibility that transcends the concerns of their own congregation and extends into visions of how the world ought to be. How these ideas become publicly manifest is as much a theological question as it is a social question.

Sociological literature has addressed how religious ideals inform a congregation's public presence.[13] From this literature a number of competing typologies have been constructed to categorize the different types of communal engagement a congregation might have in the larger society. In addition to a theological message, varying factors have been cited as critical determinants: for example, geographic locale, socioeconomic class of members, congregational size, authority structure, and human and material resources.

For the most part, these congregational typologies have been based upon cases that are both Christian and Anglo-American. Where post-1965 immigrant religious congregations are not Anglo and often not Christian, I argue that these determining factors only partially shed light on the issue.[14] Overlooking the racial and religious characteristics of new immigrant congregations neglects the way that difference mediates the sort of presence that the religious institution will have in society. Religious institutions operate in a dynamic environment whereby they are responding to a larger social context. Regardless of the intentions of a religious institution, the opportunity to enact these religious ideals in the wider society will depend on the degree of access the public grants them. It is no secret that America has a longstanding tradition of excluding those who are different from the Anglo Protestant ideal.[15] Today, religious difference continues to be an obstacle for non-Christian groups despite the rhetoric of religious tolerance and multiculturalism. For example, there is often a level of suspicion directed towards non-Christian religious groups who attempt to construct their buildings in American neighborhoods. It is not uncommon for them to have to take measures above and beyond those asked of Christian groups to secure local zoning approval of their buildings.[16] Furthermore, hostility and suspicion from mainstream America may cause immigrant religious groups to temper the zeal for their religious mission. For example, few immigrant religious institutions, Christian or non-Christian, will venture to play a prophetic role in society, despite their theological inclinations, as they don't wish to make waves in a country where they are already considered foreigners.[17] The fact of difference may also constrain the manner and extent to which immigrant religious institutions can extend their full religious mission due to the limits of their own resources to traverse the cultural divide to mainstream America.

Using the case study of Dharma Light Temple, I will address how religious and social factors shape the public engagement of an immigrant religious institution. I suggest that two simultaneous internal and external dynamics influence how an immigrant religious institution interacts with the wider society. First, building upon the sociological literature on congregations, I examine the factors that are internal to Dharma Light: its religious ideals and the cultural transferability of the strategies it employs to carry its religious mission out into society. Second, I consider the external forces of surrounding racial and religious discourses, specifically the rhetoric of multiculturalism, and how this opens and constrains possibilities for engagement in mainstream society.

SETTING

Dharma Light is located in suburban Southern California, an area that has had a high influx of immigration from Taiwan in the 1980s and early 1990s. For example, approximately 20 percent of immigrants from Taiwan to the United States have settled in greater Los Angeles County alone.[18] In highly impacted areas of Los Angeles, ethnic Chinese (primarily from Taiwan, Hong Kong, and China) can comprise anywhere from 25 percent to 50 percent of the population.[19]

Owing to the generous financial donations of their members and forward-looking leadership, Dharma Light has been able to command a significant presence in the Southern California Taiwanese community. Dharma Light is affiliated with a Chinese Buddhist order that is headquartered in Taiwan. The order has other temples located throughout the world that serve a predominantly ethnic Chinese diasporic community, the majority of devotees being from Taiwan. Dharma Light Temple has been in existence for a little over ten years, although the order has existed in Southern California for over two decades. Dharma Light has its own publishing company, which distributes religious books, newsletters, tapes, and videos in Chinese. It also has its own local radio and television shows that are broadcast in Mandarin. Dharma Light conducts most of its services in Mandarin; however, in conversation, Taiwanese is common. In addition it holds educational programs in English and Cantonese. The English programs are largely attended by the children of the Taiwanese immigrants as well as Anglo-American adults.

Members of Dharma Light reflect the general socioeconomic status of the Taiwanese immigrant community. The men are mostly well educated and hold at least bachelor's, if not advanced degrees.[20] A significant minority of the men are skilled professionals who are concentrated in the science, technology and medical industries and work predominantly outside of the ethnic community. Some, however, have experienced professional downward mobility in the process of immigration and have opted to run small businesses in the ethnic community. Immigrant women predominantly help in the family business or are full-time housewives. A very small minority work outside of the ethnic community. Most immigrants have been in the United States for at least ten years, although some, those with more advanced degrees, have typically been in the United States for twenty years or more.

RELIGIOUS MISSION: CHARITABLE ENGAGEMENT

Despite popular images of Buddhism represented by the meditating monk remote from worldly concerns, Dharma Light practices what it calls "Involved Buddhism," a Buddhism that is highly involved in the human world. Involved Buddhism is the outgrowth of a larger reform movement in Chinese Mahayana Buddhism that was started in China fifty years ago by the monk Venerable Tai Hsu. Where Buddhism in Taiwan was traditionally perceived by the public as superstitious and primarily a medium for praying for the dead, Involved Buddhism is oriented towards individual practice through daily living. Instead of rejecting the world, Involved Buddhism teaches that one truly practices Buddhism by living fully in this world.[21] This is evidenced in a saying from Venerable Tai Hsu, "When you become fully human, you will become a Buddha. That is the living meaning of truth."[22] In traditional Buddhism, practicing Buddhism referred to religious ritual with an otherworldly orientation, while Involved Buddhism claims that one can practice Buddhism through everyday activities, especially the practice of charity.

Underlying the Buddhist practice of charity is a distinct understanding of salvation that is based upon the concept of karma. Buddhists believe that beings operate in a continual cycle of rebirth whereby one's karma, the culmination of one's actions and deeds, determines the form of one's future life. Salvation for the Buddhist is attaining nirvana, or freedom from the karmic cycle of rebirth altogether. In the state of nirvana one is finally liberated from the illusions of the self and its attachments to this world, which are the ultimate causes of suffering. One works towards attaining nirvana by re-orienting one's thoughts and actions. Through practices of meditation and chanting one learns to empty the mind of illusory thoughts. Through acts of self-giving or charity, one loses the illusion of the separateness of the self.

For those who do not see attaining nirvana in this life as a reality, the more immediate goal is to at least secure rebirth into a higher realm of being. By doing good, one cultivates merit and works towards the assurance of rebirth into a higher realm. By doing bad things in this life one will earn rebirth into a lower realm. One can also accumulate merit through participation in Buddhist rituals and practice. Belonging to the Pure Land tradition of Buddhism, most devotees at Dharma Light aspire towards rebirth in Amitahba Buddha's Pure Land, a realm believed to be more conducive towards the attainment of enlightenment. In its public mission, the Dharma Light Order aspires to "establish a Pure Land on earth" through the dual process of physically transforming the world through charity and promoting internal purification through Buddhist teachings.

Given the nature of their salvation message, Buddhists regard the world and their present lives as a temporary realm where they work out their karmic debts and merits. Buddhists may be concerned about propagating the Dharma but they rarely consider it to be their primary mission in the world. The presence of other religions is in fact a good, because they recognize that all religions motivate people to act morally and ethically. Furthermore, because Buddhists believe that individuals have multiple lifetimes to attain enlightenment, there is less urgency to proselytize than in some other religions. The temple exists primarily to serve its own community of devotees. As an institution of salvation it offers both the education and ritual services that connect the individual to that which is transcendent and facilitates the cultivation of merit. To the extent that a temple, or church for that matter, focuses all of its energies on the maintenance of its own community, its engagement with those outside will be limited. But where a temple does extend itself beyond its own community, the world is a place where individuals can work out their own salvation through good thoughts and deeds. Through such acts of charity, Buddhists work for the salvation of themselves and others.

The development of Involved Buddhism has challenged the temple's traditional institutional role of merely offering sacred ritual and ceremony, expanding its concerns beyond the temple walls to those of public service and charity. While giving visitors a tour of the temple, one of the monastics explained to visitors, "We don't just sit in the forest to meditate; to isolate ourselves for our own religious practice would be selfish. We want to be involved in society." Acting similarly in this vein, the widely recognized Taiwanese Buddhist group Tzu Chi has garnered the financial support of thousands of Taiwanese in Taiwan, the United States, and abroad towards charitable activities. In Taiwan and around the world, the Dharma Light Order has made every attempt to engage its temples in the local community through charity and public service. In its mission statement, one of Dharma Light's expressed objectives is "to benefit society through charitable programs." For example, Dharma Light has been involved in local prison outreach, gang intervention, and charitable fund drives with the larger American society. It was not uncommon for monastics to pray for events remote from Southern California, such as the war in Kosovo or the shootings at Columbine High School. On the other hand, it was rare for the Christian churches to voice concern for worldly affairs that do not affect the church community.

CULTIVATING A CULTURE OF CHARITY

Among its devotees, Dharma Light attempts to cultivate an institutional culture of charity. To encourage its devotees towards greater charity in 1999, Dharma Light promoted the theme, "Three Good Movements," referring to "say good words, have a good heart, and do good things." Walking through the temple grounds, it is impossible not to notice all of the Dharma Light volunteers in their purple-vested uniforms who are attempting to put the "three good movements" into practice. In fact, at times it seems that there are more volunteers than devotees at the temple. Some are giving tours, some are sweeping the grounds, others are answering phones, working in the kitchen, managing the parking lot or running the gift shop. Dharma Light takes volunteering seriously and volunteers go through a required training course before starting their service. Furthermore, while volunteering activities might appear to be casual and fun, volunteers are hardworking and diligent in attending to their tasks. Their reasons for volunteering are multiple. Some come for social reasons, others come because they have the leisure time. Some have even admitted that they come for the vegetarian food. Whether consciously articulated or not, devotees associate volunteering with doing good and the accumulation of merit. Volunteering is mutually beneficial for both the temple and the devotee. For the temple, the presence of a readily available, trained volunteer corps is both cost-effective and convenient. At the same time, to the volunteer it offers opportunities for spiritual enhancement and merit cultivation. This became apparent in an offhand comment that a fellow kitchen helper offered one day. As the most junior volunteer I was doing the unwanted task of taking out the garbage. She remarked that doing such an undesirable chore was good for me. I asked how so. And she replied that it would help my karma and then pointed to the rest of the volunteers, who indeed knew that their acts of giving would be beneficial to their karmic balance as well.

Having cultivated a culture of charity, Dharma Light is able to mobilize this readily available volunteer corps to direct acts of charity towards the public. For example, when the temple wanted to organize disaster relief for the victims of Hurricane Mitch, the human apparatus was already in place for a timely and effective response. In a culture where good deeds are a moral imperative, people are quite willing to donate their time and money for the cause. Other examples of charity and public service work are the temple's efforts to raise money for computers and college scholarships for local high schools, donating food and clothing to an inner-city homeless shelter; donating money to a home for emotionally disturbed children; collecting food and presents for people who have family members in prison; and collecting food and clothing for victims of the January 17, 1994, earthquake in Northridge, California. In the examples given, charity is not directed only to the Taiwanese immigrant community, nor to the Buddhist community, but also to the larger local community.

INTERRELIGIOUS DIALOGUE AND COOPERATION

Another important way in which Dharma Light performs good deeds in the world is through interreligious dialogue and cooperation. Dharma Light regards the cultivation of respect and communication between different religious groups as an important step towards world peace. Sponsoring the annual "World Peace Day" and inviting leaders from different religious traditions is one example of Dharma Light initiating interreligious cooperation. In a memorial service held for victims of Taiwan's September 1999 earthquake, different religious groups from around the Southern California area were also invited to participate. In Taiwan, the Dharma Light order frequently has been the initiator of Buddhist-Catholic dialogues. The Dharma Light Temple participates in monthly Roman Catholic-Buddhist dialogues with local Buddhist and Catholic religious leaders. In addition, Dharma Light enjoys a friendly relationship with a local African American Methodist Episcopal Church. Dharma Light monks and the AME gospel choir have performed for each other's communities. The temple and church have collaborated in a charity drive against poverty in the local area.

Despite the linguistic and cultural barriers that most immigrant groups face, Dharma Light manages to exert a visible public presence in mainstream American society. Dharma Light can extend its religious mission to those outside of its ethnic community precisely because its strategies of charity and public service do not require linguistic or cultural skills. Dharma Light's charity and public service projects rarely involve extensive interactions between the lay immigrant population and the recipients of the charity. Most of the acts of generosity are in the form of donations of money or material necessities that are first gathered within the temple. Donations do not require a great deal of interaction with the larger American public. Furthermore, it is a select group of lay and monastic representatives of the temple who present the donations to the receiving party. This form of outreach is culturally transferable to non-Chinese American society.

Dharma Light also has more contact with those outside of the Taiwanese immigrant community because of its concern for interreligious dialogue and cooperation. While Dharma Light does not actively seek to promote interracial dialogue, its active mission to establish world peace through interreligious dialogue inadvertently promotes interracial interactions as well. For example, in his 1998 year-end message, the Dharma Light Master did not fail to mention that he had visited prominent Catholic and Muslim religious leaders at the Vatican and in Malaysia, respectively. The stated significance of these visits in the newsletter is explicitly religious, "We had a religious dialogue that went beyond the century. In fact world peace is not just a dream. If everyone could understand that all beings are one, and if we know how to be respectful and tolerant, then this human world will be filled with joy and harmony. There would be no war and no injustice." While motivated by religious ideals, the racial and ethnic implications are clear: a Chinese monk having conversations with a white Roman Catholic and a Southeast Asian Muslim demonstrates that world peace will be achieved through the cooperation of not only different religions, but different racial and ethnic groups as well. Particularly in the racially and religiously plural population of the United States, one cannot have interreligious dialogue without at the same time engaging other racial and ethnic groups.

GETTING ON THE INSIDE BY BEING ON THE OUTSIDE: CHRISTIANS AS RELIGIOUS INSIDERS AND BUDDHISTS AS RELIGIOUS OUTSIDERS

Internal factors such as religious mission, resources, and strategies shed only partial light on the way that immigrant religious institutions negotiate their public presence in society. External factors and social context need to be taken into account. Immigrant religious institutions, and all religious institutions for that matter, are guided not only by their religiously-defined missions, but are shaped by the dynamic interaction with their surrounding religious and social environment. Where the religious group is theologically inclined towards social engagement, I suggest that ironically it is the presence of religious difference that encourages greater engagement in mainstream America.[23] For example, in the vicinity of Dharma Light, there is a local Taiwanese mainline Christian church that has a tradition of public service and political involvement in Taiwan. Given its theological orientation it should be similarly involved in American public life as well, and yet it is withdrawn from mainstream society. The mainline Taiwanese church has not abandoned its religious mission in the world, only it continues to focus these efforts in Taiwan rather than the United States.

In the case of the Taiwanese Christian church, difference from mainstream America is diminished because it shares the same religion as a predominantly Christian United States. As a Christian institution, it doesn't pose a threat to the Christian hegemony in America. Neither does the church experience the pressure to engage in "public relations work" in mainstream America that non-Christian institutions must do to gain acceptance and favor.[24] The disengagement of the Taiwanese Christian church from mainstream American society is further reinforced by the fact that in the minds of most Americans, the association of Chinese with Christianity is incongruous and does not fit into typical religio-racial categorization. By not being sufficiently foreign as most Americans might expect, the Taiwanese Christian churches are overlooked and rendered nearly invisible. While immigrant churches might advertise themselves to the American public as ethnic institutions, the lack of distinction between the architecture of their buildings and any other Christian church makes them easily overlooked.

On the other hand, the oriental exoticism of the Buddhist temple captures the attention of most Americans and fits into the American imagination of what is Chinese. In the categories of American representation, Dharma Light symbolically represents what is Chinese more adequately than does a Christian church. Being a symbol of difference, Dharma Light must navigate within a dense forest of competing discourses advocating religious pluralism on the one hand and Christian hegemony on the other. The temple, a massive structure built in traditional Chinese architecture, faced severe obstacles from the local community in gaining permission for its construction. When arguments were raised by the local community that the temple would devalue local property or cause traffic, both members of the local community and Dharma Light devotees confided that these masked the underlying concern for the imposing presence of a non-Christian community in the town. Other arguments stemmed from misunderstandings of Buddhism, such as the unfounded fear of animal sacrifices or local residents' worries that their children would be entrapped by a "religious cult."

Sensing the antagonism from the local community, Dharma Light leaders have taken extra steps to befriend local organizations and to quell any perception of threat. In an interview with the local press the temple abbot posed the questions "What can we do to get the support of the American people?" He promised that the temple would be open for use by the community, including non-Buddhist groups, as well as be a site for running charitable programs. To build a positive image the temple holds an annual "Get to Know Your Neighbors" banquet where they invite representatives from local organizations and businesses to acquaint them with the temple community. Numerous photographs of non-Chinese at temple events are proudly displayed in the temple's monthly newsletters and publications suggesting that they are receptive to Americans. An American flag is not raised in the immigrant Christian church, however it is conspicuously present in the temple courtyard leading to the main Buddha hall. Dharma Light is also a frequent financial sponsor of local public events, such as free concerts in the park. In contrast, no immigrant Christian church makes the effort to participate in local charity events.[25] The World Peace Day, as mentioned in the opening vignette, and the charity activities to benefit local schools and non-profit organizations, are all efforts to cultivate merit, but also to cultivate acceptance by mainstream America. Buddhists would tell me that through these activities they hoped to dispel suspicions and gain the acceptance of the larger mainstream American society.

Gaining acceptance for the Dharma Light Temple means participating in mainstream American activities and "acting American." The burden of proving their Americaness was not one that the Taiwanese Christians shared because of their religious similarity with mainstream America. When asked whether their church should reach out to racial-ethnic groups of non-Chinese descent, most respondents claimed that it wasn't necessary. They had their own churches to take care of them. On the other hand, when this question was posed to the Buddhists, nearly all of them felt that it was necessary, since they were now living in the United States and they should adapt. This underlying concern to "act American" was evident in a comment that a Buddhist woman made concerning the temple's participation in the town's Fourth of July parade. They had by far the most extravagant and spectacular entry in the parade, with several dancing dragons and dozens of dancers dressed in traditional Chinese as well as Indian costumes. The woman, who had designed the costumes for the parade, told me that she sensed that they had not won a prize for their parade entry because it was "too Chinese." To her this was a legitimate reason as she added that next year she would be sure to make the costumes more American with bandannas and cowboy hats. Adapting, for Dharma Light, not only means using English and adopting the cultural trappings of a stereotypical American, but also participating in the multicultural spirit by recruiting the presence of other ethnic groups. For example, at their Chinese New Year celebration Dharma Light invited a Mexican mariachi band to perform.

At the same time that their religious difference prevents Dharma Light from being truly "American," in the age of multiculturalism, the presence of just enough difference becomes the ticket to recognition and possible acceptance. By virtue of the association of Buddhism with the Far East and Christianity with the West, the Buddhists, rather than the Christians, are the ones to be recruited and courted as the Chinese representatives at the multicultural table. Since more Taiwanese immigrants regularly attend a Christian church than regularly visit the temple, the church would be the more effective venue of the two for political campaigning. However, when local politicians want to court the vote of the immigrant Taiwanese population or publicize their multicultural platform, photographs with temple monastics are at a premium because the Buddhists are the symbolic representatives for the Taiwanese immigrant population while the Christians, who are associated with western culture, are not. Indeed, the temple and local politicians share a symbiotic relationship whereby non-Chinese use the temple to gain the favor of the Chinese immigrant population and the temple uses the attention by local leaders and figures to gain acceptance into mainstream America. Certainly this interpretation could be applied on the national level to the much-publicized case of Al Gore and the Democratic fundraising scandal with the Hsi Lai Temple.[26] Commenting on the involvement of Dharma Light in a state campaign of a non-Chinese politician, one temple devotee earnestly told me, "We just wanted to be accepted." Groups interested in cultural exchange and cultural diversity would rather seek the presence of the Chinese monk in a saffron-colored robe than a Chinese pastor in a blue business suit. Indeed, from the vantage point of those at Dharma Light, mainstream American society sends two seemingly conflicting sets of underlying messages. On the one hand there is the pressure they feel to conform to American society, and on the other hand is the message to "stay Chinese." Many Taiwanese Buddhists relayed to me how they are frequently pressured by Taiwanese Christians to convert whereas the Anglo Christians are the ones who encourage them to stay Buddhist. As one respondent told me, her Anglo Christian friend urged her to "stay Buddhist and stay Chinese," suggesting that an authentic Chinese could only be Buddhist.

Ironically, because of the public perception of religious difference, those at Dharma Light feel the need to engage in mainstream American society to bargain for acceptance. While acts of charity are certainly informed by their Buddhist understandings of karma and the desire to cultivate merit, they are also shaped by pressures from mainstream America to prove their Americaness. Having been labeled as different, Dharma Light's acts of charity are simultaneously marks of "cultural citizenship" that are no different from the philanthropic extravagance that has been demonstrated by other new Asian immigrant tycoons to high culture institutions.[27] To interpret Dharma Light's acts of charity as simply a "natural" process of assimilation into American society misses the point that their public presence is shaped by the stigma of difference and the struggle to find acceptance. Ironically, on the other hand, in a historical era where multiculturalism has taken the moral high ground, those at Dharma Light are courted by mainstream America solely on the basis of their "difference." In comparison, Taiwanese Christian churches do not have the burden to engage in public relations work among mainstream Americans to prove their American-ness. But not being perceived as "different enough," neither are they invited to participate in mainstream multiculturalism as the Buddhist Taiwanese are.

CONCLUSION

Hardly the passive sanctuary for world-weary immigrants, Dharma Light Temple demonstrates an active engagement with those outside of its sacred walls. Backed by the savvy know-how of its religious leaders and the support of a financially capable laity, Dharma Light has had a far-reaching influence on those beyond its own congregations. Certainly not all immigrant institutions are like Dharma Light. It is admittedly exceptional in having had at hand a great deal of human and material resources to build its religious empire. But what I have tried to demonstrate through the example of Dharma Light are the common constraints and inspirations which inform all immigrant religious institutions. What makes religious institutions unique is that they are not driven merely by the interests of their members, but also by transhistorical, transracial, indeed, universal ideals about the way that the world ought to be. These otherworldly religious ideals—for Buddhists, the idea of karma—drive the institutions into different mission orientations in this world. How these mission ideals practically materialize will depend upon social realities, such as the institution's resources and strategies and the reception of the community at large.

Unique to the case of Dharma Light are the historically specific opportunities and constraints on public action that multiculturalism presents in American society today. While both Dharma Light and the Christian churches command a significant presence within the ethnic community, ironically it is Dharma Light, as a religious outsider, which ventures to act publicly outside of the ethnic community. The combination of Dharma Light's religious ideals, the cultural transferability of charity, and the external pressure as Buddhists to both prove their Americaness and remain Chinese, contributes to this seeming paradox that as outsiders they are the ones to enter mainstream society. Given the past, today we regard this as an extraordinary irony, but perhaps tomorrow, as the United States grows more racially and religiously diverse, the active presence of an ethnic Buddhist temple may become part of the ordinary and commonplace.

NOTES

The data consists of ethnographic fieldwork conducted at Dharma Light Temple between January 1999 and March 2000. This included participation in volunteer activities, retreats, summer camp, religious ceremonies, religious education classes, and sutra study meetings. During this time I also conducted fieldwork at a Taiwanese Christian church as a basis for comparison. Furthermore, I conducted thirty-two in-depth interviews with devotees and monastics from Dharma Light. Respondents were recruited through snowball sampling.

Portions of this article have appeared in Carolyn Chen, "The Religious Varieties of Ethnic Presence: A Comparison Between a Taiwanese Immigrant Buddhist Temple and an Evangelical Christian Church," *Sociology of Religion* 63:2 (2002): 215–238.

1. Pseudonyms have been given to protect the identity of the institutions and individuals referred to in this article.

2. For example, see R. Stephen Warner and Judith G. Wittner, eds., *Gatherings in Diaspora: Religious Communities and the New Immigration* (Philadelphia: Temple University Press, 1998); Fenggang Yang, *Chinese Christians in America: Conversion, Assimilation and Adhesive Identities* (University Park, PA: Pennsylvania State University Press, 1999); Won Moo Hurh and Kwang Chung Kim, "Religious Participation of Korean Immigrants in the United States," *Journal for the Scientific Study of Religion* 29 (March 1990): 19–34; Pyong Gap Min, *Changes and Conflicts: Korean Immigrant Families in New York* (Boston: Allyn and Bacon, 1992); Kevin J. Christiano, "The Church and the New Immigrants," *Vatican II and U.S. Catholicism: Twenty-Five Years Later*, ed. Helen Rose Ebaugh (Greenwich, CT: JAI Press, 1991): 169–186; John Y. Fenton, *Transplanting Religious Traditions: Asian Indians in America* (New York: Praeger, 1988).

3. Yvonne Yazbeck and Adai T. Lummis Haddad, *Islamic Values in the United States: A Comparative Study* (New York: Oxford University Press, 1987); Hurh and Kim, op. cit.; Tetsuden Kashima, *Buddhism in America: The Social Organization of an Ethnic Religious Institution*, Contributions in Sociology, no. 26 (Westport, CT: Greenwood Press, 1977); Prema Kurien, "Becoming American by Becoming Hindu: Indian Americans Take Their Place at the Multicultural Table," *Gatherings in Diaspora*, ed. R. Stephen Warner and Judith Wittner (Philadelphia: Temple University Press, 1998), 37–70; Helen Rose Ebaugh and Janet Saltzman Chafetz, "Structural Adaptations in Immigrant Congregations," *Sociology of Religion* 61:2 (2000): 135–153; Luis Leon, "Born Again in

East LA: The Congregation as Border Space," *Gatherings in Diaspora*, ed. R. Stephen Warner and Judith Wittner (Philadelphia: Temple University Press, 1998), 163–196; Warner and Wittner, op. cit.

4. Warner and Wittner, op. cit.; Hurh and Kim, op. cit., Yang, op. cit.; Raymond Brady Williams, *Religions of Immigrants from India and Pakistan: New Threads in the American Tapestry* (Cambridge: Cambridge University Press, 1988); Pyong Gap Min, "The Structure and Social Functions of Korean Immigrant Churches in the United States," *International Migration Review,* 26:4 (1992): 1370–1394; Illsoo Kim, *New Urban Immigrants: The Korean Community in New York* (Princeton: Princeton University Press, 1981); Timothy L. Smith, "Religion and Ethnicity in America," *American Historical Review,* 83 (December 1978): 1155–1185; Irene Lin, "Journey to the Far West: Chinese Buddhism in America," *Amerasia Journal,* 22 (Spring 1996): 106–132.

5. Williams, op.cit.; Warner and Wittner, op. cit.; Kurien, op.cit.; Paul David Numrich, *Old Wisdom in the New World: Americanization in Two Immigrant Theravada Buddhist Temples* (Knoxville: University of Tennessee Press, 1996); Rogaia Mustafa Abusharaf, "Structural Adaptations in an Immigrant Muslim Congregation in New York," *Gatherings in Diaspora,* ed. R. Stephen Warner and Judith Wittner (Philadelphia: Temple University Press, 1998), 235–264.

6. Interpreting "congregationalism" as a natural adaptive process masks the manner in which power imposed from outside the congregation plays into internal congregational decision-making. Here I am referring to power in a Foucauldian and Gramscian sense— power not as embodied in a centralized institution or particular individual, but the assumptions of power that are embedded in our everyday cultural norms and ways of knowing and being. For example, what may be interpreted as natural processes of assimilation from the outside are regarded as strategic responses from the inside to allay the suspicions of Anglo-Americans of immigrant foreignness and difference. For example, the Japanese American Buddhist Churches of America adopted Protestant forms of worship such as meeting on Sundays, using pews, and having Sunday School to downplay the American perception that they were different and dangerous. See Isao Horinouchi, "Americanized Buddhism: A Sociological Analysis of Protestantized Japanese Religion" (Ph.D. diss., University of California, Davis, 1973); and Kashima, op.cit.

7. George E. Pozzetta, ed., *American Immigration and Ethnicity: A 20-Volume Series of Distinguished Essays: Volume 19: The Immigrant Religious Experience* (New York: Garland, 1991); Will Herberg, *Protestant-Catholic-Jew: An Essay in American Religious Sociology* (Garden City, NY: Doubleday, 1960); Oscar Handlin, *The Uprooted* (Boston: Little, Brown and Company, 1952).

8. For example, see Paul Ong and Tania Azores, "Asian Immigrants in Los Angeles: Diversity and Divisions," *The New Asian Immigration in Los Angeles and Global Restructuring,* ed. Edna Bonacich, Paul Ong, and Lucie Cheng (Philadelphia: Temple University Press, 1994), 100–132; John M. Liu and Lucie Cheng, "Pacific Rim Development and the Duality of Post-1965 Asian Immigration," *The New Asian Immigration in Los Angeles and Global Restructuring,* ed. Edna Bonacich, Paul Ong, and Lucie Cheng (Philadelphia: Temple University Press, 1994), 74–99; Timothy P. Fong,

The First Suburban Chinatown: The Remaking of Monterey Park, California (Philadelphia: Temple University Press, 1994); Lucian Mangiafico, *Contemporary American Immigrants: Patterns of Filipino, Korean, and Chinese Settlement in the United States* (New York: Praeger, 1988); Min Zhou, *Chinatown: The Socioeconomic Potential of an Urban Enclave* (Philadelphia: Temple University Press, 1992).

However, clearly not all Asian immigrants are professional and educated. There are an equally representative proportion of Asian immigrants who are unskilled and semi-skilled as well. While the Asian professional and educated class possess the skills for upward mobility, their incomes and professional status are still not commensurate with equally educated Anglos. For example, see Liu and Cheng, op. cit.; Herbert.R. Barringer, David T. Takeuchi, and Peter Xenos, "Education, Occupational Prestige, and Income of Asian-Americans," *Sociology of Education,* 63 (1990): 27–43; Henry Der, "Asian Pacific Islands and the 'Glass Ceiling': New Era of Civil Rights Activism?," *The State of Asian Pacific America: Policy Issues to the Year 2020,* ed. LEAP Asian Pacific American Public Policy Institute (Los Angeles: The Editors, 1993), 215-231; Sucheng Chan, *Asian-Americans: An Interpretive History* (Boston: Twayne Publishers, 1991); Mia Tuan, *Forever Foreigners or Honorary Whites? The Asian Ethnic Experience Today* (New Brunswick: Rutgers University Press, 1998).

9. John M. Liu and Lucie Cheng in "Pacific Rim Development and the Duality of Post-1965 Asian Immigration" make the argument that to protect its interests and to prevent the Soviet Union from gaining the upper hand, the United States invested a great deal in the educational, economic and political infrastructures of post-W.W.II Asia. One of the consequences was the rise of a professional middle class who would become the source of skilled and talented immigration to the United States after the liberalization of immigration policies in 1965. See also, Committee on the International Migration of Talent, ed. *The International Migration of High-Level Manpower: Its Impact on the Development Process* (New York: Praeger, 1970); Kuo-ting Li, *Economic Transformation of Taiwan, ROC* (London: Shepheard Walwyn, 1988); H. Brett Melendy, *Asians in America: Filipinos, Koreans, and East Indians* (New York: Hippocrene Books, 1981).

10. David A. Hollinger, *Postethnic America: Beyond Multiculturalism* (New York: Basic Books, 1995); Nathan Glazer and Daniel Patrick Moynihan, *Beyond the Melting Pot* (Cambridge MA: M.I.T. Press, 1963); Milton Gordon, *Assimilation in American Life* (New York: Oxford University Press, 1964).

11. Multiculturalism still hasn't prevented the rise of anti-immigrant sentiment in places like California. For example, campaigns for California propositions that have been detrimental to the welfare of its immigrants simultaneously appeal rhetorically to ideals of pluralism and multiculturalism. No doubt multiculturalism has increased the level of tolerance for difference in our public institutions. On the other hand, the very ubiquity of its presence is evidenced in the multiple ways that it has been reappropriated, even to the disadvantage of those to whom it claims to "celebrate." The argument might even be forwarded that the focus on the cultural aspects of difference only diverts attention from the truly subversive issue of material inequities that continue to persist among different racial groups.

12. Robert Wuthnow, *Producing the Sacred* (Urbana: University of Illinois Press, 1994).

13. Max Weber, "Protestant Sects and the Spirit of Capitalism," *From Max Weber*, ed. H.H. Gerth and C. Wright Mills (New York: Oxford University Press, 1946), 302–322; R. Stephen Warner, *New Wine in Old Wineskins* (Berkeley: University of California Press, 1988); Bryan Wilson, *Religious Sects: A Sociological Study* (New York: McGraw-Hill, 1970); David A. Roozen, William McKinney, and Jackson W. Carroll, *Varieties of Religious Presence: Mission in Public Life* (New York: Pilgrim Press, 1988); H. Richard Niebuhr, *Christ and Culture* (New York: Harper and Row, 1951); H. Richard Niebuhr, *Social Sources of Denominationalism* (New York: Henry Holt, 1929); Ernst Troeltsch, *The Social Teachings of the Christian Church* (New York: Macmillan, 1951); Nancy Tatom Ammerman, *Congregation and Community* (New Brunswick, NJ: Rutgers University Press, 1999).

14. Some scholars argue that the experience of Asian and other non-Anglo immigrants does not fit into the assimilation model of white ethnic immigrants because of the racial factor. Where white ethnics eventually could integrate and become white, non-white immigrants became racialized into an "other" category. Despite the fact that some Asians have achieved middle-class suburban aspirations, scholars argue that Asians will be unable to shed their status "foreigners" in the United States. See Tuan, op. cit., Lisa Lowe, *Immigrant Acts* (Durham, N.C.: Duke University Press).

15. Kashima, op.cit.; Horinouchi, op.cit.; Leonard Dinnerstein, ed., *Antisemitism in the United States* (New York: Holt, Rinehart and Winston, 1961); John Higham, *Strangers in the Land: Patterns of American Nativism, 1860–1925*, 2nd ed. (New Brunswick NJ: Rutgers University Press, 1981); R. Laurence Moore, *Religious Outsiders and the Making of Americans* (New York: Oxford University Press, 1986).

16. For example, recently great controversy has arisen regarding the plans for an Arab foundation to convert a church into a mosque in a suburb outside of Chicago. The city council has offered to pay the foundation $200,000 to drop the plans for the mosque. In Wichita, Kansas, residents have attempted to keep a Hindu temple out of their neighborhood. Similarly, in Irvine, California, protests have arisen concerning the building of a synagogue. See the National Conference for Community and Justice website: http://www.nccj.org.

17. Lin, op.cit.; Yang op.cit.

18. Susan B. Gall and Timothy L. Gall, eds., *Statistical Record of Asian Americans* (Detroit: Gale Research Inc., 1991).

19. Paul Ong and Tania Azores, "Asian Immigrants in Los Angeles: Diversity and Divisions," *The New Asian Immigration in Los Angeles and Global Restructuring*, ed. Edna Bonacich, Paul Ong, and Lucie Cheng (Philadelphia: Temple University Press, 1994), 100-132.

20. According to the Immigration and Naturalization Service figures from 1997, 64 percent of immigrants from Taiwan hold at least a bachelor's degree compared to 16.2 percent of the United States population.

21. Involved Buddhism's "this-worldly" orientation is not unique to Chinese Buddhism but is mirrored in contemporary Buddhist movements around the world. For example, see

the writings of Thich Nhat Hanh, who calls for an "engaged Buddhism" that is quite similar to Involved Buddhism. For scholarly accounts of socially engaged Buddhism see Christopher S. Queen and Sallie B. King, eds., *Engaged Buddhism: Buddhist Liberation Movements in Asia* (Albany: State University of New York Press, 1996).

22. According to an authority at the Dharma Light Temple, this is a quote passed down through popular oral tradition.

23. The presence of religious difference alone will not necessarily encourage engagement with mainstream America unless there exists a theologically-oriented foundation towards public engagement. For example, in the vicinity of Dharma Light there are other Taiwanese Buddhist temples whose presence does not extend beyond the ethnic immigrant community despite being "religiously different." Unlike Dharma Light, their missions are primarily to serve the existing temple community through religious education and ritual ceremony rather than through the social services as forwarded by Involved Buddhism.

24. See Carolyn Chen, "The Religious Varieties of Ethnic Presence."

25. Southern California has 100 Chinese Protestant churches compared to 32 Buddhist and Taoist temples and organizations.

26. Dharma Light respondents expressed concern over the damage the event might bring to themselves and other Chinese Buddhists in the United States. They interpreted Hsi Lai's political donations as gestures of goodwill directed towards the American government rather than the Democratic Party, per se. According to respondents' interpretations, Hsi Lai's acts of political charity were not inappropriate in themselves, but became distorted and mismanaged in the hands of political opportunists such as Maria Hsia. See also Stuart Chandler, "Placing Palms Together: Religious and Cultural Dimensions of the Hsi Lai Temple Political Controversy" in *American Buddhism: Methods and Findings in Recent Scholarship*, ed. Duncan Ryuken Williams and Christopher S. Queen (Richmond, Surrey, UK: Curzon, 1999).

27. Aihwa Ong, *Flexible Citizenship: The Cultural Logics of Transnationality* (Durham, NC: Duke University Press, 1999).

THE RACIALIZATION OF MINORITIZED RELIGIOUS IDENTITY: CONSTRUCTING SACRED SITES AT THE INTERSECTION OF WHITE AND CHRISTIAN SUPREMACY

JAIDEEP SINGH

INTRODUCTION

Among the most dynamic sources of diversity in the United States is that emanating from the numerous religious groups that are flourishing under the relative religious freedom offered by this country. While there cannot be an official state religion in the United States, Christianity has historically been given unofficial sanction and privilege in virtually every sphere of American life. Resulting from this long tradition of Christian dominance is a strong sense of entitlement and xenophobic entrenchment in significant and powerful sections of the population.

In 1997, Henry Jordan of the South Carolina Board of Education retorted to those who objected to a prominent display of the Ten Commandments in the State's public schools: "Screw the Buddhists and kill the Muslims." Jordan later explained his strong reaction in the following manner: "I was expressing frustration. . . . [Schools] can teach any kind of cult. Buddhism is a cult. So is Islam. I'm getting a little tired of it." Meanwhile, undeterred by the opposition of these "cultists," Nebraska Governor Benjamin Nelson proclaimed May 17 of the same year "March for Jesus Day."[1]

And in August 2001, Rep. Don Davis, a white, Republican state legislator in North Carolina, forwarded via email a letter to every member of the state House and Senate that stated:

"Two things made this country great: White men & Christianity. . . .
Every problem that has arrisen [sic] can be directly traced back to our
departure from God's Law and the disenfranchisement of White men."[2]

While he later distanced himself from the remarks, Davis initially explained
his reason for forwarding the email as: "There's a lot of it that's truth, the way
I see it. Who came to this country first—the white man—didn't he? That's
who made this country great."

As evidenced by these examples, religion has become a particularly powerful method of classifying the "enemy" or "other" in national life in recent
years, impacting primarily non-Christian people of color. For instance,
Muslims have become among the most demonized members of the
American polity, as a result of international events and domestic actions by a
miniscule handful of their co-religionists. In return, their religion has repeatedly been characterized in an inaccurate, misleading, and blatantly racist
fashion in the media and public discourse; their property and religious sites
have been vandalized; and their bodies have been targeted for hate crimes in
alarming numbers. As the venerable scholar Edward Said has noted, the last
sanctioned racism in the United States is that directed at followers of the religion of Islam.[3]

The validity of this statement was evident in March of 2000, when
Reverend Jerry Falwell, a powerful and influential Christian minister with a
national following, told a religion website that "the Moslem faith teaches
hate."[4] He later tried to clarify his comments by claiming that he was referring to any group "bearing any bigotry toward any human," apparently fail-
ing to see the irony in his "clarification," in which he specifically cited the
Aryan Nations and the Church of Scientology as examples of such prejudiced groups.

Noting this paradox and highlighting some possible consequences of
Reverend Falwell's bias-laden discourse, Omar Ahmad of the Council on
American-Islamic Relations faxed a letter to Falwell in which he explained
that "These offensive remarks are symptomatic of the very intolerance that
you claim Islam promotes.... Your destructive rhetoric could lead to discrimination and even physical attacks against Muslims."[5] The violent, racist
backlash mentioned by Mr. Ahmad has recurred across the nation in the
wake of the Iranian Hostage Crisis, the Gulf War, and the terrorist attacks
upon Oklahoma City, the World Trade Center, and the Pentagon.

The notion of the "Muslim terrorist" is one powerfully etched on the
minds of most Americans. The blatant racism behind this characterization,
which goes unquestioned even by the intelligentsia in American society, can

be gleaned from the complete dearth of depictions of the perpetrators of the Oklahoma City Federal Building bombing, abortion clinic bombers, and various white militia groups, as "Christian terrorists." When such acts are perpetrated by white Americans, the specificity of their religious affiliation is neither a matter of newsworthiness nor comment. The utilization of the term "terrorist" enables the facile dehumanization of the targets of that pejorative by the press and the public.

Analogously, Sikh migrants to the United States—who most Americans find indistinguishable from Muslims—have found themselves the target of racist scapegoating and media misrepresentations. The ruinous and recurring depiction of the "Sikh terrorist" was revived most recently when most of the country's major media outlets mistakenly reported that a plane hijacked in India had been seized by Sikhs.[6] Although many media outlets later apologized and printed corrections in the wake of this erroneous accusation, the hurtful initial reports only confirmed the validity of the siege mentality many Sikh Americans feel on many levels. They believe that they are second-class citizens not only because of their racial background, their accents, and their lack of English proficiency, but also because of the religion they practice. This is an especially disquieting notion to Sikhs, because a number of them came to the United States to escape the religious persecution suffered by the tiny Sikh minority in India.

The new society into which Sikh immigrants have transplanted their culture, one they perceive as hostile and forbidding to their cultural traditions, has racialized them as a result of their ostensible "racial uniform,"[7] which in the case of the Sikhs is also a religious uniform. This conflation of racial and religious identity has further convoluted the already demanding attempts of Sikh Americans to develop and crystallize a diasporic identity—one intensely informed and complicated by transnational factors—efficacious for themselves, and communicable to American society at large. The intersections of white supremacy and Christian supremacy have made the integration of Sikh Americans into the Republic all the more formidable a task.

In a fervent attempt to cling to the most salient aspects of their religio-historical identity, Sikhs have built a *gurdwara* (Sikh temple) wherever they have migrated. This has become a source of conflict in a number of communities around the country in the past three decades since Sikhs started arriving in the United States in large numbers. As a case study in this trend, I will examine the recent struggle of the Sikh community in San Jose, California to build a new gurdwara, and the highly racially-charged objections of members of the local community that opposed the construction of the new sacred site. I will examine the racialized and xenophobic aspects to the opposition of certain members of the surrounding community, linking the situation in San Jose to other struggles by Asian Americans seeking to build places of worship.

XENOPHOBIA AND OPPOSITION TO THE CONSTRUCTION OF SACRED SPACES

Silicon Valley has attracted a sizable number of Sikh Americans in the past two decades. The remarkably diverse population of the area contains sizable Sikh American and South Asian American communities, many of whom work in various sectors of the high-tech industry that propels the region's economy. However, the Sikhs in the area are visible not only behind computer terminals and in the boardrooms of computer companies, but behind the wheels of taxi cabs and the counters of convenience stores and gas stations. Their visibility and sizable presence, as well as the broad mixture of racial and ethnic groups in the vicinity of San Jose, would seem to make the likelihood of the Sikh community facing resistance in their attempt to construct a sacred site unlikely.

However, San Jose, like the rest of the nation, remains highly segregated along racial lines. The Sikhs sought to locate their new *gurdwara* in an affluent, primarily white neighborhood, and consequently became viewed as a threat by some of the residents of the locale. The visible presence of the Sikhs in the community evidently was the basis of some residents' desire to prevent them from entering their neighborhood in large numbers—a fact that became painfully evident during the contentious approval process for the new gurdwara. Nevertheless, the progressive political atmosphere in the region, as well as the general emphasis on supporting diversity by City officials and numerous faith-based community leaders, became a tremendous boon to the Sikh community as they sought support for the *gurdwara* project from non-Sikh members of the community. They formed a far-reaching coalition of political, community, and faith-based leaders in support of their cause—one that was the source of vigorous and often bitter contestation and confrontation.

The July 31, 1997, edition of the *San Jose Mercury News*, carried an article entitled "Residents Protest Temple Plans," which began with the following lines:

> People who live near a proposed Sikh temple in San Jose's Evergreen foothills packed a city hearing Wednesday to complain about the size of the sprawling structure, which some have dubbed the "Taj Mahal of the West." Opponents said the temple, however beautiful, will increase traffic and ruin the tranquility of their semi-rural neighborhood. Some fear

that the giant onion-domed facility, to be built on a 40-acre apricot orchard... will become a regional tourist attraction.[8]

This instance, when examined closely, resembles many other such conflicts faced by Sikhs, Muslims, Buddhists, Hindus, Jains, and members of other minority religions throughout the United States. The friction often boils down to a situation in which the Constitutionally-guaranteed religious freedoms of an easily differentiated, racialized community of Asian Americans are trampled by "mainstream" opponents seeking to abridge their right to build a site in which to peacefully worship and practice their religious and cultural heritage. The arguments put forth by the opponents of the construction of such sacred sites are often no more than thinly-veiled, xenophobic opposition to members of a non-Christian, racialized minority entering their community in sizable numbers. The problems faced by the Sikhs in San Jose are a classic illustration of this trend.

Since the gurdwara project met all of the City of San Jose's requirements, the city staff expressed no real opposition to the plans, and it moved quickly through the initial planning stages.[9] The development of significant community opposition appeared quite suddenly, after the process was well under way to get approval for the building of the new gurdwara.

As the date neared for the Planning Commission meeting in which the final approval for the project could be granted, the Sikhs noticed a good deal of activity in the neighborhood. They noticed people in the Evergreen community—a primarily residential enclave in the San Jose foothills, where the Sikh community purchased land on which to construct the new gurdwara—getting organized to oppose the project. The Sikhs saw provocative flyers that had been distributed to residents, alerting the neighbors to the impending building of a Sikh Temple.[10]

The opposition was led by a local real estate developer who distributed flyers through the neighborhood that attacked the gurdwara project. The flyers contained inflammatory statements like "A church the size of K-Mart is coming to the neighborhood, and it will create major traffic problems!" The rising resistance astonished the Sikhs, who had always had cordial relations with members of the surrounding community, although Sikh community leaders later admitted they had been too insular. As a result, the Sikhs were stunned that so many people were suddenly so interested in the project—and that they all viewed it negatively.[11]

At an August 13, 1997, meeting in the San Jose City Council chambers, city planning official Joseph Herwedel told a standing-room-only crowd of more than 350 people that there was no reason to deny the project approval from the City. He immediately became the target of "loud boos and mur-murs of disapproval from angry area residents. . . . The meeting was punctu-ated by shouting and catcalls. 'Put it in your neighborhood,' someone from the audience shouted. 'We don't want it in our neighborhood.'"[12]

Opponents of the gurdwara project vowed to file an appeal with the plan-ning director, and consider a lawsuit if the planning commission upheld the decision. Opposition leader Walter Neal revealed that, "they may seek an injunction based on what they see as an inadequate environmental impact report and traffic study."

The gurdwara opponents put forth five primary reasons for their opposi-tion: 1) the increase in traffic to the gurdwara would inundate the neighbor-hood with cars; 2) noise from the gurdwara would disrupt their lives; 3) the architecture would not fit into the neighborhood scheme; 4) the building would be too large and obstruct their view; and 5) tourists would flood the area because of the tremendous beauty of the new gurdwara. These ostensi-ble objections were all dismissed by the City's independent experts as being baseless, because of the numerous special precautions that the Sikh commu-nity had taken to accommodate their neighbors.

The Sikh community was shocked by the sudden groundswell of resis-tance they faced. As a *Mercury News* editorial elucidated, "The Sikh commu-nity is ready to pour a fortune into the temple and feel ambushed by the opposition, since it followed all of the city's rules in developing the plan."[13]

In order to accommodate their neighbors, the Sikhs had already agreed to putting a cap of 1500 people in the facility at any one time, as well as accept-ing restrictions on the operating hours of the gurdwara.[14] In fact, no other site of worship in San Jose has any such strictures on time of services or size of congregation applied to it. "The limit was termed 'appalling' by commis-sioner Linda Lezotte, and Gloria Chun Hoo said the Sikhs had tried to reach out to the community by even considering it."[15]

Despite all of the assurances and allowances made to prevent Sikh wor-shippers from having an inordinate impact on the community, the exagger-ated fears of Evergreen residents continued to proliferate in the media. Obviously voicing the fears of some of her compatriots, one resident claimed, in a letter published in the *Mercury News*, that, "property values will decline due to large crowds of people loitering in the neighborhood."[16]

Finally, the true basis of a large portion of the opposition was becoming apparent. To assert that Sikhs will "loiter" in the neighborhood such a dis-tance from the large parcel of land on which they have constructed their site of worship is to depict them as a gang, instead of as a highly respected religious congregation. Imagine the public outrage if the same accusation had been directed against a Judeo-Christian religious group. The racial subtext of this remark raised serious questions about the true motivation behind the opposition's tenacity, something becoming increasingly visible in their discourse of opposition.

Despite the Sikh community's assurances of good intentions and willingness to compromise, as well as numerous evidentiary contradictions presented to refute their concerns, gurdwara project opponents continued to proffer illegitimate arguments as the basis of their opposition. The intractable insistence of some Evergreen residents in clinging to discredited arguments certainly seemed informed by their own myopic experiences of attending various churches, and their obvious ignorance about Sikhs and their religious practices—which they may have perceived as something very different from the peaceful prayer and hymn-singing that constitute the majority of Sikh religious ceremonies.

In addition, their feelings of uneasiness in dealing with a group of highly visible, ostensibly different "others" played a conspicuous role in the conflict. But such explanations remain insufficient to explain the persistence of their combative stance. Other factors had to play a role in the failure of reasonable people to appreciate overwhelming evidence from so many independent sources, such as those employed by the City of San Jose, in addition to the good faith promises of the Sikh community.

THE RACIALIZED BASIS OF THE ARGUMENTS AGAINST THE GURDWARA

In a nation so obsessed with race, where many major issues of public debate become racially-tinged in some manner, one has to wonder if such impassioned opposition would have been generated if a Christian church of similar proportions were being built on the same property. The comments of some of the residents who oppose the gurdwara project bring such a proposition into serious doubt.

While most people—including many in the Evergreen community—cherish the idea of a peaceful site of worship becoming a part of their neighborhood, certain individuals in this particular instance appeared ready to use any excuse to keep the Sikhs out of their community. Dr. Loren Chan Singh sensed racial bias in segments of the opposition, albeit subtle in its use:

> On the part of some people, a lot of what they said, I felt, were just code phrases for racism. They made various excuses . . . [for opposing the gurdwara project, consisting] of different code words and phrases which

I felt [indicated] some underlying racism. It was always couched in a very diplomatic way.[17]

Dr. Gurinder Pal Singh notes that those opposed to the new gurdwara seemed determined to prevent the construction of the building, regardless of how much the Sikhs acquiesced to their demands, or offered assurances for their concerns:

> Later on, I noticed that they changed their strategy. First they were attacking the purpose of the Temple, saying this is going to be noisy. . . . Then they started saying it is going to be an ugly, monstrous building. Then once other people's opinion came out that it looks like it is going to be a beautiful structure, they said it's going to be a tourist attraction and attract too many people. I saw a constant shift in their pattern of trying to find faults which didn't exist. . . . *I saw things constantly shifting over time.* [emphasis mine][18]

This constant shifting of grievances and proffering of new complaints once previous claims had been assuaged, manifests a powerful indictment of some members of the opposition. Their true dissatisfaction obviously lay in areas other than the ostensible objections they mouthed—and repeatedly changed.

In voicing disapproval towards the construction of the gurdwara, opponents of the project repeatedly asserted the absence of any prejudice in their motives. In fact, many of the strongly worded letters to the editor published in the *San Jose Mercury News* by opponents of the gurdwara began with explicit disavowals of any racial or religious partiality. A public anti-bias proclamation became almost a prerequisite for anyone criticizing the project:

> I am certain that the Sikh community believes that the protest by Evergreen residents is due to racism or, at the very least, a negative cultural bias.[19]

> This is not a religious or cultural issue.[20]

> It's not about the Sikhs— it could be another Mormon temple or the Vatican.[21]

> "This is not a religious issue," [Jim Zito] said. "This is not a racial issue." . . . [Mr. Zito] wants people to know that his opposition has nothing to do with religion or race.[22]

Despite such strident claims, opponents of the gurdwara project repeatedly alluded to a violent conflict that had occurred in 1997 at another gurdwara, about 25 miles away. Using this isolated incident as the basis, they classified *all* Sikhs as inherently violent, and undesirable additions to the neighborhood. In fact, a lengthy piece in the *Mercury News*, focusing on a couple who live next to the parcel on which the gurdwara would be built, contained a very pointed reference to this incident, and what it supposedly revealed about the Sikhs in San Jose, and by extension, the entire world.

> In their appeal to the city, Jim and Zoe Zito cited past problems at the Sikh temple in Fremont, where members fought each other and police were called in. "The Sikh organization has established a precedent of being undesirable neighbors with incidents involving their temple in Fremont," wrote the Zitos in their appeal.[23]

Not only was Mr. Zito's racism laid bare with his words, but so was the fact that he and his wife knew almost nothing concerning the people about whom they had just issued a blanket condemnation. They were apparently unaware that they were slandering members of the fifth largest religion in the world, not some local "organization." Ironically, the article this interview appeared in was entitled: "Sikh Temple Opponents Deny Racist Motives."

The blatantly racist generalization utilized by the Zitos was repeatedly proffered by opponents of the gurdwara project. For instance, a letter to the editor published in the *San Jose Mercury News* exclaimed: "This little community is about to be hit by... potential violence from the Sikh temple gatherings."[24] Despite the fact that the Sikhs in San Jose had had no such problem whatsoever in the dozen years they had been holding religious services in the area, such rhetoric pervaded the dialogue on the construction of the new gurdwara.[25] Though sometimes just below the surface of the discourse, the language of race remained a powerful tool with which to publicly denigrate the Sikhs by guilt through racialized association.

In response to such comments, Hindu American Annie Dandavati, who led a group called Evergreen Citizens Coalition which supported the gurdwara project, issued a spirited response: "The author referred to the Sikh community as undesirable neighbors and went on to suggest that this entire community was somehow made up of outlaws."[26]

Ms. Dandavati explained, "there were a few letters that went out to some of the [San Jose] Council members that were pretty racist. . . . I remember the language in one of them. This obviously uneducated person wrote this letter saying, 'I don't want this church to be built there. These Sikh seniors, they walk around like '*crows*' [emphasis added]—because our seniors always walk in the evenings."[27] The common habit among South Asians of taking evening strolls apparently disrupted the visual image some Evergreen residents had of their community. These swarthy immigrants, with "foreign" attire, evidently did not fit into their conception of desirable neighbors.

Echoing the beliefs of the Sikh community and Ms. Dandavati, Elbert Reed, executive director of the African-American Community Service Agency, pointed towards racial motives behind the opposition to the gurdwara:

> "Whenever there's a plan for a minority church, there's always protest. . . . They have done nothing wrong. . . . I think it's going to be a plus for the community."28

Confirming the suspicions of the Sikhs and Mr. Reed, Fred Fong, an Asian American member of the opposition, uncomfortably acknowledged that the group included "some prejudiced people," but insisted that most opposed the temple for "legitimate" reasons.29

Members of the opposition even went to the length of issuing thinly veiled threats in demanding to have the gurdwara moved out of their neighborhood. Said one gurdwara opponent in a letter published in the *Mercury News*, "The Sikhs have been respected, and accepted, members of our community for many years now. We want to continue this relationship, which is why we are asking them to look for another site for their church."30 Obviously, she meant that Sikhs would no longer be granted the favor of being "accepted" by the majority community, were they to construct a new gurdwara in Evergreen.

Mr. Zito also issued a cryptic warning, one particularly disquieting in light of the hate crimes which have plagued Sikhs and their gurdwaras around the country.

> Everyone loses if this structure is built as proposed. The community will have a hard time welcoming a group [the Sikhs] which has such disregard for their quality of life.31

THE ASCENDANCE OF RACIALIZED LOGIC

Within the safe space created by the company of others who opposed the gurdwara project, the explicitly racist sentiments of several Evergreen residents flowed easily—even in the obvious presence of members of the Sikh community of San Jose. Bhupindar S. Dhillon reveals that gurdwara opponents expressed their true feelings quite freely in the early community meetings that they organized, but later tempered their language after the Sikhs began highlighting the racism explicit in their dissent. The opponents realized that such blatant racism could quickly backfire on them, and became more sophisticated in their assault.[32]

Dr. Tarlochan Singh, Chairman of the gurdwara's Public Relations Committee, attended the neighborhood meetings organized by those opposed to the gurdwara with his children, and described what he heard:

> There were all kinds of racist comments. One white woman came up with a cardboard drawing, with some characters in black, pushing daggers into each others' bodies. She was saying that this is how Sikhs fight in the gurdwara. That was the impression she was trying to create. . . . She was basically trying to scare people away, and trying to mislead them with racist stereotypes.[33]

Dr. Singh reports one of the most alarming comments he heard at one of these meetings, in which opponents of the gurdwara rarely disguised their real target: the Sikhs, not the gurdwara.

> [Someone] said, "They're going to take over the entire neighborhood, and we want a good mix in the neighborhood. We're going to have to leave and sell our houses."[34]

This statement indicates the potential for great difficulty in the new millennium for a city as ethnically, religiously, and racially diverse as San Jose. According to census data, in 1999, whites became a minority in the county of Santa Clara, which contains the City of San Jose.[35] The racial code words of seeking "diversity" and a "good mixture" in the area barely mask the ugly underside of this statement. It not only raises the ugly specter of white flight, but also attempts to give credence to the racialized image of the inundation of the neighborhood with "hordes" of Sikhs. The stark insinuation is unmistakable: that the Sikhs are unwelcome in the neighborhood, particularly in any sizable numbers.

The most prominent racist incident—and eventually the most damaging to the opposition—occurred at the City Planning Commission meeting, in front of over a thousand people and local news station cameras. A person opposed to the gurdwara project carried a large picket sign emblazoned with the words "NO SIKH JOSE." Imagine the outcry if the word 'Sikh' had been replaced with 'Jew' or 'Black.' As it was, an African American professor from San Jose City College, Dr. Merylee Rucker Shelton, saw the placard and reported the rueful incident to the City Human Rights Commission, which later sharply reprimanded the opposition.

Without taking the time to learn anything about their Sikh neighbors or their worship practices, some of the residents of the surrounding community were ready to believe the worst about this "strange-looking Other" that was "invading" their neighborhood. Echoes of present-day "white flight" resonate loudly here, but that does not fully encompass the problem. The obvious physical differences of the swarthy-skinned, dark-bearded, turban-wearing, sword-carrying, potentially fear-inspiring Sikhs presented a protuberant obstacle to imagining them as fellow citizens of the American polity. The racialization of the situation was veiled only with a very slight veneer of racial code words, and the quickly shifting objections to the gurdwara project.

Dr. Tarlochan Singh summarizes the feelings of many Sikhs:

> They never said directly that they don't like Sikhs, but that is the overall impression that we have gotten. When someone says, "We don't know these people." . . . What else do they need to know about us? We've been living here in the U.S. for about a hundred years. We've been living in this Valley for many, many decades. My grand-uncle came to this country in 1905. . . . He lived in Stockton most of his life.... [He] never went back. And these people say, "We don't know who they are"? We are human beings like any other people, and we do honest work, we pay taxes, we are law-abiding citizens, and we are very proud to be in America. . . . Simply because we look different [they do not want us here]![36]

THE FINAL DECISION

At the hearing at which a final decision was to be handed down by the City Planning Commission, the Sikh community came out en masse in an impressive show of support. Perhaps even more impressive than the over 800 Sikh supporters that turned out that day was the coalition of disparate supporters the Sikh community had patched together. A number of non-Sikh community leaders appeared at the meeting to voice their support of the project, including several Evergreen residents. Annie Dandavati recalls the strength of the broad coalition that had assembled that evening in support of the new gurdwara:

> We showed up there with a thousand people. I mean, it was awesome! I'd say 800 to 850 were Indians, mostly Sikhs, but Hindus too. And the rest were "mainstream." We had the Chairman of the local Democratic Party's Central Committee, we had the County Supervisor, we had City Council people. We had a lot of elected officials, we had a lot of com-

munity leaders, Hispanics, African Americans—all our Coalition people. And it was awesome! Everybody came and spoke and they said, this is based on discrimination and ignorance."[37]

Dr. Tarlochan Singh tells the touching story of one resident who came out to the Planning Commission meeting, to support her Sikh neighbors:

> There was a white woman—she was probably 90 or 95 years old—she came in favor of the Sikhs. She could hardly walk. She was a very old woman. She got a special hair-do on that day . . . and she spoke for a couple minutes and said she supports the Sikhs. It was so nice of her.[38]

Dr. Gurinder Pal Singh also noted that the presence of non-Sikhs was beneficial to the Sikhs' cause:

> When we went to City Hall, we benefited from a broader effort and the support of a very diverse group, which included Blacks, Hispanics, and other Asian groups. They got a number of politicians to speak in support of the gurdwara. That was very helpful.[39]

For example, "there was an African American priest who said, 'I would have an objection if they built the smallest church in the city. It is God's house. Why should it be small? It should be as big as possible!'"[40]

The following vignette from Dr. Gurinder Pal Singh, nicely sums up the sentiments of the coalition of people who spoke on behalf of the gurdwara:

> There was a Christian priest who was there of his own accord, not someone who anybody had approached to speak for us. He truly spoke from his heart. He said, "How can anybody ever say no to a house of God?" He also said, "I have a congregation of 7000 right in the same area. Why are we discriminating against them? My people come all the way from Salinas in the south and San Francisco in the north (both about 50 miles away). We never have a traffic problem. Why are we limiting them to 1500? Why are they even accepting a limit of 1500? They shouldn't! . . . Our job isn't done yet. You can't have this limit of 1500 imposed on you. If that gets set as a precedent, that would be damaging for all religious organizations. Tomorrow, they can put that on a church, or a mosque, or on anything else, and that should not be allowed. I won't let that happen." And I think he has a point.[41]

The Planning Commission of San Jose unanimously approved the gurdwara project.

RACE, RELIGION, AND INTER-RACIAL RELATIONS

While the attacks on African American churches in the South during the 1990s eventually drew attention from the nation, the travails of other congregations of color are very rarely heard. For example, in 2000, the Washington-based National Conference of Catholic Bishops concluded that Hispanics are twice as likely as other Catholics in the United States to worship in segregated, separate, and unequal settings.[42]

Several Asian American religious groups have also faced increasing discomfort from white Christians, a trend that sometimes manifests itself as opposition to attempts by Asian American congregations to construct sites of worship in predominantly white, Christian communities. In Wichita, Kansas, residents of the city attempted to keep a Hindu temple out of their neighborhood, citing parking concerns. Also in 2000, in the Chicago suburb of Palos Heights, the attempt of a Muslim group to purchase a church building and convert it into a mosque met staunch resistance from several members of the community, raising questions of religious bigotry. The 450 Muslim families in the area, most of Arab descent, were told that some city leaders had come out against the project, saying the community should instead buy the church and convert it into much-needed recreation space. The church had been for sale for two years with no previous offer from the city. The City Council even voted to offer the foundation $200,000 to drop its plans, but the Mayor vetoed the idea, calling it an insult to Muslims. During the furor, some residents of the community declared Christianity the "one true religion" and called Islam a "false religion," statements reminiscent of the arrogance and intolerance often demonstrated in such instances of Christian entrenchment.[43]

In 1978, a Buddhist group purchased a parcel of land in Hacienda Heights, in the greater Los Angeles area, less than ten miles from Monterey Park, noted for being America's "first suburban Chinatown." Located on a hill, with a picturesque view of the surrounding San Gabriel Valley, it was an ideal site for a temple. "The proposed temple, which they named Hsi Lai Temple ('Coming West Temple'), was designed to attract more believers and to promote cultural exchange between East and West."[44] But due to vociferous opposition to the temple project from local groups, the temple's construction did not begin until 1986, eight years later.

Neighborhood residents claimed that traffic would become snarled, large numbers of tourists would flood their neighborhood, and housing prices would rise (a truly remarkable point of opposition). Unfortunately, what it came down to in many instances was the fact that "many people did not want to see the establishment of a Buddhist temple in a largely Christian neighborhood, and some people interpreted the plan for the temple as a racial issue, seeing it as a means for the Chinese to build not only a temple, but to establish a dominant position in their community."[45] An issue that was, at heart, a matter of religious freedom, became starkly racialized.

In order to win the public over, Chinese Americans had to resort to measures including Buddhist monks and nuns going "door-to-door explaining their good intentions and the benefits they could bring to the neighborhood," and a petition drive to help secure permission to build. "In all, there were a total of six public hearings before the plan was finally approved. Hsi Lai Temple, the largest Buddhist monastery in the entire western hemisphere . . . has since become a tourist attraction in the valley, drawing many visitors each year from different parts of the U.S. and the world." The temple has also generated substantial revenue for local businesses, organized several charity activities, and "a New Year prayer, along with local Christian and Mormon churches, that emphasized the importance of understanding and peace in eliminating racial and religious conflict."[46]

The xenophobic resistance to the gurdwara that arose in San Jose distinctly parallels that which has confronted many other non-Christian congregations of color across the nation. In most of these instances, this antipathy is directed towards a highly visible, racialized minority group seeking to build a sacred site, in an upper-middle class white enclave.

Under most conditions, a site of worship would be welcomed into a neighborhood as an addition that could only enhance the quality of life of the area's residents, as well as positively affect the values of their property. However, the racialization of the issue prevented a sober, rational appraisal of the situation. In the case of the San Jose gurdwara, race became a seminal issue in the discourse of protest, from the general stereotyping of Sikhs as violent, unwelcome additions to the Evergreen community, to the especially egregious display of the "No Sikh Jose" at the City Planning Commission meeting.

As Elbert Reed of the African-American Community Service Agency noted above, people of color often run into what appears to be ostensibly irrational resistance when attempting to construct sites of worship. The rationale becomes much clearer when race is considered as a factor in the consternation with which some communities view such sacred sites. Numerous instances of such conflict have occurred across the country, forcing members of various Asian American groups to contend with the fears of the majority in order to exercise their right to worship as they choose.

The situation in San Jose certainly is not an isolated incidence for Sikh

Americans. In the midst of the problems the San Jose Sikhs were facing regarding the new gurdwara, one of the members of the gurdwara managing committee received a phone call from a Sikh from New York, who relayed that Sikhs in his local community had experienced very similar problems.[47] In the fall of 1998, in San Diego, California, the Sikh community engaged in a nearly parallel struggle, with remarkably similar rhetoric being employed by those opposed to the new gurdwara being designed as the Sikhs wished.

As with the San Jose case, the racist opposition painted the coming religious institution as an incongruous eyesore that belonged in India instead of an Escondido neighborhood. The comparison to Disneyland was again proffered, as was reference to the Taj Mahal mausoleum, reflecting the stereotypical impressions and limited knowledge of the area's residents about people from India.[48] The comparison of sacred sites to the aforementioned tourist attractions reflects the manner in which many Americans tend to denigrate non-Christian religions to the status of "cults," as demonstrated earlier by the comments of South Carolina's Henry Jordan. The Orientalist mindset behind this train of thought reduces the religious practices of millions of Americans to mere "spectacle."[49]

Echoing the sentiments of some of the Evergreen residents, one Escondido resident insisted, "We just don't think it is the proper place for it."[50] Again, the Sikhs publicly suggested that discrimination was a factor behind the problems they were encountering in getting approval for the new gurdwara design. An article in the *San Diego Union Tribune* said:

> Members of the society say they realize their religion is alien to most people in this country. They also suggest they are the victims of subtle discrimination . . . To buttress their argument, the Sikhs point to the presence of another church, the Apostolic Christian Church, about a block away from their site, as well as the huge commercial area that borders the residential neighborhood to the east.[51]

Pardeep Singh, of San Marcos, said the feeling now is that the domes [on the proposed gurdwara] are a must. "If the dominant alien culture starts to dictate its values on the rest, then that is nothing short of blatant discrimination," Singh said.[52]

"If we have a Home Depot in our neighborhood, how much of an eyesore is that?" said Pardeep Singh. . . . "It seems kind of discriminatory if one particular neighborhood doesn't want this because it is the Sikh culture. If this were a Catholic church, I don't think they would have the same concerns."[53]

In the summer of 2000, white resistance to the construction of a gurdwara in the District of Columbia was described in the following manner by the *Washington Post*:

> One hand was hugging the oak tree, the other held a cell phone, while above her a tree cutter in the elevated arm of a bucket truck was getting ready to start lopping branches. "I'm calling the mayor's office!" Beth Schneiderman screamed in a last-second effort to save the trees near her house. . . . Her son Daniel, 22, was hugging another oak, and a neighbor was defending a third. When Schneiderman got someone in city hall, she hollered into her phone, "This is an emergency!"[54]

In this instance, environmentalism served as the façade for the opposition of white neighbors, who went to the extent of invading the private property of the Sikhs to register their resentment towards their moving into the neighborhood. Such frenzied reactions by white adherents of Judeo-Christian religions have forced many Asian Americans to reassess the true parameters of religious freedom in this country. They note that they have not done anything illegal or immoral, yet still face such hostility from their white neighbors. They have gone through the proper channels to build their new site of worship, something very near and dear to their hearts, and something that many Sikhs consider a religious obligation.

The gurdwara in D.C. would be the first Sikh temple in the nation's capital, located on a small triangle of land the group has owned for 20 years. Said Shamsher Singh, an economist and a leader of the group, "If we did not create something which is aesthetically beautiful there, we as Sikhs would feel ashamed."[55] He went on to add, "One of the beauties of America is that it guarantees rights for everybody. The neighbors have a right, and so have we. All we are asking is equal treatment."

Echoing the reasonable voices of San Jose city planning officials, "Armando Laurenco, the city's administrator for building and land regulation, said the zoning code gives churches leeway for designs that do not conform with other building types nearby. He said the Sikhs 'are well within their rights to bring the building there.'"[56] But as in San Jose, opponents of the new gurdwara employed highly charged rhetoric in denouncing the Sikh sacred site:

> "Don't citizens count?. . . We live here, and this is the quality of life of the citizens of the District of Columbia, and we must have rights."

> The neighbors call the project a "horror" because of its size in relation to the nearby houses, which are about 34 feet tall. The temple also would not be set back from the property line on 38th Street, as every

house on the block is. While the temple would face Massachusetts Avenue, its 70-foot side wall would be built right to the line, eight to 10 feet from 38th Street. "If you walk your dog, you'll scrape your elbow," Schneiderman said.[57]

These varied, yet comparable, instances of conflict between Asian Americans and members of the dominant community illustrate a prevailing trend across the United States. As the nation increasingly diversifies, non-white members of non-Christian religious faiths are demonized in public discourse through racialized terminology by fearful white Christians. Muslim Americans have been among the most affected by this disturbing trend, augmented in severity by the particularly contentious dealings between foreign national Muslims and the United States in recent years. But, as their population has grown exponentially in recent years, other Asian Americans have increasingly faced the wrath of the white, Judeo-Christian majority. Instances of sacred site construction bring to the surface this often clandestine hostility towards an apparent "model minority."

Sikh Americans are among the religious communities of color who have suffered from this commingling of racial and religious bigotry, sometimes mistaken for Muslims, and other times singled out for abuse because of their conspicuous racial uniforms, accents, or skin color. Religion provides an additional axis of difference for Americans whose racially-informed logic prevents their recognition of Sikhs as fellow Americans.

As the country continues to diversify racially and religiously in the coming years, it remains clear that the issues of racial and religious bigotry towards minority religions—in a nation in which Christianity is the dominant, unofficial state religion—will continue to be a sore spot in non-Christian communities of color across the nation. In order to avoid increasingly rancorous conflict in the coming years, the centuries of Judeo-Christian tradition, morality, and dominance must allow space for the culturally distinct religions that accompany the increasingly racially diverse population of the United States. In addition, members of the dominant community must join with their fellow non-white Americans to battle the vicious combination of white and Christian supremacy which has plagued our nation since its birth.

NOTES

1. "News of the Week in Review," *The Nation*, June 16, 1997.
2. Estes Thompson, "N.C. Lawmaker Apologizes for E-Mail." Associated Press, August 22, 2001.

3. Sam Husseini, "Islam, Fundamental Misunderstandings About a Growing Faith," *EXTRA!*, July/August 1995.

4. Cathy Lynn Grossman, "Falwell's Remark that Islam 'Teaches Hate' Sparks Outrage," *USA Today*, March 8, 2000, p.4A.

5. Ibid.

6. See most major newspapers in the United States on December 25, 1999, for examples of this erroneous accusation.

7. The visually distinctive Sikh "racial uniform" consists of dark skin, eyes, and hair, and a turban and full beard in the case of Sikh males. The latter two items are religious articles of faith as well. The salience of this racial uniform visually distinguishes Sikh Americans in many ways from the majority, dominant group in American society.

8. De Tran, "Residents Protest Temple Plans," *San Jose Mercury News*, July 31, 1997, p. 1B.

9. Personal interview with Bhupindar Singh Dhillon, January 14, 1998.

10. Personal interview with Dr. Gurinder Pal Singh, January 16, 1998.

11. Personal interview with Bhupindar Singh Dhillon, January 14, 1998.

12. De Tran, "Planner OKs Sikh Temple," *San Jose Mercury News*, August 14, 1997, p. 1B.

13. Editorial, *San Jose Mercury News*, September 30, 1997, p. 6B.

14. Personal interview with Bhupindar Singh Dhillon, January 14, 1998.

15. De Tran, "Sikh Temple Clears Major Hurdle," *San Jose Mercury News*, October 30, 1997, p. 1B.

16. Letter to Editor by Peter Klikovits, *San Jose Mercury News*, August 16, 1997, p. 7B.

17. Personal interview with Dr. Loren Chan Singh, May 24, 1999.

18. Personal interview with Dr. Gurinder Pal Singh, January 16, 1998.

19. Letter to Editor by Dian Wilde, *San Jose Mercury News*, August 16, 1997, p. 7B.

20. Ibid.

21. Letter to Editor by Janette V. Peria, *San Jose Mercury News*, August 23, 1997, p. 7B.

22. De Tran, "Sikh Temple Opponents Deny Racist Motives," *San Jose Mercury News*, September 5, 1997, p. 4B.

23. Ibid.

24. Letter to Editor by Jeffrey Piazza, *San Jose Mercury News*, August 23, 1997, p. 7B.

25. Personal interview with Bhupindar Singh Dhillon, January 14, 1998.

26. De Tran, "Sikh Temple Opponents Deny Racist Motives," *San Jose Mercury News*, September 5, 1997, p. 4B.

27. Personal interview with Annie Dandavati, May 24, 1998.

28. Op. cit. Tran, September 5, 1997, p. 4B.

29. Ibid.

30. Letter to Editor by Elena M. Coll, *San Jose Mercury News*, October 4, 1997, p. 7B.

31. Letter to Editor by Jim Zito, *San Jose Mercury News*, August 23, 1997, p. 7B.

32. Personal interview with Bhupindar Singh Dhillon, January 14, 1998.

33. Personal interview with Dr. Tarlochan Singh, January 20, 1998.

34. Ibid.

35. Ariana Eunjung Cha, and Ken McLaughlin, "A Majority of None," *San Jose Mercury News*, April 14, 1999.

36. Personal interview with Dr. Tarlochan Singh, January 20, 1998.

37. Personal interview with Annie Dandavati, May 24, 1998.

38. Personal interview with Dr. Tarlochan Singh, January 20, 1998.

39. Personal interview with Dr. Gurinder Pal Singh, January 16, 1998.

40. Personal interview with Dr. Tarlochan Singh, January 20, 1998.

41. Personal interview with Dr. Gurinder Pal Singh, January 16, 1998.

42. "Hispanic Catholics Often Segregated," Associated Press, March 1, 2000.

43. Martha Irvine, "Mosque Issue Hits Chicago Suburb," Associated Press, July 21, 2000.

44. Wei Li, "Building Ethnoburbia: The Emergence and Manifestation of the Chinese Ethnoburb in Los Angeles' San Gabriel Valley," *Journal of Asian American Studies* 2:1 (1999): 17–18.

45. Ibid., p. 18.

46. Ibid.

47. Personal interview with Bhupindar Singh Dhillon, January 14, 1998.

48. Erik Bratt, "Sikh temple's neighbors fight addition of domes," *San Diego Union Tribune*, September 23, 1998.

49. I would like to thank and acknowledge Jane Naomi Iwamura for her help in clarifying my thoughts on the ideas presented here, as well as providing some of the language with which to express them.

50. Op. cit. Bratt, September 23, 1998.

51. Ibid.

52. Erik Bratt, "Sikhs lobby hard for domes on Escondido temple," *San Diego Union Tribune*, September 24, 1998.

53. Op. cit. Bratt, September 23, 1998.

54. David Montgomery, "Oak-Hugging Neighbors Delay Cutters; Still, Sikh Temple Is Likely to Be Built on Wooded Site in District Neighborhood," *Washington Post*, June 14, 2000.

55. Ibid.

56. Ibid.

57. Ibid.

RACE, RELIGION, AND COLONIALISM
IN THE MORMON PACIFIC

PAUL SPICKARD[1]

The large brown man closes his eyes and chants in a language few of his hearers understand. Swaying slightly, he tells of his ancestors coming to Hawai'i before written history. Of his family lines descending through centuries on Moloka'i and O'ahu. Of other lines from Samoa and Tahiti and Scotland and Germany and China. Of his grandfather chopping cane and his father planting kalo. Of his own education in La'ie, and Honolulu, and Utah. Of the glories of the Hawaiian past and the hope for national sovereignty in a Hawaiian future. Of his faith in God and his brothers and sisters to bring all this about.

As he takes a seat, the audience—nearly all Haoles (White people) from the continental United States—bursts into applause, thrilled by the performance. A pink-faced man in a white shirt and tie steps to the microphone that the chanter had not needed and welcomes them to a gathering to raise funds for scholarships for Hawaiian students at Brigham Young University-Hawai'i. He prays for the gathering. A wave of young women and men come forward to dance hula. Another Hawaiian takes the microphone. Unlike the first speaker, he is not a *kumu hula*. When the audience calls on him to chant his ancestry, he does not chant, he simply recites, in Hawaiian, his family genealogy. The audience is disappointed. But this man has much to say about building a Hawaiian studies program and raising up a generation of leaders for the Hawaiian community. Several Hawaiian students testify to the vibrancy of their faith and the excellence of the education at BYU-Hawai'i. In the end, the listeners open their checkbooks and then they go out to recruit other donors.

The interaction I have just recounted is one small example of the religious, racial, and colonial encounter that frames Mormonism in the Pacific and among Pacific Island peoples in the United States. This chapter examines how race is constructed and used by members of the Church of Jesus Christ of Latter-day Saints in the islands of the Pacific. Race and religion are bound up in colonial and anti-colonial expressions on the part of several groups of Mormons who encounter one another in the Pacific. The Church has been a force for colonialism and has expressed White American values and institutional positions that can fairly be judged to be racist. A premium has been put on encouraging Pacific Islander Mormons to shun their cultures and the needs of their communities and to seek after normative Whiteness. Nonetheless, many faithful Pacific Islander Mormons have used their connections with the Church, its resources, and even its colonial language to make a space for the empowerment of Pacific Island peoples. It is possible that some readers may take my remarks in this chapter as critical of the LDS Church or of individual Mormon leaders. That is not my purpose. The people involved here on all sides are my friends and I respect them. I intend this chapter to offer observation and reflection based on knowledge and friendship. Still, my observations are inevitably shaped by my perspectives as a non-Mormon and a scholar of ethnic studies.[2]

This chapter is based on documents from various branches of the LDS Church and on my observations during the years (1990–97) I spent as a professor and associate dean at Brigham Young University-Hawai'i. The story I will tell is centered primarily on racial encounters at BYU-Hawai'i and its fraternal twin, the Polynesian Cultural Center. However, it also relates issues there to expressions of Mormon racial formations in other parts of the Pacific and in the continental United States.[3] I would contend that issues similar to those depicted here surround the relationships between missionary churches and colonized peoples at many times in history and in many parts of the world.

The LDS Church has long had a special place in its heart for the peoples of Polynesia. This is traceable to the first generations of Mormons in the mid-nineteenth century. According to early interpretations of the *Book of Mormon,* Lehi, a Hebrew prophet, led his family and a portion of the nation of Israel on a sea journey in about 600 B.C.E. that brought them across the Pacific to South and eventually to Central America. There, his son Laman became the ancestor of the native peoples of the Americas, and also of Polynesia. There, centuries later, Christ appeared to the Lamanites and brought them true Christianity, which flourished for a time but was ultimately rejected. The Lamanites, in this interpretation, were given dusky skin as a punishment for having turned away from God, and also for having wiped out the other descendants of Lehi, the Nephites.[4]

Yet God did not give up on this people to whom he had once given a special spiritual gift. In the *Doctrine and Covenants* is recorded a revelation given to LDS founder Joseph Smith in 1828, that highlights God's special concern for salvation of the Lamanites:

> My work shall go forth, for inasmuch as the knowledge of a Savior has come into the world . . . even so shall the knowledge of a Savior come unto my people. . . . And this shall come to the knowledge of the Lamanites . . . who dwindled in unbelief because of the iniquity of their fathers, whom the Lord has suffered to destroy their brethren the Nephites, because of their iniquities and their abominations. And for this very purpose are these plates [the *Book of Mormon*] preserved, which contain these records—that the promises of the Lord might be fulfilled, which he made to his people; And that the Lamanites might come to the knowledge of their fathers, and that they might know the promises of the Lord, and that they may believe the gospel and rely upon the merits of Jesus Christ, and be glorified through faith in his name, and that through their repentance they might be saved. Amen.[5]

According to R. Lanier Britsch, the premier historian of Mormonism in the Pacific, "It is not clear from the records of the Church exactly when the leaders in Salt Lake City began thinking of the Polynesian people as descendants of Lehi," nor why they were included in the Lamanite blessing, while other Pacific peoples such as Micronesians and Melanesians were not.[6] "Because the Church believes that the descendants of Lehi are children of special promise, the leaders of the Church have expended vast amounts of manpower on missionary efforts among these people" from very early in Mormon history. Thus it was that one of the first overseas places that LDS missionaries went in the 1850s was to Polynesia, there to return to the Lamanites the true religion that they had given up centuries before. Landing first in the Tuamotu archipelago (in French Polynesia, near Tahiti), and then in Hawai'i, LDS missionaries quickly went on to Aotearoa (New Zealand), Samoa, Tonga, Fiji, and other parts of the eastern Pacific. Thus many Polynesian Mormons are third, fourth-, and even fifth- generation members of the Church. By contrast, the Church expanded into Micronesia only much later and with less enthusiasm, and has attended to the peoples of Melanesia hardly at all.[7]

The LDS Church has long had a problem about race. The Church for many years refused to grant full lay priesthood status to believers of African descent despite growing pressures for equality in the US and abroad. Finally, in 1978, God provided a new revelation.[8] Less well known than the priesthood-for-Blacks controversy are the many subtly hierarchical ways that White Mormons have relegated Asian, Latino, and Native American believers to never-formally-articulated but nonetheless real second-class status within the Church.[9]

One of the issues that frames Mormon racial expressions is a triumphal identification with the United States as a nation. The unmarked "we" at nearly all Mormon gatherings is the United States of America. It is assumed that everyone present is an American and in sympathy with the purposes of the American government, even when a majority of the gathering are not in fact from the United States. Partly, this identification with America stems from the belief that the United States has a special role to play in the world because it is the place where true religion was first returned to humankind when the golden plates were revealed to Joseph Smith. There is also an eschatological vision in the minds of many Mormons that God's kingdom will be built in the United States. And most LDS members have a sacred view of the founders of the American republic as men inspired by God, and of the United States Constitution as something approaching holy writ. It is not an accident that the first thing one sees when one enters Brigham Young University-Hawai'i is a huge mosaic depicting a gathering of Hawaiian children pledging allegiance to the American flag.[10]

One theme near the core of Mormon culture is the idea of the gathering, that Church members will come from all over the world to be in Zion, to worship at the Temple, and to build a Christian society together. It was because of this identification of the United States as the location of the promise for a bright future, and because of the theological understanding that Polynesians had a special role to play in creating that future, that the Church first encouraged Polynesian Mormons to leave their island homes and migrate to Zion. The most notorious episode was the ill-fated Hawaiian colony of Iosepa. A few Hawaiians trickled into Utah between the 1860s and the 1880s. They generally lived in Salt Lake City but were segregated from White believers. Then, in 1889, the Church fathers set aside some dusty lands in Skull Valley and told fifty Hawaiians to move out there. They were soon joined by others from Hawai'i, and in time the colony numbered nearly three hundred souls. Far from home and kin, battling a hostile climate, the Iosepa Hawaiians struggled for twenty-eight years. Scores were buried in the Iosepa cemetery before the Church abandoned the colony in 1917 and the surviving Hawaiian believers headed home to the islands.[11]

The LDS Church and its local institutional expressions, Brigham Young

University-Hawai'i and the Polynesian Cultural Center, employ religious language at every turn. That is not surprising, for these are, after all, church organizations. The University lists "religious values and intellectual values in concord" as its primary defining characteristic in its accreditation documents.[12] The alumni magazine is full of testimonies to God's faithfulness.[13] Every meeting on campus and at the PCC is opened with prayer. Religious dietary laws rule in both institutions. All the students are organized into cell groups to study the scriptures. All who work at these two institutions are expected to be faithful to their religious callings and to worship regularly. All can be called to account by ecclesiastical authorities if they fail to do so.

While it is not startling to learn that Mormons are religious, it is arresting to note that in the Pacific the religious language they use is nearly always expressed closely together with language and cultural expressions that mark race. The second defining characteristic in the accreditation report is "harmony amid diversity," and the diversity in question is clearly marked as Polynesian.[14] The alumni magazine has page after page of pictures of happy Polynesian and Asian students.[15]

The racial markings employed by White American Mormons among Pacific Islanders usually have a hierarchical nature that expresses American colonialism. In 1995, the Social Science Division put out a brochure on its majors, students, and faculty. The first picture in the brochure was centered on a White American professor in long-sleeved white shirt and tie giving lessons to a flock of brown students seated around him.[16]

The brochures put out by the university's public relations department and the alumni magazine strive to portray the university as a diverse place—and it is—but the student body is vastly more diverse than the faculty or administration. The higher one goes in the power structure, (a) the whiter the population gets, and (b) the more reluctant people are to talk about race. Roughly two-thirds of the BYU-H student body is made up of Asians and Pacific Islanders. About the same is true of the university's staff (clerks, maintenance workers, dormitory attendants, and the like). But eighty per cent of the faculty are White. At the level of deans and associate deans, two of fourteen are Pacific Islanders, one is Asian, and the rest are White.[17]

Students on campus and workers at the PCC are eager to talk about their religious lives, and they are also able to speak eloquently about racial issues. One woman student, a dancer at the PCC and a Hawaiian, wrote a protest piece in the school's literary magazine after the movie *Medicine Man* was shown on campus. She and her husband went to the movie, which portrays a blond woman in the role of a medical researcher among Indians in the Amazon jungle. The woman appears in one scene in a sports bra and shorts.

The university edited the movie, placing a black rectangle over the woman's torso to avoid offending the school's conservative audience. Yet in a scene moments later, several Indian women appeared naked, with no censorship. The student protested both the blatant racism of hiding a White woman's body while exhibiting the bodies of brown women, and also the fact that the largely brown audience was so brainwashed as to fail to notice.

There are some faculty and mid-level administrators at BYU-H and the PCC who are capable of such an analysis, but almost none will bring up such issues. At the top levels of administration that critical capability is absent. It is as if officials wish racial issues did not exist. There is a very high church official from Utah who visits the campus frequently and believes he knows it well. I have had conversations with him and have heard him speak on many occasions. He is fond of talking about the "sweet spirit" of Polynesians on campus, and of telling about a student who walked up to him and proudly showed him that he was wearing shorts that covered his knees (a campus requirement that is often ignored). This high official brought this act of sartorial obedience up again and again, for he believed it to be the epitome of life for students and faculty at BYU-Hawai'i. This is what he knows of the Pacific Islander Mormons at BYU-Hawai'i: they are faithful Mormons. Surely they are. But they are Mormons whose lives are deeply affected by structural racism and colonialism, as well as by daily encounters that have racial and colonial inflections. But of such issues, which surely are as important to their lives as long shorts, this self-confident leader has not a clue.[18]

The actual structures of power are clearly evident in BYU-Hawai'i's campus magazine. The cover of one issue shows the university's president and four vice-presidents: all are White except the vice-president for public relations. A gathering of the campus community shows a sea of brown faces staring up at a dais where sit only White people. Visiting dignitaries from Utah come in a canoe to a luau at the Polynesian Cultural Center. The servants pushing the boat are Polynesians, the hosts greeting them and bowing before them are Polynesians, and all the honored guests—judged to be spiritual superiors—are White.[19]

What top-level White leaders in the LDS Church in the Pacific will never admit is that their actions or judgments may be racially or culturally driven. They perhaps do not recognize that they place Utah culture and social structure as the highest expression of human experience and the acme of Americanism, with other cultures (and, by implication, peoples) arrayed below. The way things are done in Utah is the godly way, and all other ways are judged in comparison to that standard. For example, when I taught at BYU-Hawai'i, an edict went out specifying criteria by which faculty's work would be judged. Beyond the common academic issues of teaching, scholarship, and service, there was a moral dimension to the evaluation: faithful service in church callings, marital fidelity, and punctuality, among other habits, would be evaluated. When some islanders and others suggested that punctuality might be seen as a culture-specific virtue, that in fact it might not be seen as particularly a virtue at all in much of the Pacific, the White administrators simply would not allow the discussion.

One of the ways that the White American leaders of the LDS Church in the Pacific express a colonial attitude is by speaking as if the only, or the main, Mormons there were Haoles from the continental United States. There are several well-researched and smoothly written histories of Mormon activity in the Pacific. They have almost nothing to say about Pacific Islander Mormons. The people whose lives fill their pages are White people from Utah.[20] When White Mormons appear in such writings, their Whiteness is not marked. They are given names, personalities, and stories. When Pacific Islander and Asian Mormons appear, they seldom have names, personalities, or stories, but their race is marked. A typical caption in one book reads: "President George Albert Smith with members of the Church in Hawaii. They represent five races. Left to right, Samoan, Filipino, Japanese, Chinese, and Hawaiian." Apparently, it was Smith's name and not his race that was important, while it was the races and not the names of his colleagues that were important.[21] As Timothy Tseng notes, "To view Christianity as essentially a European religion ignores the agency of non-European subjects who creatively appropriated the symbols of Christianity for their own social and political purposes."[22] More about that creative appropriation in a moment.

It was not always this way for LDS Polynesians. There was a lot of variety to the ways that the Church dealt with the various peoples and cultures in its first century in the Pacific. For much of that time, although leadership lay in the hands of Whites sent from Utah, they were fairly open to embrace island cultures and customs, even adjusting Mormon practices to accommodate them. Thus, in Aotearoa (which Europeans call New Zealand) throughout the first half of the twentieth century, LDS missionaries took pains to learn the Maori language and services were conducted in Maori. The annual Church meeting was celebrated as the Hui Tau, "combining Maori ceremonies of greeting and hospitality with cultural displays, a strong emphasis on music and oratory, and sermons and personal testimonies in Maori and English."[23]

After World War II new Church administrators were sent out with a charge to bring Maori Mormon practices to a Utah standard. The Church in Aotearoa pursued a policy of consciously assimilating Maori believers to American Mormon culture. As historian John Garrett characterized it, the new Church "policies reflected efficiency, business ethic and the Anglo-Saxon feel of urban Salt Lake City." The top LDS leader in Aotearoa in the postwar period, Gordon Young, pronounced the hegemony: "We're not Maoris and Samoans and Tongans and Cook Islanders and Europeans. We're Latter-day Saints." That meant the Church would no longer make accommodations to Maori culture. Believers were encouraged to give up the Maori language, move into cities, ignore traditional ceremonial requirements and family obligations, wear white shirts and ties, make nuclear families, work in offices and factories, and in other ways cease to practice Maoritanga. All these changes, Maori Mormons were told, brought them closer to God's spiritual standards.[24]

Although few of the White American Mormon leaders I know would own the label or the interpretation, an independent observer might contend that they are cultural colonizers who use religion to dominate Pacific Islander Mormons on a racial basis. One can see this in the pages of the BYU-Hawai'i alumni bulletin, which tout White American business values as the acme of spiritual virtue (the Church assumes uncritically that business values are spiritual values throughout its ministries around the world). Such White American business-class values as thrift, punctuality, and nuclear family solidarity are in direct conflict with Polynesian cultural values placed on extended family obligation, sharing, and a relaxed attitude toward linear time.[25]

For decades the Church in Hawai'i gave all meaningful leadership posts to Whites imported from the continental United States, even though for some generations the majority of believers were Hawaiians and other islanders. Although that practice (not a formal policy) has relaxed somewhat in the past fifteen years, still the top Church leaders are all White and look to Utah rather than the local community of believers for guidance on all occasions. All the presidents of BYU-Hawai'i since its founding after World War II have been Haoles, and all but the current occupant of the office were shipped in from Utah to assume the office.[26]

White LDS leaders, like other conservative Whites in the islands who do not wish to recognize the racial and colonial qualities of their interactions, speak frequently of "the Aloha spirit." When Hawaiians talk of aloha, they speak of an ethic of love, caring, sharing, welcome, generosity, and gentleness, that is interwoven with family, the land, and the dignity of the Hawaiian people.[27] By contrast, when Haoles use the term, it is almost always with an undertone of complaint, as in telling Hawaiians, "You're not practicing the Aloha spirit." BYU-Hawai'i and Polynesian Cultural Center documents speak often of "The Aloha spirit," a phrase used hegemonically by Whites, Mormon and Gentile, in an attempt to force Polynesians into a posture of submission.[28]

Some Pacific Islander Mormons, for their part, wittingly or unwittingly allow themselves to be colonized. In their effort to be accepted in a White-American-defined religious community, they receive the racial message hegemonically: they take on the language, clothing, and religious manners of White American Mormonism; attempt to erase their own racial and cultural identities; and deny the colonial nature of their encounter with White power.[29]

A lot of faithful Pacific Islander Mormons have moved to Utah. The primary motive here is to be gathered near the heart of Zion, to worship at the Salt Lake Temple, and to be among like-minded people. This trend has proceeded to the point where Utah has become the state with the second highest percentage of Pacific Islander residents (after Hawai'i).[30]

Even for the majority of Pacific Islander Mormons who remain outside Utah, part of being faithful is looking like they belong in Utah. Consider a picture of a Samoan American Bishop, taken for an interview on his ministry among students. On most days he wears flowered shirts or tee-shirts, shorts, and bare feet, but for a spiritual picture he presents himself in a white shirt and tie. The accompanying article de-emphasizes racial and cultural issues; a White ward member says, "Bishop [X] doesn't favor any cultural group in the ward. He loves all of us." "Culture" is a word that LDS Church people in the Pacific use on occasions where others might use the word "race."[31]

Some observers may imagine that people like this bishop are simply deracinated cultural sell-outs.[32] Certainly, the Polynesian Cultural Center is a flavorful example of cultural colonialism. Built in the 1960s as a financial support to the college that became BYU-H, the PCC is a strange blend of anthropological museum and Disneyland. Like Colonial Williamsburg and Plymouth Plantation, the PCC is a controversial example of the marketing of human culture. Its main feature is seven "villages" representing different island groups—Hawai'i, Tonga, Samoa, Fiji, Tahiti, Aotearoa, and the Marquesas—where Pacific Islander employees don native costumes and act the way they have been taught people acted in those places once upon a time. The PCC employs several hundred BYU-Hawai'i students, most of them Pacific Islanders, to take tickets, serve meals, and perform acts of cultural representation, from singing, to carving, to climbing trees, to dancing in a splashy night show.[33]

It is easy to criticize such a feat of colonial representation. Some charge that students and other PCC workers are performing ersatz culture that they learned on the job, not back in the islands from which many of them came.

They shake their cakes for the tourists, exhibiting their bodies in scant clothing that they would be disciplined for wearing across the fence on campus. They present a static, museum-shelf version of island cultures, with all current issues, all politics, economics, and social questions bleached out. In such a view, any Pacific Islanders who participated would be judged to have sold out to the colonizers who run the show.[34]

Yet nearly all of the people who lead the PCC are capable of making an argument like this. So, too, are many of the more thoughtful student employees. However, they perceive themselves to be doing something different. The person in the Samoan village who tells jokes to the tourists in four shows daily may be exhibiting his body and playing the fool, but he is also making fun of the tourists in the subtle undertones of his patter. He is tremendously popular, and draws in tourist dollars that pay for other members of the Samoan village to go to school and earn degrees in business and chemistry. The people in the Hawaiian village refuse to entertain in such a blatantly self-exploitive fashion, but they will dance hula for tourists and teach them a few steps. What is not seen by the tourists is what happens when visitors are not around. Then, the employees of the Polynesian Cultural Center are hard at work, keeping alive and elaborating ancient traditions in dance, music, and art that have few other venues to nourish them. The chief artists, *kumu hulas*, and musicians at the PCC are among the most renowned in the world and are honored in their home countries even by anti-colonial forces. In return for entertaining the tourists, they are able to make a living at practicing their art full time. What such people are doing is using the tourist expectations encouraged by the colonial institution to make a space for themselves to do their own cultural work.[35]

The skilled artists of the Polynesian Cultural Center are almost all devoted Mormons. So is the bishop I mentioned a moment ago, and so are the chanter (also a bishop) and his colleague whose story opened this chapter. While they are all deeply committed to the LDS Church religiously, and while they are surrounded by the trappings of religious, racial, and colonial hierarchy, nonetheless they manage gently and subtly to resist racial hierarchy and colonial hegemony even while they are being faithfully Latter-day Saints. Indeed, they are able to use the language and symbols of their White-dominated religion in universalistic ways to create space and power for Pacific Islanders and point toward a postcolonial future.

The same alumni magazine that employed the language of Aloha to keep Polynesians in their place later printed an article that subtly turned that language around. In "Preserving the Language of Aloha," BYUH Hawaiians talked about their new Hawaiian language program in terms that were utterly non-threatening to White LDS hegemony. It spoke of a language

> rich in poetry, metaphor and elegance. . . . the treasure within which expressions of deep spiritual dimensions such as malama (honor), aloha (love), naʻau aliʻi (forgiveness) are analogous with basic principles of the restored gospel [Mormonism]. . . . For LDS Hawaiian youth, the newly established Hawaiian Language and Cultural Studies program at the BYU campus in Laʻie is an important—even critical—element to their education. These students are not only anxious to study their ancestral language and culture, but they appreciate the opportunity of doing so in a spiritual atmosphere where their faith in the restored gospel can be reinforced and nurtured at the same time.[36]

Here, Pacific Islander students and faculty have made a space for the building of Hawaiian cultural sovereignty, with the resources and blessings of a distinctly colonial institution, in the name of a religion in which both they and the colonizers believe deeply. In this program and in this college, they are training a generation of leaders not only for the Hawaiian community but also for several island nations around the Pacific. To my personal knowledge, BYUH alumni have been among the leaders of reform movements in Aotearoa, the Cook Islands, Samoa, Tonga, and Kiribati, and the same is surely true for other parts of the Pacific. Pacific Islander scholars and cultural experts also make use of the resources of the university and the PCC through the Institute for Polynesian Studies. Originally founded by the Church to fund White academics' studies on Pacific Islanders, it has become a fairly effective venue for bringing academic and institutional resources to the service of Pacific Islander issues. It has also placed the Pacific Islander cultural experts on a par with people with solely academic credentials.[37]

There are limits to the degree of alternative space-making that is possible, and there are tough compromises to be made. Although several Pacific Islanders have emerged at the PCC and BYU-Hawaiʻi who are eminently qualified to lead those institutions at the top level, the Church has not trusted any of them to do so. Hawaiian activists who are Church members often take abuse from both sides: from people in the community for working for the Church, and from the Church for pressing an Islander agenda. This is especially dangerous for those who are Church employees, as the LDS Church recognizes no tradition of a loyal opposition. Anyone who takes Hawaiian community needs seriously will sooner or later end up taking a position that bothers the Church, as it has for more than a century been deeply involved in colonial seizures of land and water rights.[38] Nonetheless, most of the LDS Pacific Islanders I know believe that the compromises are worth making, in service to their faith and in service to their people.

From time to time, Pacific Islander Mormons have been able to make an ecclesiastical space for themselves within the LDS Church itself, separate from the direct domination of White Mormonism. Episodically, the Church has allowed separate ethnic wards for members of recognized minority groups, including Hawaiians, Tongans, and Samoans, not only in the islands but also in California and Utah. In such wards, all the functions of leadership, from bishop to Sunday school teacher, have been performed by Islanders. Such leadership at the congregational level, however, has not translated to leadership over Whites in the Church at large.[39]

What Timothy Tseng said of Chinese American Protestants was essentially true of Pacific Islander Mormons, too: "they created space for themselves to develop a Chinese Protestant [Pacific Islander Mormon] church without yielding to pressures either to Americanize or to conform to traditional Chinese [Pacific Islander] culture."[40] It is a fragile business, however, these subtle ways by which Pacific Islander members of the LDS church have been able to carve out such institutional spaces.

If I dared have wishes for this essay, they would be three. First, I would wish that, if the essay were read by members of an LDS Church that is often hyper-vigilant for signs of rebellion, they would come to understand that the Pacific Islanders described here are not in the least rebellious, that, on the contrary, they are completely faithful Mormons in every way, even as they pursue a communal goal as Pacific Islanders that was not presented to them by the Church hierarchy. That is a tall order for a Church whose culture of agenda-setting and decision-making leaves little room for ideas to bubble up from below, but it is absolutely true and I pray they would believe it.

Second, I would hope that non-LDS Pacific Islanders, and Hawaiian sovereignty activists in particular, would come to understand that the Hawaiians and other Pacific Islanders I describe are not cultural sell-outs and pawns of imperialism. True, their deep faith leads them into engagement with a Church that has many qualities of racism and colonialism. But their posture in that Church is one of constructive interaction and vigorous advocacy for Hawaiian and Pacific people, communities, and issues, and they are very effective at those tasks.

Third, I would hope that readers outside Latter-day Saint and Pacific Islander communities would perceive that this is not just a Mormon story or a Pacific Islander story. Many of the qualities of racial and colonial hierarchy described here were equally present among Congregationalist missionaries and White church leaders in Hawai'i, and, for that matter, among

Methodists and Catholics in Africa. So, too, the careful observer can find similar engagement and turning of missionary religion to the culture and purposes of native peoples on the part of committed Christian nationalist leaders such as David Kalakaua in nineteenth-century Hawai'i, William Wade Harris on the Guinea Coast in the early twentieth century, and later Kenneth Kaunda in Zambia.[41]

NOTES

1. I offer this chapter in memory of Lance Chase and Seta Kaumaitotoia. I would like to acknowledge the many things that I have been taught over the years by LDS friends in the Pacific, including Eric Shumway, William Kauaiwiulaokalani Wallace III, Debbie Hippolite Wright, Dale Robertson, Vernice Wineera, Jon Jonassen, Charlene Keliiliki, Jeff Burroughs, Rochelle Fonoti, Max Stanton, Karina Kahananui Green, Tupou Hopoate Pau`u, Kamoa`e Walk, Blossom Fonoimoana, Dorri Nautu, `Inoke Funaki, Victor Narsimulu, and many others. Jessie Embry, Dale Robertson, and Vernice Wineera made generous gifts of research materials. Laurie Flores was one of several BYU-H students who gave me copies of the *Book of Mormon*. An earlier version of this chapter was presented to the American Academy of Religion in Nashville, November 18, 2000, where it drew helpful discussion from many in the audience including Rudy Busto, Karen Chai, Carolyn Chen, Madeline Duntley, Young Lee Hertig, Jane Naomi Iwamura, Russell Jeung, David Kyuman Kim, Fumitaka Matsuoka, Su Pak, and Lori Pierce. None of these people is in any way responsible for what I write here.

2. Nonetheless, some LDS Church leaders have a history of undue jumpiness toward even helpful observations and tend to execute the messenger. See, for example, George D. Smith, ed., *Religion, Feminism, and Freedom of Conscience: A Mormon-Humanist Dialogue* (Amherst, NY: Prometheus Books, 1994); David Clark Knowlton, "Authority and Authenticity in the Mormon Church," *Religion and the Social Order*, 6 (1996): 113-34; David Clark Knowlton, "The Freest University: Brigham Young University, Mormonism, and Authoritative Abuse" (unpublished Ms., courtesy of the author, June 1996). Therefore, insofar as possible, I will avoid using the names of particular individuals, even prominent Church officials.

3. I am not aware of any accounting of the number of Pacific Islanders who are members of the LDS Church. John Garrett estimates that in the early 1990s there were about 16,000 Mormons in Samoa and about 14,000 in Tonga (*Where the Nets Were Cast: Christianity in Oceania Since World War II* [Suva, Fiji: University of the South Pacific Institute of Pacific Studies, 1997], 391, 408). Similar numbers for other parts of the Pacific, and for Pacific Islanders in the United States, are lacking. But it is surely true that Pacific Islanders make up a larger fraction of the Church of Jesus Christ of Latter-day Saints than of any other American denomination.

4. "The Church of Jesus Christ of Latter-day Saints," *http://www.religioustolerance.org/lds.htm* (May 18, 2000); Ian Barber, "Between Biculturalism and Assimilation: The Changing Place of Maori Culture in the Twentieth-Century New Zealand Mormon Church," *New*

Zealand Journal of History, 29.2 (1995): 142–69.

5. *Doctrine and Covenants* 3:16–20. The story of Lehi and his descendants is scattered throughout much of the *Book of Mormon*; see, for example, the books of I and II Nephi, Mosiah, and Alma.

6. I recognize that such terms as "Polynesian," "Micronesian," and "Melanesian" are not Pacific Island concepts; they are ideas imported by European anthropologists. Nonetheless, they do provide a convenient way to understand which islanders the LDS Church saw as being within the special blessing and which they understood to be outside. The source of that distinction is not clear, although, given the history of church attitudes toward African-descended peoples, it might have something to do with the dark skins and kinky hair of most people whom the anthropologists reckon to be Micronesians and Melanesians.

7. R. Lanier Britsch, *Unto the Islands of the Sea: A History of the Latter-day Saints in the Pacific* (Salt Lake City: Deseret, 1984), xiv.

8. On the Church and African Americans, see Newell G. Bringhurst, *Saints, Slaves, and Blacks: The Changing Place of Black People Within Mormonism* (Westport, Conn.: Greenwood, 1981); Jessie L. Embry, *Black Saints in a White Church: Contemporary African American Mormons* (Salt Lake City: Signature, 1994); John Lewis Lund, *The Church and the Negro: A Discussion of Mormons, Negroes and the Priesthood* (1967); Lester E. Bush, Jr., and Armand L. Mauss, eds., *Neither White Nor Black: Mormon Scholars Confront the Race Issue in a Universal Church* (Midvale, Utah: Signature, 1984); Armand Mauss, "The Fading of the Pharaoh's Curse: The Decline and Fall of the Priesthood Restriction Ban Against Blacks in the Mormon Church," *Dialogue: A Journal of Mormon Thought*, 14 (Fall 1981): 41; Armand Mauss, "Mormonism and Secular Attitudes Toward Negroes," *Pacific Sociological Review*, 8 (1966); Bruce R. McConkie, "The New Revelation on Priesthood," in *Priesthood* (Salt Lake City: Deseret, 1981).

9. To take just one instance, in 1989 George P. Lee, the first Native American to become a General Authority (the top level of Mormon leadership), was excommunicated. His supporters charged that it came on account of his increasingly strident advocacy of the cause of Native Americans within the Church. David J. Whittaker, "Mormons and Native Americans: A Historical and Bibliographical Introduction," *Dialogue: A Journal of Mormon Thought*, 18 (Winter 1985): 33–64; "Press Coverage of Lee's Excommunication Ambivalent," *Sunstone*, 13 (August 1989): 47–51; Jessie L. Embry, "Reactions of LDS Native Americans to the Excommunication of George P. Lee" (unpublished ms.); Bruce A. Chadwick and Stan L. Albrecht, "Mormons and Indians: Beliefs, Policies, Programs, and Practices," in *Contemporary Mormonism*, ed. Marie Cornwall, Tim B. Heaton, and Lawrence A. Young (Urbana: University of Illinois Press, 1994), 287–309. On other racial minorities in the Church, see Jessie L. Embry, *"In His Own Language": Mormon Spanish Speaking Congregations in the United States* (Provo, Utah: Charles Redd Center for Western Studies, Brigham Young University, 1997); Embry, *Asian American Mormons: Bridging Cultures* (Provo, Utah: Charles Redd Center for Western Studies, Brigham Young University, 1999); Mathis Chazanov, "Spreading the Word:

Mormonism's Traditional Values Appeal to Converts of Many Ethnicities," *Los Angeles Times* (February 20, 1994). Chieko Okazaki is possibly the only person of color who has succeeded in consistently offering a gentle racial critique of LDS Church policies and survived in the Church; see Chieko N. Okazaki, "The Gospel and Culture: Definitions and Relationships," in *BYU-Hawai'i Profile Magazine* (Winter 1998): 16–17.

10. Some would say that scene is less about American patriotism than about commemorating the ethnic variety and intercultural aspirations of the university, but the fact remains that the flag is central to the scene. See *The State and Future of Brigham Young University-Hawai'i* (A self-study for re-accreditation by the Western Association of Schools and Colleges; La'ie, Hawai'i, December 1995), 1.

11. Dennis H. Atkin, "A History of Iosepa, the Utah Polynesian Colony" (M.A. thesis, Brigham Young University, 1958).

12. *State and Future*, 5–7 and passim.

13. It is sometimes titled *BYU Hawai'i Profile Magazine* and sometimes *BYU-Hawai'i University Magazine*.

14. *State and Future*, 8–10 and passim.

15. To take just two examples, see the covers of *BYU-Hawai'i University Magazine* for Spring 1999 and Summer 2000.

16. The division's faculty requested that this picture *not* be included because of its colonial markings, and because the White faculty member was not from their division. The publicity department overrode their request and included the colonially-inflected picture.

17. Ibid., 30-32; *BYU Hawai'i University Magazine* (Spring 1999): 12–13.

18. Hal B. Eyring, "We Greet You on This Day of Importance," *BYU Hawai'i Profile Magazine* (December 1994): 6.

19. *BYU Hawai'i Profile Magazine* (December 1994): cover, 14; (Winter 1998): 12–13.

20. Britsch, *Unto the Islands of the Sea*; R. Lanier Britsch, *Moramona: The Mormons in Hawai'i* (La'ie, Hawai'i: Institute for Polynesian Studies, 1989); Russell T. Clement, comp., *Mormons in the Pacific: A Bibliography* (La'ie, Hawai'i: Institute for Polynesian Studies, 1981); Marjorie Newton, *Southern Cross Saints: The Mormons in Australia* (La'ie, Hawai'i: Institute for Polynesian Studies, 1991); David W. Cummings, *Mighty Missionary of the Pacific* (Salt Lake City: Bookcraft, 1961); Donald R. Shaffer, "Hiram Clark and the First LDS Hawaiian Mission," *Journal of Mormon History*, 17 (1991): 94-109. Such treatment of Whites as if they were the Church in patently non-White places is not limited to the Pacific. A recent speech, broadcast to the Church worldwide, by a very high Church official, Glenn Pace, titled "A Temple for West Africa," had not a word about any West Africans, but it did include several references to White individuals in Utah and a BYU football game. General Conference April 2000, *http://www.lds.org/conference/a2000en/A2000en_2_5_Pace.html*.

21. Britsch, *Unto the Islands of the Sea*, 175. It is worth noting that all the islanders in question were also female, a condition that may have added to their invisibility as individual personalities.

22. Timothy Tseng, "Chinese Protestant Nationalism in the United States, 1880–1927," in

New Spiritual Homes: Religion and Asian Americans, ed. David K. Yoo (Honolulu: University of Hawaiʻi Press, 1999), 23.

23. Barber, "Between Biculturalism and Assimilation"; Garrett, *Where the Nets Were Cast*, 86 –88.

24. Barber, "Between Biculturalism and Assimilation"; Garrett, *Where the Nets Were Cast*, 86–88, 224–26, 385–86; Britsch, *Unto the Islands of the Sea*, 338. Barber and Garrett note that the postwar LDS policy in Aotearoa was assimilation not to New Zealand Pakeha (White) culture, but rather to U. S. Mormon culture.

25. Diana Fitisemanu, et al., "Family Dynamics Among Pacific Islander Americans," *Social Process in Hawaiʻi*, 36 (1994): 26–40.

26. It was a major victory for Pacific Islander believers that their college at last had a president who, though White and from the continental U.S., spoke an island language (Tongan) and was knowledgeable about island people. For many years the LDS Church in Hawaiʻi and elsewhere in the Pacific took pains to discourage interracial marriage between Whites and Polynesians, although there is little evidence of discrimination against couples who chose to ignore the ban. Lavar Thornock, lecture in Interdisciplinary Studies 306, BYU-Hawaiʻi, May 19, 1993; Garth Allred, "What Are Your Views on Intercultural Marriage?" *Ke Ala Kai* (BYU-H student newspaper; September 18, 1991); Garth Allred, "What Counsel Do Leaders of the Church Give Regarding Intercultural and Interracial Marriages?" *Ensign* (October 1994); John Lewis Lund, "Interracial Marriage and the Negro," in *The Church and the Negro: A Discussion of Mormons, Negroes and the Priesthood* (1967).

27. George H. S. Kanahele, *Ku Kanaka: Stand Tall: A Search for Hawaiian Values* (Honolulu: University of Hawaiʻi Press, 1986), 467–94.

28. Lori Pierce, "The Whites Have Created Modern Honolulu: Ethnicity, Racial Stratification, and the Discourse of Aloha," in *Uncompleted Independence: Racial Thinking in the United States*, ed. Paul Spickard and G. Reginald Daniel (Notre Dame, IN: University of Notre Dame Press, in press); Ron Taylor, "Door Openers and Dream Makers: Continuing the Spirit of Aloha," *BYU-Hawaiʻi University Magazine* (Spring 1999): 14–18; Eric Shumway, "Acceptance and Response to President Hunter's Inaugural Charge," *BYU-Hawaiʻi Profile Magazine* (December 1994), 16–23.

29. In the mid-1990s a Pacific Islander rose to become one of the vice-presidents of BYU-Hawaiʻi. Almost no one who knew him regarded him as possessing the intellectual or organizational skills of other candidates for the job. What he did possess was an extraordinary ability to ingratiate himself among White church leaders. He wore a white shirt and tie faithfully, and exhorted students and faculty to "raise themselves" to Utah patterns of behavior. Most observers agreed that he was hired to give brown cover for a White colonial administration. Meanwhile, at the Polynesian Cultural Center, a bright, articulate, well-educated Polynesian man took a job as the personal assistant to the Center's White president. That president was widely regarded as a nice man but sorely lacking in knowledge or understanding of Pacific peoples despite several years' residence in the islands. Nonetheless, his Polynesian assistant (and other members of the Mormon hierarchy) had to pretend he was smart and knowledgeable about Polynesian peoples

and cultures. Maintaining the pretense took such a toll on the assistant that he developed a number of physical maladies. This man's psychosomatic predicament is similar to that found by Gerald W. Mullin in slaves who had to undergo intimate daily contact with their masters; *Flight and Rebellion: Slave Resistance in Eighteenth-Century Virginia* (New York: Oxford, 1972), 80.

30. Herbert Barringer, Robert W. Gardner, and Michael J. Levin, *Asians and Pacific Islanders in the United States* (New York: Russell Sage Foundation, 1993), 275.

31. *BYU-Hawai'i Profile Magazine* (August 1998): 4–5.

32. On many occasions I have witnessed non-LDS would-be speakers for the Hawaiian sovereignty movement publicly excoriate Hawaiian sovereignty activists who are Mormons, expressing the view that it is impossible to be a Mormon and not a sellout to racism and American imperialism.

33. Max E. Stanton, "The Polynesian Cultural Center: A Multi-Ethnic Model of Seven Pacific Cultures," in *Hosts and Guests: The Anthropology of Tourism*, 2nd ed., ed. Valene L. Smith (Philadelphia: University of Pennsylvania Press, 1989), 247–62; Craig Ferre, "A History of the Polynesian Cultural Center's 'Night Show': 1963–1983" (Ph.D. diss., Brigham Young University, 1988); Vernice Wineera, "Selves and Others: A Study of Reflexivity and the Representation of Culture in Touristic Display at the Polynesian Cultural Center, Laie, Hawaii," (Ph.D. dissertation, University of Hawai'i, 2000).

34. T. D. Webb, "Missionaries, Polynesians, and Tourists: Mormonism and Tourism in La'ie, Hawai'i," *Social Process in Hawai'i*, 35 (1994): 195–212; T. D. Webb, "Highly Structured Tourist Art: Form and Meaning of the Polynesian Cultural Center," *Contemporary Pacific*, 6.1 (Spring 1994): 59–85. Cf. Elizabeth Buck, *Paradise Remade* (Philadelphia: Temple University Press, 1993). An example of the colonized and racialized situation at the PCC occurred in the mid-1990s. Outside marketing advisors, with the approval of PCC top management, took a number of pictures of the staff of the Fijian village. Their ad campaign included an invitation to an informational meeting and meal for tourist industry representatives. On the invitation's cover was a picture of several Fijian men, dressed in native costumes, holding weapons, and striking warlike poses, taken with a fisheye lens. The effect was as if the viewer were in a pot in the center of the men. The invitation read, "The Polynesian Cultural Center would like to have you for lunch." The men whose pictures appeared had no advance warning that they would be portrayed before the public as cannibals.

35. Wineera, "Selves and Others."

36. Ron Taylor, "Preserving the Language of Aloha," *BYU Hawai'i Profile Magazine* (Winter 1998): 20–23.

37. "Meeting of Minds: The Institute for Polynesian Studies Board of Fellows," *BYU Hawai'i Profile Magazine* (May 1995): 17–23.

38. Jeffrey Stover, "The Legacy of the 1848 Mahele and Kuleana Act of 1850: A Case Study of Laie Wai and Laie molo'o ahupua'a" (M.A. thesis, University of Hawai'i, 1998); J. Matthew Kester, "La'ie 'wai: A Hydrographical History of Water Use and Dispute in La'ie ahupua'a" (student paper, BYU-Hawai'i, 1999); Lance D. Chase, *Temple, Town, Tradition* (La'ie, Hawai'i: Institute for Polynesian Studies), 85–98.

39. On LDS ethnic minority wards, see Jessie L. Embry, "*In His Own Language*": *Mormon Spanish Speaking Congregations in the United States* (Provo, Utah: Charles Redd Center for Western Studies, Brigham Young University, 1997), 59–65. This is rather a different thing than the Protestant ethnic unit principle movement advocated by C. Peter Wagner in *Our Kind of People: The Ethical Dimensions of Church Growth in America* (Atlanta: John Knox Press, 1979). That was using ethnically homogeneous congregations as a marketing tool; this is using them as a tool of minority empowerment.

40. Tseng, "Chinese Protestant Nationalism," 39.

41. See Paul R. Spickard and Kevin M. Cragg, *God's Peoples: A Social History of Christians* (Grand Rapids, MI: Baker Book House, 1994), 307–19, 338–40.

PRACTICE

IMMIGRANTS' RELIGION AND ETHNICITY: A COMPARISON OF KOREAN CHRISTIAN AND INDIAN HINDU IMMIGRANTS

PYONG GAP MIN[1]

Religion plays an important role in both Asian Indian and Korean immigrants' adjustments to American society. While the majority of Indian immigrants in the United States are Hindus,[2] the majority of Korean immigrants are Protestants.[3] Many studies of Indian Hindu immigrants[4] and Korean Protestant immigrants[5] have pointed out that both groups effectively use their religions in maintaining their ethnicity. However, they use their religions in significantly different ways to preserve their ethnicity. Since Hinduism is a religion indigenous to India, Indian cultural traditions—language, food, dress, holidays, customs and values—are embedded into Hinduism. Thus, Indian Hindu immigrants can preserve their cultural traditions simply by preserving their religious faith and observing religious rituals without participating in formal religious congregations.

In contrast, Protestantism is a Western religion transplanted to Korea by American missionaries at the turn of the twentieth century and popularized only over the last thirty years. In its adjustment to Korean society, Protestantism has incorporated some Korean cultural traditions, particularly Korean Confucian and Shamanistic elements.[6] Yet Korean Protestants' religious faith and rituals are not directly related to their ethnic language, traditional food and dress, and national holidays. Moreover, as will be shown later, there are some tensions between some of the Korean Confucian and Protestant values and customs. Accordingly, Korean Christians in the United States cannot preserve their ethnicity simply by adhering to Protestant religious values and practicing religious rituals. They maintain Korean ethnicity mainly by increasing their fellowship and social networks and practicing Korean ethnic customs and values, particularly Confucian customs and values, with fellow Koreans through their active participation in an ethnic congregation.

This chapter compares Indian Hindu and Korean immigrants in the United States in their different ways of preserving their ethnicity through religion. There are four major data sources for discussions in this paper. First, a telephone survey of Chinese, Indian, and Korean immigrants in Queens, New York City, conducted in 1997 and 1998 provides data on Indian and Korean immigrants' self-reported religions and their frequency of participation in a religious congregation.[7] Second, telephone interviews with 131 Korean pastors in New York City conducted in 1989 provide information about Korean Protestant churches' fellowship and cultural retention functions.[8] Third, this investigator's participation in Korean churches provides valuable information about the nature and social functions of Korean immigrant churches.[9] Finally, this investigator's in-depth personal interviews with twelve Indian Hindu religious and community leaders conducted in 1999 provide information about Hinduism and Hindu temples, particularly in the context of New York. The main goal of this paper is to provide preliminary insights on the different ways Indian Hindu and Korean Christian immigrants use their religions to maintain their ethnicity.

THE LITERATURE REVIEW

The literature on religion and ethnicity is largely based on the experiences of the turn-of-the-century white immigrant groups. The earlier white immigrant groups—mostly Catholic and Jewish—were religious minorities in a predominantly Protestant country. Yet, these Judeo-Christian immigrant groups had much continuity with the previous Protestant immigrant groups in that they practiced their religious worship mainly through their participation in a religious congregation. Because of their congregation-based religious activities, the social science literature on religions in the United States emphasized the role of immigrant and ethnic congregations in maintaining ethnicity for immigrant and ethnic groups.[10]

Immigrant/ethnic congregations help to maintain ethnicity in two different ways. First, immigrant/ethnic churches enhance ethnicity by providing their members with fellowship and social networks with co-ethnic members. African Americans during slavery and after were alienated from white society. The black church served them as the family and community center. As W. E. B. Du Bois put it in *The Philadelphia Negro*, "its family functions are shown by the fact that the church is the center of social life and intercourse; acts as newspaper and intelligence bureau, is the center of amusement—indeed is the world in which the Negro moves and acts."[11] Meeting the need for primary social interactions is also important for immigrants who are separated from their relatives and friends with whom they maintained close ties. As one of the Hebrew words for synagogue, *Beth Haknesseth* (place of gathering), denotes, the Jewish synagogue has probably provided the most important role in providing communal ties for Jews settled in the United States, as well as in other parts of the world. It is also well known that Catholic parishes constituted territorial enclaves for many European immigrants in the latter half of the nineteenth and the early twentieth centuries.[12]

Second, immigrant/ethnic congregations contribute to ethnicity by helping members of an immigrant/ethnic group to preserve its cultural traditions. In their classic study of assimilation patterns of Catholic and Jewish immigrant groups, Warner and Srole asserted that, "the church was the first line of defense behind which these immigrants could organize themselves and with which they could preserve their group, (i.e., system), identity."[13] According to S. M. Tomasi and M. H. Engel, the Italian Catholic parishes "functioned to maintain the ethnic personality by organizing the group around the familiar religious and cultural symbols and behavioral modes of the fatherland."[14] Robert Ostergren made a similar point with regard to a white Protestant church in the Midwest: "As the center of the community life, the church was charged with responsibility of upholding the values and preserving the community with the cultural past." [15]

Contemporary Third World immigrant groups have transplanted not only Christian, but also many other non-Christian religions, such as Islam, Hinduism, and Buddhism, to the United States. Following the same theoretical perspective derived from the studies of the earlier white immigrant groups, recent studies of new immigrant groups have also stressed the ethnicity functions of immigrant congregations.[16] For example, Prema Kurien has shown how Indian Hindus use their "religious organizations as means to forge ethnic communities and articulate their ethnic identities as Indian Americans."[17] Analyzing data based on a survey of Vietnamese high school students, Bankston and Zhou have indicated that, "religious participation consistently makes a greater contribution to ethnic identification than any of the family or individual characteristics examined, except recency of arrival." [18]

As reviewed above, immigrants can meet their need for primary social interactions and preserve their language and cultural traditions effectively through their participation in ethnic congregations. Yet, many non-Western religions do not put as much emphasis on participation in a religious congregation as Judeo-Christian religions do. Hindus, Muslims, and Buddhists in particular usually practice their religion through family rituals and/or small-group prayer meetings without regularly participating in a religious congregation. The numbers of these three non-Christian immigrant religious groups have significantly increased in the United States over the last thirty years. We should not consider their lack of participation in religious congregations as an indication of their religious inactivity, particularly in connection with the role that religion plays in preserving their ethnic cultural traditions.

The significance of religion for preserving ethnic culture is that what we may call "ethno-religious" groups have huge advantages over other ethnic groups in preserving their ethnic culture through religion. They have advantages because their religious values and rituals are inseparably tied to their ethnic values, customs, holidays, food, dress, and even music and dance. Amish and Jewish groups as ethno-religious groups have been more successful in retaining their cultural traditions through religion mainly because their religious values and rituals are inseparable from their ethnic cultural traditions. Jewish religious holidays—Rosh Hashanah and Yom Kippur— have become Jewish ethnic holidays, while kosher food symbolizes Jewish ethnic food. Thus Jewish Americans have been able to retain their ethnic culture and identity mainly by preserving their Jewish religious faith and rituals, both through family rituals and ethnic congregations. Nevertheless, the focus on ethnic congregations as the major mechanism for preserving ethnic culture and identity has led researchers to neglect to examine how the association between religion and ethnic culture helps members of an immigrant/ ethnic group to maintain ethnicity, independent of their participation in congregations.[19]

INDIAN AND KOREAN IMMIGRANTS' SELF-REPORTED RELIGIONS AND FREQUENCY OF PARTICIPATION IN AN ETHNIC CONGREGATION

Table 1 shows the self-reported religions of Indian and Korean immigrants in Queens, New York City. All but two Indian respondents reported that they had a religion. Hindus compose 83 percent of the population in India,[20] although they are a minority in the state of Punjab. As expected, Hindus account for the majority of Indian immigrants (69 percent) in Queens. Indian Muslims usually use Muslim names and thus they were not included in my Indian surname sample. Given that Indian Muslims compose more than 15 percent of Indian immigrants, the proportion of Hindus may account for no more than 65 percent of Indian immigrants in Queens. The reduction of the percentage of Indian Hindus from 83 percent in India to about 65 percent in Queens is natural, considering that members of minority religious groups, such as Sikhs, Christians, and Muslims have emigrated from India in greater proportions than Hindus.

TABLE 1: KOREAN IMMIGRANTS' SELF-REPORTED RELIGIONS

Indians	Hinduism	Sikhism	Catholicism	Protestantism	Others	None
144 (100%)	99 (69%)	19 (13%)	8 (6%)	8 (6%)	8 (6%)	2 (1%)

Koreans	Protestantism	Catholicism	Buddhism	Other	None
187 (100%)	116 (62%)	32 (17%)	5 (3%)	1 (1%)	33 (18%)

Source: Telephone interviews with randomly selected Indian-, Chinese-, and Korean-surname households in Queens, New York, in 1997 and 1998.

Sikhs compose a tiny minority population in India, accounting for only 2 percent of the population. Yet, they account for over 60 percent of the population in the State of Punjab.[21] The Punjabi Sikh farmers composed the predominant majority of Indian immigrants in California at the turn of the century.[22] They are overrepresented among contemporary Indian immigrants too, as the immigrants from Punjab constitute as much as 20 percent of Indian immigrants.[23] My Queens survey shows that Sikhs make up 13 percent of Indian immigrants in the borough.

Christians, like Sikhs, represent another minority religious group in India, accounting for only 2.4 percent of the population.[24] They are heavily concentrated in three states: Kerala, Tamil Nadu, and Goa. A large number of Indian nurses have immigrated to the United States since the late 1960s, with a significant proportion of them drawing from the Christian population in Kerala.[25] My 1997–98 survey shows that Catholics and Protestants combined account for 12 percent of the Indian immigrant population in Queens, much larger than their share of the population in India.[26]

As of 2000, Christians compose about 32 percent of the population in South Korea, Protestants accounting for 24 percent and Catholics 8 percent, while Buddhists make up about 30 percent. Both Protestants and Catholics, whose numbers have gradually increased since the end of Japanese colonization of Korea in 1945, are overrepresented in the urban, middle-class segments of the population in South Korea. Korean immigrants have drawn largely from the same segments of the population. Also, Korean Christians, regardless of their urban or rural background, have responded to the U.S.-bound emigration path more favorably than Buddhists or other non-Christian Koreans because of their perception of the United States as a Christian country. Consequently, the majority of Korean immigrants were affiliated with a Protestant or a Catholic church prior to migration.[27]

Many Korean immigrants who were not Christians in Korea, including Buddhists, are affiliated with a Korean Protestant or Catholic church in the United States, because a Korean Christian church, as the major community center, provides various practical functions for Korean immigrants.[28] This means that the Korean Christian population has increased with international migration while the proportion of Korean Buddhists has significantly decreased.[29] The results of my recent survey conducted in Queens also support the previous findings that show a radical increase in Christians among Korean immigrants and the concomitant decrease in the Buddhist population *as a percentage.* Sixty-two percent of the Korean respondents in Queens and 17 percent respectively chose Protestantism and Catholicism as their main religion, while only 3 percent chose Buddhism (see Table 1).

The vast majority of Indian Hindus (77 percent) and Sikhs (90 percent) participate in an ethnic congregation (the rest of them attending a congregation mixed with other South Asians). In contrast Indian Catholics and Protestants usually participate in ethnically mixed or non-ethnic congregations. The lack of Indian pastors, Indian immigrants' multilingual background, and their fluency in English all seem to explain why almost all Indian Christian immigrants in Queens participate in an ethnically mixed or a non-ethnic congregation.

The tendency of Korean Christians to participate in an ethnic congregation is even much greater than that of Indian Hindus or Sikhs who practice their indigenous religions. All but two Korean respondents—one Protestant and one Catholic—reported that they participated in a Korean congregation. This finding is not surprising at all, considering that Korean immigrants, coming from a culturally homogeneous society, participate in an ethnic congregation to enjoy fellowship with other Koreans and to maintain Korean culture through them.[30] The tendency of nearly all Korean Christian immigrants to participate in an ethnic congregation sets them apart from other Asian Christian immigrants. Not only Indian Christians, but also other Asian Christian immigrants tend to participate in a predominantly white congregation. For example, more than 80 percent of Filipino immigrants are Catholics, but my conversations with Filipino community leaders indicate that the majority of them attend non-ethnic churches.

There are two major reasons why almost all Korean Christians attend a

Korean congregation. First, there are enough Korean pastors and Korean churches to provide Korean immigrants with native-language services. Because Koreans have one language, they have a huge advantage over other multi-lingual Asian immigrant groups, such as Indian, Filipino, or Chinese immigrants, in establishing their own churches. Proportionally, more pastors have emigrated from South Korea than any other occupational group. In fact, one could say that there are too many Korean pastors in the Korean immigrant community, which has contributed to the increase in the number of Korean immigrant churches by causing existing churches to split into more churches.[31] There are approximately 600 Korean churches in the New York-New Jersey metropolitan area alone, serving a Korean American population of perhaps as many as 180,000 people.

The other major reason Korean immigrants prefer a Korean church is their need for a communal bond. Due to their uprooting experiences, all immigrants seek a communal bond by establishing ethnic organizations. Yet, the need for a communal bond is strong especially for Korean immigrants because of their cultural homogeneity, and greater language barrier and other adjustment difficulties. Because of their cultural homogeneity, Korean immigrants try to confine their social interactions largely to fellow Koreans and stick to Korean language, customs, and values.[32] Further, most Korean immigrants have severe language barriers and other adjustment difficulties due to cultural differences. Given their cultural homogeneity and culture shock, we can easily understand why Korean Christian immigrants prefer a Korean congregation.

Korean Christians, especially Korean Protestants, participate in an ethnic congregation not only in higher proportion, but also far more frequently than Indian Hindus. As shown in Table 2, 82 percent of Korean Christians —84 percent of Protestants and 72 percent of Catholics—attend a religious (ethnic) congregation once a week or more often. In contrast, only 22 percent of Indian Hindus go to a temple weekly, while 46 percent go there a few times a year or less frequently.

The differences in worship style between Christian religions and Hinduism mainly explain why Korean Christian immigrants participate in a religious congregation far more actively than Indian Hindus. While Christians, especially Protestants, perform religious services mainly in a church as a group, Hindus usually have worship at home individually or in a small-group setting. In fact, several Indian informants told me that Hindus in India less frequently participate in a temple than Indian immigrants in the United States do.[33]

Yet, Korean Christian immigrants participate in a religious congregation far more frequently than even other Christian immigrant groups. Table 2

TABLE 2: INDIAN HINDU AND KOREAN CHRISTIAN IMMIGRANTS' FREQUENCY OF PARTICIPATION IN A RELIGIOUS CONGREGATION

	Less than once a year	Once or a few times a year	Once or twice a month	Once a week or more often
Indian Hindus 99 (100%)	21 (21%)	25 (25%)	31 (31%)	22 (22%)
Indian Christians 16 (100%)	3 (9%)	3 (9%)	3 (19%)	7 (44%)
Korean Christians 147 (100%)	5 (3%)	6 (4%)	16 (11%)	120 (83%)

Source: Telephone interviews with randomly selected Indian-, Chinese-, and Korean-surname households in Queens, New York, in 1997 and 1998

also shows that only 44 percent of Indian Christian immigrants go to church at least once a week. Results of the national studies of racial and ethnic Presbyterians also show that Korean Presbyterians participate in a congregation far more frequently than Black, Latino, or white Presbyterians.[34] Korean Christian immigrants' active participation in a Korean church can be explained by a combination of the social and psychological functions of Korean ethnic churches.[35] Since a Korean immigrant church serves as a Korean community center by providing all kinds of services, it is practically difficult for a Korean immigrant family to survive without attending a Korean church regularly. But the Korean church's various social functions alone may not be enough to make approximately two-thirds of all Korean immigrants participate in it weekly. Because of their great adjustment difficulties—including their language barrier and long hours of work in general and their experiences with downward mobility in social status in particular —most adult Korean immigrants may turn to religion to find new meaning in their lives.

KOREAN IMMIGRANTS' ACTIVE PARTICIPATION IN ETHNIC CHURCH FACILITATES THEIR FELLOWSHIP AND RETENTION OF CONFUCIAN CULTURE

We have noted above that Korean Christian immigrants participate in an ethnic congregation far more frequently than Indian Hindus do. Korean immigrants' active participation in an ethnic congregation contributes to their ethnicity by increasing their ethnic networks on the one hand and by helping them to preserve Korean cultural traditions on the other.

As previously noted, one major reason why a predominant majority of Korean immigrants actively participates in a Christian ethnic congregation is their need for primary social interactions that stems from their sense of alienation from the larger society. Korean immigrant churches are organized and operate in such a way that they indeed meet this need for communal bonds. All Korean churches have a fellowship hour after the Sunday service during which church members exchange greetings and enjoy informal talks with their "brothers and sisters." Almost all Korean churches provide refreshments during the fellowship hour. Twenty-eight percent of the Korean churches surveyed in 1989 were found to provide a full lunch or dinner after Sunday service. In these churches, each member prepares Korean meals on a rotating basis. Almost all Korean churches surveyed also have parties after services to celebrate important Korean traditional and Christian holidays. In addition, most small-scale Korean churches have birthday parties for children and elderly people, with cakes, food, and gifts prepared.

Large Korean churches are less effective than small churches for meeting the needs of Korean immigrants because they do not provide for an intimate social environment. Yet, even large churches have made adjustments to facilitate the immigrants' primary social interactions. Korean immigrant churches usually divide church members into several different groups by their area of residence and help each group to hold regular district meetings called *kuyok yebae*, or "cell group" meetings.[36] Nearly 80 percent of the surveyed Korean churches in New York City were found to have district groups, with each group usually holding a meeting once per month. A district meeting combines a religious service and a dinner party at a member's private home, which provides district members with ample opportunity for informal social interactions.[37]

Korean congregations also contribute to maintaining Korean ethnicity by helping to preserve Korean cultural traditions. First of all, the Korean language and customs are more strictly observed inside the church than outside of it. Sermons are given in Korean in all main services prepared for immigrants. As shown elsewhere, even children's services are provided bilingually or in Korean more often than in English.[38] Many Korean children practice the Korean language to attend a Korean-language or bilingual service. Moreover, about half of all Korean churches in New York provide a Korean language program for second-generation Korean children. Korean language programs provided by Korean churches are vital to the second generation's language retention, because the vast majority of Korean children (about 80 percent) attend an ethnic church every week. Several Korean churches in New York provide summer schools—ranging from two weeks to two months—

focusing on teaching the Korean language and culture that target not only the children of their church members, but also other Korean children.

Exposure to Korean culture is not limited to the Korean language. All Korean immigrant churches celebrate not only religious holidays, but also all Korean traditional holidays (Lunar New Year Day and *Chuseok*, the Korean Thanksgiving Day, in particular) and national holidays (the March-First Movement Commemoration Day and the Korean Independence Day). On traditional Korean holidays, churches serve a variety of traditional Korean foods, with many church members wearing traditional Korean costumes. Almost all Korean immigrant churches celebrate the year-end party at a member's private home on New Year's Eve, and participants usually play a traditional game called *yoot* at the party.

Korean pastors often emphasize Korean values in their sermons, and this is another way Korean churches contribute to preserving Korean culture and identity. Korean pastors as a group seem to be more conservative than other college-educated Koreans in their attitudes toward American mass culture in general and American youth culture in particular. Many Korean pastors tend to think that American society, which originated from the migration of Puritans from European countries, is turning against Christian values. They argue that Korean traditional values, such as respecting parents and other adults, are more consistent with Christian values than American "individualism." They frequently tie certain Korean traditional values to a paragraph from the Bible and preach to their church members to preserve those Korean values to live as sincere Christians.

Confucianism, which was transplanted from China in the fourth century, has had a powerful influence on Korean culture. Respect for the elderly and subordination of women to men are two central elements of the Confucian ideology as applied to Korean society. These Confucian cultural elements are incorporated into Korean Christian religions, particularly in church hierarchies.[39] Under the impact of Korean Confucian cultural traditions, Korean immigrant churches are hierarchically organized based on age and gender. A small number of ordained elders, who usually hold the position until they retire, exercise a great deal of power and authority in Korean immigrant churches. An analysis of comparative data reveals that elders in Korean Presbyterian churches are significantly older than elders in other churches and include many fewer women, and that women elders have higher levels of education than men elders.[40] The 1999 Korean Churches Directory of New York shows that women serve as the head pastors only for four out of the nearly 600 churches, although women are more active in Korean immigrant churches than men.[41] Women are usually involved in fundraising, prayer meetings, and visiting the sick—all directly related to women's traditional roles as nurturers and caretakers—while men hold important positions that involve decision-making in organizational and financial affairs.[42]

INDIAN HINDUS MAINTAIN ETHNICITY THROUGH PRESERVATION OF RELIGIOUS VALUES AND RITUALS

We earlier noted that Indians participate in a religious congregation much less frequently than Korean Christians. Indian Hindus' lack of participation in a religious congregation is reflected in the small number of Hindu temples. The Indian population in the New York–New Jersey metropolitan area is twice as large as the Korean population. But there are only about 25 Hindu temples in the area, compared to approximately 600 Korean churches.

One major reason why the Indian community has a small number of Hindu temples compared to churches in the Korean community is that it costs a lot of money to build an "authentic" Hindu temple that requires unique architectural designs and sculpture. In contrast, Korean Christian immigrants use American church buildings or rent private buildings for services. My 1989 survey showed that only 24 percent of Korean churches in New York had their own building and that the rest either used American churches (59 percent) or rented private buildings (17 percent). Indian immigrants also have greater difficulty establishing their Hindu temples than do Koreans partly because there are many variations, regional variations being the most significant, in Hindu religious forms—language, rituals, deities, sacred texts, and religious values. Indian Hindus speak dozens of languages. The New York–New Jersey area contains the largest Indian community in the United States. Yet, even in New York, there may not be enough Telugu- or Bengali-speaking Hindus for their own local-language temples in a particular locale.

Hindu temples usually provide religious services Friday evenings, throughout Saturday and Sunday, and Monday evenings. Indian Hindus go to a temple on one of these days depending upon convenience. But most Hindus go to a temple only on several religious holidays per year. A Hindu priest and college teacher of Hinduism told me that participants in Hindu temple services do not consider themselves "members of a congregation" because they have neither exclusive relations with the temple nor close social relations with other participants in it. Unlike Korean Christian churches, Hindu temples do not provide various practical services—immigration orientation, job referral, family counseling, and after-school programs—for the participants. By virtue of a large number of medical professionals available, a

Hindu temple usually provides a health clinic once a year. But there are no more social services for the participants than that. When called upon, priests in a temple visit Hindu families to preside over many religious rituals that are given following life cycles. But these families who request services do not have to be participants in the temple. A Hindu family that regularly goes to a temple often has a special ritual under the guidance of a priest in a separate room in the temple with their relatives and friends invited. But this is an individual family affair to which other participants are not invited. Thus a Hindu temple is much less important for providing social services and fellowship for the participants than a Korean Christian church is.

Although a Hindu temple is not significant as a social center, it is an important cultural center for Indians. Indian Hindus can maintain ethnic and subethnic cultural traditions through their participation in worship there because their religious worship is inseparably tied to their culture. First of all, the temple itself, with its traditional Indian sculptures, symbolizes Indian culture. For religious services, participants read scriptures written either in Sanskrit, an ancient Indian language, or translated into a local language. They sing, pray, and chant in either language. The deities they worship are closely related to their local culture and history. The religious values Hindu priests advocate, such as non-violence, peace, truth, and duty, symbolize Indian national values. On major Hindu holidays, a larger number of Hindu immigrants go to a temple, usually accompanied by their children, to celebrate these holidays. By celebrating their religious holidays in the United States, American Hindus celebrate their Indian national holidays.

Few colleges and universities in the United States offer any of the Indian languages because of Indians' multilingual backgrounds, while numerous colleges and universities offer three East Asian languages (Chinese, Japanese and Korean). Thus second-generation Indian students are at a disadvantage for learning their native language. But most Hindu temples provide a Sanskrit and/or a Hindi/local language class for second-generation children. They also offer courses to teach Indian children Indian dance and music. Thus Hindu temples play an important role in teaching the second generation their languages and culture. Because of the complexities of religious rituals performed, only a small fraction of Indian children participate regularly in religious services performed in a temple.[43]

As noted above, only 22 percent of Indian Hindu immigrants go to a Hindu temple every week or more often. Their children, according to my informants, participate much less frequently than their parents. If participation in a religious congregation is the only way members of a group can maintain their ethnicity through religion, then Indian Hindus have disadvantages compared to many Christian immigrant groups in general and Korean Christian immigrants in particular. However, almost all Indian Hindus, regardless of their participation in a temple, have a family shrine to worship deities and perform religious rituals. Hindus worship individually at home every day, usually after bathing.

They also perform a number of religious rituals following changes in a person's life cycle. For example, when a child is born, they have a ceremony to shave him or her completely. When the baby becomes one year old, they have another ceremony to start the baby on solid food. When the baby turns three, they have another ceremony to teach him or her the alphabet. At the age of twelve, they perform another ritual to induce him or her to the study of scriptures. Hindu norms require more complicated ceremonies at the time of marriage and death. My informants told me that most Hindu families perform some of these ceremonies at home, usually under the guidance of a priest. They also celebrate Hindu religious holidays at home. Many Hindu families remain vegetarian following Hindu rules. Because these Hindu rituals and values are uniquely Indian, they can maintain their ethnic cultural traditions effectively by practicing Hinduism.

CONCLUSION

Scholars of religion and minority and immigrant groups have long taken for granted the positive effects of an immigrant or ethnic group's religion on its ethnicity. Yet they may not have taken pains to explain how a religion helps immigrants and members of an ethnic group to *maintain* their ethnicity. Theoretical discussions about how religions help to maintain ethnicity in the United States are largely based on turn-of-the-century, congregation-based, Judeo-Christian immigrant groups. As a result, researchers at least in the United States have emphasized the role of immigrant and ethnic congregations in the preservation of ethnicity for those groups. Also recognized—but less emphasized—is the fact that many non-Protestant white ethnic groups, including the Amish and the Jews, have maintained their ethnicity through preservation of their religious values and rituals. It has been possible for them to do so mainly because of the inseparable connection between their religious values and rituals, and their ethnic culture.

In maintaining their ethnicity through religion, all religious groups utilize both mechanisms—participation in an ethnic congregation and the association of religious faith and rituals with ethnic culture—to some extent. But some religious groups depend upon one mechanism to a far greater extent than the other. As examined in this chapter, Indian Hindu immigrants maintain their ethnicity largely through preservation of their religious values and rituals at home without actively participating in an ethnic congregation. In contrast, Korean Christian immigrants maintain their ethnicity mainly through their active participation in an ethnic congregation.

It is important to note that Korean immigrants actively use their Christian congregation as a place for fellowship and preservation of Confucian culture. Yet, even more important to note is that their religious practices do not directly help them to maintain Korean culture and identity because of their weak connection between the religious practices and Korean folk culture. The literature founded on congregation-based, Judeo-Christian, white ethnic groups leads us to conclude that Korean immigrants have a huge advantage over Indian Hindu immigrants in retaining their ethnicity through religion because they participate in ethnic congregations far more actively than Indians. However, Indian Hindus have an advantage over Korean Christians in maintaining their ethnic culture and identity through religion mainly because Hinduism is their native religion. Their religious faith and rituals are inseparably tied to their language, values, customs, food, and holidays.

NOTES

1. This is a revision of the article published in the *Bulletin of the Royal Institute for Inter-Faith Studies* 2 (2000): 121–140. Also, different versions of this chapter were presented at the following three conferences; the Conference on "Korean and Korean-American Christianity" held at University of Illinois at Urbana-Champaign in October 1999; the Conference on "Migration and Culture Contact: Patterns of Confrontation and Coexistence in a Changing World" held in Amman, Jordan, in October 1999; the Annual Meeting of the Eastern Sociological Society held in Baltimore, in March 2000.

2. John Fenton, *Transplanting Religious Traditions: Asian Indians in America* (New York: Praeger Publishers, 1988), 28.

3. Won Moo Hurh and Kwang Chung Kim, "Religious Participation of Korean Immigrants in the United States," *Journal for the Scientific Study of Religion,* 29 (1990): 19-34; Pyong Gap Min, "The Structure and Social Functions of Korean Immigrant Churches in the United States," *International Migration Review,* 26 (1992): 1370–94.

4. Fenton, *Transplanting Religious Traditions;* Prema Kurien, "Becoming American by Becoming Hindu: Indian Americans Take Their Place at the Multicultural Table," in *Gatherings in Diaspora: Religious Communities and the New Immigration,* ed. R. Stephen Warner and Judith G. Wittner (Philadelphia, PA: Temple University Press, 1998), 37–70; Prema Kurien, "Gendered Ethnicity: Creating a Hindu Indian Identity in the United States." *American Behavioral Scientist* (1999): 648–670; Prema Kurien, "'We Are Better Hindus Here': Religion and Ethnicity among Indian Americans," in *Religions in Asian America: Building Faith Communities,* ed. Pyong Gap Min and Jung Ha Kim

(Altamira Press, 2002); Raymond Williams, *Religions of Immigrants from India and Pakistan* (New York: Cambridge University Press, 1988).

5. Ai Ra Kim, *Women Struggling for a New Life: The Role of Religion in the Cultural Passage from Korea to America* (Albany, NY: State University of New York Press, 1996); Jung Ha Kim, "The Labor of Compassion: Voices of 'Churched' Korean American Women," *Amerasia Journal,* 22 (1996): 93–105; Ho-Young Kwon, Kwang Chug Kim, and Stephen Warner eds., *Korean Americans and Their Religions: Pilgrims and Missionaries from a Different Shore* (University Park, PA: Penn State University Press, 2001); Pyong Gap Min, "Cultural and Economic Boundaries of Korean Ethnicity: A Comparative Analysis," *Ethnic and Racial Studies,* 14 (1991): 225–41; Min, "Structure and Social Functions of Korean Immigrant Churches"; Eui-Hang Shin and Hyung Park, "An Analysis of Causes of Schisms in Ethnic Churches: The Case of Korean-American Churches," *Sociological Analysis,.* 49 (1988): 234–48.

6. Donald Baker, "Christianity," in *An Introduction to Korean Culture,* ed. John H. Koo and Andrew Nam (Elizabeth, NJ: Hollym, 1997), 170–200; Andrew Kim, "Korean Religious Culture and Its Affinity to Christianity in South Korea," *Sociology of Religion,* 61 (2000): 117–134.

7. The survey was conducted as a part of a larger study that compares Chinese, Indian and Korean immigrants in New York in ethnic attachment. Using twenty prominent Chinese, Indian, and Korean surnames, 600 households for the three groups—200 for each group—were randomly selected in 1997 for a telephone survey from the 1997 Queens Borough public telephone directory. In 1998, the same survey with the same sample size was repeated to double the number of the respondents. As a result, 166 Chinese, 144 Indian and 187 Korean adult immigrants (household heads or their spouses) were successfully interviewed by six Queens College students who were perfectly bilingual.

8. The 1988 Korean Churches Directory of New York, published by the Council of Korean Churches of Greater New York, was used as the sampling frame. The directory included 290 Korean churches in the New York-New Jersey metropolitan area. 165 of the 290 churches were located in the five New York City boroughs. This investigator and two Korean bilingual students successfully interviewed 131 of the main New York City pastors by telephone.

9. He regularly participated in two Korean Protestant churches in Atlanta and one church in New York between 1975 and 1993. Between 1991 and 1992, he served as the principal of the Korean language school established in a Korean church in New York.

10. Andrew Greeley, *Why Can't They Be Like Us? America's White Ethnic Groups* (New York: E. Dutton & Company, 1971); S. Rosenberg, *The New Jewish Identity in America* (New York: Hippocrene Books, 1985); Timothy Smith, "Religion and Ethnicity in America," *American Historical Review,* 83 (1978): 1155–85; R. Stephen Warner, "Work in Progress toward a New Paradigm for the Sociological Study of Religion in the United States," *American Journal of Sociology,* 98 (1993): 1044–93; R. Stephen Warner, "The Place of the Congregation in the American Religious Configuration," in *American Congregations, Vol.2: New Perspectives in the Study of Congregations,* ed. James Wind and James Lewis (Chicago: University of Chicago Press, 1994), 54–99.

11. W. E. B. Du Bois, *The Philadelphia Negro* (New York: Schocken Books, 1967), 201.

12. R. M. Links, *American Catholicism and European Immigrants* (Staten Island, NY: Center for Migration Studies, 1975).

13. W. Lloyd Warner and Leo Srole, *The Social Systems of American Ethnic Groups* (New Haven: Yale University Press, 1945), 160.

14. S. M. Tomasi and M. H. Engel, *The Italian Experience in the United States* (Staten Island, NY: Center for Migration Studies, 1970), 186.

15. Robert Ostergren, "The Immigrant Church as a Symbol of Community and Place in the Upper Midwest," *Great Plains Quarterly*, 1 (1981): 229.

16. Carl Bankston III and Min Zhou, "Religious Participation, Ethnic Identification, and Adaptation of Vietnamese Adolescents in an Immigrant Community," *Sociological Quarterly*, 36 (1995): 523–534; Helen Rose Ebaugh and Janet Saltzman Chafetz, *Religion and the New Immigrants* (Walnut Creek, CA: Altamira Press, 2000); Hurh and Kim, "Religious Participation of New Immigrants"; Kurien, "Becoming American by Becoming Hindu"; idem., "Gendered Ethnicity"; idem., "'We are Better Hindus Here'"; Min, "Cultural and Economic Boundaries of Korean Ethnicity"; idem., "Structural and Social Functions of Korean Immigrant Churches"; Williams, *Religions of Immigrants*; Fenggang Yang, *Chinese Christians in America: Conversion, Assimilation, and Adhesive Identities* (University Park, PA: Penn State University Press, 1999), 132–162.

17. Kurien, "Becoming American by Becoming Hindu," 59.

18. Bankston III and Zhou, "Religious Participation, Ethnic Identification, and Adaptation," 530.

19. The following are exceptions: Ana Maria Diaz-Stevens, *Oxcart Catholicism on Fifth Avenue: The Impact of the Puerto Rican Migration upon the Archdiocese of New York* (Notre Dame, IN: University of Notre Dame Press, 1993); Ebaugh and Chafetz, *Religion and the New Immigrants*, 391–392; Anthony Orsi, *The Madonna of 115th Street: Faith and Community in Italian Harlem, 1880–1950* (New Haven: Yale University Press, 1985); Nancy Wellmeier, "Santa Eulalia's People in Exile: Maya Religion, Culture, and Identity in Los Angeles," in *Gatherings in Diaspora*, 97–122.

20. Williams, *Religions of Immigrants*, 37.

21. Ibid.,

22. J. M. Jensen, *Passage from India: Asian Indian Immigrants in North America* (New Haven: Yale University Press, 1988), 41.

23. Williams, *Religions of Immigrants*, 37.

24. Ibid., 103.

25. Sheba George, "Caroling with the Keralites: The Negotiation of Gendered Space in an Indian Immigrant Church," in *Gatherings in Diaspora*, 265–94.

26. In-Sook Han Park and Lee-Jay Cho, "Confucianism and the Korean Family," *Journal of Comparative Family Studies*, 26 (1995): 225–38.

27. Various survey studies conducted in Los Angeles, New York, Chicago and Seoul have shown that 50–55 percent of Korean immigrants attended Christian churches in Korea. See Hurh and Kim, "Religious Participation of Korean Immigrants," Pyong Gap Min and Dae Young Kim, "Intergenerational Transmission of Religion and Culture: Koreans

in New York," Paper Presented at the Annual Meeting of the Association for the Sociology of Religion, Washington, DC, August, 2000; In-Sook Han Park, James Fawcett, Fred Arnold, and Richard Gardner, "Koreans Immigrating to the United States: A Pre-Departure Analysis," Paper No. 114 (Honolulu: Population Institute, East-West Center), 60.

28. Min, "Structure and Social Functions of Korean Immigrant Churches."

29. Hurh and Kim, "Religious Participation of Religious Immigrants"; Min and Kim, "Intergenerational Transmission of Religion and Culture."

30. Min, "Cultural and Economic Boundaries of Korean Ethnicity"; idem., "Structures and Social Functions of Korean Immigrant Churches."

31. Shin and Park, 1988; R. Stephen Warner, "Korean Immigrant Church as Case and Model," in *Korean Americans and Their Religions*, 33.

32. Min, "Cultural and Economic Boundaries of Korean Ethnicity."

33. Kurien, "Becoming American by Becoming Hindu"; idem., " 'We are Better Hindus Here'."

34. Kwang Chung Kim and Shin Kim, "The Ethnic Role of Korean Immigrant Churches in the U.S.," in *Korean Americans and Their Religions*, 82.

35. Ibid.

36. Victoria Hyunchu Kwon, Helen Rose Ebaugh, and Jacqueline Hagan, "The Structure and Functions of Cell Group Ministry in a Korean Christian Church," *Journal of the Scientific Study of Religion*, 36 (1997): 247–256; Min, 1992.

37. Ibid.

38. See Min, "Structure and Social Functions of Korean Immigrant Churches."

39. Baker, "Christianity" 170–200; Park and Cho, "Confucianism and the Korean Family."

40. Kim and Kim, "Ethnic Role of Korean Immigrant Churches," 84.

41. Results of a survey conducted in 1997 show that 79 percent of Korean immigrant women in New York, compared to 67 percent of men, were Christians. See Min and Kim, "Intergenerational Transmission of Religion and Culture."

42. A. Kim, *Women Struggling for a New Life*, 76.

43. According to Hindu religious leaders, less than 10 percent of Hindu high school students in New York go to a temple every week. Indian religious leaders consider simplifying Hindu rituals to attract more second-generation children.

CREATING THE SACRED:
ALTARS IN THE HINDU AMERICAN HOME

SHAMPA MAZUMDAR AND SANJOY MAZUMDAR

INTRODUCTION

Religion and Immigrant Communities

Religion, according to Peter Berger "serves to maintain the reality of that socially constructed world within which men exist in their everyday lives."[1] Symbolic interactionists, such as Berger, acknowledge that as a human construction the social world is "inherently precarious and transitory." Religion, by "placing human phenomena on a cosmic frame of reference," legitimates "humanly defined reality to ultimate, universal and sacred reality," thus giving it a cosmic status.[2] When people are uprooted and separated from their familiar, taken-for-granted social world, they experience feelings of rootlessness, of not belonging, anxiety, and alienation. It is not surprising then, that throughout history, immigrant groups have turned to religion to ease the pain and stress of transition and transplantation, to reconstruct and find meaning in a new social world and to legitimate and sustain their newly created social reality.[3] Describing the role of religion in immigrant lives Randall Miller writes:

> Religion was intertwined and imbedded in the psyche, the folk life, the very identity of each immigrant. It gave meaning, a system of moral values, self-definition, and community to the immigrants. It ordered their internal private world and the world outside the family. Thrown into close proximity with competing cultural and linguistic groups in indus-

trial, urban America, the immigrants turned to religion, the very bone and sinew of ethnicity, to shore up communal ties.[4]

Immigration then, according to Timothy Smith[5] is a "theologizing experience." Though immigrants cognitively transport their religion with them they leave behind their "objectivations"[6] of the sacred, such as their churches, synagogues, temples, sanctuaries, pilgrimage sites, altars, and icons. Arriving in a new land, one of their first steps is the recreation of these objectivations.[7] For the community of believers, recreation of these objectivations both in public space (temples, churches, mosques) and in private space (family altars) represents not only a significant step in the transplantation of religion but also is fundamental to the sustenance of religion itself. Yet, re-creations, in private space, have not received adequate scholarly attention.[8]

Here we are concerned with altars and shrines in private space and the role they play in identity formation.[9] It is useful to examine domestic altars and shrines for the following reasons:

First, it extends the literature from its preoccupation with the dominant Euro-American paradigm to include alternative forms of discourse. Because of its Euro-American bias and model, the focus of much scholarly inquiry has been on the public, institutional, congregational, and visible aspects of religion—with a near total neglect of the private, the non-congregational, the personal, and the not so visible. Thus although congregational religions such as Judaism, Christianity, and Islam and their collective sacred spaces of synagogues, churches and mosques[10] have been studied, altars and shrines and other important objectivations of religions such as Hinduism and Buddhism have been largely ignored.

Second, a study of altars focuses attention on home-based religion, on everyday family practices and rituals that help create religious reality without the mediation, assistance, and involvement of ritual specialists and clergy. Specifically, it emphasizes the need to understand the informal mechanism of religious socialization, one that is based on learning through observation and participation in home rituals with parents as teachers.

Finally, it suggests that, despite scholarly aversion, religion ought to become an important component of Asian American studies. In this we agree with David Yoo that religion "merits serious study in its own right as a force that shapes, transforms, and unifies as well as divides Asian American communities," and thus should not be "subsumed under other categories."[11] It is important to recognize here that, despite the predictions by some regarding the erosion of religion,[12] religion and the sacred continue to hold meaning[13] and exert influence in a post-modern world.[14] In fact, it has been suggested that the religious identities of certain diasporic populations become more important in diaspora than in their native contexts.[15]

HOMES AS SACRED SPACE

In several societies, the home is the locus of many socio-religious rituals, which by their very nature impart sacredness to the home. Lord Raglan in his book *The Temple and the House* provides many cross-cultural examples of this. To Raglan, homes in traditional societies are "sacred because they are places where divine beings whether gods or ancestral spirits are worshipped."[16] Mircea Eliade calls the manifestation of sacred in a place or object a "hierophany."[17] Not only is home sanctified by the presence of hierophany, it can also be made sacred by the performance of specific rituals.[18] Many researchers have studied different aspects of this sacred quality. Pierre Bourdieu's[19] 1973 analysis of the Berber house points to the importance of appropriate orientation of home. David Saile[20] describes house building rituals among the Pueblo, rituals that seek supernatural assistance to make home sacred, safe, and habitable for its occupants. In similar fashion, Graeme Hardie[21] analyses the protective and consecration rituals among the Tswana, while Eleftherios Pavlides and Jana Hesser[22] describe sacred objects, spaces, and rituals of the traditional Greek house.

Home is sacred to Hindus; it is the place where household deities are worshiped, where a Hindu is "able to communicate with the other world, the world of divine beings or ancestors,"[23] where sacred events in the life of a Hindu, such as initiation rites and marriage, are celebrated.[24]

This chapter focuses on Hindu immigrant family and home, and the creation of the sacred at the individual and familial level. Through a study of family shrines, it describes the process of religious transplantation and transformation, the sacralization of space, and the use of this sacralized setting for the socialization of children into their religious identity. It concludes with a brief comparative analysis of the domestic articulation of the sacred by other religious groups.

THE HINDU IMMIGRANT HOME IN AMERICA

The Hindu immigrant community in Southern California is a relatively new immigrant group, having arrived in large measure following changes brought by the Immigration and Reform Act of 1965. Separated from their familiar, taken-for-granted, social world, the immigrant Hindu population faced both unfamiliar values and traditions, as well as hostility and suspicion towards their religion. In the early years, creating sacred public spaces such as temples was not foremost in the mind of the Hindu community for several reasons. First the community was small and dispersed. Second, many Hindus came to this country as students with some uncertainty about their future. They could be classified as sojourners with no long-term plans for settling down.[25] Third, even those Indians who came to reside permanently were in the early years focused on material success and gaining a financial foothold in the new country.[26] Fourth, unlike Jews, Christians, and Muslims, congregational prayers at the temple on mandated days were not a requirement for Hindus. Fifth, the Hindu religion had few conceptual similarities with the prevailing Judeo-Christian traditions, thus making its transplantation in the public arena more difficult. Unlike Jewish, Christian, or Muslim practice, Hinduism was non-congregational, lacked a singular text comparable to the Bible, and focused on multiple manifestations of a single god. These differences left the Hindu religion and its sacred spaces more open and vulnerable to overt public hostility and negative attention. Sixth, services traditionally provided by Hindu temples were markedly different from those provided by churches and synagogues. Temples in the Hindu tradition served primarily as ritual and cultural centers. By contrast, Christian churches and Jewish synagogues provided important public social service to their community of believers, helping newcomers find "jobs, food, shelter and acceptance."[27] There was, thus, an immediate need among Jews and Christians to set up churches and synagogues in a new setting.[28] Hindu temples, on the other hand, had neither the history nor the institutional set-up needed to provide social services. Due to a different approach and format, which did not see these functions as important, there was no immediate urgency among Hindus to establish temples. Finally, the Hindu religion had a long and well-established tradition of home based rituals and daily practices at the family shrine.[29]

For a Hindu in America, a sacralized home, however, took on added meaning. A Hindu in India was surrounded by the familiar sights and sounds of his or her religion. There were the sacred rivers, mountains, cities, pilgrimage centers, domestic shrines, and the many temples ranging from simple roadside shrines, to midsize neighborhood temples, to grandiose complex structures. Here in America, a sacred geography was largely missing. Temples were often far away and required a long commute. Roadside shrines and neighborhood temples were lacking. Home then became for many the primary focus for the practice of religion and the maintenance of religious identity.

In the next section, we focus on the creation of the sacred in the immigrant home. This is described through the establishment of the altar as well as the performance of ritual—both of which are pivotal in the transplantation of religion.

CREATING THE SACRED

The *pooja* area (prayer, religious, or ritual space) is the most sacred space in the Hindu immigrant home. This is where a permanent altar is established and religion is practiced on a daily basis.

Several general considerations provide guidance for selecting the most appropriate space for the family altar in the immigrant home. Locational norms derived from Hindu principles of purity and pollution require that its sanctity be protected from pollution and defilement. The risk of ritual pollution is minimized if this area is removed from easy access and entry by visitors who may pollute unknowingly and inadvertently. This issue becomes particularly important in immigrant homes where visitors to the home may not be Hindus and may include people not knowledgeable about the rules. The discomfort associated with non-Hindus coming into contact with the altar is illustrated through the following example: Bijoya's family had lived in the United States for almost two decades. Their altar was located in a deeply recessed alcove in the corner of the living room. While in some ways the alcove was "convenient" for the placement of the altar, it allowed for no visual privacy. People walking into the house were curious about the altar and the anthropomorphic forms the family worshiped, such as Durga with her ten hands, Ganesha with his elephant head, and so on. The family expressed concern that non-Hindu children unaware of the Hindu rules of purity and pollution would touch the altar with their shoes on and hands unwashed.

Seclusion to reduce opportunities and chances of pollution is an important consideration. Unlike Catholic altars, which are usually given a place of prominence in the living room open to public view, the Hindu altar is rarely made visible to the public and outsiders. Hindus try never to locate the *pooja* area near the entryway, nor in the middle of the traffic flow of the home. The ideal is to have the altar in an enclosed space, visible only to family and intimate friends and those who are knowledgeable about the purity and pollution rules. Furthermore, seclusion of the *pooja* area enables *pooja* activities to continue even when visitors are present.

Separation from areas considered impure or polluting is also important. The *pooja* area and altar are not located near areas considered unclean, such as kitchen trash, bathrooms, the kitchen sink, and so on. Preeti, a college student, recalled her mother's discomfort with the initial location of their *pooja* area because it was too near the kitchen sink, and thus in close proximity to dirty dishes. In another example, Gita relocated her shrine from her kitchen to her bedroom because in her small kitchen, the trash bin would often come uncomfortably close to her shrine area. Additionally, it is considered preferable not to have the altar located downstairs or under stairways even though these spaces could afford visual privacy, as this would be a sign of great disrespect since the possibility of a person walking over one's deities would be symbolically inappropriate.

A variety of devices are used to maintain the sacrality of altar spaces. They are: (a) complete spatial separation; (b) incorporation into other sacred spaces; and (c) symbolic separation.

a) Complete Spatial Separation

In some homes there is a complete spatial separation of the sacred. The altar is enshrined in a separate, enclosed space, usually located on a separate floor far from the entryway and living room. In one example, a family built at the back of their house a separate structure in the architectural form of a miniature Hindu *mandir* (temple). Although separate, its entrance was through the interior of the house; it was thus both separate and connected. It was the repository for the family deities and icons, some of which were transported from India to be ritually consecrated and installed in this domestic temple. This elaborate creation of the sacred was however an exception. Although many families ideally wished to locate their shrine in a separate enclosed space, many lacked the room to do so. Some transformed a spare bedroom or a study into a *pooja* room. Another common strategy was to convert a walk-in closet into a *pooja* room. Although limited in floor space and somewhat confined, this allowed for the same degree of seclusion, enclosure, and privacy.

Inside a *pooja* room is placed a *mandapam* (altar), which can vary in shape, size, and form. Framed pictures and paintings of Hindu deities and saints adorn the walls. The *pooja* room is also the repository of several sacred objects and artifacts, such as sacred texts, brass and silver lamps, bells, incense, and camphor, as well as small silver and brass utensils for ritual offerings. In some homes, the *mandapam* is elaborate and designed to resemble a miniature Hindu *mandir* (temple). In other homes, it could be a simple raised platform or a tiered shelf. On the *mandapam* are placed the family deities. This could include pictures and figures of Hindu gods and goddesses, saints, and other divine beings. Also placed there are sacred mementos and relics from pilgrimages to sacred places in India. The *pooja* space is kept scrupulously clean, minimally furnished, and as uncluttered as possible. There are no chairs and sometimes no carpeting; family members sit on the floor or on prayer mats. An attempt is made to create a serene and tranquil setting conducive to prayer and meditation. One housewife described her *pooja* room to be her "sanity space." Sunanda, a college student, provides a detailed description of her family's shrine:

> In my house we have a separate room for prayer . . . There is a rug on the floor in front of it. In the shrine we have a few pictures of some of the gods. Also, we have statues and many books are present as well. There is incense, flowers, a bell and many shelves that has books . . . On the walls . . . we have big pictures of different Hindu gods. The room seems to have its own essence. When you walk into it you cannot hear all of the noises of the house. It is the quietest and most peaceful place in the house.

In the context of the prayer room and the *mandapam* (altar), it is important to emphasize that the artifacts placed on the *mandapam* have a different ritual status than the other Hindu artifacts found elsewhere in the home, hanging on the walls, entryways, and so on. They are usually not removed from the altar and used as decorative art. All utensils and cleaning materials used for the altar are kept strictly separate and used only for sacred rites and never for secular purposes. The cloth for cleaning the altar is not used to clean anything else. Special silver plates, glass and other utensils are used exclusively for serving food to the gods. Candles for prayers are stored separately from candles used for secular purposes such as for dining. Matches used for lighting incense, lamps, and candles in the *pooja* room are also separate.

b) Incorporation into other Sacred Spaces

In those homes where limitations of space (such as the lack of separate rooms, availability of walk-in closet space, or lack of possibility for expansion) make complete spatial separation in private, enclosed space difficult, care is taken to incorporate the *pooja* area in other sacred spaces. Some families locate their altars in the kitchen.[30] Since the kitchen is usually located towards the interior of the home, location here reduces easy accessibility. Hindu kitchens are required to be scrupulously clean and therefore the chance of ritual pollution is minimized.

c) Symbolic Partitioning

When complete spatial separation or incorporation into other sacred areas is difficult, a third strategy used is symbolic partitioning. A ritually neutral area such as a study or a family room, master bedroom or spare bedroom is divided into sacred and neutral areas with the shrine being placed in the symbolically defined sacred zone. Anjali describes how symbolic partitioning is used:

We have a den in our house and a part of it is dedicated to our shrine, the other part has an office desk, a closet and a bookshelf. We will never wear our shoes in that room nor will we ever have alcohol in that room.

RITUAL OBSERVANCES

Once created, the *pooja* area becomes the setting for the enactment of ritual. Rituals in the immigrant household can be categorized into daily individualized rituals and periodic, congregational rituals. Here, we will focus only on daily, individualized rituals.

The immigrant families studied took time regularly to honor their deities and express their devotion. This show of devotion is called *bhakti*.[31] For an immigrant Hindu devotee, *bhakti* is expressed through hospitality rituals.[32] In Hinduism, Gods are treated as revered guests and the *pooja* rituals symbolize hospitality rituals.[33] As in the temple, so also in the home, *pooja* is a ritual process involving bathing or cleaning the deities, anointing them with fragrant sandalwood paste, decorating with fresh flowers, offering *prasadam* (food such as fruits and nuts), lighting *dhoop* (incense), *karpuram* (camphor), *deepam* or *deewa* (lamps), and providing entertainment through singing *bhajans* (devotional music). Family members also read from a sacred book or use prayer beads, or recite the names of their deities. The *pooja* rituals culminate with *pranaam* (body prostration) to their deities.[34] There is then a "sensuous" nature to Hindu worship, which Diana Eck further elaborates:

> It is sensuous in that it makes full use of the senses—seeing, touching, smelling, tasting and hearing. One "sees" the image of the deity (darsan). One "touches" it with one's hands (sparsa) . . . one "hears" the sacred sound of the mantras (sravana). The ringing of bells, the offering of oil lamps, the presentation of flowers, the pouring of water and milk, the sipping of sanctified liquid offerings, the eating of consecrated food-these are the basic constituents of Hindu worship, *puja*.[35]

From the above, it is clear that Hindu rituals are multisensory, involving speaking, singing, reading, hearing, seeing, smelling, touching, tasting, and eating. It is through full employment of the senses that daily rituals help to create religious reality. As Barbara Myerhoff[36] asserts, "in ritual not only is seeing believing, doing is believing." Martin Buber provides the example of wearing Sabbath clothes and feeling "holy":**

> If you put on sabbath clothes and sabbath caps it is quite right that you had a feeling of sabbath holiness.[37]

This is true for Hindus as well. The daily rituals create the feeling of holiness for them. Vivek describes the sacredness created by the ringing of bells in his family's *pooja* room:

> In the room there [are] glass bells that you shake . . . as you say your prayers and its kind of sending the vibrations to god and around the room and that it's a holy place. The idea behind it is that you don't have to go to temple to pray. . . .

Some families took the time to conduct a complete set of *pooja* rituals, but others performed only discrete segments of it. Indira describes her daily rituals in the following way:

> During prayer I sit on the floor with my hands folded and my eyes closed. My prayers last for 5 to 10 minutes, it is not very long at all.

Anjali, on the other hand uses prayer beads and repeats a particular prayer:

> I use a bracelet of 21 beads and I would count my beads. I would say the same thing over and over . . . I don't know the translation of it (it is only four lines), but ever since I was a baby we had to say it daily . . . and now it is a habit. It is meaningful to me for the fact that I grew up with it and it's always been a part of my family.

Vivek's *pooja* rituals involved sitting on the floor and reading out of sacred texts.

Rituals also play an important role in the socialization of children. They teach, inform, and clarify Hindu beliefs for the younger generation. Two twenty-year-old females describe the instrumental role played by their mothers in introducing them to their religious beliefs, through the practice of daily rituals. According to Nanda, it was her mother who first introduced her to the daily rituals of *pooja*. She recalled being ten or eleven when her mother taught her how to clean the altar, put in fresh flowers, and light the lamp. Similarly, Padma was deeply influenced by her mother's religiosity. Though the whole family is fairly religious, it is her mother who takes time every morning and evening to pray and meditate. She uses prayer beads, recites prayers—and never leaves home before completing her morning prayers. Following her mother's example, Padma now tries to pray every day. Although this is difficult when she is in her college dormitory she makes up for it by praying longer when she is home on weekends. Although in most immigrant families it is the mother who is primarily responsible for the main prayer rituals, in some families it is the father who takes the primary role. For second-generation Hindu children, daily *pooja* rituals at home at the altar played an important role in their identity formation. When they moved away from home to go to college several of them set up their own altars. For example, Vivek had a picture of *Hanuman* (the monkey god), Pratima had a picture of *Ganapati* (the elephant god), and Devika had a picture and some holy ash. While these altars were not as elaborate as the ones in their parental homes, and consisted usually of a picture or a statue, they facilitated their practice of religion and sustained their Hindu identity. Sometimes practice of religious ritual became difficult in college. Vivek described one such problem:

> I used to have incense in my room last year at the dorms. But the R.A.
> got all mad because she thought I would burn down the hall but I think
> I should get some for this year.

Even though daily rituals play an important role in the transplantation of religion at home, immigrants make accommodations. First, is the *contraction* of daily rituals. For working couples, rituals on weekdays are shortened but not neglected. They involve offering flowers, lighting incense, and doing *namaskaram*, that is, bowing before the altar in the morning. The evening rituals involve lighting lamps and incense. Daily rituals on weekends are longer and more detailed. One family has specifically instituted the practice of having "family ritual time" in front of the altar every Sunday. Students living in dormitories often shorten their daily prayers. For example, according to Pratima, her daily prayers in the dorm lasted five minutes while at home she would pray for forty-five minutes. A second accommodation is the *combination* of rituals. Morning and evening rituals are both performed in the evening. Preeti's mother, a working woman, is an example. She is usually rushed for time in the morning and typically showers after work in the evening. It is after her evening shower that she sits before the altar and performs both her morning and evening rituals. A third accommodation involves *temporary suspension* of ritual activity during the week. Many students who live in dormitories fall into this category. While in the dorm, they do not take time to perform their daily rituals. Ritual behavior is reinstated when they return home on weekends. Fourth is *delegation* of ritual responsibility. Elderly family members are delegated the responsibility of conducting the daily rituals. Deepak's mother is one such example. For her, there is no "short-cut" in everyday rituals. All rituals are enacted with meticulous detail. Her grown-up children feel reassured that one of their family members is conducting all the rituals in the proper way.

DISCUSSION

This study leads to several important conclusions regarding the religious lives of immigrants. First, it documents the importance of home and domestic religion. While the public and congregational aspects of religious behavior are easily observable and have been studied by scholars in great detail, the private, individual, and familial everyday practices have been largely ignored or minimized. This scholarly skew does injustice to religious traditions such as Buddhism, Hinduism, and Zoroastrianism, which unlike the Judeo-Christian and Islamic traditions do not mandate specific days of the week for congregational worship. Studying only their congregational rituals and gatherings in public sacred space then, provides an incomplete conceptualization allowing only partial understanding of these religions. As this study has shown, home shrines and home worship can be complex, detailed, and multi-layered and ought to form a focus of scholarly inquiry in their own right. Second, it demonstrates the spatial and ritual component of domestic religion. Spatially, it describes how Hindus create sacred space in their homes in America in accordance with the Hindu rules of purity and pollution and use strategies ranging from complete spatial separation to symbolic separation. Once created, these sacred spaces became the setting for daily, multisensorial ritual behavior. And yet, here too accommodations are made and rituals modified and adapted to life in America. For Hindu immigrants then, home is not just a secularized dwelling—it is imbued with religious meaning. Hindu families attribute religious meaning to their homes by placing religious objects on their doors and walls, by creating a family shrine, and through daily ritual of prayer and worship. Third, a sacralized home facilitates religious learning. It is here that children are socialized into their religious identity. Within the privacy and security of their homes, immigrant children observe and participate in the practice of their religion without fear, suspicion, ridicule, curiosity, scrutiny, or discrimination. They can celebrate religious holidays and engage in the daily rituals of their religion. It is here that they learn the textual and contextual aspects of religion; they read from their sacred texts, memorize the formal prayers, and sing the devotional songs. This early socialization in domestic space has long-term consequences for identity formation in the second generation. As this study has demonstrated, several students who have moved away from home to go to college have set up simple altars and continue their daily practice of religion even though in an abbreviated fashion. They are more diligent about daily personal, individual prayer than they are about temple visits and temple rituals.

Other immigrant groups also use the domestic setting to recreate the sacred. Sikh homes are sacralized with pictures of Sikh Gurus, particularly Guru Nanak and Guru Gobind Singh, as well as paintings and pictures of the Golden Temple of Amritsar. As in Hindu homes, Sikhs also create a sacred niche or prayer area where, under a decorative silk canopy, they place the Guru Granth Sahib, the Sikh holy book.[38] South Asian Muslims are another example. Unlike Hinduism, Islam strictly prohibits the use of human or animal representation. Allah (God), the Prophet, humans, and animals are not depicted in sculpture, painting, or statues, and so these are absent in Muslim homes. Instead, homes are sacralized with calligraphic inscriptions from the Quran, pictures of the *kaaba* (the sacred shrine of Islam in Mecca), and pictures of famous mosques and pilgrimage sites sacred to Muslims.[39] Vietnamese Buddhist families have an altar with statues of Buddha and framed pictures of ancestors placed on it.[40]

A sacralized home thus plays an important role in the development of the religious self. For diasporic populations, the public symbols of religion in their native contexts are noticeably lacking. Lacking are the neighborhood temples and mosques, the familiar sound of temple bells, or the call to prayer from the mosque; and familiar sights such as religious processions. Home then becomes the "visual articulation"[41] of religion; and sacred objects, icons and artifacts act as reminders and become the medium for religious teaching, expression and identity.[42]

NOTES

1. Peter L. Berger, *The Sacred Canopy: Elements of a Sociological Theory of Religion* (Garden City, NY: Doubleday, 1967/1969), 42.
2. Berger, *Sacred Canopy*, 35–36.
3. The following authors have all addressed this issue: John Fenton, *Transplanting Religious Traditions: Asian Indians in America* (New York: Praeger, 1988); Andrew M. Greeley, *The Denominational Society: A Sociological Approach to Religion in America* (Glenview, IL: Scott, Foresman, 1972); Oscar Handlin, *The Uprooted: The Epic Story of the Great Migrations that Made the American People* (Boston: Little Brown, 1951); Will Herberg, *Protestant, Catholic, Jew: An Essay in American Religious Sociology* (Garden City, NY: Doubleday, 1955); Won Moo Hurh and Kwang Chung Kim, "Religious Participation of Korean Immigrants in the United States," *Journal for the Scientific Study of Religion* 29:1 (1990): 19–34; Randall M. Miller, "Introduction," in Randall M. Miller and Thomas D. Marzik, eds., *Immigrants and Religion in Urban America*, (Philadelphia: Temple University Press, 1977); Teklemariam M. Woldemikael, *Becoming Black American: Haitians and American Institutions in Evanston Illinois* (New York: AMS Press, 1989).
4. Miller, "Introduction," xv.

5. Timothy L. Smith, "Religion and Ethnicity in America," *American Historical Review* 83 (December 1978) 1155–1185.

6. Berger, *Sacred Canopy.*

7. Will Herberg, *Protestant, Catholic, Jew: An Essay in American Religious Sociology* (Garden City, NY: Doubleday, 1955).

8. Exceptions of scholars who have looked at altars in immigrant homes in some detail are: E. Allen Richardson, *East Comes West: Asian Religious and Cultures in North America* (New York: Pilgrim Press, 1985); John Fenton, *Transplanting Religious Traditions: Asian Indians in America* (New York: Praeger, 1988); and Kay T. Turner, *Beautiful Necessity: The Art and Meaning of Women's Altars* (New York: Thames and Hudson, 1999). For studies of Hindu altars, see Shampa Mazumdar and Sanjoy Mazumdar, "Of Gods and Homes: Sacred Space in the Hindu House," *Environments* 22:2 (1994): 41–49; Shampa Mazumdar and Sanjoy Mazumdar, "Sacred Space and Place Attachment," *Journal of Environmental Psychology* 13:3 (1993): 1993, 231–242; Shampa Mazumdar and Sanjoy Mazumdar, "Women's 'Significant Spaces': Religion, Space and Community," *Journal of Environmental Psychology* 19 (1999): 159-170.

9. Data for this paper was collected primarily through interviews. Writings by ethnic group members, personal and autobiographical writings, and autoethnographies (D.J. Jones, "Towards a Native Anthropology," *Human Organization* 29 (1970): 251–259; David Hayano, "Auto-ethnography: Paradigm, Problems, and Prospects," *Human Organization* 38:1 [Spring 1979]: 99–104) were also used. Magazine and newspaper articles published by the immigrant community were examined and served as sources when appropriate descriptions were provided.

10. Several scholars have looked at this issue. Some of them are: Yvonne Y. Haddad and Jane I. Smith, *Muslim Communities in North America* (Albany: State University of New York Press, 1994); Helen Rose Ebaugh and Janet S. Chafetz, *Religion and the New Immigrants* (Walnut Creek, CA: Alta Mira, 2000); Barbara D. Metcalf, *Making Muslim Space in North America and Europe* (Berkeley: University of California Press, 1996); Rogaia M. Abusharaf, "Structural Adaptations in an Immigrant Muslim Congregation in New York," in R. Stephen Warner, and Judith G. Wittner, eds., *Gathering in Diaspora: Religious Communities and the New Immigration* (Philadelphia: Temple University Press, 1998); R. Stephen Warner and Judith G. Wittner, eds., *Gathering in Diaspora: Religious Communities and the New Immigration* (Philidelphia: Temple University Press, 1998).

11. David K. Yoo, ed., *New Spiritual Homes: Religion and Asian Americans.* (Honolulu: University of Hawai'i Press, 1999), 9.

12. Phillip E. Hammond, ed., *The Sacred in a Secular Age* (Berkeley: University of California Press, 1985); Bryan Wilson, "Secularization: The Inherited Model," in Hammond, *The Sacred in a Secular Age.*

13. Hans J. Mol, *Identity and the Sacred* (New York: Free Press, 1976).

14. Yoo, *New Spiritual Homes;* Warner and Wittner, *Gatherings in Diaspora.*

15. See for example the following: Warner and Wittner, *Gathering in Diaspora;* Raymond B. Williams, *Religions of Immigrants from India and Pakistan: New Threads in the American*

Tapestry (Cambridge, MA: Cambridge University Press, 1988); Ebaugh and Chafetz, *Religion and the New Immigrants.*

16. Lord Raglan, *The Temple and the House* (New York: W.W. Norton, 1964), 14.

17. Eliade, Mircea, *The Sacred and the Profane: The Nature of Religion* (New York: Crossroad, 1959); idem., *Symbolism, Sacred and the Arts*, ed. Diane Apostolos-Cappado (New York: Crossroads, 1985).

18. Eliade, *Sacred and Profane*, 108.

19. Pierre Bourdieu, "The Berber House," in Mary Douglas, ed., *Rules and Meanings* (Hammondsworth, UK: Penguin, 1973).

20. David G. Saile, "The Ritual Establishment of Home," in Irwin Altman and Carol M. Werner, ed., *Home Environments* (New York: Plenum, 1985).

21. Graeme Hardie, "Continuity and Change in the Tswana's House and Settlement Form," in Altman and Werner, *Home Environments.*

22. Eleftherios Pavlides and Jana Hesser, "Sacred Spaces, Ritual and Traditional Greek House," in Jean-Paul Bourdieu and Nezar AlSayyad, eds., *Dwellings, Settlements and Traditions: Cross Cultural Perspectives* (Lanham, MO: University Press of America, 1989).

23. Eliade, *Sacred and Profane*, 107.

24. Mazumdar and Mazumdar, "Sacred Space and Place Attachment"; idem, "Of Gods and Homes"; idem., "Women's 'Significant Spaces'."

25. Usha R. Jain, *The Gujaratis of San Francisco* (New York: AMS Press, 1989); Fenton, *Transplanting Religious Traditions.*

26. Jain, *Gujaratis of San Francisco*; Fenton, *Transplanting Religious Traditions.*

27. Miller, "Introduction," xv.

28. Oscar Handlin, *The Uprooted* (Boston: Little Brown 1951); Herberg, *Protestant, Catholic, Jew*; Miller, "Introduction."

29. Miller, "Introduction," xv; Mazumdar and Mazumdar, "Sacred Space and Place Attachment"; idem., "Of Gods and Homes"; idem., "Women's Significant Spaces'."

30. See also Mazumdar and Mazumdar, "Of Gods and Homes."

31. Diana L. Eck, *Darsan: Seeing the Divine Image in India* (Chambersburg, PA: Anima Books, 1981), 37.

32. Sunita Ramaswamy and Sundar Ramaswamy *Vedic Heritage*, (Saylorsburg, PA: Arsha Vidya Gurukulam, 1993).

33. See also Ramaswamy and Ramaswamy, *Vedic Heritage*; Eck, *Darsan.*

34. See also Eck, *Darsan;* Ramaswamy and Ramaswamy, *Vedic Heritage.*

35. Eck, *Darsan,* 9.

36. Barbara G. Myerhoff, "We Don't Wrap Herring in a Printed Page," in Sally F. Moore and Barbara G. Myerhoff, eds., *Secular Ritual* (Aasen, Netherlands: Van Gorcum, 1977), 223.

37. Quoted in Myerhoff, "We Don't Wrap Herring," 223.

38. Gurinder S. Mann, "Sikhism in the United States of America," in Harold Coward, John R. Hinnells, and Raymond B. Williams, eds., *The South Asian Religious Diaspora in Britain Canada and the United States* (Albany: State University of New York Press, 2000).

39. Regula B. Qureshi, "Transcending Space: Recitation and Community among South Asian Muslims in Canada," in Barbara D. Metcalf, ed., *Making Muslim Space in North America and Europe* (Berkeley: University of California Press, 1996).

40. See Ebaugh and Chafetz, *Religion and the New Immigrants.*

41. Qureshi, "Transcending Space."

42. Ibid.

IDENTITY

THE CROSS AND THE LOTUS:
CHANGING RELIGIOUS PRACTICES AMONG
CAMBODIAN IMMIGRANTS IN SEATTLE

THOMAS J. DOUGLAS

This paper is based on research that I conducted in the Cambodian community of Seattle, Washington in the summers of 2000 and 2001. It is part of a larger research project in which I am comparing the Cambodian communities of Long Beach, California, and Seattle Washington. In 1995 I first worked as a volunteer at a Long Beach Cambodian nonprofit agency in their tutoring and mentoring program. I was doing it for school credit at the time and I initially thought that my primary interest in Cambodian communities was related to the issues facing Cambodian youth, such as high school drop-out rates, poor academic performance, gangs, drugs, alcohol, violence, teen pregnancy, etc.

However, as I came to know the staff at the center I became intrigued by how many of them either said that they were Christians now or had been practicing Christians in the past. It surprised me because here was a Cambodian agency clearly devoted to preserving Cambodian culture and identity among Cambodian immigrants and yet the majority of the Cambodian staff had links with Christian groups. I found this situation to be something of a paradox. May Ebihara, the only American anthropologist to work in Cambodia prior to Pol Pot's infamous regime, stated that, "To be Khmer is to be Buddhist".[1] Yet, at this Long Beach center I found Cambodians dedicated to their community who did not, at least at first glance, seem to support Ebihara's claim. However, as I learned more about both the Long Beach and Seattle Cambodian communities, I came to realize that religion and religious identity were playing a very complex role.

In the following sections, I first provide a brief background of the events that led to the development of Cambodian refugee communities in the U.S. Then, I present some ethnographic data about refugee Cambodian churches and temples where I have been conducting research. Next, I describe a Seattle Cambodian community event that revolves around religious tradition. Fourth, I turn to the life-stories that Seattle-area Cambodian immigrants have told me about their own religious experiences and beliefs. It is these stories and the accompanying talk, which, I believe, provides the most insight into the complex meanings and roles of religion in the lives of these immigrants. These stories all center around the key-words of contemporary capitalism: choice, freedom, value, and risk. Finally, in my analysis I suggest that these stories should not be taken simply as a reflection of religious belief but as a commentary on the refugee experience in American society. They form a discourse that counters mainstream assessments of Cambodians as impoverished dropouts still suffering under the legacy of the Killing Fields in the form of post-traumatic stress disorder. I will argue that the complex and apparently contradictory religious affiliations and practices of Cambodian immigrants speak to their efforts to create meaning and especially value in the context of their experience as refugees and their insertion into a particular form of United States capitalism at the turn of the millennium.

A BRIEF BACKGROUND

In 1975, the United States removed its last military forces from South Vietnam. On April 17, 1975, the Khmer Rouge entered Phnom Penh,[2] and took control of Cambodia.[3] The first wave of refugees left Cambodia at this time. About 6000 Cambodian refugees came to the United States in 1975 and a few thousand more came over the five following years. However, the great outpouring of Cambodian refugees was yet to come.

The Killing Fields
After taking over Phnom Penh, the Khmer Rouge began systematically to destroy anyone who had been associated with the old regime. Anyone known to have more than a nominal amount of education, who wore glasses, or who had in some way worked for the former government was killed. Not even temple monks were spared. This "purge" by the Khmer Rouge resulted in the deaths of perhaps 2 million Cambodians.[4]

However, in January 1979, Vietnamese invaders overthrew the Khmer Rouge. As a result of the Vietnamese invasion, many Cambodians fled to the

Thai-Cambodian border. Hundreds of thousands sought refuge, and a window of opportunity for escape was temporarily created during the confusion that followed the invasion as the new Vietnamese-controlled Cambodian government came to power.

In 1980, approximately one-tenth of the entire population of Cambodia was seeking refuge across the Thai border. Although the Thai government initially sought to prevent these "illegal immigrants" from entering their country, it eventually bowed to international pressure and agreed to establish refugee camps with UN assistance.[5]

Welcome to America
Between the years of 1980 and 1990, over 100,000 Cambodian refugees entered the United States.[6] This coincided with the great migration of other Southeast Asians. fifty percent of all Southeast Asian immigrants entered the U.S between 1980 and 1984.[7] By 1990, according to U.S. Census data, there were 147,411 Cambodians refugees living in the United States.[8]

The Seattle Setting
The Greater Seattle area has a Cambodian population of approximately 5,000 immigrants and their U.S. born children. Many Cambodian immigrants arrived in Seattle as a result of the Khmer Guided Placement Project (KGPP). The KGPP was created by the Office of Refugee Resettlement (ORR) in 1980 because of concerns that the newly arriving waves of Khmer refugees would overburden areas, such as Long Beach, California, where large numbers of refugees had already settled in the late 1970s. The KGPP plan was to place Cambodians refugees without sponsoring relatives in 12 different project sites that would divert them from "impacted" areas. It was hoped that these new Cambodian communities would become self-sufficient and secondary migration to the impacted areas would be prevented.[9] The Office of Refugee Resettlement had designated the Puget Sound area as a refugee destination point, and many immigrants were initially placed there. However, in spite of the goals of the KGPP, according to my informants living in Seattle, the number of Cambodian immigrants in the area has slowly declined as Cambodians immigrants have moved on to places like Southern California.

CAMBODIAN TRADITIONAL RELIGIOUS PRACTICES: MERIT, SOCIAL STATUS, AND GENDER RELATIONS

Theravada Buddhism is the dominant religion of Cambodia.[10] Sri Lanka, Myanmar (Burma), Laos, and Thailand also follow this tradition. However, in

Cambodia, religious beliefs and practices are also influenced by spirit worship and Brahminism that had been the basis of earlier forms of Khmer worship.[11]

Theravada Buddhism is concerned with notions of earning merit in this life, which is believed to affect one's karma in the next life. Various acts can be done to gain merit, and the elderly often spend a great deal of time in the temples where they accumulate merit that will improve their karma in preparation for their next life.

The concept of merit is central to Cambodian Buddhist beliefs.[12] Good works produce *bon* and bad works produce *bap*. According to this philosophy, those in authority should have accumulated a lot of bon in order to have their current power. Thus, traditionally the Cambodian king is believed to have his authority because he accumulated a large amount of merit in his past lives. Cambodian immigrants in Seattle have created two Khmer temples or wats in which to celebrate in order to maintain Khmer Buddhist practices and to promote proper behavior (dhamma) and acts of merit.

KHMER TEMPLES: MONKS AND ACHARS

The temple in White Center, a relatively low-income area in West Seattle, is called *Wat Khemarat Pothira*. One of the monks explained to me that this means "The Khmer Boddhi Tree Pagoda." This temple was originally a two-story single-family home on a very large lot. The large front room has been converted into an internal worship area and there are several bedrooms for the monks within the house, as well as a good size bathroom and kitchen. The temple also has a large canopied outdoor area for worship and other community events. In the rear yard, under some trees behind the temple are a couple of very small sleeping rooms, perhaps eight feet by eight feet. Monks who wish to focus completely on meditation and study use these outer sleeping quarters.

During one visit it was explained to me that, ideally, a temple ought to have at least three monks: a head monk, a right-hand monk, and a left-hand monk. The right-hand monk is destined to eventually become the new head monk. The left-hand monk will eventually move up in status to become a right-hand monk. However, the total number of monks at a temple might vary from one to over one hundred. The total number of monks living in a temple is determined by how many the community can support. This temple had six monks during the summer of 2001. Seattle temple leaders make requests to the U.S. immigration department to allow a new monk to emigrate from Cambodia to their temple when they feel they can support another one.

At the temple I was told that there are traditionally three sets of monks in Cambodian society. There are lower order monks, or novices, that are referred to as *Samanera* (pronounced as Sam-a-nay). These are traditionally teenage boys who serve in the temples to honor their parents. They don the saffron robes, take vows, and their participation in the temple brings merit to their parents. Prior to the 1950s, service as a monk was often the only education that a Cambodian man ever received. A Samanera's time in the temple generally lasted from a few months to a couple of years. Traditionally, after serving as a Samanera, a young man would see to the business of finding a wife.

There is another type of lower order monk, referred to as *Moke-Pluhng*. These men are commonly referred to as "fireside" monks. Fireside monks take on this role when a relative or close family friend has died. They dress all in white and traditionally stand next to the corpse as it is cremated on the firebed. Afterwards, they spend time meditating for the dead and accumulating merit for the soul of the deceased. A Moke-Pluhng's period as a monk typically only lasts a matter of days.

The higher order of monks is called *Bikkhu*. A man may not become a Bikkhu until he is 21 years old, although Cambodians often count the time spent in the womb as part of one's age, so by American reckoning a man may become a Bikkhu at 20 years of age. According to my informants, a man must first be ordained as a Samanera, and then, after he has continued his studies and he is of the proper age, he may be ordained as a Bikkhu. One head monk told me that any man may become a monk, but he must give up sexual relations to do so. A married man may only become a monk with the agreement of his wife. Furthermore, a man may quit his monk's position at anytime.

There is also a certain type of layman known as an *achar* (pronounced as "ah'–tcha") associated with the temples. The achars perform ceremonies and chants that will increase the merit or bon of worshippers. An achar sometimes performs a chant or ceremony by himself, but often works in tandem with the monks. Besides serving Khmer worshippers, an achar often helps to raise money for the temple. At a Khmer temple in Tacoma, I attended a "flower money" ceremony where the achar worked with the monks to raise thousands of dollars for new temple building additions. Having noted that all of the achars that I had met were elderly males, I asked one head monk if only males were permitted to become achars. Interestingly, the chief monk told me that a woman could conceivably serve as an achar, but that this would be very difficult because a woman must know all the rules and be educated in the ways of the temple. However, there are elderly women or nuns who serve the temple, who help care for its maintenance and care for the monks who reside there.[13]

"TALK" ABOUT MONKS AND TEMPLES

During my research, I quickly learned that it is not unusual to hear accusations within Cambodian communities that one temple or another has succumbed to corruption or that some group of monks is not keeping their vows. Furthermore, I also found that it was not unusual to hear talk by Cambodian immigrants about their concern over a general decline in the morality of Khmer monks in both the US and in Cambodia.

Various informants told me that monks were lazy, corrupt, or no longer working to help their community. I heard accusations that monks and temples were secretly growing rich and that they no longer cared about the common people. I frequently heard about monks who broke their vows. I was told that in Cambodia monks would change their clothes and engage in the pleasures of brothels by night. I heard similar stories about monks in the U.S. I also occasionally heard stories about monks that engage in homosexual behavior. I heard such talk from both self-identifying Buddhist and Christian Khmer immigrants.

The chairman of one Cambodian nonprofit organization in Seattle, a Buddhist, told me one afternoon that Cambodia needed a strong leader like China's deceased revolutionary leader, Mao Zedong. I was surprised. I expected him, as a refugee from the Khmer Rouge and a Buddhist, to be strongly anti-Communist and anti-Mao. So I asked him what he thought about Mao's policy on religion. I mentioned that since he was a Buddhist I did not expect that he would appreciate Mao's treatment of religion. He replied that Mao had just wanted to get rid of the Christian churches in China, but Mao was not against Buddhism. I told him that I believed Mao was responsible for the closure of many Buddhist temples in China. He then responded that Mao was not against Buddhism, but rather that he was against the system of monks who "just sit in the temple and don't work."

This informant's support for Mao was unusual among Cambodian refugees I spoke to, yet our conversation did demonstrate that he, like many other Cambodian immigrants, both Christian and Buddhist, is questioning the value of the traditional Khmer religious system. Over and over again I found that many Cambodian immigrants openly questioned both the personal integrity of the monks and the role and value of the traditional system of monks and temples. I will return to this topic in my conclusion.

EVANGELICAL CHURCHES

Buddhism is not the only religion in which Cambodian immigrants are engaged. I have found that there are Christian churches thriving and growing in the hearts of Cambodian communities. Whether or not these churches compete with Khmer Buddhist temples for believers is something that I think will become clear later in this paper.

The Good News Church in the White Center district of Seattle is across the street from the Park Lake public assistance housing where many immigrant Cambodians live. At Good News, the Sunday School service begins in the afternoon, followed by the main service. During the services, children often play outside in the playground or downstairs in the basement. In both churches and temples, I have observed that any Khmer child who is able to walk seems to come and go at will.

Though I attended the Good News Church alone, a Khmer man in his thirties quickly approached me. His name was Marin. Marin told me that the Khmer congregation at the Good News Church currently has no pastor. The former pastor left to become a missionary in Cambodia (I found this to be a fairly common scenario among Khmer Christian churches). This church has had no permanent pastor for the past four or five years. Currently, the Cambodian church elders lead the congregation in conjunction with a white missionary, James, and his Cambodian wife, both on hiatus from Cambodia. Marin told me that the elders run their church, not the pastor.

Marin said that currently the church elders rotate the responsibility for teaching the congregation. "Everybody has their chance," he told me. While Marin told me about his church, Jenny, the missionary's wife, was leading the service. She opened with prayer, and then led in singing, accompanied on the guitar by her Caucasian husband. This was followed by her message from the Bible, during which she often stopped to ask questions from those in attendance. Her questions were predominately answered by women in the congregation, who made up the majority of the audience.

During Jenny's presentation, Marin asked me what I thought about Cambodian churches. I told him that I was surprised by how active the women were in these churches. I could tell by the look on his face that he was unhappy with my response. Marin immediately told me that women were only allowed to teach in the church, not to preach. He said that women cannot govern the church and are not allowed to be church elders. Marin told me that their church followed the teachings of Paul, which do not allow women to preach or lead the church. Up to this point, I had assumed Jenny was giving the sermon, only then did I learn her presentation was considered only Sunday School "teaching" and that there would be a sermon, presented by a male church elder, after a short break. Just as in traditional Khmer religious practices, women were not considered to be the appropriate leaders of this Christian congregation.

PCHUM BEN: A KHMER FESTIVAL

Pchum Ben (also spelled in the literature as Prachum Ben) is the annual Festival for the Dead, when Cambodian families make offerings to the dead, visit the temples and provide gifts to the monks. Those who donate to the monks earn merit (bon) or good karma for their actions. Large feasts are also held at this time to honor the dead. Aside from the yearly Pchum Ben Festival, families also hold small death anniversary celebrations annually in their own homes to honor their own deceased ancestors. Both Pchum Ben and these familial death anniversaries are traditional Khmer religious events. Yet, I found in my research that both self-described Christians and Buddhists participate in them. Pchum Ben might be compared to "All Soul's Day," and offerings and prayers are made in temples and homes for all of the dead at this time.

During my first fieldwork trip to Seattle, the Cambodian agency where I worked as a volunteer decided to host a Pchum Ben Festival for the Khmer community. It had to be scheduled for the afternoon of the last day of the Pchum Ben period so that the monks would be free to attend. The biggest obstacle was finding a large building in which to host the event. The director at the agency managed to rent a local Salvation Army gymnasium for the event. The pastor of the Salvation Army was reluctant to permit this. In speaking to him and his assistant I realized that this pastor was not particularly thrilled about having a Buddhist event hosted in his facility. However, his assistant, determined to maintain good relations with the Cambodian community, assured the pastor in the presence of myself and the Cambodian agency director that this event was really not a religious one but rather a "cultural" festival. Of course, neither the director nor I said anything to discount the assistant's comment, and we were quite appreciative of his intervention. As an anthropologist, I realize that sometimes discretion is the better part of valor. So I bit my tongue and did not strive to alter either the pastor's or his assistant's perspective that "culture" and "religion" are easily distinguishable entities.

An achar, dressed in the traditional attire of a white shirt and black pants, and four monks in their saffron robes were brought to the Salvation Army gymnasium the afternoon of the event. A large dais was created under the basketball hoop at one end of the gym where the monks were seated and a small Buddhist altar with statue, incense, and candles was erected. Carpets were laid on the floor where worshippers could kneel and participate in the chanting. Before beginning, the director of the local Cambodian agency invited everyone, specifically calling on both Christians and Buddhists, to come forward and participate in the event. While many attendees did come and kneel on the carpets in front of the altar, others simply sat in their chairs and waited for the "religious" part of the festival to be over. The achar opened the event with Pali chants and was soon followed by the monks. The congregation also joined in the chants, which they knew from memory. Monks burned incense during the chants, and one issued water blessings over the crowds from a wand that he held. The chanting lasted 30 or so minutes, then the monks ate and returned to the temple.

As at any Khmer celebration, enormous amounts of food were brought and consumed at this Pchum Ben event. Traditionally, no one is supposed to eat before the monks. However, many people at the festival did not follow this rule and went ahead and started eating before the monks arrived. The monks were late to the event and people became hungry. One woman, who ate before the monks, told me in a defensive tone that she was hungry and "it was the monks' own fault that they were late." However, her husband, who was in charge of organizing the festival, waited to eat until after the monks had finished their meal.

Along with the eating, there were several hours of live Cambodian music, singing, and dancing. Cambodian youth dressed in Islamic costumes presented what the director called "ethnic Cambodian dances." Their performance was based on dances from the minority Khmer Islamic tradition. I asked one of the festival coordinators why Islamic dances were being performed at this Buddhist festival. The answer he gave me was that they simply wanted to perform these ethnic dances as part of the overall celebration. No one other than myself seemed perplexed by this.

After the dance performance, a live band took over and played many traditional and contemporary Cambodian songs. The band members were performers from one of the local Cambodian discotheques. People of all ages danced while colored lights and a fog machine added to the overall ambience. The Salvation Army gymnasium was transformed from a Buddhist place of worship into a Cambodian nightclub for the rest of the evening.

CHANGING PRACTICES AND NEW CHALLENGES

How are we to explain the relationship between Cambodians' self-declared identities as Christian or Buddhist and their crossover participation in events like Pchum Ben and Christian worship services? To help understand this, in the following section I will present some brief snap-shots from the life-stories and religious "talk" that I gathered from my informants. Though their stories are often quite different, I suggest that there is a unity to these stories that I will address in the conclusion of this work.

Andy

Like many Cambodians I met in Seattle, Andy and his siblings initially told me that their family is Buddhist. However, after a seeing him regularly for a month or so at the center where I volunteered, I noticed that Andy started showing up wearing a cross. When I asked him about it, he told me that his mother had given the gold necklace to him. In fact, Andy's mother, who both owned and worked in a small sewing factory next door, wore a cross as well, but she also had a small Buddhist shrine above her workstation. Her daughter, Vanny (Andy's sister), told me that her mother had sometimes gone to a Christian church. I told Vanny that I thought her family was Buddhist, but she said that they considered both Buddha and Jesus to be good. "It's the same thing," Vanny told me. A couple of days after the Pchum Ben Festival, Andy and his two younger brothers started wearing Buddhist pendants around their necks. They told me that their mother had just purchased them after the recent Buddhist holiday.

Frienda

I met Frienda through tutoring her son. Frienda told me that she converted to Christianity while in a Thai border refugee camp. Frienda was bored with camp life and found Christian meetings to be a pleasant diversion, though her parents disapproved of them. She said that at the meetings she could sing and dance, things that she told me she was normally restricted from doing in her own culture. She also said that there were boys at the meeting. She was normally restricted from meeting boys at home, and she said that she enjoyed meeting boys at the church meetings. However, she also expressed to me that she felt the evangelical meetings were a safe place to interact with boys. She felt that there was nothing indecent about meeting boys at church. She told me that traditional Cambodian society was too restrictive in its treatment of young women.

Frienda told me that though initially she went to the church for excitement, eventually she became a Christian believer. Frienda is the only member of her family to convert to Christianity. The rest of her family is not pleased with her conversion. To this day she says that her parents refer to her as being "hard-headed." She regularly prays for the conversion of her family members.

Frienda eventually entered the U.S. illegally, but she found a Cambodian man to marry her and give her legal status. However, in doing so she seemed to compromise her principles because she married a Buddhist rather than a Christian. She told me that she prays for her husband's salvation. Her son has been raised as a Christian and attends church regularly with his mother. Her son, who is in grade school, even asked my own mother (who was visiting Seattle at the time) to pray for his father's salvation.

BOPHA AND SOTHEA

One morning I was driving two Cambodian women downtown to enroll in an employment program. The younger woman, Sothea, had only been in the U.S. for about a year or so. She had been brought to the U.S. from Cambodia as a bride to marry a Cambodian immigrant living in Seattle. The older woman, Bopha, was a grandmother and had lived in the U.S. since the 1980s. While in the car, the subject of religion came up among us. The two women had very different ideas about religion. I asked Bopha (the older woman and long-time U.S. resident) if she raised her children in the U.S. to be Buddhist or Christian. She was very firm in her reply, "Buddha is better." However, she told me that her sister has converted to Christianity and has told Bopha that she too ought to convert since they now live in America.

Sothea, the younger woman, was of a different mind. She said that she enjoyed going to both Buddhist temples and Christian churches and that she wanted to experience it all. She told us that she wants to learn to "see what is good about both [Christianity and Buddhism]." I had mistakenly expected Sothea, as a recent immigrant, to be more conservative about her religious practices than Bopha. Obviously, I was wrong. Bopha also hangs an image of Qin-Yin, a Vietnamese goddess, on the mirror in her car.

Polina

I met Polina at the children's Khmer language classes that are held at a Seattle temple during the summer. She brought her preschool-aged daughter to the classes. Polina had immigrated to the U.S. as a young girl and spent several years in South Carolina before moving to Seattle. While living in South Carolina, she told me that many Cambodians she knew were attending a Baptist church there. However, she said that the Cambodian leader at that Baptist church received more money if he was able to bring in a larger Cambodian congregation. Consequently, she told me that she thought he might have just been in it for the money.

She told me that she became heavily involved in an Assembly of God church. She participated in that church faithfully before her marriage. She told me that many mainstream, American Christians would consider any other non-Christian religious activities, such as Buddhism, to be from the Devil. However, she felt that Buddhism and Christianity are the same. She told me that both emphasize the same moral system, don't kill, don't steal, etc. She said that she believed that the biggest difference between Christianity and Buddhism was that Christians do not know when the Second Coming of Christ would be—"no man can tell"—but that

Buddhists knew exactly when the next Buddha would arrive. When she married, she no longer attended a Christian church because her husband is Buddhist. However, she still believes that Christianity is good and that it is basically the same as Buddhism. But she also told me that honoring the ancestors and Buddha is extremely important to Cambodians. She said that many Cambodians do not want to give that up. She said that there are some, who she referred to as "true Christians," who quit honoring the ancestors, but many others who do not.

Dara

I met Dara while attending a Flower Money ceremony (*Bon Phkai Phratt*) at a temple in Tacoma. I was taking some pictures inside the temple and he approached me in a very friendly manner and said, "I was Christian like you. I believe in both." He told me that he had been in the U.S. for fifteen years now and that he had attended a Christian church for about a year after arriving in the U.S. Like both Polina and Vanny, Dara said that Buddhism and Christianity are the same. He then explained to me that both Buddhism and Christianity were concerned with the same moral system, don't kill, don't steal, be honest, be respectful, etc. Dara said that if you follow these rules, if you live a moral life, "then you will be lucky."

Venerable Sophan

Venerable Sophan is a Bikkhu (higher order) monk at a Seattle temple. I met Venerable Sophan at the children's Khmer language classes being taught at his temple. He was the instructor. He agreed that I could come and sit in on the lessons if I would help provide snacks for the children; this I found to be a very amicable arrangement.

One hot August afternoon, while Venerable Sophan was discussing some of the importance of dhamma with me, I mentioned to him that I had learned that many Cambodian immigrants were involved in both Buddhism and Christianity, and I wondered what he thought of that situation. He responded by saying, "God and God not fighting together. Buddha does not fight with Jesus. Hindu, Muslim, Buddhism, all religion is good." He then told me that if you choose to do good, not to steal, not to kill, etc., then it does not matter to what religion you belong.

He then told me about a funeral in Aberdeen, a town about a two-hour drive west of Seattle, at which he and the other monks had chanted. This funeral actually took place in a Christian church! However, Venerable Sophan told me that the deceased had been both a Christian and a Buddhist and had wanted both ceremonies performed at his death. So, Venerable

Sophan told me that he and the other monks performed at this funeral just as they would have done for any Khmer Buddhist. He told me that even though this funeral was in a Christian church, he and the other monks did everything that they would ordinarily do for any Buddhist believer.

Sophanny

Sophanny graduated from high school a year early but did not head straight into college the following fall semester. After graduation, his mother reminded him that when he was five years old he had promised to become a monk. As mentioned earlier, youths in Cambodia traditionally spend time as lower order monks (or Samanera) but this rarely occurs in the U.S. As a child, Sophanny had never been very involved in Buddhism, however, he agreed to keep his childhood promise, and he was ordained at one of the Seattle Khmer temples. He was the only Samanera at his temple. He spent three months living at the temple, studying, meditating, and keeping his vows. Sophanny told me that sometimes it was hard work, and at other times it was quite boring, but he was glad for having had the experience. He said that he now has a much greater understanding of Buddhism and now considers himself to be more than a nominal Buddhist. He told me that prior to his monkhood, he was more interested in science than in religion. He wanted to know about natural laws, empirical proof, and cause and effect, something that he had previously believed to be incompatible with religion. However, he told me that he now believes that Buddhism is very much like physics. He explained to me that Buddhism's explanation of the universe resonates strongly with current physics theories. For Sophanny, Buddhism is a rational religion in tune with the scientific world.

THE HEGEMONIC FORCE OF SOCIAL INSTITUTIONS—
MENTAL HEALTH, CAPITALISM, AND RELIGION

Most of the literature on globalization and transnational movements of peoples has ignored the role of religion in this process. It focuses on transnational businesses and economies, the movement of labor and capital, or national responses to the changing hegemonic forces at work in the world. David Harvey, in his 1989 work *The Condition of Postmodernity*, does mention a rise in fundamentalist religious activities as a result of the postmodern crisis and globalization pressures, but the immigrant Cambodians I have worked with do not clearly fit that model.[14] They are not rejecting an old religion in favor of a new one; rather many are conflating the boundaries of both, creating a new social and religious space.

Cambodian immigrants are under both tacit and explicit pressures to conform to a Westernized work ethic. Explicitly, some Cambodian youth are introduced to work via Christian churches that encourage them to raise funds for summer camp by sponsoring a church car wash or bake sale. At one Long Beach church, the main congregation, which consists of predominately white members, was asked by the pastor to please hire Cambodian church youth to do odd jobs or other tasks in their homes. This was so that the church's Cambodian youth would earn money in order to be able to participate in short-term summer missionary work in Cambodia. This is in stark contrast to the Cambodian Buddhist tradition where young Cambodian male initiates are given rice bowls for the purpose of begging.

I believe that the negative talk that I previously described in connection with the Khmer monastic system is, at least in part, a reflection of a growing tacit acceptance of a Westernized work ethic by Khmer immigrants. This work ethic demands a particular form of goods or services as the evidence of real labor. Both Buddhist and Christian Khmer immigrants openly question the value of the monastic system. Perhaps monks don't do any "real" work? What product or service do they provide? As a result, the work of Buddhist monks is devalued. Khmer monks become characterized as greedy, lazy, and corrupt. Are monks a boon to or a parasite on Cambodian communities? This is one of the questions that Cambodian immigrants and their families struggle with as they engage in new cultural values and strive to preserve old ones.

Since their arrival in the U.S., Cambodian immigrants have been under the intense scrutiny of the American public's gaze. Like other Southeast Asian refugees, they have been overtly studied, examined, and researched since their arrival on U.S. shores. Social Science literature claims that Cambodian immigrants are the most depressed, the most likely of all Southeast Asian immigrant groups to suffer from post traumatic stress disorder, and the most likely to suffer from refugee neurosis and cultural maladaptation. The psycho-medical community blames this pathology on the Cambodian immigrants' experiences under the Khmer Rouge. It has created measures of "acculturative stress," "trauma," and "cultural adaptation" to verify its claim that Cambodian immigrants are suffering from higher rates of mental health problems than any other refugee group.[15] The psycho-medical community has constructed the Cambodian immigrant acculturative experience as inherently pathological.

Churches, mutual assistance agencies, schools, and social welfare programs use their relationships with Cambodian immigrants to instill practices of self-discipline among these refugees in an effort to help them to adapt to American culture. These structures incorporate a capitalist logic that pre-

sents work and gainful employment as a moral issue through both their ideologies and practices. In some cases I fear that these institutions are using a
priori assumptions of the Khmer Rouge experience to gloss "undesirable"
Cambodian immigrants' behaviors as pathological. I believe that these institutions can inadvertently pathologize Cambodian Americans who do not
demonstrate particular Western capitalist forms of self-discipline. Cambodian immigrants who do not readily adapt to American style capitalist
production are likely to be labeled as mentally unstable, depressed, malad-
justed, or suffering from PTSD.

But Cambodians also use these "disciplining" organizations for their own
ends. They use their relationship with the churches and other agencies to
produce informal social and economic networks. These agencies provide a
gateway to social services and legal aid. One Cambodian father and community leader told me that Khmer children who attend Christian churches will
be more successful in school and find better jobs when they are adults.

A POST-HOLOCAUST CAMBODIAN SEARCH FOR MEANING

Cambodians manifest some of the worst fears of the postmodern age.
Cambodians experienced the complete failure of modernity when their society collapsed in 1975. Democracy, capitalism, science, and religion all failed
to prevent the terror that followed. For four years, from 1975–1979, the
Cambodian people lived in abject horror and endured a holocaust that ranks
among the worst in the history of the world.

In Cambodia's past, the Khmer monarchy, the French colonial period, the
re-introduction of self-rule, U.S. intervention, and a Marxist state committed to mass genocide all ended in failure. The current state is one where a
short-lived democratic government has given way to a coup d'etat, powered
by a repressive military force under the direction of Hun Sen, a former
Khmer Rouge party member and Vietnamese political puppet. Capitalism
threatens to enslave rather than liberate Cambodians as sweatshops proliferate across Southeast Asia. The Cambodian nation today struggles to maintain an image of democracy and support for human rights even as internal
politics threaten to undo whatever positive changes have been made in the
two past decades. The intervention of the UN and Western powers has done
little to stabilize the lives of Cambodian people.

Among Cambodian Americans life is far from easy. Unemployment,
drugs, alcoholism, spouse abuse, youth gangs, violence, low literacy, depression, post-traumatic stress disorder and gambling addictions all plague
Cambodian American communities. Cambodian immigrants and their

families have been left with little certainty in their lives. All their values from the past and present are being called into question. They are struggling with an age-old question, "Is there any meaning to life?" In the context of post-modern capitalism they ask, "Do I have any value?"

Yet, simultaneously, they are open to new opportunities and ready to create new spaces for themselves socially, intellectually, and individually. As demonstrated in the life stories that I have presented, many Cambodian immigrants are searching through religious traditions as, Sothea put it, to "find what is good in both." Many are not providing a religious mandate to their children because they believe they should not force them into a religious belief system. One Cambodian father said to me, "Let [the children] choose their way."

Among Cambodian immigrants, traditional Cambodian holidays and events are never simply Buddhist activities, rather at these occasions they seek to accommodate a variety of religious participants. Both Christian and Buddhist Cambodians are attending religious festivals where Islamic dance is included as part of the celebration. There is an emerging identity among Cambodians in the U.S. where being a Buddhist–Christian or Christian–Buddhist is part of the identity of being a Cambodian American.

Finally then, I think that it is no longer safe to claim that among Cambodian immigrants to be Khmer is to be Buddhist. Rather, I think that it is more appropriate to say that to be a Cambodian immigrant is to be seeking, building, and creating. Being a Cambodian American is to be searching for answers, and searching for one's own value, in a capricious and insecure world. Current immigrant Cambodian religious beliefs, practices, and participation are a reflection of this seeking. The fact that many Cambodian immigrants are engaging in both Buddhist and Christian belief systems manifests their drive to create a space for themselves, as Cambodian Americans—a desire to derive their own meaning in life.

NOTES

1. May Ebihara. "Svay, A Khmer Village in Cambodia" (Ph.D. diss., Columbia University, 1968).
2. The Khmer Rouge, led by Pol Pot, installed Cambodia's Prince Sihanouk as a nominal leader. Sihanouk had fled to China after Lon Nol's U.S. supported coup in 1970. However, in 1976, Sihanouk resigned his position with the Khmer Rouge due to his outrage over the violence of the regime. He became a prisoner of the Khmer Rouge until the Vietnamese invasion of Cambodia in 1979. Sihanouk was crowned king of Cambodia on September 24, 1993.

3. Usha Welaratna, *Beyond the Killing Fields: Voices of Nine Cambodian Survivors in America* (Stanford, CA: Stanford University Press, 1993), 19–23.

4. Ibid.

5. Scott Shaw, *Cambodian Refugees in Southern California: The Definitive Study* (Hermosa Beach, CA: Buddha Rose Publications, 1989) 11–13. Hereafter cited in text as Shaw. Cf. Welaratna, 186.

6. Larry Hajime Shinagawa. "The Impact of Immigration on the Demography of Asian Pacific Americans," In Bill Ong Hing and Ronald Lee, (eds.) *Reframing the Immigration Debate.* (Los Angeles: LEAP Inc. and UCLA Asian American Studies Center, 1996), 103.

7. Paul Ong, Dennis Arguelles, Susan Castro, Bruce Chow, Chanchanit Hirunpidok, Tarry Hum, Winnie Louie, Erich Nakano, and Roderick Ramos. *Beyond Asian American Poverty* (Los Angeles: LEAP Inc., 1993), 331.

8. Shinagawa, "Impact of Immigration," 103.

9. Robert G Bruce, *A Preliminary Assessment of the Khmer Cluster Resettlement Project: Final Report.* (Washington D.C.: Office of Refugee Resettlement, 1982), iii. Cf. Sharon Kathleen Ratliff, "Caring for Cambodian Americans: A Multidisciplinary Resource for Helping Professionals" (Ph.D. diss., Ohio State University, 1995), 4.

10. See for example: Craig B. Bagdasar, "Khmer Conflict Style: Cultural Foundations and Forms of Resolution" (Ph.D. diss., The Union Institute. 1993), 57; May Ebihara, "Khmer," in *Refugees in the United States: A Reference Handbook,* David W. Haines, ed., (Westport, CT: Greenwood, 1985), 127–147; Nancy Smith-Heffner, *Khmer American: Identity and Moral Education in a Diasporic Community* (Los Angeles: University of California Press, 1999), 21.

11. Usha Welaratna, "Cambodian Refugees in California: After the Holocaust" (M.A. thesis, San Jose State University, 1989), 73–73. Ebihara, "Svay" 364; Bagdesas, "Khmer Conflict Style," 58; Sue Needham, "Literacy, Learning and Language Ideology; Intracommunity Variation in Khmer literacy Instruction" (Ph.D. diss., UCLA, 1996), 86.

12. Ebihara, "Svay," 313; Welaratna, "Cambodian Refugees," 72–73.

13. Cf. Nancy Smith-Hefner, *Khmer American: Identity and Moral Education in a Diasporic Community* (Los Angeles: University of California Press, 1999), 27; and Judy Ledgerwood, "Changing Khmer Conceptions of Gender: Women, Stories and the Social Order" (Ph.D. diss., Cornell University, 1990), 34, for further discussion of women's roles in Khmer temples.

14. David Harvey, *The Condition of Postmodernity* (Oxford: Basil Blackwell, 1989).

15. See for example: Rita Chi-Ying Chung and Marjorie Kagawa-Singer, "Predictors of Psychological Distress among Southeast Asian Refugees," *Social Science Medicine* 36:5: 631–639; Carolyn D'Avanzo, Barbara Frye, and Robin Froman, "Culture, Stress and Substance use in Cambodian Refugee Women," *Journal of Studies on Alcohol* (July 1994): 420–426; Tali Karin Walters, "Acculturative Stress, Social Support and Trauma in a Community Sample of Cambodian Refugees" (Ph.D. diss., Boston College, 1994); Gary James Rezowalli, "Acculturation and Distress among Cambodian Refugees," (Ph.D. diss., Pacific Graduate School of Psychology, 1990).

"TO BE BUDDHIST IS TO BE KOREAN": THE RHETORICAL USE OF AUTHENTICITY AND THE HOMELAND IN THE CONSTRUCTION OF POST-IMMIGRATION IDENTITIES

SHARON A. SUH

INTRODUCTION

> If I stayed in my country, I would not even work like this or have such a hard time. I started out here in labor work. I started as a box boy at a supermarket and then a warehouse man, and then a stock man. Well, I could not stand this kind of work. Then I became a real estate broker and then, well here I am now. If I had stayed in my own country, I am sure that I would have been in a better position than I am now!

Steven Lee, a forty-seven year old Korean immigrant arrived in the United States in the early spring of 1971 with his wife who dreamed of coming to America since college. Although he had no interest in leaving Korea where he worked as a civil servant, Lee gave in to his wife's desires to immigrate for "a higher level of opportunity and because she figured that the U.S.A. would be a wonderful land." Like many new immigrants, Steven had a difficult time adjusting to his new surroundings and did not speak English when he first arrived. Although he had a high status job in Seoul and a master's degree, he learned that his previous credentials carried little weight in the Los Angeles work force.

Lee characterizes his immigration as a downward turn in economic opportunities as well. Fully expecting to obtain a high paying job in the U.S., Steven maintains that even after developing his English skills to fluency, he was still passed over for jobs based on his race. He explains:

> White people [Americans] think with their noses high in the air. They even behave that way too. Ever since we [Koreans] came here we started our own businesses and worked for large companies. But even when we work, they always think that Orientals are not worthy of consideration for promotions. Really, I have experienced that before. I have argued with them and talked to them about it. I used to ask them, "Hey, what's going on? I am the priority here and I am the one supposed to be promoted." But they wouldn't consider me at all. Even though I had a college degree, they wouldn't consider me for the promotion.

Steven currently does not utilize any of the skills he learned from his master's degree in public administration. In this respect, Steven's condition and his frustration with his status in the U.S. reflects what sociologist Won Moo Hurh considers a psychological crisis, "when the immigrants perceive limitations to occupational and social mobility in their adopted country. Furthermore, the perception of the glass ceiling in one's occupational career is certainly a painful and demoralizing experience."[1]

However, in order to combat this psychological and emotional stress, Lee has turned to a local Korean Buddhist temple, Sa Chal, in Los Angeles's Korean district, where he has found other co-ethnic men in similar situations. While Lee worships and prays with a community comprised largely of first-generation Korean Buddhists, it is primarily the temple's political projects related directly to Korea that Lee and other men at Sa Chal turn to for support. At the temple, Lee has found a group of first-generation Korean immigrant men who share a similar political interest in Korean reunification and North Korean famine relief projects that the temple's abbot strongly supports. It is also within this group that Lee and other participants seek to address the struggles that often accompany settlement into a new country. In this chapter, I note that projects connected to the homeland through the religious congregation can provide a sense of self-enhancement for individuals who thus create identities for themselves that are defined by the homeland rather than by the new land. This reference to the homeland as the primary identity marker finds expression in Lee's statement, "I am Korean, I am a Korean, I could not be an American. I am a Korean living in America."

The immediacy of the homeland plays a crucial role in the psychological adjustment of many recent arrivals following the act of immigration. While it is certainly true that a transnational context for migration has always existed for immigrants to this country, today's immigrants like Steven Lee are aided by a certain immediacy to the homeland which helps mediate the experience of adapting to a new environment. In this chapter, I examine the ideological and psychological implications of transnational identification in a religious context by focusing on Sa Chal temple.[2] Based on interviews conducted with members of this religious organization compiled between June 1997 and June 1999, I show how participation in an ethnic religious organization allows recent immigrants to view themselves in relation to their homeland as Koreans and how such participation affects their experiences of immigrant life. As a component of this study, I also show how politically-related temple projects are coded male by practitioners and enable the construction of a male subjectivity vis-à–vis the homeland and conventional Korean norms as a point of reference.

SA CHAL TEMPLE

Sa Chal is the country's largest lay-centered Korean Buddhist temple and is located in the heart of Koreatown. Established in 1974 in a former Jewish synagogue, Sa Chal's main activities include weekly dharma services, memorial rites, ancestor worship, a library, art gallery, and a social services center aimed at a primarily first-generation Korean American clientele. Like many immigrant religious institutions in the U.S., Sa Chal provides a central venue through which Korean Americans may develop and experience social cohesion and ethnic identification, particularly as mainstream American institutions cannot always fulfill culture-specific needs. Consequently, the temple becomes the focal point for all religious and much of the social interaction for its members.

On any given Sunday from 11:00 AM to 12:30 PM, the main worship hall of Sa Chal is filled with eighty to one-hundred members; of that group, only fifteen to twenty percent of the members are male. The gendered space and larger percentage of women present in the temple is typical of any Sunday at Sa Chal, especially when there are no outside speakers invited as guest lecturers and no special events like the Buddha's birthday to celebrate. That women comprise the majority of the weekly worship services is well acknowledged and expected by men and women alike. The only times when the percentage of men equals or outnumbers that of women in Sa Chal are during reunification meetings and other politically-related events sponsored by the temple where it is clear that these meetings are considered "men's space." In this study, I suggest that men's participation at Sa Chal is deeply tied to a desire to raise self-esteem and assert authority by creating male spaces and social selves in the temple as they renegotiate their identities following their arrival in the United States.

During my two years of research amongst Buddhists at Sa Chal, I often asked members to explain the discrepancy in men's and women's attendance at worship services. The varieties of responses offered were based primarily on references to the putative attributes of each gender. While some women claimed that men were too arrogant to bow down to the Buddha, others maintained that men lacked the time to come to temple since they worked all the time. Others believed that men chose not to attend temple simply because there were not enough fellow men around with whom they could socialize. Men, on the other hand, either tended to claim that the temple's programs did not appeal to their intellectual curiosity, or did not provide them with enough opportunities for leadership roles. In many ways, these responses reflect men's desires to have more social prestige and responsibility in their ethnic institution in a manner similar to that of Korean Christian churches that reserve lay leadership positions as deacons, elders, and ushers for men alone.[3]

In men's responses, women were characterized as more faithful and more connected to the family's religious identity since they had more free time and because they had no other culturally acceptable means of letting go of stress. Female Buddhists were also held to enjoy more devotional forms of Buddhism that the temple offered over a more intellectual, philosophical and, therefore, male approach to Son (Zen) Buddhism. Furthermore, women's practices at Sa Chal were associated with a lower form of religiosity characterized as emotional, sensitive, dependent, and oriented towards the good fortune of the family. Through this contrast between rational and devotional styles of worship, men at Sa Chal thus distinguish between what they consider a "higher" form of religion centering around more cerebral activities like meditation, and a "lower" feminine form of practice based on bodily activities like prostrating, chanting, and praying in front of the Buddha during worship services. Thus, since men were posited to be more interested in an intellectual understanding of religion, the body was viewed as secondary to the practice of meditation and "awakening the Buddha nature." I found that in drawing these distinctions, men create a stereotypical view of women's religious practices as devotional although the women themselves do not see their practices as mere devotion.

According to many of the men that I interviewed at Sa Chal, immigration has a tremendous impact on self-esteem, especially for those who have moved from previous positions of high Confucian social status and professional respect in Korea. Upon arrival in the United States, many male participants like Steven Lee have experienced limited social mobility and inverted status and are unable to maneuver easily through the American system. I suggest that this downward turn in social, economic, and political status serves as a motivating factor for men's engagement in those activities sponsored by the temple that facilitate a strong psychological and emotional connection to Korea. Furthermore, these activities are generally aimed at the exclusion of women and directly influence the construction of a male subjectivity and reconstruction of a post-immigration identity. Central to this reconstruction of male identity is the creation of a transnational identity, which, as I show, enables men at Sa Chal to view themselves as Koreans rather than Korean Americans. That is, men in this study assert their identities through religious activities that establish a strong connection with the place of origin and construct distinctly male spaces for themselves in the temple in response to the vicissitudes of immigration to the new country.[4] At the same time, in asserting a transnational Korean identity in the U.S., many male members of Sa Chal further claim that by remaining Buddhist in the U.S. they remain more loyal and more "authentic" Koreans—in contrast to their male counterparts in the Korean American Christian churches.[5]

By participating in the temple's political activities, men at Sa Chal temple assert a transnational Korean identity that emerges as a direct response to their ethnic minority status in the U.S. and their religious minority status within the Korean American community. Throughout my interviews with male participants, I discovered that many members of Sa Chal do not desire to become full American citizens; rather, they are tied to an ideological translocal Korean identity.[6] Thus, for someone like Mr. Yang who immigrated to the U.S. in 1983, the idea of American citizenship holds very little appeal because he still considers himself a Korean and not a "Korean American." Even after living in the U.S. over fifteen years, he has yet to apply for citizenship and admits that he still pays "more attention to news and happenings in Korea than in America—Korean 70 percent and American about 30 percent." For some male members, "becoming American," is the last thing they desire despite the fact that many of these men do not wish to move back to Korea. Rather, they keep themselves ideologically tied to the homeland as an identity marker even as they work for economic success in America; in many ways, this transnational identification reflects the isolation many immigrants experience in the U.S. As Mr. Yang aptly puts it:

> For someone like me, I am just here alone with all my family in Korea. My mother lives there, my relatives are there and so even though I live

here [with my wife], it's lonely and so you really have to worry a lot about yourself.

The desire to remain focused on Korea as a main source of identity and reference despite living in the U.S. for a number of years thus exists as an option for many immigrants who have not experienced a positive sense of adjustment to life in the U.S. For most of these men, a positive transition into American culture requires something more than economic success and determination that they seek at the temple.

"TO BE BUDDHIST IS TO BE KOREAN"

According to David Jeon, a forty-seven year old temple member who came to the U.S. in 1987, "to be Buddhist is to be Korean." Throughout our interview, he explains how Buddhism existed in Korea before Christianity and also insists that most of Christianity is derived from Buddhism since he believes that the Bible contains passages very similar to Buddhist scriptures that were written "way before the time of Jesus." His comments equating Buddhism with an "authentic Korean identity" reflect not only his unquestioned Buddhist faith but also a more common disappointment and perhaps even envy of the increasing numbers of Korean Christian churches in the United States shared by members of this temple.

Currently he owns a marketing company that he runs with a fellow Buddhist member of Sa Chal and spends most of his time socializing and working with temple members. During the weekdays, male friends from the temple can usually be found in his office chatting, drinking tea, working on new business ideas, and discussing temple affairs. Like many men at Sa Chal, most of David's social life revolves around Buddhists at the temple. In addition to being an active member at Sa Chal, David is also heavily involved with the temple's famine relief efforts to North Korea and serves as a main administrator for the One Korea Buddhist Movement, USA. As an organization that raises funds for famine relief in North Korea, the One Korea Buddhist movement is also tied to reunification efforts and established the Diamond Noodle Factory just outside of Pyongyang in 1998. The noodle factory is a joint venture between the abbot of Sa Chal, David, and his older brother, a leading Buddhist figure in South Korea.[7]

As a main figure in the famine relief project and reunification endeavors within the Buddhist community, David devotes most of his time to the transnational Korean community and maintains significant ties to Korea by traveling back and forth from South Korea, the U.S. and North Korea.

Although he has lived in the U.S. since the mid 1980s, like many of the men interviewed in this study, he claims that he has no desire to become an American citizen, nor of obtaining citizenship rights like voting or financial assistance in the future, for he still sees himself as "a Korean always." Another factor contributing to his refusal to apply for American citizenship is his sense of disappointment over his son's involvement in "American" gangs and his disrespectful "un-Korean" behavior towards his father. Furthermore, following the Los Angeles disturbances of 1992, David has developed a strong distrust of the U.S. government and the police department based on their slow response to the violence that erupted in Koreatown.

When asked about his involvement in the temple's efforts in North Korea, David expresses a widely held view amongst men when he claims that he became an important figure in the reunification and famine relief movement out of nationalistic pride. Over tea he explains:

> Because of the political motives of the Christians in Korea during the [Korean] war and the lack of nationalistic pride amongst Korean Christians who have been duped by Westerners and the Korean obsession with PX culture, Korean Christians in Korea and in the United States have lost their history and their culture. There is no philosophy among Christian converts! They were all obsessed with the material value of PX culture during the Korean War and the influence of the Salvation Army and other Christian groups who brought in specialty foods that later ended up on the black market. They also brought in special gifts for kids at Christmas time and ended up creating this love for Western things!

David argues that Korean Christians have been so heavily influenced by Western powers that even today they lack pride and a sense of loyalty to their own country of origin. In response to this situation, David has devoted himself to spreading Korean Buddhism throughout North Korea, South Korea, and the United States. In so doing, he also asserts his own identity as a Buddhist and as a nationalistic Korean in contrast to the Korean Christians who have, as he puts it, "betrayed their country." David then reiterates, "to be Buddhist is to be Korean," and, similarly, that "to be Korean is to be Buddhist."

The notion of the betrayal of the Koreans is a commonly expressed sentiment among many of the participants in this study. In addition to blaming the West and Christianity for the lack of nationalistic pride amongst Korean Americans, I found that reunification and famine relief efforts are heavily driven by memories of a past that still looms large in the minds of many

Korean immigrants—the Japanese occupation of Korea from 1910–1945. David himself refers to this period as the "Japanese brainwashing of Koreans." In his view, historically the Japanese (even before the occupation) had criticized Korean Buddhist monks and during the Japanese Occupation, Korean monks were forced to marry like the Japanese Buddhist monks. David explains in an excited voice:

> During the occupation, the Japanese forced the monks to marry so that they couldn't rebel if they were tied down with wives and children! Because of this brainwashing, after the occupation, the Korean Christians like Syngman Rhee started criticizing all the monks' departure from celibacy, which proved for Christians that Buddhists were not 'pure' anymore! Then, since the Christians only believed in one god, then the Buddhists were thought of as devils!

David thus equates Buddhism with a strong sense of nationalism and a Korean identity that has been attacked not only by the Japanese imperialists but also the Christians attracted by the West. Interestingly, his equation of Buddhism with Korean nationalism seems to altogether exclude the historical relationship between Korean Christianity in the U.S. and Korean nationalism in the early part of the twentieth-century.

For men like David Jeon, the establishment of the Diamond Noodle Factory can be understood in relation to the political desire for reunification between North and South Korea that is espoused by some temple participants, even if this desire is more ideological than actual. In fact, there are many who support the efforts out of a desire to "help our people" and for a reunification of the two countries. As his friend Jae Woo, a Korean immigrant student, claims, "Every Korean wants Tong-il [reunification] at heart." For many Koreans in the Los Angeles Koreatown district, reunification plays a key role in their ethnic identification, for they self-identify first and foremost as Koreans or Koreans living in America rather than as Korean Americans. As such, this transnational identification as Korean is related to the exertion of political agency amongst immigrants who do not have much political clout in the U.S.

Although David never explicitly discusses his sense of dislocation in the United States, the fervor of his critiques against Korean Christians in America and his daily struggles with his son reveal, nonetheless, some of the main motivations for his participation in Sa Chal. Although he criticizes the Korean Christians for their material success and "selling out" to American culture, it is hard to see how someone who works seven days a week in his own business cannot help but feel at least slightly envious of the financial support offered by other religious organizations outside one's own. These contributing factors have thus led him and others at Sa Chal to reject the notion of becoming an American citizen and embrace a more transnational identity.

IMPLICATIONS OF TRANSNATIONAL IDENTIFICATION

As I have shown above, for many immigrants, the narrative of "becoming American" is non-essential to the development of a post-immigration identity. It is in a transnational context that identity formation, agency, and self-esteem emerge for many male immigrants in their assertions of a Korean identity. In supporting famine relief and taking active roles in promoting reunification by attending meetings, staging protests, or even traveling to North Korea, many Korean American men are involved in an assertion of Korean identity and nationalism while continuing to live in the United States. Male support of such activities thus ties them closer to the Korean community and a strong ethnic identity. For many men at Sa Chal, the claim for identity and agency is made not as American citizens but as transnational Koreans—part and parcel a response to the conditions of immigrant life often experienced as displacing. Thus, in this context, the Buddhist temple serves as the site for the production of an alternative form of identity outside of any distinct claim to an American identity.

Viewing oneself in relation to the homeland and in relation to political and relief issues back home through the temple provides an individual with an opportunity to express agency and confidence while living in the host country. In fact, some scholars even reject "immigrant" as an analytically appropriate term because it implies a "permanent rupture" and separation from the homeland and obscures the everyday reality of life in the United States, which continues to be heavily tied economically, politically, and ideologically to the country of origin.[8] Through their participation in political programs at the temple, many male Buddhists in the United States are able to assert a political agency that they do not experience in the host country given their minority status and inability to fully assimilate. When I polled members of the temple, I have found that most men consider themselves fully Korean with very little interest in in-depth integration into American culture. Many feel isolated from mainstream society or excluded due to racism and language problems; upon arrival in the United States, many immigrants experience downward social mobility and are unable to maneuver easily through the American system. This downward status is one of the primary factors motivating an immigrant to continue to look back to the homeland as a source of reference and engage in transnational activities.

Hence, many men at Sa Chal actively support reunification and famine relief as a way of combating or offsetting the crisis in status upon arrival in America. I did note, however, that the few men who were in higher paying professional jobs tended to speak of themselves as Korean Americans rather than Koreans, which indicates that social and economic standing has an effect on how immigrants may classify themselves.

Sociologist Luin Goldring points to a similar phenomenon found in the Mexican American community where Mexican immigrants look to and maintain close social ties with the country of origin by sending remittances, supporting local and political projects back home, and even returning with gifts.[9] Goldring outlines three main reasons for maintaining these transnational ties: (1) the ability to increase social status within a transnational context; (2) the individual may change his or her own status in the host country by taking part in home-based or transnational activities and become key players in a different social context; and (3) transnational organizations may offer organized resources that permit the development of alternative hierarchies where individuals are viewed in relation to those back home rather than in the host country.[10] Despite the appearance of permanent settlement in the United States, such border crossings are an integral part of the immigrant experience.

Goldring's study further indicates that immigration and transnationalism affect men and women differently. For many of the female participants in her study, immigration was often perceived as beneficial to their self-esteem. For example, women often gain greater status within the household prior to their own immigration when they are responsible for taking care of the household and family during their separation from their husbands who have migrated in search of employment first. In addition, many Mexican women find that working in the U.S. provides them with previously unknown opportunities for advancement and the enhancement of self-esteem. For men, however, the social setting of the host country makes it almost impossible for them to retain their status particularly when they lack the political power and agency they had as Mexican men back home.

Similarly, Ai Ra Kim attributes the rise of male leadership and worship in Korean American churches to this lack of power in America, for the church provides a context in which men can reassert their agency and political power. In her study of the role of the Korean church in Korean immigrant social lives, Kim asserts that:

> Churches confer social status and positions of leadership upon adult members. This function is highly important, especially for men. Most

Korean men, except for those in prestigious professions such as medicine, law and big business, find their social status has been denigrated after immigration; their traditional egos and pride become damaged. Korean churches help heal their psychological wounds by giving men recognition and power within the church leadership and bureaucracy through the position of lay-elder and lay-deacon, board member and trustee. Most of the staff and administrative officers of ethnic Korean churches are men. In particular, being an elder grants prestige and power to a man: elders exercise tremendous power inside and outside the church, and almost all elders are men. Also most of the celebrities in the Korean communities are elders of their churches. In this sense, men still control the reins of power in Korean community. The church reflects traditional Confucian Korean cultural/social structure and system.[11]

Kim's work indicates that the religious institution plays a key role in sustaining Korean identity and gender relations despite the transition to a new country. While men may view the church as a source of power through the conferral of lay leadership roles, the Buddhist temple lacks specifically ritualized roles for men. Hence, most men presently at Sa Chal occupy the few administrative opportunities available (e.g., volunteer accountant) or pursue leadership roles in temple-supported programs outside of the worship service.

This continued tie to the homeland enables many men at Sa Chal to alter their social landscape in the U.S. and actively engage in nationalistic or political processes related to Korea that they do not have access to yet in the U.S. Thus, although men may be less visible at the temples and less inclined to worship publicly with the women, they are more willing to take active part in reunification and famine relief than women are in Sa Chal. I do not wish to suggest that developing a transnational identity is merely a simplistic way to combat alienation but, rather, that perhaps such an identity has developed as one type of coping mechanism and method of adaptation that has previously been overlooked. Thus, transnationalism can be said to "resist or raise their social standing and validate their [men's] self-esteem."[12] While male members are said to be embarrassed to bow down in full prostration in the company of women, they are nonetheless active in Sa Chal's academic lectures and political activities. While these activities do not exclude religious and spiritual motivations, of course, they do indicate that men are involved in creating alternative forms of practice that are more suitable to meeting their psychological needs.

CONCLUSION: BROADER IMPLICATIONS OF TRANSNATIONALISM AND RELIGION

By taking a lead role in relief efforts to North Korea through the noodle factory and the coordination of a support network between the U.S. and South Korea, Sa Chal extends beyond the traditional model of assimilating immigrants to American life by providing a specific avenue for the maintenance of ethnic identity and active involvement in the homeland. As a new post-1965 immigrant institution, Sa Chal is by nature involved in transnational activities and consists of members who cross national borders at least once a year and do not really consider themselves Americans; rather, they are more tied to an ideological translocal Korean identity. Like the Italian Harlem church studied by Robert Orsi, the temple brings together immigrants and their children through ceremonies and services to provide an essential link to the homeland.[13] Unlike earlier immigrants of European descent, however, the new post-1965 Immigration Act Koreans are better able to transport themselves back to the homeland through the advent of telecommunications, computers, and numerous flights back and forth from Asia. This very immediacy of the homeland and ability to exist almost simultaneously in the homeland and the new land has obviated the need for many new immigrants to even worry about full-scale assimilation to American society.

It is in the context of transnational immediacy that the cultural practices of identity formation, memory, and resistance can take place for many new immigrants. Excluded or marginalized from the American mainstream, new immigrants have sought different means of developing subjectivity outside of the narrative of American citizenship.[14] For Koreans at Sa Chal, the claim for identity and agency is made not as American citizens but as transnational Koreans—this claim for hybrid identity is a response to the conditions of immigrant life often experienced as displacing. In other words, for many recent immigrants, the ethnic congregation serves as the site for production of an alternative form of identity outside of the claim to an American identity.

As indicated in this study, there are ethnic stakes at hand in transnational famine relief movements that have implications beyond the material both abroad and at home, in the global *and* the local context. These implications have different meanings for the different parties involved at the temple and in the Korean community. In supporting famine relief and taking active roles in promoting reunification by attending meetings, staging protests, or even traveling to North Korea, many Korean American Buddhists I have spoken with are involved in an assertion of Korean ethnicity and nationalism while continuing to live in the United States. Through the establishment of the Diamond Noodle factory and children's relief movement, Buddhists in the

United States are able to assert a political agency that they do not experience in the U.S., given their minority status and inability to fully assimilate. While there is a tendency to assume that all immigrants desire and follow the same trajectory to full scale participation in American culture and the benefits of citizenship embarked upon by early groups of European immigrants, this assumption does not take into consideration that such a trajectory is not easily followed by all immigrants, nor even necessarily desired.

The continued tie to the homeland also enables Koreans to alter their 'social landscape' in the U.S. and actively engage in nationalistic or political processes related to Korea that they do not have access to yet in the U.S. As noted earlier in this study, Sa Chal mediates the process of immigrant adaptation yet, unlike any other U.S.-based temples and churches, this Los Angeles congregation takes on the role of a transnational site which impedes what is often accepted as the inevitable and eventual assimilation of the immigrant. What this emerging transnational identification signifies is that religion plays numerous roles in immigrant lives and that there are more processes at play than assimilation and ethnic enclaving for new immigrant congregations in the United States. The temple and many of its members, following many years of adjustment in Los Angeles, has been able to extend its gaze back home, a transition also reflected in the larger history of the Korean community in America. Immigrant religious organizations are self-reflexive in their response to congregational needs. Religion therefore reflects the patterns and demands of adaptation to the new land as well as the continued maintenance of religious and cultural traditions. In Los Angeles, the temple becomes the symbol of home and continues to mediate this relationship through transnational activities and is bringing about a new function of religion.

NOTES

1. Won Moo Hurh, *The Korean Americans* (Westport, CT.: Greenwood Press, 1998), 143.
2. I have deliberately changed the name of the temple where I conducted my research to "Sa Chal" which is a generic term in Korean for "temple." I have also changed the names of all interview participants in this study for the purpose of anonymity.
3. Sociologists Eui Hang Shin and Hyung Park attribute Korean immigrants' attachment to ethnic churches to the marginal man theory and maintain that since Koreans have suffered in America because of their racial marginality, "Korean churches are the primary sources of comfort and compensation for Korean immigrants." See Eui Hang Shin and Hyung Park, "An Analysis of the Causes of Schisms in Ethnic Churches: The Case of Korean-American Churches," in Seong Hyong Lee and Tae-Hwan Kwak, eds., *Koreans in North America: New Perspectives* (Seoul: Kyungnam University Press, 1988), 235–36.

Furthermore, the churches become very popular amongst the male population of Korean immigrants, for "[s]ince a great majority of Korean immigrants are deprived of status competition in the broader society, their competition supplies a meaning to life, [and] a means for feeling important." See Shin and Park, 235–36. Male Buddhists at Sa Chal are aware of the leadership and status competition offered by the church and maintain that the temple should provide similar opportunities for lay men to take on some of the responsibilities for temple administration held by the monastics.

4. Sheba George points to a similar phenomenon amongst Keralite men in a Christian immigrant church who seek to negotiate and expand their roles in the church by taking over the activity of caroling and cooking at public events. In this study, George maintains that men's activities are to be seen in direct relation to gendered patterns of immigration from India where women and wives tended to immigrate first and earn higher incomes than their spouses who follow. For further inquiry see Sheba George's "Caroling with the Keralites: The Negotiation of Gendered Space in an Indian Immigrant Church," in R. Stephen Warner and Judith G. Wittner, eds., *Gatherings in Diaspora: Religion and the New Immigration* (Philadelphia: Temple University Press, 1998), 265–294.

5. Throughout this study, I discovered that most members of Sa Chal have had at least one experience in a Korean American Christian church either through family members who had converted following immigration or through Korean immigration-related social services that the members had previously utilized. Furthermore, many members of Sa Chal continue to do business within the ethnic community and encounter Korean American Christians on a daily basis. One of the unfortunate results of this interaction is that many Buddhists are unwilling to admit their religious affiliation out of fear of jeopardizing their business opportunities.

6. Unlike earlier immigrants of European descent, the new post-1965 Immigration Act Koreans are better able to transport themselves back to the homeland through the advent of telecommunications, computers, and numerous flights back and forth from Asia. Furthermore, as John Lie claims, "it is no longer assumed that immigrants make a sharp break from their homelands. Rather, pre-immigration networks, cultures and capital remain salient. The sojourn itself is neither unidirectional nor final. Multiple, circular and return migrations rather than a singular great journey from one sedentary space to another, occur across transnational spaces. People's movements, in other words, follow multifarious trajectories and sustain diverse networks." John Lie, "From International Migration to Transnational Diaspora," in *Contemporary Sociology* 24:4 (July 1995): 304.

7. The Diamond Noodle factory was established in order to provide sustenance to North Koreans living in and around the Sariwon area just an hour's drive from Pyongyang. According to David the noodle factory is the result of many years of negotiation with the North Korean government. Currently, Sa Chal's abbot and David are the main fundraisers for the project in the U.S., and David's older brother is the main fundraiser in Korea.

8. Linda Basch, Nina Glick Shiller and Christina Szanton-Blanc, *Nations Unbound: Transnational Projects, Postcolonial Predicaments and Deterritorialized Nation-States* (Langhorne, PA: Gordon and Breach, 1994).

9. Luin Goldring, "The Power of Status in Transnational Social Fields," in Michael Peter Smith and Luis Eduardo, eds., *Transnationalism from Below* (New Brunswick, NJ: Transaction Press, 1998).

10. Goldring, "The Power of Status."

11. Ai Ra Kim, *Women Struggling for a New Life: The Role of Religion in the Cultural Passage From Korea to America* (Albany: State University of New York Press, 1996), 67.

12. Goldring, "The Power of Status."

13. Robert Orsi, *The Madonna of 115th Street: Faith and Community in Italian Harlem, 1880–1950* (New Haven: Yale University Press, 1985).

14. Lisa Lowe, *Immigrant Acts: On Asian American Cultural Politics* (Durham, NC: Duke University Press, 1996).

REFLECTION

STAKING A CLAIM ON AMERICAN-NESS:
HINDU TEMPLES IN THE UNITED STATES

HIMANEE GUPTA

An intricately-carved tower rises amid the Allegheny foothills east of Pittsburgh, marking the entrance to the Sri Venkateswara temple, one of the most visited public places for Hindu worship in the United States. The temple occupies ten acres in suburban Penn Hills, and draws thousands of visitors each year. Dedicated June 30, 1976, it has four priests in residence and a daily schedule packed with religious services. On weekends, cultural activities join the schedule: lectures by artists and religious leaders visiting from India; musical performances; religious instruction for children and teens; classical dance. For special religious festivals, priests from the parent temple in Tirupati, India, are flown in to officiate lavish services.

For many Hindu immigrants, such temples in diaspora have grown into gathering places to gossip, share movie videocassettes, and talk about the latest Indian fashion trends, while their American-born children study Indian languages or learn such cultural arts as classical dance. In addition, such temples are like tourist sites, offering Indians in diaspora an opportunity to blend a summer vacation with a spiritual experience. The Sri Venkateswara temple in Pittsburgh is especially noteworthy in this respect. With an annual income of $1 million, it is among the wealthiest Hindu temples outside India. It also is regarded as a must-visit spot for Indians who reside on the East Coast, in the Midwest, and even in India itself. Its greatest selling point is its promise of an authentic Indian experience. Many, in fact, report that going inside the temple feels like being back in India again.[1]

This temple, like others in the United States, figures prominently in arguments that post-1965 Indian immigrants have come of age in the United

States. The Sri Venkateswara temple's wealth, awesome structure, and no-expenses-spared attitude toward the performance of Hindu rituals symbolize the affluence that these immigrants have attained. Many scholars suggest that Indians, having achieved material success, now are eager to establish a social toehold in America in a culturally resplendent way. Others suggest these houses of worship help children understand their Indian heritage. As one frequent attendee put it, "I want my children to get exposed as much as possible to our culture. . . . I think if we take them to the temple one hundred times, at least once something might go into the child's head."[2]

However, such sites represent more than the wealth of Indian immigrants. Temples also have come to help define what it means to be Indian in the United States. Since the early 1980s, the site where an Indian cultural identity unfolds has been undergoing a change of venue, moving from the privacy of homes to more public spaces. The building of temples reflects this spatial shift, as participation in religious activities plays an increasingly visible role in influencing how Indian communities throughout the United States define what constitutes being an Indian. Yet, an outward display of a religious identity in such settings as temples marks a potentially problematic shift in the conceptualization of community. It represents a definition that is more static, less fluid as these immigrants strive to make their status more solid.

Nearly 1.7 million Asian Indians reside in the United States, according to the 2000 census. Most are believed to be Hindu.[3] Among those who are, one finds an incredible array of styles in which the faith is conceptualized, practiced, and folded into individual identities. Yet, just as the rhetoric of an increasingly powerful Hindu nationalist movement in India draws momentum from a claim that the cultural grounding of India has been tied historically to a Hindu ethos, many images of Indians in mainstream America center on Hinduism. This external categorization of Indian as Hindu cannot help but affect how Indians in the United States not only are defined by mainstream Americans but also define themselves.

When the Sri Venkateswara temple in Pittsburgh was built, there was only one other Hindu temple of note in the United States. By the mid-1980s, the number of temples had increased to nearly fifty, and as Raymond Brady Williams notes, most communities in the United States with at least a hundred Hindu families were either building temples or planning to do so.[4] While these temples might provide an aesthetically pleasing display of one aspect of an Indian cultural identity, their very visibility on the American landscape could make that cultural identity—which is a largely upper-caste, upper middle-class Hindu identity—the dominant, if not only, way in which Indians in the United States are defined, both internally and externally.[5] John Fenton, for instance, likens the building of temples to the symbolic staking of a claim on a foreign land. Territorializing land as sacred property in such a way declares "the country is now also an Indian-American land."[6] Because Hindus make up the majority of Indian immigrants in the United States, non-Hindus must cooperate with that Hindu majority in order to further a sense of Indian American unity.[7] Such a pan-Indian identity is of critical importance to the many less-economically privileged and less talked-about Indians in the United States. For it has arisen at least partly through the 1980 change in census designations that gave Indian residents minority status, allowing them to qualify in the United States for affirmative action hiring and other benefits.

Studies on the building of temples and other houses of worship by immigrant communities in the United States tend to regard such sites less as spaces for sacrality and more as sites where ethnic communities can establish a place in an American multicultural scene.[8] Through this process, the argument goes, immigrants resist assimilation into a homogenized American identity. Ethnic community-based forms of worship enable immigrants to achieve a balance that Indians often describe among themselves as the "best of both worlds"—economic success without a loss of cultural distinctiveness. What this argument fails to note is the political implication of projecting an immigrant presence in such a publicly visual way, especially when that representation of a non-Western faith becomes the most recognizable marker of the ethnic group.

In India, Hindus make up eighty-five percent of the population. Nevertheless, temples compete for spiritual space with mosques, gurdwaras, and houses of worship from numerous other faiths. In the urban colonies of New Delhi, for instance, it is not unusual to be awakened at dawn by a clamor of religious noise: the clanging of temple bells, the singing of hymns, the muezzin calling Muslims to prayer. By contrast, in the United States, where Indians make up less than one percent of the population, the cacophony of religious noise within this community is effectively silenced by the majority Hindus who dominate, numerically and economically. Williams argues that religion helps immigrants adapt to a new society because it is regarded as an accepted mode for establishing a distinct community identity in the United States. Yet, over the past four decades, the Indian immigrants that have been most successful at fostering a sense of community in a manner that is meaningful within the broader fabric of mainstream America have been Hindus.[9]

The potential hardening of an Indian American identity along a Hindu line comes as Hindu nationalists in India contend with increasing political clout that non-Hindus are not truly Indians, even if they can trace their birth and/or ancestry to India. The Hindu nationalist movement has found receptivity particularly among voters in India who share the same caste, class, and religious affiliations as their affluent counterparts overseas. The defining of Indian as Hindu has served to categorize those who follow other faiths, particularly Islam and Christianity, as non-Indian. It also has led to a misinterpretation of Hinduism itself, defining it primarily along a particular brahmanical line.[10] That rearticulation of Hinduism suppresses the vast array of beliefs and practices within the faith. In doing so, it evokes an Orientalist rendering of Hinduism that gained currency during the British colonial era and was transported to the United States via such experiences as Swami Vivekananda's visit to Chicago in 1893.[11] That such a standardizing process is occurring in the United States as well as India threatens to undermine the freedom to define one's self as one pleases while exacerbating tensions between the different culturally defined groups who fall under the general category of Indian. In Atlanta, for instance, a cultural center that was to represent a variety of Indian cultural traditions became an almost exclusively religious center after economically powerful Hindus in the city's Indian community insisted that religion and culture were inseparable. Their position alienated Sikhs, Christians, and Muslims after the center's architectural drawings included space for a temple but none for a gurdwara, church, or mosque. While the center has drawn substantial support from Hindus in Atlanta, few non-Hindu Indians have patronized it since it opened.[12]

The Hinduizing of India's public cultural and social spaces and the accompanying Hinduizing of Indian identity in the United States carries further ramifications. Anecodotal evidence suggests the Hindu nationalist movement in India draws at least some support from upper-caste Hindus in the United States.[13] However, by understanding the desires that feed Hindu nationalist support in the United States, one might be able to channel those sentiments toward a political consciousness that challenges the movement. Such a possibility lies in understanding what motivates the building of lavish Hindu temples in affluent communities outside India, and in so doing, considering the consequences of how these acts standardize the identity of the Indian immigrant self.

THE MEANING OF MULTICULTURALISM

To look at temples in such a way, it helps to understand how Indians in the United States are situated within the discourse of American multiculturalism. The idea of what it meant to be an American underwent a profound change in the 1960s that was tied to ethnic activism generated through the Civil Rights movement as well as to new immigration laws that allowed large numbers of non-white professional and technically-skilled migrants to enter the United States. The new definition of American can be seen as a shift from the idea of America as melting pot to one of a society based on multiculturalism. On one level, that is positive. It allows all people residing permanently in the United States to be American, if being American is an identity that all choose to inhabit. Multiculturalism, however, shares some commonality with the melting pot idea, even as it appears to be its antithesis. In coining the phrase "melting pot," Jean de Crevecoeur described "the American" as emerging out of a melting pot of Europeans from a diversity of backgrounds. Crevecoeur envisioned one nationality formed by a multiplicity of cultures. Likewise, multiculturalism dictates that non-white immigrants who cannot melt into a racialized white American self can become American by obtaining U.S. citizenship—or even merely a green card—while retaining their distinct regional, linguistic, religious and other identities. The credo of multiculturalism is that it is not unity through assimilation but unity through diversity that makes America great. Yet, even as it promotes diversity, multiculturalism tends to lead to some losses of diversity.

How is this so? In what Verne Dusenberry calls the "logic of multiculturalism," America is not a nation of cultures but a nation of nations. Such a framework suggests that several melting pots, rather than one melting pot, have come to comprise American-ness.[14] This process constitutes part of what Yen Le Espiritu has described as the formation of a panethnic community, "a politico-cultural collectivity made up of peoples of several, hitherto distinct, tribal or national origins." Espiritu, in her discussion of Asian Americans as a panethnic community, argues that governmental and other institutional classifications of peoples tend to "lump" distinct ethnicities together as one. This lumping, she suggests, leads to all Asian Americans being treated "as if they were the same," and in turn enables a politically disenfranchised group to develop a sense of community solidarity.[15] Through this process, Stephen Cornell suggests that external categorizations and self-imposed definitions work together in a positive sense to enable those with a diversity of backgrounds to embrace a newer, broader ethnic identity.[16] As a result, immigrants from India who settle in the United States all become Indian—that is, Indians within an American framework.

Multiculturalism emphasizes the idea of many cultures, all separate, all equal. In doing so, it makes an ethnic identity appear synonymous with a cultural one. This often leads to a tightening of the link between culture and nationality. In the America I grew up in, for instance, it was not relevant whether one was Punjabi, Bengali, Gujarati, or of any other regional background. What mattered was that if we were of Indian ancestry, we were Indian. This knowledge was passed on to children like me by parents like mine who upon arrival in the United States had begun to be identified and to identify themselves as simply Indian, rather than employing the numerous regional, linguistic, or other criteria that denote identity categories in India.

Along these lines, geographers Surinder M. Bhardwaj and N. Madhusudana Rao have shown that the Indians who immigrated to the United States between 1965 and 1980 produced the most geographically dispersed ethnic community in America. But despite the geographic diversity, the community of Indians that began forming in the United States after 1965 has been economically quite homogenous. Bhardwaj and Rao note that Indians not only identified strongly with the American middle class but also cast their desire to immigrate and establish new lives in the United States in terms of bourgeois self-interest.[17] That self-interest underwent a change in its articulation as a booming post-World War II economy began to slow in the mid-1970s just as the idea of multiculturalism began to take root. At that point, the definition of self grew more strongly Indian. This process was aided by the addition of an "Asian Indian" category to U.S. census forms in 1980.

Thus, regardless of whether Indians in the United States see themselves as Indians in a nationalist sense or in an ethnic/cultural sense, their identity as a community has come to be a cultural one linked to what is seen as the "culture" of India. Through this process, the diversity of cultures that represent Indian-ness is quietly suppressed.

RESISTING ASSIMILATION

When immigrants arrive in the United States, they often suffer an identity crisis. Such a crisis is perhaps particularly acute for Hindus from India who are thrust out of an environment where they were a numerical majority and into one in which they are both an ethnic and religious minority. Isolated in an alien setting and unaccustomed to the norms of their host society, religious ritual becomes a way of recouping a sense of self. Soon after settling into new homes, Indian immigrants typically set up a small shrine in the kitchen, a spare closet or a separate room. If they are Hindu, the shrines generally consist of a small table or chest upon which the images of a few favored deities are placed, along with a candle or incense burner and containers for rice and roli (the red powder used in personal pooja). Non-Hindus also create shrines featuring photos or images of religious figures, while Muslims often create a space to perform namaz (initial act of prayer and worship).[18]

Using religious practice to formulate an identity of self lets Indians establish an easy fit within a multicultural America. Fenton suggests that during their first several years in the United States, Indian immigrants—regardless of their religious affiliation—see the time that they devote to quiet prayer or meditation less as a religious practice and more as a spiritual one. Fenton notes that many of his Atlanta area respondents devoted part of each day to personal worship but did not consider themselves particularly religious. Based on this, he suggests that an assertion of being overly religious would link Indian immigrants with a dominant American understanding of Hinduism as cult-like that had been perpetuated by sects such as the International Society of Krishna Consciousness through the 1960s and 1970s.[19] Such an association would hurt the immigrants' image as professionally skilled, Westernized contributors to an expanding U.S. economy by making them appear unable to assimilate.

The defining of private worship practices as spiritual in an Indian sense but not religious in a non-Western sense allows an Indian self to emerge that is, as the "best of both worlds" term would suggest, like the average American—but not entirely so. Private prayers give immigrants a daily association with a cultural memory and let them distance themselves from the perceived cult images that Hinduism had attained in the United States, ensuring that the multiculturalism in which they participate is palatable within mainstream America. At the same time, prayers subtly link immigrants to a community of believers, providing a fertile ground in which the seeds for formulating a sense of self and an affiliation with a particular community can flourish.

FROM PRIVATE TO PUBLIC

In the home, prayer retains some fluidity. For the only relationship that exists during the practice is the one between a higher being and the self. Since a higher power is largely self-defined, especially in a private ritual practiced at home, it allows one to define one's self without turning to an intermediary, such as a scriptural text, a worship schedule or a religious leader. However, personal expressions of faith have taken on a more static feel as the number of Indians in the United States has increased, causing some immigrants to feel pressured to practice religion "properly."

Describing religious traditions among Indian immigrants as "made in the U.S.A.," Williams notes that most of the post-1965 immigrants came to the United States with little, if any, specialized knowledge of scripture.[20] As a result, religious practices often were based on memories of how rituals were practiced among families at home. However, because the memory of India is less accessible to children, immigrants often seek out more structured forms of practice as families form. At this point, families typically begin meeting regularly for prayer groups or to study certain scriptural texts such as the *Bhagavad Gita*. In addition, immigrants turn to recognized religious authorities such as Brahman priests to gain a more accurate understanding of Hinduism.

The use of priests increased in the 1980s as the number of Indian immigrants clustered around major cities swelled. As priests received more requests to preside over rituals celebrating such events as the birth of a child, a wedding, or a move into a new home, a sort of mini-enterprise developed in which the priests would offer their services, sometimes for a fee. In the process, the practice of Hinduism took on a more standardized form, even as it sought to be established as a community affair.[21]

Yet, standardization often generates dissent. Like the stifling of diversity that occurs through the formation of panethnic identities within multiculturalism, the presence of priests and the invocation of rituals centered on a formal understanding of scriptural texts alienated many Hindus, particularly those who were not brahman by caste, not upper middle-class, and not direct emigrants from India. This led to two things: a rise in sectarian groups and the development of a new form of Hinduism in America. Williams describes the latter as ecumenical Hinduism, a practice that tries to draw together a diversity of Hindu practices through a congregational form of religion that mimics the Christian church. Such a form of Hinduism had flourished initially when a few immigrant families in a given city would gather for prayer meetings or other services. By the early 1980s, however, ecumenical Hinduism had "become a conscious strategy to develop a new form of Hinduism among immigrants."[22]

MAKING INDIANS HINDU

The Hindu nationalist group Vishwa Hindu Parishad—whose U.S. branch is known as VHP of America—has played a critical role in developing ecumenical Hinduism in the United States. Its activities have had a decided effect not only on how Hinduism has come to be defined in the United States but also on making "Hindu" and "Indian" nearly synonymous.

The VHP initially was established in India in 1964 with a mission of uniting all Indians. It opened its first chapter in the United States in 1970 and devoted much of the first decade of its existence to promoting Hinduism among diasporic Indians. It currently has branches in forty states.[23] The VHP's interest in reaching out to overseas Indians is linked to the political context of a newly independent India. Although Hindu nationalism was intertwined in both resistance to and accommodation of the anti-British struggle in the late nineteenth and early twentieth centuries, the idea of a Hindu nation received little public support in the early years of an independent India largely because of the 1948 assassination of Mahatma Gandhi by a Hindu nationalist supporter. Lacking respectability at home, the VHP turned to the Indian diasporic community, advertising itself as an organization that could help immigrants maintain a tie to a community that they, upon migrating, had lost.

The VHP of America strives to promote Hinduism in the West. Its local branches sponsor lectures on Hinduism, yoga workshops, and summer camps and conferences for Indian youths. The group also encourages overseas Hindus to support social-service projects in India, and it often launches fund-raising drives to help victims of earthquakes, floods, and other natural disasters in India.[24] While not formally involved with politics, much of the VHP's rhetoric encourages Hindus in the United States and elsewhere to use their devotion to Hinduism as a means of improving the economic condition of their counterparts in India. Although the VHP defines a Hindu as a person who follows the ethical and spiritual values developed in Bharat (a name used to refer to India in a spiritual, emotive sense), it often excludes Indians who are Muslim and Christian from this category of Hindu. VHP of America leader Yash Pal Lakra, for instance, has suggested that while all persons of Indian origin can identify themselves as Hindu, Muslims cannot because Islam originated outside the subcontinent.[25]

This linking of Indian to Hindu fits well within the multicultural American framework. Because Hindus represent the majority of Indians in the United States and because Hindus represent the majority of India's citizens, both groups—those who remain in India and those who have left—can assert that the national cultural identity of India is essentially Hindu. While all-India associations stress the culture and arts of India in an official secular way, many make use of distinctly Hindu motifs. Though Hindus often do not notice the linkage, much as whites in America generally fail to detect the subtle racisms that non-whites experience, non-Hindus are quite aware of it.

BUILDING A TEMPLE

Most accounts about the origin of the Sri Venkateswara Temple in suburban Pittsburgh begin with a dream a couple had in 1971. The couple was watching a bharatnatyam performance at the University of Pittsburgh, and was so moved by the pleasing image it evoked that they wanted their daughters, aged nine and seven, to study the dance. The couple invited the performer over for dinner and persuaded her to start a dance class for Indian girls in the community. By early 1972, twenty girls were taking classes, which met in the basement of an Indian businessman's warehouse. Parents who transported children to the class began using the opportunity to gather for a community puja, and before long, a makeshift shrine had been put into place. This led to dreams of building a real temple. A steering committee was formed and fund-raising began.[26]

The desire for a temple evoked many sentiments: an emotional need for spiritual fulfillment, a wish to nurture a cultural identity, an interest in passing on a religious practice to an American-born generation. At the same time, there was a deep-seated interest in asserting a public identity in Hindu as well as Indian nationalistic terms. Aparna Rayaprol quotes a woman who was involved with the initial planning as saying the period was "very emotional." Rayaprol writes:

> It was the time when India was at war with Pakistan over the issue of Bangladesh and immigrant Indians living in the United States ... experienced a great deal of stress. The sense of insecurity engendered by a tumultuous political event (the war) pushed the Hindus further into concretizing their rather abstract vision of a temple on the mountain top. During the period of revivalism and nationalism in India, there was a celebration of Indian culture that included several definitions of Hinduism. Similarly, during the time of political crisis in South Asia, the immigrant Hindus took on the act of temple building.[27]

The initial project seemed to fit nicely into an assertion of community and self within a multicultural framework. But, just as dissent often lurks within claims of unity through diversity, tensions developed among those involved with the Pittsburgh project. In the spirit of ecumenical Hinduism, the Pittsburgh group had planned a design that would accommodate a number of deities as well as several different forms of worship. As the planning committee began looking for funding, they discovered that the Tirumala Tirupati Devasthanam in the southern Indian state of Andhra Pradesh would help finance temples outside of India as part of a mission to promote globalized dharma, much as the VHP calls for world Hindu unity. The foundation typically provides up to $150,000 per project, usually in the form of temple architects, masons, and craftspeople who build and supply images, temple stones, and implements for worship.[28] However, it also controls how temples it supports are developed. It expects them not only to follow the design of the Tirupati temple but also to be associated with a sole presiding deity, Sri Venkateswara, one of the many incarnates of Vishnu. After seeing the Pittsburgh group's plan, the Tirumala Tirupati Devasthanam sent a letter back saying it was unacceptable. This led to a split between North and South Indians in the community and prompted several key players to resign from the project.

By this point, the group already had purchased land in the suburban town of Murraysville. That site has since been developed into a Hindu-Jain temple. Though it features deities from a variety of traditions, it draws primarily worshippers from northern India. Four miles away, the Sri Venkateswara temple uses rituals that follow the traditional patterns established in Tirupati. Most of its devotees and supporters are from the southern Indian states of Andhra Pradesh, Karnataka, Kerala, and Tamil Nadu.

TEMPLES AND IDENTITIES

What might this experience suggest about the construction of Indian-ness, and Hindu-ness? Can the decision by South Indians in Pittsburgh be attributed to a desire to resist assimilating into an all-India identity that was being shaped along the lines of the North Indians? Did the refusal by North Indians to support a project that would be tied to a specific regional tradition and presiding deity grow out of a fear that a South Indian viewpoint would dominate the definition of Indian that the temple would represent?

Rayaprol attributes the split to regional difference. Unlike temples in the north, medieval South Indian temples were not just sites for worship but centers of economic, political, and administrative power. Similarly, South Indian rulers helped develop centralized temple structures around the identity of a particular deity. According to Rayaprol, the Tirumala Tirupati Devasthanam inherited this tradition and plays a key role in social, cultural, and educational activities throughout southern India and elsewhere today. "It is this culturally inherited experience of the South Indian tradition backed strongly by the financial and religious support from Tirupati that has made it possible for the establishment of South Indian temples in the Indian diaspora."[29]

Pittsburgh's Sri Venkateswara temple evokes envy for its beauty and wealth, and the Tirumala Tirupati Devasthanam has supported temple projects elsewhere in the United States. However, the assertion of such a leadership role does not mesh comfortably with Hindus in other communities who, Williams argues, are anxious to ensure that temples built in North America convey a pan-Indian spirit. He quotes one leader of a Hindu

Temple Society in Dallas-Fort Worth as saying: "In ten years the children will not think of themselves as Gujarati, Tamil, or Hindi (speakers), but as Indian and they will need a unified group."[30]

While inclusiveness is to be applauded, it does tend to echo the VHP's motto of strength in unity. Children who can trace their identity to India need only know that they are Indian; other identities—Gujarati, Punjabi, etc.—are irrelevant. One might ask whether this idea forces assimilation into a designated multicultural niche, leading to an erasure of a more richly-varied cultural background in the process.

Temples built in the United States in such localized traditions as the Sri Venkateswara can resist this homogenizing. But do they? Often, the participants regard these temples and their participation within them as enactments of cultural practices that are not representative just of a particular locality in India but of all of India. Rayaprol notes that while her respondents feel a strong affiliation with localized identities, they also cultivate a national image of India within the Sri Venkateswara temple itself. One woman who organizes tours of the temple for tourists and school groups, for instance, told Rayaprol that she felt it was "her 'duty' to educate 'outsiders' about the rich heritage of India and help establish deeper roots for Hinduism outside India."[31] Such representations suppress the Sri Venkateswara temple's distinctive identity in favor of a more general Indian one that fits in a multicultural America.

CONCLUSION: UNDERSTANDING TEMPLES

It appears that temples—as a public expression of an Indian immigrant self —do not promote diversity. Instead, they stifle it within a multiculturalist discourse that tends to render the culture and nationality of immigrants to the United States as inseparable. Does this mean multiculturalism should be discarded as a framework for understanding how American society is structured in the early twenty-first century and how varied communities of immigrants fit into that structure? Hardly. Multiculturalism, by recognizing that all cultures, all differences have value, provides persons of non-white, non-Christian ancestry a more humane way to exist. Its classification of all peoples as equal and its tendency to suppress diversities within its multi-cultures are problematic. Yet, awareness of the process of suppression that occurs within multiculturalism provides a means through which one can begin to question the categories it creates.

Hindu temples in the United States draw their support from an economically- and socially-dominant Hindu majority. As such, they represent an Indian identity on an American landscape. They appear to challenge the idea that an American identity is a white, Western, generally Christian identity. We should accept this as a positive rearticulation of American-ness. Yet, we should recognize that this resistance challenges primarily the assimilative ideal of Americanism, not the idea of assimilation itself. Temples let Indian immigrants continue to be Indian. In so doing, they can convey a sense that being authentically Indian means embracing both the cultural traditions and religious practices that the temples perpetuate. One must ask, what are the consequences of such a message?

Indians in the United States represent a vast array of regional, linguistic, and religious backgrounds. However, just as "all Asian Americans have been lumped together and treated as if they were the same," through governmental and institutional systems of classification,[32] Indians in the United States are categorized in similarly homogenizing terms. Much of the stifling of difference has come from mainstream perceptions of Indians as well as institutional classifications. However, this essay has argued that some of that stifling process is abetted by the numerically- and economically-dominant upper-caste Hindus in the United States. As the dominant group of Indians in the United States, this group will pursue a pan-Indian sense of unity when it suits its interests, such as in the lobbying for an Asian Indian census category in 1980. However, when it comes to establishing what that unified Asian Indian identity means, it is this group that insists upon and generally succeeds in defining it. The building and representing of temples as a cultural symbol of Indian-ness is but one sign of this.

The identity of Indian American is diverse, much more diverse than the exotic image of Hindu spirituality evoked by the temples would suggest. Bringing this point to light means understanding each temple that is built on U.S. soil for what it is—a representation of a particular form of Hindu practice, not a cultural marker of an overarching pan-Indian ethnic and cultural identity. This not only would require us to treat an ethnic and religious identity as if each were separate but also would encourage us to evoke one of Hinduism's strongest features. That is recognition that the spiritual encompasses multiple meanings. Through this, one can embrace the value of diversity that multiculturalism conveys and also insist that identity categories remain open to constant reinterpretation. One also can regard worship as practice that encompasses a multiplicity of beliefs. In the case of immigrant Indians, one must insist that being Indian does not mean being Indian in one particular Hindu way.

NOTES

1. For descriptions of the temple, see its website (http://www.svtemple.org); Fred Clothey, *Rhythm and Intent: Ritual Studies from South India* (Bombay: Blackie & Son Publishers, 1983), 77–100; Vasudha Narayan, "Creating the South Indian 'Hindu' Experience in the United States," in *A Sacred Thread: Modern Transmission of Hindu Tradition in India and Abroad*, Raymond Brady Williams, ed., (New York: Columbia University Press, 1992), 147–176; Aparna Rayaprol, *Negotiating Identities: Women in the Indian Diaspora* (New Delhi: Oxford University Press, 1997), 28–40; and Raymond Brady Williams, *Religions of Immigrants from India and Pakistan: New Threads in the American Tapestry* (Cambridge, UK: Cambridge University Press, 1988), 55–69.

2. Rayaprol, *Negotiating Identities*, 70.

3. Firm figures on the number of Hindu Indians are not available. Fenton estimated that Hindus made up 65 percent of the Asian Indian population in the United States, as of 1980. The Learning Network (http://www.infoplease.com/ipa/AO193644.html) estimated the overall Hindu population in the United States at 950,000 as of mid-2000, compared with 795,000 in 1995.

4. Williams, *Religions of Immigrants*, 55. Several organizations have temple directories, but the number of temples listed varies widely. A directory sponsored by the VHP of America (www.mandirnet.org/temple-list.html) lists 99 sites, representing mainly North Indian traditions. A Tamil electronic library (www.geocities.com/Athens/5180/temple.html) lists 136 temples and a third directory (http://monishrai.tripop.com/temple.html) lists 274. Harvard University's Religion and Pluralism Project (www.harvard.edu/~pluralism) lists 530 Hindu religious centers in its directory, 86 of which include the word temple in the formal name.

5. Joanne Punzo Wagehorne links the temple-building boom in the United States to other periods in Indian history where the construction of temples was tied to assertions of Hindu identity as well as competitions for dominance among caste groups. "The Diaspora of the Gods: Hindu Temples in the New World System 1640–1800," *Journal of Asian Studies* 58:3 (1999), particularly pp. 649–650, 654, 673–677, 682–683.

6. John Fenton, *Transplanting Religious Traditions: Asian Indians in America* (New York: Praeger Books, 1988), 173.

7. Ibid., 156.

8. See *Gatherings in Diaspora: Religious Communities and the New Immigration*, R. Stephen Warner and Judith G. Wittner, eds. (Philadelphia: Temple University Press, 1998).

9. Despite their longer history in the United States, Sikh immigrants, as a group, generally are less numerous and economically privileged than the upper-caste Hindus who have taken advantage of the professional skills categories that were established after 1965 to emigrate from India for economic and social betterment. Gurdwaras have not attained the same external prominence as temples for this reason, and among mainstream Americans, often are seen as the same thing as a Hindu temple.

10. Orientalist depictions of caste in the colonial era and anthropological renderings of the concept in the post-colonial era are vigorously debated in the scholarship on Indian his-

tory. Susan Bayly offers an excellent overview in *Caste, Society and Politics in India from the Eighteenth Century to the Modern Age* (Cambridge, UK: Cambridge University Press, 1999). Sumit Sarkar shows how the idea of caste has interacted with Hindu nationalist politics in India in "Indian Nationalism and the Politics of Hindutva," in *Making India Hindu: Religion, Community, and the Politics of Democracy in India*, David Ludden, ed. (New Delhi: Oxford University Press, 1996), 276–277. A few scholars have explored how caste plays into the articulation of Indian identity as Hindu in the United States. See Susan Koshy, "Category Crisis: South Asian Americans and Questions of Race and Ethnicity," *Diaspora* 7:3 (1998); Prema Kurien, "Becoming American by Becoming Hindu: Indian Americans Take Their Place at the Multicultural Table," in *Gatherings in Diaspora: Religious Communities and the New Immigration*, 58–60; and Arvind Rajagopal, *Politics after Television: Religious Nationalism and the Reshaping of the Indian Public* (Cambridge, UK: Cambridge University Press, 2001), 244–250.

11. For a description of the interplay between Orientalist thought and the defining of Hinduism in the United States in the late nineteenth and early twentieth centuries, see Vijay Prashad, *The Karma of Brown Folk* (Minneapolis: University of Minnesota Press, 2000), 11–45.

12. Fenton, *Transplanting Religious Traditions*, 151–162.

13. See Sadanand Dhume, "No Place Like Home: Hindu Nationalism Draws Strength from U.S. Supporters," *Far Eastern Economic Review*, Feb. 25, 1999; Himanee Gupta, "Illuminating India: How a South Asian Diaspora Helps Build a Hindu Nation," *Sagar* 6 (1999); Biju Mathew and Vijay Prashad, "The Protean Forms of Yankee Hindutva," *Ethnic and Racial Studies* 23:3 (2000); and Arvind Rajagopal, "Transnational Networks and Hindu Nationalism," *Bulletin of Concerned Asian Scholars* 29:3 (1997) and "Hindu Nationalism in the U.S.: Changing Configurations of Political Practice," *Ethnic and Racial Studies* 23:3 (2000).

14. Verne Dusenberry, "A Sikh Diaspora? Contested Identities and Constructed Realities," in *Nation and Migration: The Politics of Space in the South Asian Diaspora*, Peter van der Veer, ed., (Philadelphia: University of Pennsylvania Press, 1995), 24.

15. Yen Le Espiritu, *Asian American Panethnicity: Bridging Institutions and Ideas* (Philadelphia: Temple University Press, 1992), 2, 159.

16. Stephen Cornell, "Discovered Identities and American Indian Supertribalism," in *We Are a People: Narrative and Multiplicity in Constructing Ethnic Identity*, Paul Spickard and W. Jeffrey Burroughs, eds. (Philadelphia: Temple University Press, 2000), 99–102.

17. Surinder Bhardwaj and N. Madhusudana Rao, "Asian Indians in the United States: A Geographic Appraisal," in *South Asians Overseas: Migration and Ethnicity*, Colin Clarke, Ceri Peach and Steven Vertovec, eds. (Cambridge, UK: Cambridge University Press, 1990).

18. Fenton, *Transplanting Religious Traditions*, 69.

19. Ibid., 57–58.

20. Williams, "Sacred Threads of Several Textures," in *A Sacred Thread: Modern Transmissions of Hindu Traditions in India and Abroad*, Raymond Brady Williams, ed. (New York: Columbia University Press, 1992), 230.

21. Williams, *Religions of Immigrants*, 31.

22. Ibid., 50.

23. For more on the VHP's overseas activities, see (www.vhp.org) and (www.vhp-america.org).

24. See (www.vhp-america.org).

25. Yash Pal Lakra, "Let Us Call Ourselves 'Hindu Americans,'" *Hinduism Today* (October 1997), 9.

26. Clothey, *Rhythm and Intent*, 177–178; Rayaprol, *Negotiating Identities*, 27.

27. Rayaprol, op. cit., 90–91.

28. Williams, *Religions of Immigrants*, 58–59.

29. Rayaprol, op. cit., 28–29.

30. Williams, op. cit., 62.

31. Rayaprol, op. cit., 75, 91.

32. Espiritu, *Asian American Panethnicity*, 159.

COMMUNITY

WHY CAN'T THEY JUST GET ALONG?
AN ANALYSIS OF SCHISMS IN AN INDIAN
IMMIGRANT CHURCH

SHEBA GEORGE

As many unsuspecting worshippers stood participating in the Sunday morning communion service in an Indian immigrant orthodox church, some church members escorted police officers into the church and pointed out particular men who were alleged trouble makers. The officers took these men out of the church and began to search them for weapons as the singing and chanting of the congregation became replaced by shocked silences and cries of fear and outrage. This incident was the final point in a series of conflicts in this immigrant church that resulted in a schism and the formation of a new congregation.[1]

While employing the aid of the state in settling internal politics is extraordinary, that the schismatic model of church formation has become the norm among the Orthodox Indian Christian immigrants in the U.S. is even more phenomenal. In India, it is usually the diocesan bishop who arranges for the establishment of a new parish by calling together the petitioning parishioners and assigning a priest to be vicar at the new location. In the U.S., it appears that most new congregations are formed as the result of political splits within existing congregations, and mostly initiated by the laity and clergy. The tendency for congregations to split over non-doctrinal issues is a growing concern that many church leaders raise. While I do not have the exact numbers of congregations that have formed as a result of splits, informed church leaders at national meetings indicate that it is a common pattern in most metropolitan areas where there is more than one congregation. Even though the diocesan center in New York State does not have an official count of the number of American immigrant congregations out of the fifty-six that were formed as the result of schisms, it would be unusual to find *any* second or third congregation in a given area to have a non-schismatic origin. In this paper, I will examine the gendered and racialized conditions of immigration and settlement that, coupled with organizational changes in the American setting, produce the phenomenon of schisms in the immigrant Indian Orthodox congregations in the U.S., which is exceptional relative to the church in India.

Splitting within immigrant churches is not unique to the Orthodox Indian Christians. For example, there is an emerging body of literature about Korean Christianity in the U.S. that analyzes the issue of splitting in Korean American churches.[2] Shin and Park, in an important study titled "An Analysis of Causes of Schisms in Ethnic Churches: The Case of Korean-American Churches," explain the splitting in terms of both supply and demand as well as the heterogeneity of the immigrant population. The abundant supply of immigrant clergy is a main condition for the feasibility of schisms leading to new congregations. The marginal status of Korean immigrants in the U.S. creates a demand for alternate status positions within the community leading to a greater demand for more status-granting institutions such as congregations. Finally, the heterogeneity in characteristics of church members leads to the need for different members to create their own space, in which they can worship and praise fellowship with those like themselves.

Additionally, Shin and Park find that the tendency to split varies by whether the Korean immigrant congregation is affiliated with a larger denomination in the United States. Within Christian tradition, there are three general church polities or governing forms. The Episcopal polity is the most hierarchical order, with bishops on top followed by elders or priests, and then deacons. The Presbyterian polity holds that presbyters, or general assemblies of elders who are all equal in Christ, should govern the church. Finally, the Congregational polity looks to the single congregation with the leadership of the pastor to decide all controversies and govern itself. In the Korean case, Shin and Park argue that, ". . . the knowledge that the higher organization (presbytery) will review the merits of the important decisions of a congregation tends to discourage the potential challenges on such issues, thus promoting the unity of a congregation."[3] That is, if the congregation is affiliated with the Presbyterian Church, for instance, the well-defined procedures for resolving disputes that denominational organizations have are likely to deter schisms.

Given this reasoning, one would expect schisms to be the exception rather than the norm in the Orthodox Church, since they are part of an episcopal polity where bishops have supreme control over congregational decisions. Why would the Orthodox Indian Church, relatively more hierarchical in its organization and administration, experience schisms as the rule in the formation of new congregations?

After giving a brief background of the immigration of this community and of Indian Orthodox Christianity, I look at how the different incentives in participation for both the male laity and the clergy in the U.S. immigrant congregation is shaped by the nature of the Kerala Christian immigration. Because of their loss of status relative to the women in the community as well as their marginalization as racial minorities in the economic, social, and political arenas of the host society, they look to the immigrant congregation to recoup their losses. While the increased incentives for lay and clerical participation in the U.S. fuel the politics of schisms, I argue that the changing organizational structure of the immigrant church also contributes to its factious nature. The new institutional autonomy at the local congregational level in the United States, coupled with incomplete institutionalization and a consequent decrease in control at the U.S. diocesan level are among the necessary conditions for the proliferation of schisms in these immigrant churches. In what follows, I begin by looking at the conditions of immigration and the gendered patterns of life in the church.

IMMIGRATION AND CHURCH LIFE

A shortage of nurses in the United States in the 1960s resulted in the increasing recruitment of foreign nurses, especially from Asian countries. Immigration increased substantially for Indian nurses after the 1965 liberalization of immigration policy. By the late 1970s, immigration of Indian nurses to the U.S. was only exceeded by that of Filipina nurses.[4]

The Kerala Indian Christian community in the United States is unique among Asian Indian immigrants in the prominent role that women played in the immigration process. Whereas in the case of most other immigrant groups, the men immigrate first, in the case of Kerala Christians, female nurses have come first and later sponsored their husbands and families. Typically, the men waited in India with the children until they were allowed to join their wives, who were already working in the United States and supporting the household through remittances. In other cases, single women went back to India with their green cards and found husbands with whom they could return. In this immigration experience, conventional roles were partially reversed for men and women. [5]

Since the women were the primary agents of immigration, their husbands and male kin were dependent on them when they joined them in the U.S. The dependence of the men on the women often went beyond the financial aspect to include orientation in American society. Because they immigrated prior to the men, the women of the community were initially more proficient in dealing with the American society. Furthermore, the jobs most men obtained were of lower status and income than their wives had. The difficulty in transferring Indian degrees, credentials, and work experience to the U.S. context often left the men in the position of having to start all over again. They typically had to relocate for their wives' job conveniences and re-educate themselves in new trades and professions to become employable.

Although many of the women worked in India and contributed financially to the household income, they did not play the primary role there that they did in the immigration and settlement process. Low incomes and unstable employment in usually secondary labor market jobs left many men with few opportunities for public participation and access to leadership positions. As immigrants, they had little entrée into the political and social structures of the wider American society. Men not only lost autonomy and patriarchal status in the immigration process but they also lost their sense of belonging and felt very isolated in the U.S. Whereas the women experienced upward mobility and an increase in general status, many men in the community became downwardly mobile and lost status in the immigration experience.

Since Orthodox Indian Christians are Syrian Christians, it is important to take a brief look at the history of Syrian Christianity in India. Syrian Christians from Kerala, the state at the southernmost tip of India, claim their descent from the early converts of the apostle Thomas who, tradition has it, was martyred in southern India in 72 AD. These Christians of Kerala are called Syrian not because they have Syrian ancestry but rather because they use Syrian liturgy. Syrian missionary influences which started in the seventh century led to the establishment of the church under the patriarch of Antioch, with a liturgy that still retains some Syriac.

Over the centuries, the Syrian Christians became divided among themselves into different denominations. There are Catholics, Eastern Orthodox, as well as Protestants of every stripe who claim a Syrian Christian ancestry.

The Orthodox Syrian Christian church of India is one such denomination in this Indian Syrian Christian tradition. It broke off ties with Antioch in 1912 and is currently led by a patriarch from Kerala.[6]

The gender roles and ideology in the Orthodox Church are starkly delineated and enforced. For example the congregation is physically separated by sex. The men and boys sit on the left and the women and girls on the right side during a service. In the Orthodox Church, women do not have any official roles in the three-hour-long Sunday morning service other than joining in communal responses including hymns. Furthermore, women and girls must cover their heads during the service, and they receive communion and final blessings only after all the men and boys have taken their turn.

As in India, men assume the administrative and ritual roles within a gender-specific division of labor. Only men and boys can be altar helpers or assistants to the priest. They can formally lead the congregation in responses and enter the altar area, which is off limits to all women and girls. Because they are polluting by nature, the women in the church cannot enter the altar area or touch the garments of the priest. Because the consequences of their sex include menstruation, they will defile that which is holy and are therefore barred from contact with all that is holy.[7]

Women also do not have many leadership positions available to them in the administration of the church. Lay membership in the Orthodox Church is designated on a family basis with the male head of the household being the representative with the right of suffrage in general body meetings of the congregation. In fact, only males over twenty-one years of age have a vote in the general body meetings. The lay administrative body is made up of an elected male managing committee, which includes the treasurer and the secretary. Women are therefore not present in administrative capacities except in the areas of child education, food production, and church sponsored women's groups. For instance, women may become Sunday school teachers but they cannot be elected to the managing committee of the congregation. There is a service/prayer group for women called the Martha Maria Samajam (group) that offers some office-bearing positions for women but the president of this group in every congregation is the vicar, a male.

For my current project, I examined the gender dynamics in this community by doing ethnography in an immigrant Orthodox Church in a major metropolitan area in the United States.[8] Using the congregation as a base, I have conducted interviews in the homes of members of the congregation. I have also attended national church conferences and spoken with many priests and leaders in the church and larger the community of Kerala Christians in the U.S. In what follows, I will examine the different incentives for increased lay and clerical participation that has led to the congregation becoming an almost exclusively male-run sphere.

LAY AND CLERGY PARTICIPATION IN THE UNITED STATES

Because of the highly heterogeneous nature of Kerala society, with large numbers of Hindus, Muslims, Christians, and even a small Jewish community, religion is an important identity marker for Keralites. Furthermore, the history of colonization in Kerala was an additional factor that contributed to the importance of religion in this region. Especially in the case of the Orthodox Christians in Kerala, "the true Orthodox Christian faith" had to be frequently defended from the colonizing Protestant and Catholic influences of the Portuguese, Dutch, and English. While the denomination one belongs to becomes an important source of identity, this privilege is reserved for males as women are expected to join the denomination of their husbands upon marriage.

In Kerala, the church one belongs to is the essential basis for social life. In an interview, one immigrant man explained why a person had to belong to a church in Kerala when he said,

> In our home [Kerala)], if we don't stay in a church, it is a great problem. If we have children, we need to baptize. If we die, they won't bury you. When you go to get married, that is a problem. We will be brought down. You have to obey and go along with them. We have to go along with the church or we become people without anything. If a death happens in your family and the church does not do the burial, where do you take your dead body? Do you understand? That is the problem. So you have to obey and get along over there.

Contrastingly, in the United States, the same man explained why it was different:

> [In the U.S.,] there is more freedom. If I don't want to go to one church, I can go to another church or I can stay away from the church. The church will not put any force on me. . . . We can do whatever we want. It's OK if we don't go to church. It's OK if we stand up against the church. The church cannot bring us down or bend us. [In Kerala,] it is not like that.

Despite there being "more freedom" in the United States from the dictates of the church, most male immigrants report higher levels of church participation. The role of the church as the main source of community life continues in the U.S. and is intensified since there are not many other options for social life for immigrants.[9] Most immigrants continue to depend on the church for the conducting of their marriages, baptisms, and funerals, and the blessing of new homes and cars. But there are some clear differences in lay participation in church life in the U.S. that sheds light on the phenomenon of splitting.

Most of the immigrant male lay members reported a significant increase in participation in church life after immigration. Because immigration is often what historian Timothy Smith calls a "theologizing experience,"[10] the increased participation of the immigrants in religious institutions can be attributed to the alienation inherent to the immigration experience. For Kerala Christian men, immigration results in loss of status relative to their pre-migration economic positions and relative to their wives. Like the Korean immigrants, the Kerala Christians, as racial minorities, also experience marginalization vis-à-vis the larger U.S. society. With limited opportunities for civic participation in the wider American society, the religious congregation becomes the ideal place for immigrant men to recover their lost status through increased participation.

First, many immigrant congregations endeavor to forge a social and religious space in the new setting that reproduces what has been left behind in the imagined homeland. In many ways, the immigrant congregation attempts to create an untainted "little Kerala"—an "extended family" for its members experiencing alienation in the wider American society. As Mr. Varghese, one of the men I interviewed, put it, "The church is a community —it is a place where once a week or once a month you can share your sorrows or happiness."

During both happy and sad times, individual members share the events of their lives with the church family. Beaming parents bring huge birthday cakes for the whole church to celebrate the important first birthday of their child. The housewarming party is usually a communal celebration that takes place after the house blessing ceremony conducted by the priest. Death or illness—even of relatives in Kerala—summons up an immediate network of support. Church members gather together at the home of the bereaved or sick member to offer spiritual consolation and material aid.

Another interviewee, Mrs. Simon's complaint about her husband highlights the importance of church participation for immigrant men. " . . . As for me," she said, "I told my husband, 'Don't join all these (political) parties and groups in the church. Just go to church, pray and come back. Why go for these parties? I don't like that.' But he says, 'I have to have a niche here somehow. At least I have three to four people with whom I can talk now.' . . . ." Without extended family or friends, and often without a satisfying job, "having a niche " becomes crucial for the men.[11] The church becomes important as proxy for the missing extended family relationships that make up the fabric of social relations in Kerala, especially for the men who suffer greater losses in the immigration process.

Second, church leadership positions, which inherently signify status relative to Kerala, become a means of compensating for the loss of status for the Kerala Christian men. Back home in Kerala, leadership roles in the church are reserved for socially and economically prominent male members of the community, so that lay leadership is associated with high status. Mr. Lukos, for example, was proud to be from a family that could trace back its active role to the first churches of Indian Orthodoxy in the seventh century. Just as for Indian Syrian Christians in Kerala, the Church was the umbrella under which family and individual identities are formed and reputations are won or lost, so for immigrant Kerala Christians in the United States, the immigrant congregation becomes the venue for status claims.

The congregation offers leadership to some men and a sense of community to others. More generally, and this is the third compensatory role, the congregation has always been a place of male privilege. Besides marginalization vis-à-vis the larger society, the immigrant Orthodox men also experience downward mobility relative to their wives who tend to be more economically stable than they are. The church is one space where women are forcibly silenced and where men are the official voices representing the family. In a number of interviews, both men and women explained the level of combative church politics and increased male participation in the church by saying what is apparently accepted in the community. In an interview, one woman advanced it as an explanation for why the men do not allow the women to speak in public forums at church. As she put it, " It is those people who don't have status at home that find it in the church. They don't have any status at home. They don't have any status at their workplaces. It is only in the church that no matter what they say, nobody can throw them out—they can voice all their opinions."

Thus, we see that the immigrant congregation offers a unique setting for men to attempt to restore their lost status and their self-esteem. To compensate for demotion in the labor market and the family, they utilize the church space to assert their leadership, to develop a sense of belonging, and to secure their exclusiveness. To counteract their racial and economic marginalization in the wider American society, the immigrant men look for opportunities for civic participation in the congregation. Splits in immigrant congregations allow more male members to actively participate in various leadership roles. Because the new split-off groups tend to be small, the vigorous participation of male members becomes crucial to the survival of the split-off congregations. The people involved in such splits probably feel a sense of importance as key players shaping events.

Along with the increase in the male lay participation in the U.S. congregation, there is also a convergent increase in the availability of immigrant clergy. Much as in the Korean case, the increased demand for status positions among lay members is paralleled by an increased supply of priests in the U.S. Unlike Catholic priests, Orthodox priests are allowed to marry and fifty-seven of the sixty-two Orthodox immigrant priests in the U.S. are married. Not unlike their male parishioners, most of the priests immigrate to the U.S. when their wives, who are typically nurses, sponsor them.

These clergy suffer a similar loss in status relative to the larger society and their wives. Furthermore because most congregations cannot afford their upkeep, they cannot be full time priests and must find other work during the week. As a result, it becomes a very important identity issue for the immigrant priest to have a congregation where he can conduct mass on Sundays and maintain his vocational status.

Moreover a priest has the additional incentive of the financial income that comes in the form of the monthly congregational contribution as well the individual donations accompanying the administration of priestly duties. Therefore priests often play an important part in the splitting of congregations. If there is a thriving congregation in a particular area and a new priest immigrates to that area, chances are that within a few years he will find a dissatisfied group of people in the existing congregation who will precipitate a split.

Whereas the male laity's and clergy's increased incentives for participation in the immigrant congregation is fuel for the politics of schisms, it is the changes in organizational structures and the incomplete institutionalization of the immigrant church that allow for the possibility of schisms in the first place. In the next section, I will look at the organizational differences in the U.S. that contribute to greater autonomy at the local level coupled with a decrease in diocesan control. First, I will examine the change in organization of the local religious body from parish to congregation. Necessary legal incorporation at the local level cements the greater autonomy of the immigrant congregation. But there is a concurrent decrease of control at the diocesan level, especially in the church's inability to control the random immigration of priests which points to its incomplete institutionalization in the U.S.

ORGANIZATIONAL DIFFERENCES: INCREASED LOCAL AUTONOMY AND
DECREASED DIOCESAN CONTROL

In Kerala, each diocese of the Orthodox Church is made up of parishes or administrative units that are geographically designated. Membership in a parish is dependent on where the member lives. The church constitution allows a change in membership only under specific conditions that maintain control of lay processes within the church hierarchy. For example, in case of a need for membership change, the church constitution specifies that

> A member of one Parish Church can either become a permanent member of another Parish Church or if he resides temporarily in another place for [his] profession, [he can] become temporarily a member of the Parish Church there, with the permission of the Vicar of the Parish church he leaves and the Vicar of the Parish church he joins and the respective vicars shall report to the respective Diocesan Metropolitan about such leaving and joining.[12]

Whereas churches in Kerala function according to the episcopal model, immigrant Orthodox churches in the U.S. seem to be organized around the congregational model, which require the churchgoer to choose between different options. The ability to choose the congregation to which one will belong at the individual level is not available to most Kerala Orthodox Christians. Even when there were historical schisms in the Kerala Orthodox church, it was typically entire extended families or whole neighborhoods that supported one side or another. But in the typical large U.S. metropolitan areas where most immigrants live, the Orthodox Indian churchgoer is faced with having to make a choice from among several congregations up to as many as sixteen in the greater New York and New Jersey area.

The Orthodox immigrant congregation in the United States fits into sociologist Steve Warner's definition of a typical American congregation as a voluntary religious community. As Warner puts it,

> To say that the congregation is a voluntary community is to say that mobilization of members must rely on idealism or personal persuasion rather than coercion or material incentives, but voluntary also signifies, particularly in the U.S., that the congregation cannot assume the loyal adherence of its members as if they were all part of the same tribe; it must actively recruit them.[13]

Whereas the Kerala parishioner is born into his parish because of geographical dictates and tradition, the U.S. churchgoer has fewer such stipulations to regulate his church attendance. He may become tied to his congregation because of political and financial commitments, often made during the schismatic origins of the congregation, that continue to remain crucial to its survival. Thus, it is not unusual to find some immigrant churchgoers driving long distances to attend one congregation when there may be another much closer to their homes. And because these ties are voluntarily made, they can also be broken in the same manner.

And whereas Kerala parishes can take their membership for granted, in the U.S., congregations must compete for membership. One Kerala immigrant who had been in the habit of visiting more than one congregation in the city where he lived told me about a priest from one of the congregations who telephoned him to make him choose one he was going to attend. One priest told me that he was accused of trying to steal members from another congregation because he allowed these members to join his congregation without a letter from their previous vicar.

The transformation of the "ascribed" Kerala parish into the "achieved" and voluntary immigrant congregation in the U.S. sets the stage for increased autonomy at the local level and allows for the possibility of schisms.[14] Furthermore, the convention of religious incorporation in the U.S.—a practice alien to Kerala churches—cements local autonomy by placing legal authority over congregational property in the hands of the board of trustees in each congregation. Although church property is owned at the local level by parishes in Kerala as well, the force of custom typically places the authority over such property in the hands of the diocesan bishop, who is symbolically handed the key of the parish upon its consecration.

A relatively recent incident in one American city exemplifies the increase in autonomy for the immigrant congregation and served as a rude awakening to church officials, both in India and in the U.S. In the fall of 1993, the American diocesan bishop was scheduled to visit a church in the New York area where he was going to oversee the appointment of a new priest whom he had assigned to the congregation. The priest who was leaving had requested a transfer because he had become frustrated with the politics in the congregation. When the bishop arrived at the church with the new priest in tow, he found members of the congregation gathered at the front of the church after having locked and blocked the gate to the property. They turned him away citing that the church was their private property under the existing U.S. laws of incorporation.

This incident induced the shocked church synod to create an official certificate of incorporation exclusively for U.S. congregations that regularizes this process and makes such congregations subject to the church constitution and by-laws of the American diocese. However, American congregations continue to retain greater autonomy relative to their parish counterparts in Kerala. In addition to the managing committee, most U.S. congregations have to elect an extra administrative body in the board of trustees, which consequently makes available additional church leadership positions to male lay members. The U.S. diocesan bishop, in an interview, called it a parallel system where the board of trustees is legally responsible for the congregation, whereas the managing committee deals with the more mundane matters.

While the new practice of religious incorporation and the change in the organization of the religious body from parish to congregation increases local autonomy, there is a coinciding decrease in diocesan control. For example, as noted above, the random immigration of Orthodox priests is a problem facing the church that illustrates the loss of control at the diocesan level and signifies the incomplete institutionalization of the church in the U.S.

In Kerala, priests are assigned to particular parishes and are rotated every three years to other parishes in the diocese. If a priest desires to transfer to a different parish, he must get the permission of the bishops from both dioceses in question. Priests are paid a salary from a pooled diocesan fund that is collected from all the parishes in the diocese. The diocesan fund supplements the deficit in the budgets of smaller parishes that cannot afford the salary for their priests.

In the U.S., priests are not assigned to congregations but randomly immigrate depending on the opportunities that become available to individuals. Furthermore, because U.S. congregations tend to be small and few in number and because the diocese does not have control over the schisms in the congregations, it is not able to institutionalize a system of consistent financial compensation for the priests that would allow them to dedicate themselves solely to their vocation. Again as mentioned above, almost all of the priests in the U.S. are employed in typically low status secular jobs and most are primarily dependent on their wives' nursing jobs. Furthermore, the immigrant priests are not capable of the mobility necessary for assigned rotation within the diocese as is customary in Kerala. Instead, they become invested in particular congregations, often shifting the focus of their allegiance from the diocesan bishop to the lay leadership of the congregations so as to remain permanent vicars. Consequently, the American diocese seems to be less capable of regulating the role of immigrant priests in congregational formation and politics signifying its inability to exercise episcopal control and pointing to its incomplete institutionalization in the U.S.

CONCLUSION

In this chapter, I have attempted to understand the phenomenon of schisms in the immigrant Indian Orthodox congregations in the U.S., which is exceptional relative to the church in India. I have argued that the gendered and racialized aspects of immigration and settlement for this community has shaped the particular nature of the lay and clergy participation in immigrant congregations. Whereas the male laity's and clergy's increased incentives for participation in the immigrant congregation is fuel for the politics of schisms, I have asserted that it is the changes in organizational structures and the incomplete institutionalization of the immigrant church that allow for the possibility of schisms in the first place. I have shown how the change in organization of the local religious body from parish to congregation along with the practice of congregational incorporation in the U.S. contribute to greater autonomy at the local level. But there is a concurrent decrease of episcopal control at the diocesan level especially in the church's inability to restrain the random immigration of priests.

At this point, we are left with the question that I posed in the introduction to this chapter: Why did the reputed episcopal control and discipline fail to function in the American diocese of the Indian Orthodox Church? On one hand, it may have been the lack of visionary leadership that resulted in the random immigration of priests and the subsequent problems leading to loss of diocesan control.[15] On the other hand, many in the church accuse the first bishop of the church in North America of having had ambitions of enlarging the diocese by increasing the number of congregations and eventually splitting off from the mother church. The bishop who resigned from his office as head of the U.S. diocese in 1993 was allegedly attempting to promote a separation from the mother church in India so that he could become the leader of an independent church in the U.S. Part of his alleged strategy was to encourage the splitting of congregations so that he would have a greater number of congregations under his jurisdiction.

Whether the breakdown of authority in the church resulted from lack of visionary leadership or the Machiavellian vision of one bishop is a highly political issue that is difficult to assess. But it is clear that the phenomenon of splitting in the immigrant Indian congregations has to be seen as also resulting from the convergence of lay and clerical needs at the local level, shaped by a gendered pattern of immigration and the racialized marginalization of these immigrants in the United States.

NOTES

1. In the interviews that I conducted with over sixty members of this congregation, I was not able to get a consensus on what precipitated this incident, why these men were targeted, whether the police actually found any weapons on them and what the role of the priest was in this incident. However, there was general agreement that this incident did occur and that it was the culmination of a series of bitter struggles that finally led to the splitting of the congregation.

2. See Eui Hang Shin and Hyung Park, "An Analysis of Causes of Schisms in Ethnic Churches: The Case of Korean-American Churches," in *Koreans in North America*, S.H. Lee and T. Kwak. eds. (Seoul: Kyungnam University Press, 1988); Won Moo Hurh & Kwang Chung Kim, "Religious Participation of Korean Immigrants in the United States," *Journal for the Scientific Study of Religion* 29 (1990): 19-34; Pyong Gap Min, "The Structures and Social Functions of Korean Immigrant Churches in the United States," *International Migration Review*, 26:4 (1992): 1370–1394.

3. Shin and Park, "Causes of Schisms," 246.

4. Tomoji Ishi, "Class Conflict, the State and Linkage: The International Migration of Nurses from the Philippines," *Berkeley Journal of Sociology* 32 (1987): 281–312.

5. See Sheba George, "Caroling with the Keralites: The Negotiation of Gendered Space in an Indian Immigration Congregation," in *Gatherings in Diaspora: Religious Communities and the New Immigration*, R. Stephen Warner and Judith G. Wittner, eds. (Philadelphia: Temple University Press, 1998).

6. For an in-depth description of the history and organization of various Christian groups in Kerala as well as the immigrant congregations in the United States, see Raymond Williams, *Christian Pluralism in the U.S.: The Indian Immigrant Experience* (Cambridge: Cambridge University Press, 1996).

7. In 1987, the church synod revised the constitution to permit females under the age of five to be brought to kiss the altar along with the male children during baptism ceremony. That the church chose the age of five is not accidental. Females under the age of five are seen as nonsexual.

8. See Sheba George, "When Women Come First: Gender and Class in Transnational Migration among Indian Christian Immigrants" (Ph.D. diss., University of California, Berkeley, 2001.)

9. There are Kerala cultural organizations that also provide a space for immigrants from Kerala to get together and socialize. But these cultural gatherings occur a few times a year as compared to the weekly opportunities for fellowship provided by the church. Consequently, for Kerala Christians, the immigrant church continues to be a main space of social life.

10. Timothy Smith, "Religion and Ethnicity in America," *American Historical Review* 83 (1978): 1155–1185.

11. While immigrant women also miss their extended families and experience the congregational space as one for community and belonging, they have other options for community such as with co-ethnics in their work places. I discuss this difference at length in

"When Women Come First: Gender and Class in Transnational Migration among Indian Christian Immigrants."

12. From *The Constitution of the Malankara Orthodox Syrian Church* (Kottayam, Kerala, 1967), Section 2-A, 9: 2.

13. Stephen R. Warner, "The Place of the Congregation in the American Religious Configuration," in *American Congregations, Vol 2, New Perspectives in the Study of Congregations*, James Wind and James Lewis, eds. (Chicago: University of Chicago Press, 1994), 63.

14. From Talcott Parson's sociology, "ascribed" refers to those characteristics with which we are born such as race, sex and national origin and "achieved" refers to characteristics over which we have some control such as occupation and education. See Talcott Parsons, *The Social System* (Glencoe, IL: The Free Press, 1951), Chapter 2.

15. Elsewhere I have argued that in its disproportional dependence for financial support on the American diocese, the mother church in Kerala often allows individual members and congregations in America to bend the rules, which contributes to the breakdown of authority. See George, "When Women Come First."

NEW ASIAN AMERICAN CHURCHES AND SYMBOLIC RACIAL IDENTITY

RUSSELL JEUNG

INTRODUCTION

"My mom comes here, so I come."
>—*Joe's reason for attending a Chinese American church*

"It fits my lifestyle."
>—*Mae's reason for attending an evangelical Asian American church*

"The pastor has a passion for social justice and it attracted me."
>—*Larry's reason for attending a mainline Asian American church*

Chinese and Japanese congregations have existed in the San Francisco Bay Area since 1853 and 1877, respectively.[1] Today, I estimate 24,000 people worship weekly at 180 Chinese Christian churches and about 2,000 congregate at 18 Japanese churches in the San Francisco Bay Area.[2] These numbers make religious institutions the largest voluntary association within these ethnic communities where people have regular, face-to-face interaction. The church, it might be claimed, is the community's primary social institution in maintaining ethnic solidarity and promoting ethnic identity.[3] Joe, for example, attends Chinese Grace Church (CGC), which has served the Chinese American community for over a century. Living by himself, he visits the church to see his parents and enjoys the extended family ties within this church.

Today, however, a remarkable new movement is emerging. Asians of different ethnicities now congregate and worship together in pan-ethnic Asian American churches. In fact, half of the 44 churches I studied in the San Francisco Bay Area target Asian Americans instead of focusing on a single ethnic group. The number of pan-ethnic Asian American congregations in the San Francisco Bay Area has grown from one in 1989 to five in 1993 and twenty-two in 1998. As congregational entrepreneurs, Christian leaders have chosen a newly constituted racial group as their spiritual market niche.[4]

Why would Christians meet together along racial lines instead of ethnic lines? In this chapter, I argue that Asian American pan-ethnicity is a symbolic racial identity. Rather than utilizing ethnic cultural ties to draw people to church, new pan-ethnic congregations organize around different definitions of Asian American identity. Specific characteristics and experiences symbolize these identities. Evangelical Asian American churches see Asian Americans as young professionals and appeal to the lifestyles of their target group, to persons like Mae. Mainline congregations understand Asian Americans as a marginalized racial minority. Their concern for social justice attracts members like Larry, who want to empower the community.

To understand the differences between ethnic and the new pan-ethnic congregations, I interviewed forty-four ministers within this region.[5] Half are ethnic-specific and the other half self-identify as Asian American. And to further explore how symbolic racial identities may differ, I compared evangelical Asian American churches with mainline ones. Thirty-one of the study's participants identified as evangelical or fundamentalist and thirteen claimed to belong to a mainline denomination.[6] I then conducted participant observation at one mainline and one evangelical Asian American congregation to explore how different symbolic identities affect church programming, worship style, and group solidarity. This chapter will discuss the differences between ethnic and pan-ethnic churches, as well as explore the nature of symbolic racial identity in greater detail.

CHINESE AND JAPANESE AMERICAN ETHNIC CHURCHES

When I visited Chinese Grace Church (CGC), I was struck by the Chinese architectural motifs that conveyed the tranquility of a Chinese walled home with courtyard. One enters through a rounded moon gate into a small vestibule with a goldfish pond. Within the main sanctuary, curved lanterns hang from the ceiling and the walls are inscribed with Chinese characters of grace and blessing.

After a high school Sunday School class as we headed down to the worship service, the young teacher announced, "Time to practice our Chinese." A collective groan of resignation rose up among the kids. They all chafed at the thought of a long service that had two sermons—one in Cantonese and one in English.

By reaching out to Chinese or Japanese Americans, ethnic-specific congregations draw together around a common denominator, an ethnic heritage that people share. Mobilization of church activities and efforts around this common background establishes among the people a sense of extended family. Within ethnic-specific congregations, even the architecture and artwork pay homage to the group's culture. Furthermore, in the type of congregational programming, worship style, and commitment to church, traditional ethnic values permeate the congregations.

With the mission to serve an ethnic population, the ethnic church reproduces and transmits ethnic language and cultural traditions. Like other ethnic churches in the United States, every ethnic-specific congregation in this study offered some language instruction for native-born children and many sponsored cultural festivals and events. As the minister at CGC explained, these kinds of programs are ubiquitous:

> We have a Saturday morning Chinese language program that every Chinese church seems to have in that form or other. There's an element of holding onto your culture, especially for later generation kids to learn Chinese and to be around other Chinese kids.

Many ministers note that members may come as much for the cultural and social activities of the church as the spiritual ones. Parents might send their children to church language schools but not attend worship services or visit churches only on special occasions. One pastor cited attendance numbers to illustrate the popularity of these ethnic programs over traditional, Western Christian festivities:

> Last year, we did Halloween, Thanksgiving, Christmas and we were having like 40, 50 kids. When we did Mochizuki, we had 120 kids. So what does that tell me? Should we try to do this ethnic stuff or should we do this plain wrapper Christian stuff? We did 40, 50, 60 when we did Christian stuff and we had a bigger number with ethnic stuff, so. . .

Cultural orientations affect the style of worship as well. Pastors observe that the hierarchical, authoritarian relationships that Asians have within their family appear in how they relate to God and the pastor. At CGC, the minister observed the difference between the worship service and the fellowship time, a socializing period following the end of worship:

> The main way that I see the worship being affected is that to me, it's more traditional and formal than what I'm used to. I see element of culture in that because Chinese culture is more hierarchical and traditional in that sense. There's such a sense of being quiet and reverent before God.

> The fellowship time is just so loud. But the worship time is the time to be together. Worship is a time of reverence before God is the impression I have. I know that's certainly been so at other congregations. I think the seriousness of the liturgy is what hits me. The sermon is oftentimes more intellectual, not as personal, and I find that to be . . . . sort of a distance. It adds to the distancing of worship.

Singing and prayers at worship services at Chinese and Japanese American ethnic congregations tend generally to be more reverential and subdued. Again, traditional formality of relationships and passive instruction from authorities influence how the members respond in worship.

Not only does ethnic culture affect church programming and worship style, but it also becomes the basis of church community and solidarity. Chinese-and Japanese American members at these churches bring distinct cultural orientations that shape how they approach group efforts and church gatherings. For example, members can expect that everyone, including the children, will participate within group activities. Like the young man at CGC, a member's motivation to attend and participate comes from a sense of familial responsibility and obligation. One Chinese American minister complained,

> The issue of obligation, shame and duty has been the fuel that has run this church for the past sixteen years. And it works for the second generation because they drink that in with their mother's milk. So they tend to filter their spirituality through duty and obligation.

> And I think one of the felt needs of the Taiwanese is like, "Man, we've been serving and we don't have a life. We don't have any life other than this little, stinkin' church. They sacrifice all these things thinking that that's their Christian duty. But really, they've been given over to a family system.

In fact, this sense of duty and obligation derives from Shinto, Buddhist and Confucian ethics as well. By mobilizing upon these Asian values, Christian churches employ a cultural resource to build solidarity.

My contention is, however, that this cultural solidarity is waning as Asian Americans acculturate more and more.[7] For evangelical Asian Americans, their distinct group identity as "Asian American" is merely symbolic; the cultural content of their church experience is not much different from other evangelicals of their class background. Why then, do they distinguish themselves from other evangelicals?

EVANGELICAL ASIAN AMERICAN CHURCHES

Even though I was driving into an ordinary parking lot next to a functional, plain stucco building, I knew I arrived at an Asian American church, this one being Faith Evangelical Church (FEC). It was as if I was at a dealership for new and used Hondas. Furthermore, every third car had a license plate of the owner's alma mater: UC Berkeley, UC Berkeley, UC Davis, UCLA, UC Berkeley, Stanford.

As I enter the lobby, smiling greeters welcome me and hand me a program. The carpeted all-purpose room held two huge speakers and a huge screen where songs' lyrics are projected. Without any other symbols or adornment, the room seems set up more for a concert than a sanctuary where sacred rituals are practiced.

The worship part of the service is lively, upbeat, and focused. We sing the same simple Vineyard song three or four times before the worship team transitions into the next song that is also repeated three or four times. These contemporary praise songs speak of God's love and power on our behalf. Everyone stands, many with eyes closed and concentrating on the experience of God's "awesome" presence.

As this story exemplifies, church at evangelical Asian American congregations looks very different from an ethnic-specific one. These churches reflect very little of their ethnic culture and much more of the American evangelical subculture and the members' lifestyle. Ethnic-specific Asian congregations, especially their worship services, tend to be impersonal, formal, and hierarchical. Yet these Asian American congregations have adopted postmodern evangelical practices and are therapeutic, informal, and casual.[8] More than one minister commented that his church was so denuded of traditional ethnic influence that its worship and programs looked like any other evangelical church. He noted

> In terms of our English-speaking Chinese, if you came to our service for
> a period of time—and you could do it with your eyes closed—I'm not
> sure you would note there was anything Chinese.

In programming, evangelical pan-ethnic congregations adopt practices from contemporary evangelical mega-churches. The programs of evangelical

Asian American congregations have shifted from having a traditional Sunday School format to sponsoring small groups and occasional retreats and conferences that better fit their members' schedules. Small group meetings have become the primary vehicle through which evangelical churches evangelize and cultivate fellowship. Groups of seven to fifteen meet weekly in person's homes to study the Bible, share their week's experiences, and pray. All the evangelical Asian American congregations have adopted this format, also known as cell groups, in their own church structure. One pastor, whose church has grown from 8 to 120 in just one year, reached out to people by organizing a flower arranging group, an investors' group, and a Monday Night Football group. These groups are not tied to anything ethnic or cultural, but oriented around lifestyle affinities.

Similarly, the conferences and retreats sponsored by churches tend to be generic and not particularly affirming of specific, ethnic cultural practices. FEC encouraged its members to attend two weekend conferences that were only two weeks apart from each other. At one, six hundred Asian American men joined together for a conference modeled after Promise Keepers Conferences. The use of the Promise Keepers format again illustrates how pan-ethnic congregations utilize and accept teachings and trends from the broader, American evangelical subculture.

So what made an Asian American men's conference distinct, and for that matter, pan-ethnic congregations uniquely tailored to serve Asian Americans? The conference's workshop topics provide insight on this matter. Not only are evangelical churches programmatic, but they also are highly therapeutic and oriented towards meeting the emotional and psychological needs of individuals. Asian American evangelical ministers also focus on the development of the individual. As a result, they see Asian Americans as a group in terms of people with particular family dynamics and psychological issues. They note that since Asian American parents raise their children with high expectations, their offspring often must deal with issues of self-worth and perfectionism. The workshops, led by Christian psychologists, counselors, and pastors, included "Perfectionism," "How To Keep Your Cool," and "When West Meets East: Connecting with our Fathers." The coordinator of the men's conference explains:

> There are whole cultural nuances for Asian American men that are different than men in general in the United States. Stuff like self-esteem, how to be a godly husband in an Asian cultural setting where there are more family issues that Asian men have to face. Issues of work—a lot of Asian men feel like they're in a glass ceiling and how do you deal with

those kinds of issues—how do you deal with perfectionism, being a workaholic, those kinds of things. Obviously there's a lot of common ground.

Worship at evangelical Asian American congregations differs from that in ethnic-specific congregations as well. Given the Asian Americans' need for emotional healing, Asian American pan-ethnic congregations seek to create worship services that mediate a direct, intimate experience with God. This pastor contrasts the reverent, fearful attitude that the older generation maintains with the American-born generation's desire for personal encounters with God:

> We want to be more experiential. The Chinese would say we have to be more solemn and reverential in order to worship and experience and appreciate God, which is fine. But as I said, for those of us in the English congregation, we want something more energetic and that was a big thing. It wasn't a centerpiece, but it was very important that that keeps going.

The worship style that works in mediating Asian American evangelicals' experiences with God is clearly a Southern California cultural sensibility that is being exported around the world. The fact that Asian Americans seem to respond to it and shy from more traditional forms found in ethnic churches indicates that this cohort has indeed acculturated.

Ministers provide activities that meet the schedules, social needs, and interests of young urban professionals in order to secure commitment from Asian Americans who no longer feel a familial responsibility toward church. The other symbolic identity marker for Asian American evangelicals is their professional lifestyle. At church, one can meet friends of similar backgrounds who enjoy common pursuits—skiing, basketball, eating out. One can also join other parents who want to raise their children with the same class aspirations. Indeed, as the woman explained, the new evangelical pan-ethnic church "fits her lifestyle." One small group fellowship, on successive weekends, went skiing, biking to Angel Island, skydiving, and singing at a karaoke club. Like other contemporary evangelicals, these Asian Americans have accommodated to the culture around them and seek to maintain a lifestyle consistent with their professional class background.

Evangelical Asian American churches attempt to establish a product that meets the demand of their market. Thus, instead of the preservation of ethnic culture playing a primary role in the activities of the church, accommodation to mainstream therapeutic and consumer culture shapes the new pan-ethnic congregations. By identifying psychological needs and social needs that Asian Americans have and seeking to satisfy them, evangelical Asian American congregations also establish a new symbolic, pan-ethnic identity. The pan-ethnic identity promoted in mainline Asian American churches, however, revolves around the marginalized minority status of Asian Americans. How do these different symbolic boundaries for Asian American pan-ethnicity influence the life of the church?

MAINLINE ASIAN AMERICAN CHURCHES

The first Sunday of the month is always Memorial and Communion Service Sunday at Park Avenue United Methodist Church (PAUMC). Near the organ in the front is a table with a vase. During the memorial remembrances, names of church members who have passed away are called out. When a person is announced, a child goes up and places a flower in the vase in his or her memory. The child then joins the deceased's family or widow in the pews. A moment of silence is observed and then the next name is called out. After the pastor speaks a little about these members, a memorial hymn closes this portion of the service.

Members of Park Avenue United Methodist Church (PAUMC) understand Asian American pan-ethnicity much differently from their evangelical sisters and brothers. They view Asian Americans as a racial minority group with a common history of cultural oppression and racism. As people who have been marginalized and pressured to assimilate, they believe the church is called to rally around social justice issues and to affirm one's ethnic and racial identity. The worship service at evangelical Asian American churches encourages individual intimacy with God. Here, on the other hand, the liturgy aims to resonate with members' sense of Asian heritage and community. As a result, PAUMC's innovative memorial remembrance has become a regular ritual. The pan-ethnic subculture that emerges within this type of congregation is a hybrid of ethnic traditions, American multicultural innovations, and racial concerns.

The programs and activities of mainline Asian American churches reflect these emphases on justice and multiculturalism. Mainline congregations do have small groups, Bible Studies, and conferences like the evangelical ones, but they are not as popular as the ethnic and social programming of the church. Mainline pan-ethnic congregations, like ethnic-specific ones, celebrate ethnic holidays and festivals. Yet they sponsor these events, not so much for cultural preservation, but for ethnic reinvention.[9] Denied culture, language, and a sense of community in the United States, native-born Asian Americans have had to re-establish and reclaim ethnic pride to feel accepted and at home. They do so through ethnic reinvention, the resurrection of former traditional practices to strengthen one's ethnic identity.

Mainline ministers observe that later generations of Chinese and Japanese Americans have acculturated to such an extent that they no longer have much attachment to their ethnic heritage. American host society initially sought to exclude Asian immigrants but later developed policies to assimilate the native-born generations. As a result, Asian Americans may experience marginalization both in mainstream American society and within their own ethnic communities. The lack of cultural and linguistic competencies precludes them from full participation and authentic group identity. One priest observed:

> [Chinese Americans] feel they are afraid of being rejected. They are afraid they are looked down on because they are not American, not Chinese. They are called Chinese Americans but what are Chinese Americans? Chinese? American? They have to find what side they are on.

To address these issues, mainline pan-ethnic churches actively teach about groups' heritages and promote ethnic celebrations to families who understand little of their background. Furthermore, to become pan-ethnic and incorporate members of different Asian ethnicities, congregations have utilized a variety of ethnic traditions. At PAUMC, the pastor explained how the congregation has embraced both Chinese and Japanese traditions:

> I think because we've been a Japanese church, we need to affirm more of the Chinese presence. We're really starting to do that with little things, like with the Lunar New Year thing. What's it mean if you're Chinese and you're coming to a church that's Japanese and there's a lot of reference to Japanese things? We really need to be more intentionally inclusive about the Chinese members, about affirming what's going on in their lives.

Another distinctive aspect of the programming of mainline Asian American churches is their commitment to community concerns. For example, PAUMC is a congregation with a strong social activist agenda. As the sponsor of the denominational Community Developer's program, it has spawned several organizations and initiatives. In its efforts to promote racial justice, the church helped to create the Organization of Asian Americans (OAA), the Coalition for Racial Equality (CORE), and the town's Multicultural Center all within a period of six years. In addition, the church supports a Japanese American ethnic organization, an affordable housing group, and a collaborative with Asian Mental Health Services. Through these types of ministry, PAUMC reinforces its members' identity as racial minorities entitled to an institutional voice.

The worship liturgy at mainline Asian American churches also exemplifies the hybridized nature of pan-ethnicity. As well as celebrating core Asian values and practices, Asian American mainline ministers infuse regular Christian rituals with Asian American meanings, symbols, and elements. The memorial service at PAUMC demonstrates how mainline Asian American liturgy involves a reinvention of ethnic practices and the establishment of new ones. The aim of the memorial is to acknowledge the presence of loved ones that have passed away, to connect the children with the elderly, and to respect the Asian practice of ancestor reverence. Additionally, the church integrates the memorial, which is primarily seen as an Asian practice, with its Christian communion practice. Pastor Bill of PAUMC noted that his members were taught that Christian and Asian spiritual practices were antithetical. The incorporation of the memorial into the church service, on the other hand, is official recognition of the people's popular religiosity. The memorial expands their understanding of communion by likening it to an Asian memorial. He said,

> I blend it in with communion. Because in a way, communion is like a memorial. And so when we can blend, it's like we're just doing a worship service and we're not worshipping our ancestor, but we're remembering people and understanding that we have a paradigm that makes sense for us. It's saying that part of your life is part of your whole life and it's affirmed here.

To build pan-ethnic solidarity, mainline Asian American churches emphasize Asian Americans' common racial history and lift up community role models. Several ministers recounted the frequent Asian American experience of being categorized and treated as a foreigner in this country. One minister explained that his congregation founded an Asian American church to acknowledge and affirm Asians' experience in the United States:

> It was an understanding that second and third generation English-speaking Asians have more in common than they do different. Ancestrally, there's a difference. But the Asian American experience had very similar qualities when you look at the history of being in America.

> The need we were trying to meet was to create a place where Asian American experience would be a regular part of the life of this community. That history, field trips, activities, programs were a regular part of it.

To remember and celebrate that experience, the church took visits to Locke, an old rural Chinatown, and to Angel Island, the entry site for most Asian immigrants.

To build community at PAUMC, the pastor often refers to role models within the Asian American community, such as Fred Korematsu who resisted internment orders. According to the pastor, Korematsu is a hero to all Asian Americans because he took a stand for his beliefs. Similarly, the pastor pointed out activists in the congregation who work for community non-profit organizations. These persons are role models of people who not only experience discrimination, but also challenge it. Similarly, sermon topics on environmental racism, immigration issues, and affirmative action acknowledge the common concerns of Asian Americans as racial minorities.

To sum, the symbolic markers that Asian American mainline liberals use to distinguish Asian Americans from others are the racialized experiences of forced assimilation and marginalization. To address these issues, they employ ethnic traditions and values to recover a sense of wholeness and community. The formation of mainline Asian American congregations seeks to prevent acculturation into the mainstream American religious landscape and to establish a group identity that integrates one's faith and one's heritage.

CONCLUSION: THE NATURE OF SYMBOLIC RACIAL IDENTITY

Asian American pan-ethnicity, as a symbolic racial identity, is a remarkable, new phenomenon. The establishment of new Asian American churches reveals three significant characteristics about the nature of symbolic racial identity. First, ministers as cultural entrepreneurs define the group boundaries of Asian Americans with specific sets of symbols. This process of self-definition transforms the term, "Asian American" from a political, racial category to a pan-ethnic identity. Second, these symbols are subjectively meaningful and so salient that congregations can establish new institutions mobilizing around this identity. And third, symbols are subject to manipulation and re-articulation. As a result, Asian American pan-ethnicity is an evolving identity contingent upon one's institutional and historical context.

First, pan-ethnic churches in this study organize around sets of symbols that are self-defined and not around fixed cultural traits. Some theorists of race and ethnicity assert that Asian American pan-ethnicity is founded upon a common culture that the various ethnic groups share. For example, Pyong Gap Min suggests that Chinese, Japanese, and Korean Americans are more likely to affiliate with pan-ethnic organizations than other Asian ethnic groups might because they share cultural and physical similarities, such as a

Confucian worldview.[10] Indeed, pan-Asian congregations are more likely to have these three groups while South Asians, Southeast Asians, and Filipinos do not affiliate with pan-ethnic organizations as often.

However, the differing evangelical and mainline definitions of the group, "Asian American," demonstrate that pan-ethnic identities are fluid and subject to self-definition. Unlike ethnic culture, which hearkens to a tradition and heritage, pan-ethnicity requires re-invention and hybridity. Pan-ethnicity theorists write that racial group formation is an ascriptive process in which the state establishes racial categories by lumping groups together.[11] Yet the process of racial formation not only involves the assignation of a category, but also the claiming of an identity.

Ministers are doing just that, claiming Asian American identity as their own and defining for themselves what it means. Using representative experiences as symbolic markers, they define group boundaries of who belongs to this group and what distinguishes them. Evangelical Christians suggest that Asian Americans organize around the common upbringing and the professional status of Asian Americans to build their churches. In contrast, mainline Asian American Christians highlight the marginalized status and the cultural heritages of Asian Americans to mobilize around community concerns. Leaders of both groups claim this identity in strategic ways so that they can build their congregations and develop legitimacy among their members.

By consciously organizing themselves to meet the perceived needs of this grouping, congregations engage in collective self-definition and identity work. Through programs, teachings, and activities, these churches maintain and reinforce these identities. The Asian American subculture that emerges includes conferences dealing with Asian American psychology, and liturgies combining Asian sensibilities with Christian rites.

Second, racial symbols define one's identity and establish group solidarity by evoking strong emotional attachments. Similar to the notion of symbolic ethnicity, a symbolic racial identity deals more with the expressive feeling of connection to a group than actual ethnic cultural commonalties.[12] This subjective identification to the group and its symbols can have powerful consequences by eliciting strong sentiments, providing a sense of belonging, and securing group loyalty.

Theories of white symbolic ethnicity argue that this type of group identity involves only an intermittent, shallow, and voluntary feeling of connection to an ancestral group. For example, Irish Americans only identify as Irish during St. Patrick's Day. However, symbolic identity for racial minority groups may not be that shallow or non-consequential as these theorists suggest.[13] A symbolic racial identity may be based on only occasional experiences where race becomes salient, but these incidents are deeply significant.[14] The experiences that are symbolic of Asian Americans' identities, such as the pressure to do well in school or being treated as a foreigner, recall powerful memories and represent distinct group membership. Even though these experiences are not exclusive to Asian Americans, ministers see that this symbolic identity is common among Asian Americans and useful in mobilizing new groups.

Third, symbols are not fixed, but are subject to infusions of new meaning and reinterpretation. Symbolic racial identities may also be recast when certain symbols become less salient and new ones emerge within a group. The formation of Asian American pan-ethnicity is thus a process that allows for new reconfigurations and boundaries. Two stories illustrate how Asian American pan-ethnicity emerges.

In May, evangelical Grace Faith Church (GFC) sponsored one of its largest events of the year, a Christian seminar entitled, "Living Free in Christ: A Life Impact Workshop on Resolving Personal and Spiritual Conflicts." The speaker preached that a new identity in Christ could provide us a sense of significance, acceptance, and security that the audience felt they lacked. To experience the freedom that God provides, Christians need to renounce old lies and claim the truths of the gospel. The first step is to "renounce your previous or current involvement with satanically-inspired occult practices and false religions." Experiences to renounce include fortune telling, New Age activities, magic eight ball, spirit worship, Buddhism, and the religion of martial arts. The latter three "false religions" are traditional Asian beliefs that the families of GFC Christians hold. Embracing a Christian identity, in this case, entails a renunciation of one's ancestral heritage and perhaps, the practices of one's immediate family.

A few miles away, at the same time, PAUMC was sponsoring one of its largest events of the year as well. PAUMC holds its annual Spring Bazaar and the focus is on its teriyaki chicken, which competes with other Japanese and Asian American churches for the claim of "Best Teriyaki Chicken." Originally begun in 1959 as a traditional Doll Festival similar to ones held in Japan, this bazaar is now one of the church's main fundraisers and ethnic events that draws in old members and guests.

Upon learning the origin of the festival, the pastor also provided a theological interpretation for the event. He suggests that the community bazaar is not just a cultural event or economic fundraiser. As the community here gathers together to work and celebrate just as Jews do in the Feast of the Passover, they also share stories of their past and the oppression they encountered on the way. The bazaar itself, when people come together in sacrifice, represents the Asian American community. The pastor wrote,

> In the gathering of the people, the Spirit of Christ will remind us that life is born of sacrifice. But in our story, the sacrificial Spirit of Christ is not the "Lamb of God," but of course, the "Chicken of God."
>
> As people gather to eat their chicken teriyaki lunches, through the eating and the fellowship, in the festivity and the storytelling, the Spirit of the community of the faithful will be remembered as a new community is born.[15]

Indeed, new communities—Asian American pan-ethnic ones—have been born. The bazaar has become a pan-ethnic tradition used as a means to understand how God builds solidarity among a new community of people. As Asian American ministers do their religious work and develop their congregations, they also construct new symbolic boundaries for Asian American pan-ethnicity. By renouncing old ways, such as spirit worship, they foster "new identities in Christ." This new identity encourages emotional health and relationships that are free from dysfunctional shame or guilt. Through the re-invention of ethnic traditions as Christian ones, such as the Doll Festival, they reclaim the past and instill a new sense of connection with it. This new identity, instead of being marginalized, celebrates one's heritage. And by articulating new religious ideas, such as the teriyaki Chicken of God, they provide symbols that draw together a new racial group in formation. They have taken the concrete experiences of Asians in the United States and fashioned symbol identities of their own. Asian American pan-ethnicity, then, is not just an abstract concept, but also a subjectively meaningful identity that continues to be re-interpreted each time that congregations meet.

NOTES

1. Dr. William Speer founded the Presbyterian Church in Chinatown in 1852 and Kanichi Miyama founded Pine United Methodist Church in 1877. Both were originally located in San Francisco Chinatown and both still exist.
2. Statistics on weekly participation are derived from estimates from my research and James Chuck's study, "An Exploratory Study of the Growth of Chinese Protestant Congregations" (Berkeley, CA: Bay Area Chinese Churches Research Project, 1996).
3. In fact, 55.6 percent of Nisei and 35.2 percent of Sansei belong to a Japanese American church or temple but only 3.5 percent and 3.7 percent respectively belong to a non-

Japanese or Asian American church. See Stephen Fujita and David O'Brien, *Japanese American Ethnicity: The Persistence of Community* (Seattle: University of Washington Press, 1991).

4. The emergence of pan-Asian American congregations has attracted the attention of the media. Ryan Kim, "Asians Seek United State," *San Francisco Chronicle*, August 2, 2001; Tini Tran, "Pan-Asian Churches Emerging," *Los Angeles Times*, March 8, 1999; and De Tran and Ariana Cha, "Congregations at the Crossroads: Asian American Christians Leaving Their Parent's Style of Worship Behind," *San Jose Mercury News*, April 12, 1998.

5. Possessing the oldest and one of the largest concentrations of Asians in the United States, the San Francisco Bay Area structures pan-ethnic formation through its politics and its economy. Within the Bay Area, Asians make up 31 percent of San Francisco County, 20 percent of Alameda County, and 26 percent of Santa Clara County.

6. American Christians fall into two basic groups, with mainline, liberal, and progressive Christians within one institutional field; and conservatives, evangelicals, pentacostalists, and fundamentalists within another. See Robert Wuthnow, *The Restructuring of American Religion* (Princeton: Princeton University Press, 1988); James Hunter, *Culture Wars: The Struggle to Define America* (New York: Basic Books, 1991); Wade Clark Roof *A Generation of Seekers* (New York: Harper Collins, 1993).

7. In particular, 1.5 generation (those born overseas and raised here) and later generations of Asian Americans are less likely to have traditional cultural viewpoints and patterns; See Alejandro Portes and Ruben Rumbaut, *Legacies: The Story of the Immigrant Second Generation* (Berkeley: University of California Press, 2001).

8. Mark Shibley, *Resurgent Evangelicalism in the United States: Mapping Cultural Change since 1970* (Columbia, SC: University of South Carolina Press, 1996); Don Miller, *Reinventing American Protestantism: Christianity in the New Millenium* (Berkeley, University of California Press, 1997).

9. Kathleen Neils Conzen, David Gerber, Ewa Morawska, George Pozzetta, and Rudolph Vecoli, "The Invention of Ethnicity: A Perspective From The U.S.A." *Journal of American Ethnic History* 12 (1992):3–42; Joane Nagel, "Constructing Ethnicity: Creating and Recreating Ethnic Identity." *Social Problems* 41 (1994):152–177.

10. Pyong Gap Min, "Ethnicity: Concepts, Theories and Trends," in *Struggle for Ethnic Identity*, ed. Pyong Gap Min and Rose Kim (Walnut Creek, CA: AltaMira Press, 1999); Lavina Dhingra Shankar and Rajimi Srikanth eds., *A Part, Yet Apart: South Asians in Asian America* (Philadelphia: Temple University Press, 1997).

11. David Lopez and Yen Le Espiritu, "Panethnicity in the United States: A Theoretical Framework," *Ethnic and Racial Studies*, 13 (1990): 198–224; Michael Omi and Howard Winant, *Racial Formation in the United States*, (New York: Routledge, 1994).

12. Herbert Gans, "Symbolic Ethnicity: The Future of Ethnic Groups and Cultures in America." *Ethnic and Racial Studies* 2 (1979); Mary Waters, *Ethnic Options* (Berkeley: University of California Press, 1990).

13. Lillian Rubin, *Families on the Fault Line: America's Working Class Speaks about the Family, the Economy, Race and Ethnicity* (New York: Harper Collins, 1995), 194.

14. Mia Tuan suggests that Asian Americans who congregate in non-ethnic activities, such as

Asian American volleyball leagues, do so to maintain a meaningful, distinct identity. Mia Tuan, *Forever Foreigners or Honorary Whites? The Asian Ethnic Experience Today* (New Brunswick, NJ: Rutgers University Press, 1998)

15. Michael Yoshii, "The Buena Vista Church Bazaar: A Story Within a Story" in *People on the Way: Asian North Americans Discovering Christ, Culture and Community*, ed. David Ng (Valley Forge, PA: Judson Press, 1996), 60.

LEGACY

TRANS-PACIFIC TRANSPOSITIONS: CONTINUITIES AND DISCONTINUITIES IN CHINESE NORTH AMERICAN PROTESTANTISM SINCE 1965

TIMOTHY TSENG

When Rev. James Y. K. Tan arrived in Boston on Nov. 19, 1958 to lead the Chinese Christian Church of New England's ministry to recent immigrants from Toishan, he had been warned about its minister. This pastor's "doctrinal and theological beliefs and his ministerial style were very different from ours," evangelist Newman Shat confided to him earlier.[1] Rev. Tan was not at all certain the congregation would embrace him. He was not sure he could supply the required five reference letters. Providentially, the church and its "theologically-suspect" pastor called him and processed his immigration papers.

At the time, the Chinese Christian Church of New England was the only Chinese ministry in the Boston area (today there are more than seventeen). But its senior minister could not speak the dialects of the Cantonese and Toishanese population. When he asked Rev. Shat to recommend a minister for these communities, James Tan, then a pastor at a Chinese church in Yokohama, Japan, was tapped. Tan noted that only about 8,000 Chinese lived in Boston's tiny Chinatown, not including the dozens of students enrolled in Boston's famous colleges and universities. From the outset, Rev. Tan felt that the senior minister's motive for bringing him to Boston was to establish a financially independent congregation rather than attending to the spiritual needs of the Chinese people. "The Sunday morning services were held in Cantonese with about thirty or forty people in attendance," Tan observed, but "the evening services were held in English and were attended mostly by non-Chinese." These evening services were a revelation to him:

> The atmosphere was not that of a worship service. It turned out that this pastor organized and held seminars about China and its culture, such as customs, marriages, politics, and other related topics . . . Oriental crafts and chopsticks were sold after these seminars and a Chinese dinner usually followed. Tickets to these seminars and dinners were sold to American churches and organizations. Churches were also welcomed to invite this pastor and his wife to give these seminars and, as a result, they were kept very busy doing this. In addition, this pastor would rent a hall at the John Hancock Building to hold celebrations for Chinese New Year and other Chinese festivals. Tickets, again, were sold and usually, these events were well attended since there were many people who were interested in the Chinese culture.[2]

According to Tan, the senior minister was not in touch with the Cantonese and Toishan people and received little sympathy in return. He also felt that the church had neglected the many overseas Chinese students in Boston area universities and colleges. "I found that [the students] were very lonely here in America," Tan noted.

> They were having a difficult time adjusting because of differences in the language, culture, and customs. In addition, they felt that their spiritual needs were not being met. The American churches they attended were doctrinally sound but the students just did not seem to be able to have a close fellowship with the rest of the congregation, probably because of language difference.[3]

Pastor Tan worked with Chinese campus minister Ted Choy to help form a Chinese Bible Study ministry.[4] This ministry soon grew to an average weekly attendance of over fifty and drew students from the universities and colleges around Boston.

At this point the differences between the senior minister and Tan were revealed dramatically. According to Tan, the pastor often argued with the students at these meetings over "doctrinal differences and his liberal interpretation of the Bible." For instance, the students were impressed by the Gospel accounts of Jesus healing the sick and casting out demons. But the senior pastor refuted these "miracle" accounts, chastened the students for their ignorance of Jewish culture, and offered naturalist explanations. As a result of these debates, the leaders of the Bible Study group decided to stop holding their meetings at the Chinese church for the sake of doctrinal purity.

After only two years into his ministry, James Tan concluded that he could no longer stay at the church. He believed that neither the Chinese community nor the students wanted to join the church, so he was unable to help increase its membership. Furthermore, the senior minister felt that Tan's theology was thirty years behind the times. Tan's only reason to stay was to provide financial support for his family. Claiming that he and the senior pastor parted on good terms, he resigned and embarked on a new church plant in Boston's Chinatown in 1961. From this effort emerged the Boston Chinese Evangelical Church, a vibrant ministry that continues to minister among working class immigrants and affluent suburban commuters. This church, along with seventeen other Boston-area Chinese evangelical congregations that sprung up in the 1970s and 1980s, has captivated the hearts and spirits of many post-1965 Chinese immigrants.[5]

If pastor Tan was better acquainted with the senior minister, he did not reveal it in his autobiography. Dr. Peter Shih was actually quite passionate about Chinese Christianity. In 1953, he was appointed by the National Council of Churches research bureau to conduct a survey of Chinese churches in the United States and Hawaii.[6] According to a promotional flyer, Shih graduated with "first honors" from Nanking Theological Seminary and was the pastor of "the largest church in Hangchow, China" for three years where he preached "to over one thousand people every Sunday morning." Between 1935 and 1939, Shih was a "missionary fellow at the Union Theological Seminary in New York City" and a "Chinese Missionary to America sponsored by the World Fellowship for Christian Evangelism." During those four years, he toured the United States and Canada, "traveling over one hundred thousand miles appearing before countless audiences." Before coming to Boston, he was "for eight years Dean and Professor in West China Union Theological Seminary in Chengtu." Described as a "profound student of Chinese history and philosophy" and "one of the best scholars in Chinese classics," Shih was also considered a gifted orator who addressed "U.S. Senators and House of Representatives" in Washington, D.C. over breakfast.[7] Dr. Shih's gregarious personality and networks among mainline Protestants may have been an asset for him among the older Chinese American churches, but it scarcely impressed Rev. Tan and his evangelical peers.[8]

James Tan's unhappy entry into an existing Chinese church with historic ties to mainline American Protestantism, his subsequent separation, and his successful efforts at planting an independent and evangelical congregation is paradigmatic of the transformation of Chinese Christianity in North America since World War II. In the 1950s, Chinese American Protestantism was a mere handful of small Chinatown missions in large urban centers.

Most of these congregations depended heavily upon "mainline" denominational support. Their ministers studied at "mainline" seminaries and some of them became denominational leaders. Though the Chinese population in the United States had increased from a low of 85,000 in 1920 to over 237,000 in 1960, most of the growth was attributed to the American-born Chinese population rather than immigration.[9] Many assumed that the American-born would quietly assimilate into the mainstream of American religious life and questioned whether the ethnic Chinese (i.e., Chinese language) congregations would survive after integration.

But by 1998, there were over 1,000 Chinese churches and Christian organizations in the United States and Canada (785 congregations in the United States alone).[10] While most mainline denominations have also experienced an increase of Chinese congregations, the majority of the Chinese churches are independent or affiliated with evangelical denominations.[11] Even those within the mainline denominations are becoming increasingly "evangelical" in orientation. Paralleling the emergence of Chinese wealth in the Pacific Rim, many congregations have developed large memberships (over 500) and have become very affluent and highly educated.

This impressive growth is usually attributed to the large number of Chinese who have migrated to North American shores in recent years.[12] Throughout the 1950s and '60s, refugees, immigrants, and students from Taiwan, Hong Kong, Singapore, Thailand, the Philippines, Malaysia, Indonesia, and other countries with significant Chinese populations (i.e., the Chinese Diaspora) trickled into the United States and Canada.[13] But after the 1965 Immigration Act placed the number of migrants from Asian nations on equal footing with the European quota and after the thawing of Cold War tensions between the Peoples' Republic of China and the United States in the 1970s, Chinese immigration surged and fueled the growth of Chinese American Protestantism.

But numerical growth and elevated economic status offer limited insight into the internal transformation of Chinese Protestantism in North America. One of the most significant changes has been the "transposition" of Chinese Protestant ethos and theological identities from one that was mainline and ecumenical to one that is overwhelmingly evangelical. Chinese Protestant congregations have always been the most socially active, and perhaps, the "predominant religious institutions among the Chinese in America."[14] But unlike the past, most congregations today adhere to biblical inerrancy and require their pastors to be trained at "acceptable" evangelical seminaries. Many are apathetic towards or suspicious of mainline Protestant organizations such as the National Council of Churches of Christ and Union

Theological Seminary in New York City. Rev. Tan and his colleagues would not be disappointed by this development, for they sought to emancipate the "pure" gospel from a Chinese Christian liberalism that allied itself to the social, political, and religious elite in China and the United States.

What accounted for this movement of Chinese Protestantism in the United States away from mainline denominational affiliation towards an independent and evangelical orientation? Some may note the similarity between the rise of Chinese American evangelicalism with the growth of American evangelicalism since the 1960s. There are, indeed, parallels between this Chinese "transposition" and Christian Smith's account for the continuing viability of American evangelicalism. Smith contends that

> evangelicalism capitalizes on its culturally pluralistic environment to socially construct subcultural distinction, engagement, and tension between itself and relevant outgroups, and this enhances evangelical-ism's religious strength. The evangelical movement, we have claimed, flourishes on difference, engagement, tension, conflict, and threat. Its strength, therefore, should be understood as the result of the combination of its socially-constructed cultural distinction vis-à-vis and vigorous socio-cultural engagement with pluralistic modernity.[15]

Fenggang Yang's sociological study of an evangelical Chinese congregation in Washington, D.C. supports this view. The church provides a context for the construction of a distinctive subcultural identity that blends traditional Chinese culture with elements of American evangelicalism.[16] Such a distinct identity thrives in a contemporary setting of political uncertainty in China (and, I would add, the Chinese Diaspora) and American cultural modernization. The social climates where contemporary Chinese find themselves favor the success of evangelical institutional outreach efforts.[17]

Clearly the construction of a distinct religious identity has been a major factor in the success of Chinese evangelicals. Rather than rejuvenating the denominationally affiliated Chinese church or joining mainline denominations, the path chosen presumed significant enough differences between evangelical and mainline Protestant Chinese to warrant separation. In the case of a number of older Chinese churches such as the Chinese Christian Union Church in Chicago and the Chinese Christian Church and Center in Philadelphia, conservative evangelicalism has become the dominant theological ethos.

But Yang's study focuses on one congregation in the early 1990s and ignores the implications of historical changes and theological differentiation. He is right to posit the changing Chinese context and changing Chinese

Diasporic identity as external factors that have shaped and continuing to shape a distinctive Chinese evangelical identity, but he does not explore the internal history of the Chinese Protestants themselves or the historical contexts. Furthermore, while Yang gives some attention to developments in China, his research (like most sociological literature of immigrant religious communities) remains "America-centered" and does not given enough attention to the Diasporic contexts from out of which have come most of the Chinese Protestants that he studied.[18] Ironically, scholars of Chinese Christianity also tend to ignore the Chinese Diaspora. Studies of religious Chinese in the Diaspora are rare. Yet one cannot fully understand the transformation of Chinese North American Protestantism without understanding how deeply ingrained the Diasporic experiences were for the post-1965 Chinese immigrant.

TRANSPACIFIC TRANSPOSITIONS: RELOCATING CHINESE NATIONALISM

Sociological studies notwithstanding, I argue that the Chinese Communist victory in 1949 was a decisive catalyst which "transposed" Chinese Protestant nationalism in the Diaspora into a "different key." The Communist triumph shattered the hopes of mainline Protestants who sought to accommodate Christianity to Chinese society while making China Christian. Before 1949, Chinese Protestant leaders in China and the Chinese Diaspora were among the most active nationalists.[19] Indeed, recent studies have noted the central role that religion (and Protestantism, in particular) has played in the formation of nationalist sentiment and the drive for modernization in several Asian countries.[20] The religious nationalism of Chinese Protestants was a trans-Pacific ideology that helped galvanize efforts to topple the Ching regime at the turn of the twentieth century and to build a modern China under Kuomingtang rule in the 1930s. Among the predominantly Mandarin-speaking and well-educated leaders, there was a tendency towards theological liberalism. Chinese Christian liberals tended to blur the distinction between culture and state, and thus gave relatively uncritical support of the Chiang regime while fundamentalists sharpened the distinction. But strong anti-imperialist and nationalist sentiments were present even among theologically conservative Christians. All felt pressured to support a state-centered nationalism under the Kuomingtang and some actively promoted it.[21]

For the Chinese outside of China who had acquired "pariah capitalist" status in their host societies, the Communist victory was undesirable. Their situation was made precarious as Chinese Diasporic communities found themselves squeezed into a three-way political vise. Communist animosity towards capitalism and religion in general (and Christianity in particular) made it impossible for Diasporic Chinese to return home. Though exiled to Taiwan, Chiang Kei-shek's Kuomingtang efforts to control the Diasporic Chinese communities was also distasteful. Finally, the rise of Southeast Asian nationalism and Cold War anxieties in North America put Chinese in a precarious relationship with their host societies. Hence the political consciousness and nationalist fervor of Diasporic Chinese communities was muted in the 1950s and 1960s. After 1949, state-oriented sense of Chinese identity gave way to one that was more culture-centered. Wang Gungwu believes that Diasporic Chinese have recently started to "distinguish between Chinese culture and the Chinese state, and many now identify with the culture and not the Chinese regime."[22] The transposition of the trans-Pacific Chinese nationalism into a "cultural key" is a particular Diasporic contribution to an evolving trans-national Chinese identity.[23]

This change was certainly true of Diasporic Chinese Protestants as well. During the anti-Christian movements in the 1920s, the costly struggle against Japan in the 1930s, and the devastating loss to the Communists, "state-centered" religious nationalism all but vanished in the Chinese Christian Diaspora by mid-century.[24] The Communist victory left a vacuum of liberal and state-oriented leaders and created opportunities for conservative and "separatist" evangelicals to thrive. Since 1949, Diasporic Chinese Protestants have focused their energies on proselytizing and building Chinese congregations. The exclusive attention to the "Chinese people" underscores the continuity of a nationalist sentiment altered only by its focus on Chinese cultural identity and a self-consciously apolitical posture. With the "loss" of China, many Chinese felt like "abandoned orphans" amidst the newly created Asian nation-states, British-controlled Hong Kong, KMT-dominated Taiwan, and North America. Thus, it is understandable why many were attracted to the "world-denying" features of separatist evangelicalism. Separatist evangelicalism was best suited for the tremendous dislocation experienced by Chinese all over the world. In sum, socio-political dislocation led to religious relocation among Chinese Protestants.

BEFORE TRANSPOSITION: CHINESE NORTH AMERICAN PROTESTANTS BEFORE 1949

Because there was a history of Chinese Protestantism in the United States prior to the Communist victory, the transformation of the Chinese church was quite dramatic, if not painful. Had immigrant pastors such as James Tan exhibited more sympathy towards the history of the North American Chinese churches, their development may have been completely different.

One can only speculate what might have happened if he had seen Rev. Shih as not merely a flamboyant elitist leader, but as someone who cared deeply enough about the Chinese Church in America to expend hundreds of volunteer hours and to travel thousands of miles to help the National Council of Churches Department of Urban Ministries conduct its survey of the Chinese Churches in the United States in 1955. The only female Chinese Christian eader Rev. Tan was probably aware of was Christiana Tsai, who was living with returning missionaries in Pennsylvania. He probably did not know about Dr. Mabel Lee of the Chinese Baptist Church of New York City, who earned a Ph.D. in economics at Columbia in 1923. He was probably not aware that she had been an outspoken suffragist during her college years at Barnard College, had "hobbed-nobbed" with renowned liberal literati Hu Shih, and tried to develop her congregation into a social service ministry.

Prior to 1949, North American Chinese Protestants were vocal advocates of democracy and modernization in China. In the late 19th century, they appropriated pre-fundamentalist evangelical theology for revolutionary politics and socio-political reform. They also collaborated with mainline American Protestants to struggle for civil rights through the U.S. legal system. Influenced by radical abolitionist biblical hermeneutics and the ideology of Victorian domesticity, Chinese Christians considered themselves the vanguard of China's awakening from feudalism. Through mainline Protestant lenses, they urged China to join the world of modern nations.

By the time Pastor Tan arrived in Boston, Chinese Protestantism in the United States and Canada had undergone a remarkable transformation from overwhelmingly male missions to family-centered congregations. The "bachelor missions" themselves did not really exist until after the Chinese were segregated into urban Chinatown enclaves in the late nineteenth century. By then, Chinese women were barred from immigrating to the United States and Chinese immigrants were barred from naturalization.[25] Anti-Chinese discrimination in the United States, recognition of the Ching regime's impotence in the face of Western imperialism, and its defeat at the hands of Japan in 1894 awakened a revolutionary consciousness among "bachelor" Christians. They utilized the missions as centers for organizing and mobilizing support for revolutionary goals and the 1905 boycott of United States goods. Chinese Protestants found allies in sympathetic white Protestants who helped voice their concerns and gain some political clout.[26] North American Chinese Protestant men were iconoclasts. Not satisfied with the Baohuanghui's reformist agenda, they were the among the first in the Chinese Diaspora to advocate replacing China's monarchy with a democratic, modern, and Christian political system.[27] Indeed, Dr. Sun Yat-sen, considered by Communist and Nationalist Chinese alike as the father of modern China, and a fugitive from Ching dynasty for his revolutionary activities, found Chinese "bachelor" missions in North America welcome places of refuge, political activism, and fund-raising.

Though they were revolutionary iconoclasts, their organizational structure was not novel to these men. All-male associations flourished throughout China's halting, yet turbulent, struggle to enter the modern world. Such fraternal associations were especially popular among men who were marginalized from the Chinese family structures in China and the Diaspora. Looking at Chingquing, China, in the 1940s, Lee McIsaac notes that

> For men living in a society that validated few alternatives to marriage and family life, widespread bachelorhood had deep emotional and practical ramifications and contributed to the growth of sworn brotherhood organizations. Their association with a long and glorious tradition, as well as they popular image as a refuge for just and righteous men who found themselves pushed to the margins of society, meant that fraternal organizations were uniquely suited to playing an important role in helping to fill this void.[28]

Many fraternal associations were both religious and rebellious, thus, perceived as threats to the Chinese state.

> By providing an alternative to the models of kinship and society defined by Confucian ideology and promoted by the Chinese state, and by glorifying the bonds of loyalty and commitment to righteousness that had brought them together, fraternal organizations inevitably weakened the ties of loyalty to the family and the state that were the cornerstone of Confucian ideology. Moreover, sworn brotherhood constituted a powerful bond among men that enabled them to resist the intrusion of more formal forms of state power.[29]

It is not surprising that Chinese Protestant "bachelor missions" appeared similar to the politicized and religious fraternal orders indigenous to China, especially in a setting where marriage and family life were drastically limited.[30]

If the "bachelor missions" at the turn of the century helped awaken a muscular and masculine revolutionary nationalist consciousness among North American Chinese, the "domestication" of these missions in the 1920s and 1930s engendered both Chinese woman's social awakening and the identity discourse of second generation Chinese-Americans. This later development, in turn, generated a greater sense of ambivalence towards China among Chinese Protestants. "Bachelor" Protestants who viewed the missions as vehicles for spiritual and political activism did not invest in them as centers for family life. It would not be until the population of Chinese women and American-born increased that these missions began to resemble family-centered congregations.

Though still ensconced in nationalist discourse, greater attention was given to Chinese Protestant women and the second generation's experiences between the two World Wars. In part, this was a response to Americanization efforts in the 1920s that pressured all immigrants to demonstrate their "assimilability." Mainline Protestant women missionaries brought greater public awareness to the plight of many Chinese women prostitutes whose unfortunate circumstances they believed could be redeemed by Christian conversion and assimilation into a "normal" American-style family life. When Chinese nationalism assumed anti-Christian sentiments in the 1920s, missionaries could point to the faithful second generation who were raised in Chinese Christian households and therefore becoming just like "normal" American youth.[31] In fact, the Oriental Sociological Survey in the early 1920s concluded that the second-generation Chinese would inevitably assimilate.[32]

Finally, as the promotional efforts that linked Chinese missions in America to the missionary enterprise in China started to fall on deaf ears in the 1920s and 30s, denominational supervision of the missions was transferred to the Presbyterian and Methodist home mission boards. Reflecting the era's isolationist mood, many mainline Protestants lost interest in foreign missions during this period and were more concerned about integrating the immigrant population.

As Chinese missions became family-centered congregations, immigrant and American-born women found in them sources of empowerment and leadership development. Most white women missionaries prescribed domestic roles for Chinese women, yet their very presence and leadership roles in the congregations and community inspired a generation of civic-minded Chinese women. Judy Yung and Peggy Pascoe, for instance, have noted the importance of the Chinese congregations in the cultivation of Chinese women's leadership and family life in San Francisco's Chinese community.[33] Though most women supported the Chinese nationalist efforts during the Sino-Japanese war, it became clear that their interests were better served in North America than in China. Unlike the men, whose nostalgia for China included the benefits of a relatively traditional and patriarchal family, Chinese Protestant women had more to gain in the United States. They had greater personal choices and better opportunities to build families and community life free of the male-dominated Confucian ethos. Thus, their presence and eventual dominance in mid-century Chinese Protestant congregational life contributed to the decline of state-centered Chinese Protestant nationalism.

Because American immigration laws excluded Chinese until 1943, both the female and second-generation population grew proportionally. A generation of American-born Chinese had come of age in the 1920s and 1930s, and by 1940 outnumbered the immigrant population. They helped create a more stable Chinese American family life. The American-born Protestants also organized youth conferences in Lake Tahoe, California and Silver Bay, New York, which helped affirm their ethnic identity and cultivated a new generation of church leaders. Mainline Protestants applauded and supported these efforts, for most of these American-born young people appeared to have assimilated into American life despite growing up in Chinatown. In addition to recreation, the American-born Chinese found opportunities in these conferences to discuss current social issues, matters of "Chinese-American identity," and theological questions. The Chinese Christian Youth conferences provided an arena for "Americanized" Chinese who were conscious of job and housing discrimination to reflect on their place in American life. The youth were exposed to a brand of religious liberalism that encouraged the youth to devote their lives to civic service in China or the United States.[34] Few actually went to China because the Sino-Japanese conflict and the Chinese Civil War exacerbated the already difficult conditions there. Though most felt warmed by calls for patriotism, even more were inspired to integrate American society by seizing post-World War II opportunities to work and live outside of Chinatown. The East Coast conferences ceased operations by 1963 and were displaced by the fundamentalist Eastern Chinese Bible Conference. The West Coast conference continues to meet, but, like the East Coast conference, it appears to have lost its religious orientation. Nevertheless, these conferences were instrumental in shifting the focus of the Chinese churches in the United States away from a China-centered nationalism.

INTERLUDE: MAINLINE CHINESE AMERICAN PROTESTANTS SINCE THE COMMUNIST REVOLUTION

By mid-century the change from revolutionary bachelors' missions to family-oriented congregations was undermining a nationalism that focused on the Chinese nation-state and placed China as the geographical center of Chinese identity. But so long as China existed as a supportable nation-state, it was impossible to completely suppress this type of nationalism. This was especially true for congregations historically affiliated with mainline American Protestantism. Mainline Protestantism inculcated a concern for civic life and nation as an essential part of one's religious responsibility. Therefore, many mainline Chinese Protestants considered the support of China a part of their religious duty until the Communist victory. Today, the focus on China has waned considerably among mainline Chinese Protestants, but the concern for civic life remains one enduring feature that distinguishes it from evangelical congregations.

The Chinese Communist victory and subsequent expulsion of missionaries delivered a crippling blow to an already faltering mainline foreign mission enterprise in China. As interest in the China missions waned in the 1930s, so did interest in ministering to Chinese in the United States. In Philadelphia, Chicago, and Boston, for instance, Chinese union congregations were created from the merger of Chinese Sunday Schools or missions supported by different denominations. Following the drastic reduction of all immigration in 1926, mainline Protestant home mission policies also began to view segregated ethnic congregations as temporary and undesirable enclaves. Mainline Protestants advocated racial "integration" in the 1950s and pressured Asian American congregations to erase their ethnic identification. For instance, the Methodist Oriental Provisional Conference, which was comprised of Chinese, Filipino, and Korean congregations, was disbanded in 1956, as was the Pacific Japanese Provisional Conference in 1964. The member congregations of these ethnically distinct conferences then merged into regular Annual Conferences.[35] The American Baptist Home Mission Board did not replace Dr. Charles Shepherd, Superintendent of Asian American Baptist ministries, when he retired in 1956. After the concentration camp experiences, Japanese American Protestants who abandoned their ethnic communities and entered into the mainstream of American Protestantism were accorded great recognition and praise for modeling integration. In their efforts to combat racism, mainline Protestants supported unidirectional integration policies that sought to erase racial identities. This, in turn, led to a period of benign neglect of Chinese American Protestants in the 1950s and 1960s, just as Chinese immigration started to grow again.

Ironically, these policies effectively disenfranchised a generation of Chinese church leaders and pastors. Despite the promise of integration, very few Chinese seminary graduates became ministers in predominantly Caucasian congregations. Virtually no denominational resources were made available to start new congregations that could effectively minister to the growing Chinese immigrant population. Hence, Chinese American seminary graduates found few pastoral positions in mainline Protestant affiliated congregations. According to Jonah Chang, the assimilation policies of the United Methodist churches were so devastating that

> there was no single new church organized, no single new minister recruited, no single gathering of clergy and laity of fellowship or encouragement held. There was a total absence of plan or goal for ministry. The morale of Asian American ministers and lay people was very low, their sense of isolation pervasive.[36]

Furthermore, Chinese American church leaders could no longer look to China as an outlet for their ministerial and missionary zeal as they did before World War II. The Chinese Communist government was becoming openly hostile towards religious institutions, particularly those with European or American roots.[37]

Complicating matters for Chinese American Protestants in the middle decades of the twentieth century was a suspicion of Chinese in the United States after the People's Republic of China entered the Korean conflict. The Cold War climate contributed greatly to the suppression of Chinese nationalism and pressured Chinese Americans to demonstrate their loyalty to the United States. It was therefore not surprising when the National Council of Churches of Christ in the United States sponsored a survey of Chinese congregations in 1953, the first since Protestant home mission boards had sponsored the "Oriental Race Relations Survey" in response to a renewed nativism in the 1920s.[38] The 1953 study relied on the sociological theories that guided the earlier survey. It too attempted to prove Chinese American loyalty, cultural amiability, and the inevitable erasure of Chinese ethnicity. The study registered 43 Protestant Chinese congregations in the United States, most of which were believed to be in decline. As the American-born integrated into the mainstream workforce and the suburbs, it appeared that Chinatown churches would be rendered superfluous. Only recent migrants from China (such as refugees from the Chinese Civil War) would need a distinctively Chinese congregation. Despite some signs to the contrary, the report was convinced that the end of the Chinese American experience was "assimilation."[39]

When the study was presented to a national Chinese Christian Conference in San Francisco in 1955, its conclusions about the continued viability of the Chinese Church in the United States left the delegates in stunned silence.[40] Only one-tenth of the 118,000 Chinese in the U.S. were Christians, the report asserted.

> Few of the churches are self-supporting; few exert much influence in the Chinese community. No more than a dozen of the 60 ministers are

American-born—this after a century of Christian work, during which at least three generations of young people have grown up within the churches. That few of them choose the ministry as a life work can perhaps be explained by the further facts revealed in the survey: the Chinese churches are inadequately staffed, housed and financed; their programs are generally weak and ineffective; their ministers are expected to live on barely a subsistence income.[41]

Despite the pressure from the denominations to assimilate Chinese congregations, the pastors and lay delegates at the conference decided to form an ecumenical organization called the National Conference of Chinese Christian Churches, Inc. CONFAB, as it was called, sought to carve out a space where Chinese congregations could continue to receive the attention and support of mainline denominations. It has met on a triennial basis and continues to draw participation from Chinese churches affiliated with mainline Protestantism.

Mainline Chinese American church leaders were clearly not receptive to erasing their ethnicity and merging with "neighboring Caucasian churches" at the 1955 conference. Memories of past racial discrimination were not easily forgotten. "Wary of ventures" that would result in the "loss of identity and . . . sense of security which comes from having their 'own' organization," they worried that

> overtures stressing 'brotherhood' may prove fickle; they cannot forget the unbrotherliness of Christian Americans who thrust all people of Japanese descent from their west coast homes at the onset of World War II.[42]

Nevertheless, the Chinese representatives recognized that the suburban exodus and cultural assimilation of their American-born children was contributing to the decline of Chinatown ghettos. Yet, this came at a psychological cost to the American-born, who exhibited "symptoms of disorganization of personality and of family loyalty and unity." They also recognized the "influx of China-born or China-raised immigrants, many of them refugees of the communist revolution." Because these refugees had greater social status and education than the earlier immigrants they did not relate well to the established Chinese in America. These challenges illustrated the need to maintain viable ministries for Chinese immigrants and the American-born.[43]

At the next CONFAB gathering, Rev. Edwar Lee (1902–1996) gave a presentation that questioned the belief that the "exclusively" Chinese church would disappear. Though he noted that racial difference was one factor for the slower rate of "integration and amalgamation" among the Chinese when compared to European immigrants, he offered Chinese cultural tenacity and the continuing stream of Chinese immigration as the most important reasons. The heart of his defense of cultural particularity was a theological justification for non-Western indigenous expressions of Christianity, something that mainline Protestant missionaries affirmed as early as 1938. "It is antagonistic to Christian philosophy that all should subscribe to the doctrine of uniformity," he noted. "Christianity is one great fellowship of love throughout the whole wide earth, and it is a fellowship in the unity of diversity." Furthermore, many feel that American Christianity seeks to do little more than preserve the "American Way of Life. "Such can hardly be said to be truly Universal Christianity." Lee's point was that the proliferation of different cultural expressions of faith actually makes American Christianity better. Perhaps reflecting his sentiments about the recent disbanding of the Methodist Oriental Provisional Conference, Lee sounded a theme that seemed a decade ahead of its time: "Integration is desirable so long as it is truly voluntary." He then speculates that perhaps "one of the reasons why the Chinese churches in America are a small minority group among the Chinese in America is because we are too American. The Chinese Christian church has been looked upon by the Chinese community as a foreign institution, and its impact on the culture of the Chinese in America has, therefore been small."[44]

The irony was that Edwar Lee was an American-born Chinese pastor. He was one of the first English-speaking Chinese ministers in the United States. Trained in a liberal Protestant seminary, he became a prominent United Methodist leader among the Chinese Protestant community. Lee's calling to ministry was a response to the neglected American-born generation in Chinese churches in the 1930s. He was one of the founders of the Lake Tahoe Chinese Christian Youth Conferences and CONFAB.[45]

Lee influenced a younger generation of American-born Chinese ministers who valued their Chinese heritage highly. The Rev. Dr. James Chuck, senior minister for over forty years at the First Chinese Baptist Church of San Francisco, mastered the Chinese language and continues to conduct field research among the Chinese in the San Francisco Bay Area. Rev. Dr. David Ng (d. 1997) was the first Chinese senior minister in a predominantly Caucasian Presbyterian congregation. Later he became a Christian Education curriculum specialist for the Presbyterian Church, U.S.A. Though Ng's ministry career was devoted to service in his denomination, much of his energies went to developing Christian education curricula that was sensitive to Asian Americans.[46]

CONFAB and the English-speaking Chinese American Protestant leadership helped many Chinese congregations resist their denominations' assimilation policies in the middle decades of the twentieth century. But their resistance to assimilation was not a declaration of independence from denominations that could no longer see the viability of ethnic-specific ministries. It was motivated by past experiences of racial discrimination, the practical reality of a steadily growing Chinese immigrant population, and a vision for a Christian unity without cultural erasure. Many leaders were also influenced by the Civil Rights movement and Asian American activism.[47] By working with other ethnic Asian Protestants, Chinese American Protestants helped create caucuses within the mainline denominations and groups such as the Ecumenical Working Group of Asian Pacific Americans, the Pacific American Center for Theology and Strategies at the Graduate Theological Union (Berkeley, California), and Pacific American and Canadian Christian Education project in the 1970s.[48] None of these endeavors sought to separate from the mainline denominations. Rather, they struggled to make their denominations more responsive to Asian American representation and ministry needs. In general, these efforts have helped to reverse mainline assimilationist policies. Most mainline Protestant organizations now have significant Asian American presence and provide programs for Asian American ministries.

What many white Protestants could not see at the time was that Chinese American resistance to assimilation was itself a very American democratic practice. Chinese and other Asian Protestant demands for self-determination and representation demonstrated how thoroughly assimilated they were to the mainline denominational contexts. Though Edwar Lee and other Chinese American Protestants might have resorted to the defense of Chinese culture, their willingness to engage their denomination's structure and process illustrates how Americanized they truly were. Indeed, one of the largest challenges facing mainline Asian American caucuses today is integrating new immigrants who have not had the same history with their denominations as the previous generations of Asian American Protestants.

This point was not lost on the Chinese evangelicals who migrated to the United States in the 1960s. While Edwar Lee defended the continued existence of exclusively Chinese churches, the new evangelicals planted many congregations that were not merely exclusively Chinese, but also separatist in outlook.

THE EMERGENCE OF CHINESE AMERICAN EVANGELICALISM

To understand the origins of Chinese American evangelicalism, one must look to the populist revivals that swept through China during the early twentieth century and through the Chinese Diaspora by mid-century. Since the late nineteenth century, the predominant mainline Protestant missionary strategy had centered on gaining the approval of Chinese elites. Thus, mainline Protestant missionaries focused their work on education and hospital care in urban settings. By contrast, a number of more theologically conservative missionary agencies, notably Hudson Taylor's Chinese Inland Mission, entered rural communities and continued their focus on winning converts. Canadian Presbyterian Jonathan Goforth embraced Pentecostal fervor as a leader in the 1908 Manchurian revivals and eventually separated from his sponsoring Presbyterian mission agency. Though spurred on by European and American missionaries, this evangelical revivalist tradition was in fact an indigenous form of Chinese Christianity. The revivalists were able to tap into the millennial yearnings and popular religiosity of ordinary Chinese people. They spoke to the "heart" during turbulent times through emotional sermons.[49]

This is not to suggest that mainline missionaries and their Chinese coworkers stopped proselytizing. Notable evangelists from mainline settings such as John R. Mott and Sherwood Eddy of the Y.M.C.A. effectively evangelized Chinese students in the 1910s and inculcated many with a social gospel orientation. By the 1920s, however, there was noticeable cleavage between mainline and revivalist Chinese Protestants that mirrored the growing chasm between American fundamentalists and liberals. As mentioned earlier, the mainline orientation remained open to engagement and care for the civic and political arenas, thus creating a theological "bridge" for Chinese Protestants to participate in public life. These Christians embraced China's modernizing projects and were open to liberal theologies despite their evangelical orientation.[50]

Among the revivalist Chinese, separation from the public arenas became a mark of one's Christian identity. Separatism appealed to the rural masses, in part, because it reinforced their sense of spiritual superiority in the face of actual social and political marginalization. These dynamics were also to be found among the Diasporic Chinese revivals during the Sino-Japanese conflict and after the Communist Revolution. Evangelical separatism comforted the Chinese in Diaspora who felt alienated from China and their host country. Politically, most detested Chinese Communism, were less than enthusiastic about the Kuomingtang in Taiwan, and felt ambivalent about the British colonial rule in Hong Kong. As refugees and exiles, separatist evangelicals during mid-century were assured that they were a chosen remnant that yearned for the conversion of Chinese to their brand of Christianity.

The loss of China to the Communists in 1949 greatly deflated the "civic" voice among Chinese Protestants throughout the Diaspora and brought about an anticlimactic end to years of patriotic zeal. European colonial withdrawal from a revolutionary Southeast Asian situation after the Second World War resulted in the formation of several new nation-states. Nine million Diasporic Chinese who had played ambiguous roles as merchants and laborers under colonial rule now found themselves in precarious political positions in the face of Southeast Asian nationalism. This situation was exacerbated by waves of Chinese refugees fleeing Communist rule. Between the 1930s and the late 1970s, however, migration from China was still "extremely limited." Historian Lynn Pan observes "movements from peripheral Chinese territories, Hong Kong and Taiwan began again in earnest in the late 1970s." By 1980, 21.8 million Chinese lived in the Diaspora (not including Taiwan and Hong Kong). The population would reach 30.7 million by 1990, mostly in Southeast Asia.[51] Though often perceived as a "pariahs" in their host societies the diasporic Chinese developed strong merchant networks which eventually led to a large accumulation of capital and engaged in different levels of political participation. But, whether they lived under the defeated Nationalist Regime in Taiwan, in British-controlled Hong Kong, the United States, or in societies ripe for ethnic conflict such as Malaysia, Indonesia, or the Philippines, Diasporic Chinese were indeed a people without a nation they could call their own. This experience alone sharply differentiated the Disaporic Chinese experience from that of the mainland Chinese.[52]

From the ashes of failed religious nationalism a vibrant young cohort of evangelicals emerged who pinned their hopes on the Chinese Diaspora rather than China. While this vision centered on Chinese people rather than the nation, there always remained a hope that China's doors would once again be open to the free proclamation of their gospel. Most of the revivalists and pastors who eventually came to the United States spent a significant amount of time in the Diaspora even if they were born and raised in China. Through the middle decades, as "nation state-centered" Chinese identity in the Diaspora was being transposed to a "culture-centered" one, revivalists such as John Sung, Andrew Gih, Torrey Shih, Thomas Wang, Moses Chow, and Christiana Tsai defined a generation of Chinese Protestants who had little interest in politics or mainline Protestant institutions. Rather, because their nationalism was politically circumscribed, any nationalistic expression was channeled through a focus on evangelizing exclusively to the Chinese in the Diaspora. This separatist ethos was instrumental in shaping a religious community that resisted engagement with its surrounding social settings and contexts. Thus, post-World War II Chinese Protestant immigrants have had little interest in the existing Chinese Protestants or their history.

The Diasporic experiences of these Protestant leaders and those who migrated to the United States in the 1950s and 1960s dramatically reshaped the character of Chinese evangelicalism in North America. Though the Chinese population in the United States was not large in the 1950s, the revivalists saw an opportunity to build a support base for their Diasporic ministries there. Andrew Gih [Ji Zhi-wen] (1901–1985), probably the best-known Chinese Diaspora evangelist, honed his revivalist preaching skills with the "Bethel Worldwide Evangelistic Band." Between 1931 and 1935 the band "had traveled over 50,000 miles, visited 133 cities, and held almost 3,400 revival meetings."[53] The Bethel band was a ministry of the Bethel Mission in Shanghai, "an independent and self-sustaining holiness enterprise . . . founded by Phoebe and Mary Stone, two Chinese sisters who were medical doctors, and by Jennie Hughes, an American." All three had separated from Methodist "modernism" to start the mission, which developed a hospital, church, and Bible training school for evangelists and pastors. A number of members of the Bethel Band became successful pastors in the United States. Torrey Shih (d. 1984) started the Overseas Chinese Mission, the largest Chinese congregation on the East Coast. Philip Yung Lee (1911–1993), a gifted musician and minister, was pastor of the Chinese Presbyterian Church in Los Angeles (now True Light Presbyterian Church) in the 1940s and the Chinese Christian Union Church in Chicago in the 1950s, important years in the histories of these churches as they distanced themselves from their mainline Protestant origins and became decidedly evangelical.[54] Though John Sung [Song Shangjie](1901–1944) was a more famous member of the band, it was Andrew Gih's organizational skill that distinguished him from Sung and the other band members. During the Sino-Japanese conflict and after the Communist Revolution, Gih devoted himself to evangelizing the Chinese in the Diaspora. His missionary organization, Evangelize China Fellowship, Inc. (EFC), built churches, orphanages, and schools while creating a vast network of Chinese Christians in the Diaspora. His notoriety placed him in the company of fellow revivalists J. Edwin Orr and Billy Graham.[55] Eventually ECF established its main headquarters in Southern California.[56]

Though itinerant revivalism among the Chinese was inspired by Anglo-American evangelists, it took on a different character as a result of Gih's endeavors. Here, the evangelist was also a networker, church planter, and an organizer. In the 1960s, Moses Chow and Thomas Wang would employ a similar model and build the two largest Chinese para-church organizations in North America. Unlike the historic Chinese churches that originated with the support of mainline denominations and white missionaries on the Pacific West Coast, these indigenous ministries were started in Detroit, Michigan and Washington, D.C. Ambassadors for Christ, Inc. (AFC) started as a campus ministry that targeted the growing number of Chinese students from Hong Kong and Taiwan. One of its founders, Rev. Moses Chow, had been a pastor among the Chinese in Shanghai, Indonesia, and Japan before his call to help start the nondenominational Chinese Christian Church of Greater Washington, D.C., a Mandarin-language congregation. The itinerant networking required of campus ministry work often clashed with the demands of local church ministry. So after five years of work with both the church and AFC, Chow left the congregation and devoted his energies to the campus ministry. Under Chow's leadership, AFC took Christiana Tsai's ministry under its wings and expanded its work to that of providing resources and conferences for Chinese congregations.[57]

Chinese Christian Mission (CCM) was originally a small congregation led by Thomas Wang in Detroit, Michigan. In 1964, CCM merged with the Chinese Bible Church of Detroit. This freed "brother" Wang to promote missions among Chinese churches and Christian campus groups. That year, he toured the Northeast in a white Rambler with a large sign affixed on it that read in Chinese and English: 'CHRIST RETURNING—REPENT, BELIEVE.' At Plymouth Rock, Massachusetts, he reflected on the meaning of America with an unabashed conservative Christian jeremiad:

> In 300 years God had made this nation the strongest, the richest and the greatest in the world. There is hardly any country that has not been directly or indirectly helped by this Republic. Yet, in recent years, which the uprise and advance of sin, unbelief and secularism, there is a sharp decline and retreat of the influence, honor and integrity of America (sic).
>
> God's blessing is being forced to withdraw. We as Chinese Christians feel it is our obligation to do everything we can to sound out the warning and to call AMERICA TO REPENTENCE.
>
> We believe, in spite of sin and vices, today, America is the only (or the last) stronghold of freedom, justice, democracy and Christian principles. If America sinks, the Free World follows. Christians! Awake![58]

Over the next two years, Wang traveled thousands of miles across the United States to deliver his prophetic, if not apocalyptic, message. In CCM's English language newsletter, *Challenger*, he denounces the ecumenical movement, liberal theology, the new morality, Roman Catholicism, the removal of prayer from public schools, and a host of other signs of American spiritual complacency.[59] Remarkably, by 1967, the tone of Wang's pronouncements had changed considerably. A more sophisticated analysis of the missionary relationship with Chinese people is made:

> One of the things that annoy Asian intellectuals is the very subtle but insistent refusal by westerners to accept Asians as Asians and as equals. Unfortunately, this has also been one of the fatal inconsistencies of western missionaries as a whole. Having the Gospel first does not presume superiority over the ones to whom the Gospel is imparted. It should be a state of obedience to the One Who gave the commission and privilege.

> It would not be an exaggeration to say that such inequality accounts for at least some of the basis for anti-western feeling in Asia today. The Communist regime in China didn't need much to arouse pent-up emotions against the west.[60]

Wang remarks that the missionary must identify with the other by crucifying the self and wonders why "westerners always try to absorb and engulf Chinese Christians into their own patterns and program?" Declaring proudly that 85% of CCM expenses is supported by Chinese Christians, Wang declares that Chinese Christians are no longer satisfied with a "sit-listen-follow pattern" of relationship and "want a share of the action in worldwide missions in general and a major role in missions to their own people in particular."[61]

This particular issue of *Challenger* marks a turning point in CCM and Wang's story. Like Ambassadors for Christ, Chinese Christian Mission experienced significant growth in the 1970s and 1980s. Both para-church organizations provide local church resources, but CCM has placed greater emphasis on sending missionaries to the Chinese Diaspora. The pages of *Challenger* rarely ever became as polemic or apocalyptic as it was during its early years. Since 1967, Thomas Wang has become more involved with mainstream evangelicalism and is recognized as one of its leaders.

By the 1970s the Chinese itinerant evangelists and organizers discovered that the congregations they served were no longer as conservative, separatist, or homogenous as an earlier generation of dislocated Chinese were. Though many were refugees in the 1950s, by the 1960s, younger Chinese in the United States had become better educated, more sophisticated, and more affluent. The trickle of immigrants in the 1940s and 1950s became a tide of well-educated and highly skilled professionals from several Asian countries. Campus Chinese Bible study groups in the 1960s and 1970s were transformed into congregations filled with wealthy families in the 1980s and 1990s. Many Chinese congregations have been planted in suburban enclaves, thus diluting the urban focus of older congregations. Furthermore, the influx of Chinese immigrants from a diversity of Asian nations (and more recently from mainland China) is diversifying these younger Chinese churches and adding another layer of complexity to the growing intergenerational tensions.

Despite changes since the 1970s, Chinese evangelicalism has left an indelible mark on Chinese American Protestantism. "Separatist" evangelicals have helped define Chinese American Protestantism as a strongly pietistic and independent faith community. Consequently, their suspicion of mainline or denominational Protestantism extends even to their American-born children and is affecting Chinese congregations with historic ties to mainline denominations. One repeated Chinese evangelical critique of mainline Protestantism is its doctrinal impurity and lack of religious zeal. Evelyn Shih did not like social gospelers and the older ministers who preached cold, rationalistic messages. Leland Chinn recalled that many of the members of the Chinese Union Church in Chicago attended merely to socialize in the early 1950s, though he was conscious of the anti-Chinese backlash that had occurred in the wake of the Korean War. Bernadine Wong grew up in a mainline Baptist church, but required a more full conversion before she could claim her faith.[62]

The "separatist" outlook also conformed to the independent and anti-denominational spirit that pervades Chinese Christianity. James Chuck's detailed study of the growth of Chinese congregations in the San Francisco Bay Area is very revealing. Before 1950, there were only 15 congregations. By 1996, the number of churches has grown tenfold to 158. This growth is not surprising. Nationwide, there were over 1,100 Chinese churches and Christian organizations in 1995—reflecting an almost twenty-fold growth.[63] What was surprising was that over one-third of the Bay Area Chinese churches have no denominational affiliation. Furthermore, these congregations attract more than 50% of the Chinese worship attendance.[64]

Despite these tendencies, Chinese American evangelicals have attempted to build towards some unity. In the 1970s, evangelicals set themselves apart from the CONFAB-related churches and organized their own "ecumenical congress." The first North American Congress of Chinese Evangelicals (NACOCE) met on Dec. 25–30, 1972 in California. Over 300 Chinese church leaders participated in this meeting, whose theme was "Spiritual

Unity and Awakening."[65] Three additional congresses were held in 1974, 1978, and 1980 before NACOCE was integrated into the Chinese Coordination Centre of World Evangelism (CCCOWE), an umbrella organization serving Chinese evangelical churches worldwide. Despite the early excitement over NACOCE, efforts to bring about greater unity and cooperation among Chinese American evangelicals have failed.[66] Tensions between advocates for Presbyterian or Baptist congregational governance in many newly-formed Chinese congregations created a divisive atmosphere among Chinese church leaders.[67] Furthermore, the English-speaking Chinese leaders sought greater voice within NACOCE in 1974, resulting in intergenerational conflicts that continue to persist.[68] Since the 1980s, the vision for a united Chinese evangelical effort has fragmented. Though Chinese church splits are more rare today than in the past, inter-generational conflicts and the diversity of Chinese sub-groups have made it very difficult for any unity on a national scale.

CONCLUSION: ANOTHER TRANSPOSITION?

Despite separatism's ability to help Diasporic Chinese weather the storm of sociopolitical dislocation, it has not been able to generate any unified Chinese Christian public witness and fails to appreciate the significance of the historical development of the Chinese mainline Protestant experience. One of the consequences of the transpacific transposition of Chinese Protestantism has been a singular focus on Chinese people in the Diaspora to the exclusion of the historical and social realities they inhabit. In other words, separatism supplies the ideological structure for the formation of distinctive ethno-religious identities during periods of great turbulence— but offers few resources for Chinese evangelical engagement in their host societies.

In 1970, James Chuck offered a similar assessment in his presentation before the Chinese Christian Union of San Francisco. Noting the promise of the new Chinese evangelical presence, he also warned of its potential divisiveness over theological differences. In an effort to reconcile the Chinese evangelical with Chinese mainline Protestant, he suggested that the central function of the church was evangelism, which is "nothing less than the totality of all that the church does." The church's main task is to call people "to respond in love and trust to God through Christ," a "deeply personal, even mystical" relationship with the Divine. At this point, Chuck offers a telling critique of separatist evangelicals. Although "faith is intensely personal,"

it is *never private*. Much harm has been done to the Christian cause with
the uncritical identification of the personal with the private. True faith
always seeks to find ways of expressing the love of God in love for
neighbor. The Christian lives a "separated" existence only in the sense
that his life is *different* from, or *distinguishable* from that of the world;
but the Christian never lives *apart* from the world. He is *in* the world
but not *of* it. He relates to the world as salt, light, and leaven.

Chuck recognized that the church was criticized for not being "sufficiently
concerned about the large social issues such as injustice: war, the pollution of
the environment, etc." and being "preoccupied exclusively with personal
morality and the salvation of the individual's soul." He attributed this to the
unfortunate fundamentalist-liberal controversy where "commitment to Jesus
Christ in a deep personal sense and concern for the world and its needs are
seen as opposites." "Why could we not have said," he ponders, "that the
more deeply we are committed to Christ, the more we will be committed to
the world and its needs? And conversely, the more we are committed to the
world and its needs, the more we will see the need for the new life in
Christ."[69]

Chuck's call for a more holistic Chinese Christian ministry in the 1970s
probably fell on deaf ears among those who viewed separation as a fundamental Christian tenet. However, since the late 1980s, Chinese evangelicals
who are more sensitive to historical and social contexts have started to
reclaim "civic duty" as a part of Christian responsibility. In part, this
increased sensitivity is related to the recognition that the growth of Chinese
wealth and social status demands Christian response to the poor. Despite
continued political uncertainties around the future of Chinese in China and
the Diaspora, Chinese congregations (especially in North America) have
grown large and secure enough to begin to engage the evils of poverty,
according to Peter K. Chow. Assuming that Jesus' bias is *for* the poor, Chow
asserts that, "in building pre-dominantly middle-class churches, we must be
missing out a lot of blessings of the Kingdom. . . . In seeking the next great
shower of blessings, should we not consider an approach which can more
effectively bring the gospel to the poor?" Chow's remarkable article includes
a biblical study of poverty—an economic analysis that critiques the U.S.
dominated global capitalism, and offers models of ministry and Christian
education that incorporate these critical issues.[70]

Chow's article illustrates that the separatist ethos within Chinese evangelicalism may be waning as many of its leaders now encourage civic responsibility. For example, the influential First Evangelical Church Association in

Southern California publishes a magazine that incorporates a call for social engagement. Some leaders from this association have also formed Chinese Christians for Justice, an educational ministry that advocates for Chinese evangelical participation in social justice issues. At every Ambassadors for Christ triennial missionary conference, there are speakers and workshops that address social justice issues. There is even room among Chinese evangelicals for a discussion about gender equality and the ordination of women.[71]

Part of the reason for this development can be attributed to the popularity of socially conscious Evangelicals such as Tony Campolo, Jim Wallis, Stephen Mott, and Ron Sider.[72] The 1979 opening of Communist China to the West, the 1989 T'ienaman Square incident, and the 1997 return of Hong Kong to China have also played a part in awakening the social consciousness of many immigrant Chinese evangelicals. Though China's return to international prominence has sparked intense debates over the Diasporic Chinese Protestant relationships with the Chinese Christian Council and the "house churches," there is no doubt that China as a nation-state is once again emerging as a concern. Chinese evangelicals are beginning to reflect on their history and role in China and North America.[73] Second-generation Chinese evangelical leaders have not, in general, exhibited a similar social consciousness.[74] But among immigrant Chinese evangelicals, this renewed interest in "civic duty" confirms the argument in this chapter that links nationalism and social responsibility. It is possible, therefore, that a new transpacific transposition is underway which may reconcile Chinese evangelicalism with a history and tradition of Chinese Protestant social responsibility.

NOTES

1. James Y. K. Tan, *Grace Upon Grace,* trans. Vitus Cheng (Hong Kong: China Alliance Press, 1993), 132, 133.
2. Tan, *Grace Upon Grace,* 140–141.
3. Tan, *Grace Upon Grace,* 144.
4. Choy later distinguished himself for his campus ministry among Chinese students which eventually led to the founding of Ambassadors for Christ, Inc., one of the larger and well-known Chinese para-church organizations. Ted Choy (with Leona Choy), *My Dreams and Visions: An Autobiography* (Winchester, VA.: Golden Morning Publishing, 1997).
5. Tan, *Grace Upon Grace,* 148–149.
6. Horace R. Cayton and Anne O. Lively, *The Chinese in the United States and the Chinese Christian Churches: A Statement Condensed for the National Conference on the Chinese Christian Churches* (National Council of Churches of Christ in the U.S.A., 1955); Wilber Wong Yan Choy, "Survey Needs of Christian Chinese," *Christian Century,* 72 (June 15, 1955), 14–15.

7. "Doctor Peter Y. F. Shih" Promotional Flyer, Edwar Lee Collection, Box #2, folder 4. Asian American Studies Library of the University of California, Berkeley (Berkeley, California).

8. Mainline Protestantism refers to the historical denominations that initiated the Protestant mission efforts to China in the nineteenth century such as Presbyterian, Congregational, Methodist, and Baptist.

9. Bill Ong Hing, *Making and Remaking Asian America Through Immigration Policy, 1850–1990* (Stanford: Stanford University Press, 1993), 48.

10. *1998–1999 Directory: Chinese Churches, Bible Study Groups, Organizations in North America* (Paradise, PA: Ambassadors for Christ, Inc., 1999). *1994–1995 Directory: Chinese Churches, Bible Study Groups, Organizations in North America*, (Paradise, PA: Ambassadors for Christ, Inc., 1995).

11. Fenggang Yang, *Chinese Christians in America: Conversion, Assimilation, and Adhesive Identities.* (University Park, PA: Pennsylvania State University Press, 1999), 7.

12. Impressive as it is, Chinese growth pales when compared with Korean Protestant growth in North America. In 1970, there were only 75 Korean churches in the entire United States. Astonishingly, more than 2,200 congregations could be identified in 1998. Won Moo Hurh, *The Korean Americans* (Westport, CT: Greenwood Press, 1998).

13. One could say that North America is also part of the Chinese Diaspora, but for our purposes, it will refer to countries other than China that provide significant Chinese immigration to North America.

14. Fenggang Yang, *Chinese Christians in America,* 7.

15. Christian Smith, *American Evangelicalism: Embattled and Thriving* (Chicago: University of Chicago Press, 1998), 153.

16. Fenggang Yang, *Chinese Christians in America.*

17. Fenggang Yang, "Chinese Conversion to Evangelical Christianity: The Importance of Social and Cultural Contexts," *Sociology of Religion* (Fall, 1998) *http://www.findarticles.com/cf_0/m0SOR/n3_v59/21206031/print.jhtml.*

18. By posing the "oriental problem" as a question of whether Asians could overcome their "foreignness" and assimilate into American life, missionaries and sociologists betray their "American-centric" biases. Timothy Tseng, "Ministry at Arms' Length: Asian Americans in the Racial Ideology of Mainline American Protestants, 1882–1952," Union Theological Seminary, May, 1994; Henry Yu, *Thinking Orientals: Migration, Contact, and Exoticism in Modern America* (New York: Oxford University Press, 2000).

19. Timothy Tseng, "Chinese Protestant Nationalism in the United States, 1880–1927," *New Spiritual Homes: Religion and Asian Americans*, ed. David Yoo (University of Hawai'i Press, 1999): 19–51; Wing-hung Lam, *Chinese Theology in Construction* (Pasadena, CA: William Carey, 1983). Lam employs H. R. Niebuhr's "Christ and Culture" categories to interpret the various Chinese Christian responses to the "Chinese Renaissance" and nationalism. For more historically grounded studies, see Jun Xing, *Baptized in the Fire of Revolution: The American Social Gospel and the YMCA in China, 1919–1937* (Bethlehem, PA: Lehigh University Press, 1996) and Samuel D. Ling, "The Other May Fourth Movement: The Chinese 'Christian Renaissance,' 1919–1937" (Ph.D. dissertation: Temple University, 1981).

20. Jon Thares Davidann, *A World of Crisis and Progress: The American YMCA in Japan, 1890–1930* (Bethelehem, PA: Lehigh University Press, 1998); Peter van der Veer and Hartman Lehmann, eds., *Nation and Religion: Perspectives on Europe and Asia* (Princeton: Princeton University Press, 1999); Anthony D. Smith, *Nationalism and Modernism: A Critical Survey of Recent Theories of Nations and Nationalism.* (New York: Routledge, 1998).

21. For a discussion about how state-centered nationalism transformed Chinese definitions of womanhood from one subject to 19th Century Chinese kinship systems to one circumscribed by the Communist state see Tani E. Barlow, "Theorizing Woman: *Funü, Guojia, Jiating,*" in *Body, Subject, and Power in China,* ed. Angela Zito and Tani E. Barlow (Chicago: University of Chicago Press, 1994), 262–63.

22. Wang Gungwu, "Among Non-Chinese," in *The Living Tree: The Changing Meaning of Being Chinese Today,* edited by Tu Wei-ming (Stanford: Stanford University Press, 1994): 145. See also Wang Gungwu, *China and the Chinese Overseas* (Singapore, 1990); Wang Ling-chi and Wang Gungwu, eds., *The Chinese Diaspora: Selected Essays. Volume 1* (Singapore: Times Academic Press, 1998); Lee Kam Hing and Tan Chee-Beng, eds., *The Chinese in Malaysia* (New York: Oxford University Press, 2000); Daniel Chirot and Anthony Reid, eds., *Essential Outsiders: Chinese and Jews in the Modern Transformation of Southeast Asia and Central Europe* (Seattle: University of Washington Press, 1997).

23. Kevin Doak advocates broadening recent theories on nationalism that have focused on the concept of nation as a socially constructed, invented, or imagined identity. Citing Homi K. Bhabha's *The Location of Culture* (London: Routledge, 1994), Doak suggests that a national culture may be located in places other than the state—at least in the case of Japan. I think this can be said of Chinese cultural nationalism in the Diaspora, too. Kevin M. Doak, "What Is a Nation and Who Belongs? National Narratives and the Ethnic Imagination in Twentieth-Century Japan," *The American Historical Review* 103:2 (April, 1997). 283–309.

24. This form of nationalism, however, was demanded of all people by the Chinese Communist government. Chinese Protestant leaders, for the most part, successfully negotiated these demands. Philip L. Wickeri, *Seeking the Common Ground: Protestant Christianity, the Three-Self Movement, and China's United Front* (Maryknoll, NY: Orbis Books, 1990).

25. Sucheng Chan, ed., *Entry Denied: Exclusion and the Chinese Community in America, 1882–1943* (Philadelphia: Temple University Press, 1991).

26. Charles J. McClain, *In Search of Equality: The Chinese Struggle against Discrimination in Nineteenth-Century America* (Berkeley: University of California Press, 1994).

27. L. Eve Armentrout Ma, *Revolutionaries, Monarchists, and Chinatowns: Chinese Politics in the Americas and the 1911 Revolution* (Honolulu: University of Hawai'i Press, 1990), gives more detailed coverage of Chinese Protestant involvement via the *Chung Sai Yat Po.* Him Mark Lai, "The Kuomingtang in Chinese American Communities before World War II," in *Entry Denied: Exclusion and the Chinese Community in America,* Sucheng Chan, ed. (Philadelphia: Temple University Press, 1991), 174.

28. Lee McIsaac. "'Righteous Fraternities' and Honorable Men" Sworn Brotherhoods in Wartime Chongqing," *American Historical Review* 105:5 (December, 2000): 1653.

29. Lee McIsaac. "'Righteous Fraternities' and Honorable Men" Sworn Brotherhoods in Wartime Chongqing," *American Historical Review* 105:5 (December, 2000): 1654. David Ownby, *Sworn Brotherhoods and Secret Societies in Early and Mid-Qing China: The Formation of a Tradition* (Stanford, CA: Stanford University Press, 1996).

30. Similar dynamics appear in the study of the Chinese Handlaundry Association. Renqui Yu, *To Save China, to Save Ourselves* (Philadelphia: Temple University Press, 1992).

31. Note Charles Shepherd's two works, *The Ways of Ah Sin* and *Yim Yuk Loy*, as illustrations of this.

32. Henry Yu, *Thinking Orientals.*

33. Judy Yung, *Unbound Feet: A Social History of Chinese Women in San Francisco* (Berkeley: University of California Press, 1995) and Peggy Pascoe, *Relations of Rescue: The Search for Female Moral Authority in the American West, 1874–1939* (New York: Oxford University Press, 1990).

34. Paul Louie, "Chinese Christian Youth Conferences in America, with a Focus on the East Coast," *History and Perspectives 2001: Chinese America* (San Francisco: Chinese Historical Society of America, 2001), 47–58.

35. Jonah Chang, "Movement of Self-Empowerment: History of the National Federation of Asian American United Methodists," in *Churches Aflame: Asian Americans and United Methodism,* ed. Artemio R. Guillermo (Nashville: Abingdon, 1991), 136.

36. Jonah Chang, "Movement of Self-Empowerment," 136–137.

37. Philip L. Wickeri, *Seeking the Common Ground,* gives a fairly balanced account of Chinese Communist attitudes towards Chinese Christianity.

38. Henry Yu, *Thinking Orientals.*

39. Horace R. Cayton and Anne O. Lively, *The Chinese in the United States and the Chinese Christian Churches: A Statement Condensed for the National Conference on the Chinese Christian Churches* (National Council of Churches of Christ in the U.S.A., 1955), 69–73.

40. This conference for Christian workers among the Chinese population in North America was organized by a core of San Francisco-based Chinese clergy. Chinese clergy in San Francisco have worked collaboratively since 1916. *Chinese Christian Union of San Francisco, U.S.A.: 80th Anniversary Souvenir Book* (Chinese Christian Union of San Francisco, 1996).

41. Wilbur W. Y. Choy, "Survey Needs of Christian Chinese," *Christian Century,* 72 (June 15, 1955): 14.

42. Ibid.

43. Ibid.

44. Edwar Lee, "The Future of the Exclusively Chinese Churches in America" *Chinese America: History and Perspectives, 2001* (San Francisco: Chinese Historical Society of America, 2001): 59–62.

45. Interview with Edwar Lee in Oakland, California (July 5, 1996). Moonbeam Tong Lee, *Growing Up in Chinatown: The Life and Work of Edwar Lee* (Brisbane, CA: Fong Brothers Printing, Inc., 1987).

46. Interview with James Chuck, Berkeley, CA (Oct. 5, 1998); David Ng, *People on the Way:*

Asian North Americans Discovering Christ, Culture, and Community (Valley Forge, PA: Judson Press, 1996). R. Stephen Warner's *New Wine in Old Wineskins: Evangelicals and Liberals in a Small-Town Church* (Berkeley: University of California Press, 1988) gives some account of Ng's ministry at the Caucasian congregation.

47. William Wei, *The Asian American Movement* (Philadelphia: Temple University Press, 1993).

48. Jonah Chang, "Movement of Self-Empowerment: History of the National Federation of Asian American United Methodists," in *Churches Aflame: Asian Americans and United Methodism,* ed. Artemio R. Guillermo (Nashville: Abingdon, 1991), 135–154.

49. Daniel Bays is one of the leading authorities on Chinese Evangelicalism, See "The Growth of Independent Christianity in China, 1900–1937," *Christianity in China: From the Eighteenth Century to the Present,* ed. Daniel Bays (Stanford, CA: Stanford University Press, 1996), 307–316; "Christian Revival in China, 1900–1937," *Modern Christian Revivals,* ed. Edith L. Blumhofer and Randall Balmer (Urbana, IL: University of Illinois Press, 1993), 161–179; and "Chinese Popular Religion and Christianity Before and After the 1949 Revolution: A Retrospective View," *Fides et Historia: Journal of the Conference on Faith and History* XXIII:1 (Winter/Spring, 1991), 69–77.

50. Many Chinese Christian leaders studied at New York's Union Theological Seminary in the 1920s–1940s. For a discussion of Chinese students in North America, see Timothy Tseng, "Religious Liberalism, International Politics, and Diasporic Realities: The Chinese Students Christian Association of North America, 1909–1951," *Journal of American-East Asian Relations* 5:3–4 (Fall–Winter, 1996): 305–330.

51. Lynn Pan, ed., *The Encyclopedia of the Chinese Overseas* (Cambridge, MA: Harvard University Press, 1999), 58.

52. Daniel Chirot and Anthony Reid, *Essential Outsiders: Chinese and Jews in the Modern Transformation of Southeast Asia and Central Europe* (Seattle: University of Washington Press, 1997); Wang Ling-chi and Wang Gungwu, eds. *The Chinese Diaspora: Selected Essays,* vol. 1. (Singapore: Times Academic Press, 1998); Lee Kam Hing and Tan Chee-Beng, eds., *The Chinese in Malaysia* (New York: Oxford University Press, 2000).

53. Daniel H. Bays, "Christian Revival in China, 1900–1937," 172.

54. Lily Lee, *The Life and Times of Reverend Philip Yung Lee* (Nanjing: Nanjing Amity Printing Co., Ltd., n.d. 1994?).

55. Orr was also the chronicler of Billy Graham's Los Angeles crusades. Joel A. Carpenter, *Revive Us Again: The Reawakening of American Fundamentalism* (New York: Oxford University Press, 1997), 211–231.

56. Paul Szeto, ed., *Higher Ground: ECF 50th Anniversary Jubilee Celebration* (Monterey Park, CA: Evangelize China Fellowship, Inc., 1997).

57. Moses C. Chow (with Leona Choy), *Let My People Go! Autobiography* (Paradise, PA: Ambassadors for Christ, Inc., 1995). See also Ted Choy (with Leona Choy), *My Dreams and Visions: An Autobiography* (Winchester, VA: Golden Morning Publishing, 1997). Fenggang Yang studies the Chinese Christian Church of Greater Washington, D.C. in his *Chinese Christians in America: Conversion, Assimilation, and Adhesive Identities* (University Park, PA: Pennsylvania State University Press, 1999).

58. *Challenger* (May 20, 1964).

59. Gleaned from 1964–1966 issues of *Challenger*.

60. *Challenger* (Mar/Apr 1967).

61. Ibid.

62. Evelyn O. Shih, *Love is Forever* (Hong Kong: Chinese Alliance Press, 1981), 25: Evelyn O. Shih, *Torrey Shih: The Lord's Servant* (Kowloon: Chinese Alliance Press, 1994); Leland Chinn, "Abounding in the Work of the Lord for Seventy-five Years," *Diamond Anniversary Commemorative Issue of the Chinese Christian Union Church of Chicago: 1915 to 1990* (Chicago: Chinese Christian Union Church, 1990); Interview with Bernardine Wong (July 1, 1996).

63. See note # 10.

64. James Chuck, "Growth of Chinese Protestant Congregations from 1950 to Mid-1996 in Five Bay Area Counties," *History and Perspectives 2001* (San Francisco: Chinese Historical Society of America, 2001), 63–73.

65. Though its organizers conceived of the idea of NACOCE at the InterVarsity Christian Fellowship sponsored missions conference in Urbana in 1969, evangelicals had been involved with "conciliar" type efforts since the World Congress on Evangelism in Berlin (1966) and the U.S. Congress on Evangelism (1969). These efforts culminated in the Lausanne Congress on World Evangelism (1974) and have continued since then.

66. NACOCE Update, vol. 3 (Jan. 1980).

67. Fenggang Yang documents some of this tension in his study of a Chinese congregation near Washington, D.C., *Chinese Christians in America: Conversion, Assimilation, and Adhesive Identities.*

68. The formation of the Fellowship of American Chinese Evangelicals (FACE) in 1979 was a direct result of efforts to give English-speaking Chinese evangelicals greater voice. Dialogue and debate were carried by Chinese Christian Mission's *Challenger* Magazine and FACE's *About Face.* Some of the articles were compiled in *A Winning Combination: Understanding the Cultural Tensions in Chinese Churches* (Chinese Christian Missions, 1986).

69. James Chuck, "Where are the Chinese Churches Heading in the 1970's?" Private paper presented before the Chinese Christian Union of San Francisco, Feb. 28, 1980.

70. Peter Chow, "Good News to the Poor: A Perspective on Church Growth, Social Ethics, and Christian Education," *Chinese in North America* (Jan.–Feb., 1989), 3–10.

71. For example, see the Social Concern issue of the *Bulletin: First Evangelical Church Association* (April 1999); Dr. Paul Sui, "The Social Responsibility of the Church," in the newsletter of the Chinese Bi-cultural and Pastoral Ministries Program of the Alliance Theological Seminary (Spring, 2000); Cecilia Yau, Dora Wang, Lily Lee, *A Passion for Fullness: Examining the Woman's Identity and Roles from Biblical, Historical, and Sociological Perspectives* [in Chinese]; Grace Ying May & Hyunhye Pokrifka Joe, "Setting the Record Straight: A Response to J. I. Packer's Position on Women's Ordination," *Priscilla Papers,* 11:1 (Winter 1997).

72. Janet Furness and Timothy Tseng, "The Reawakening of Evangelical Social

Consciousness" in *The Social Gospel Today,* edited by Christopher Evans (Louisville, KY: Westminster/John Knox, 2001): 114–125.

73. Wing Ning Pang, "The Chinese American Ministry," in *Chinese in North America* (Jan.–Feb., 1989): 11-17; Rudolf Mak, "The North American Chinese Church and Missions: Lessons from a Historical Analysis," *Chinese Around the World* (May, 2001): 4–13. See also Samuel D. Ling, "The Other May Fourth Movement: The Chinese 'Christian Renaissance,' 1919–1937"; and Wing-Hung Lam, *Chinese Theology in Construction* (Pasadena, CA: William Carey Library, 1983).

74. The ambiguity that surrounds American-born or raised Chinese can be seen in Clarence Cheuk, "Our Enigmatic Generation: A Second Generation ABCX Perspective," in *The "Chinese" Way of Doing Things* ed. by Samuel Ling (San Gabriel, CA: China Horizon, 1999), 3–14.

TULE LAKE PILGRIMAGE: DISSONANT MEMORIES, SACRED JOURNEY

JOANNE DOI, M.M.

INTRODUCTION

In July of 1996, I embarked on the Tule Lake Pilgrimage with academic interest as a graduate student and member of the broader Japanese American community. To my knowledge at that time, I had no direct relatives who had been detained at Tule Lake during World War II. My research indicated that as a Segregation Camp, the sociopolitical climate of Tule Lake was the most polarized and conflictive of the ten "camps," with eruptions of strikes, and the imposition of detention and torture. To fully comprehend any of the particular U.S. concentration camp realities, it was important to understand the significance of Tule Lake. My objective interests soon encountered deeper layers. I was truly embarking on a pilgrimage, both inner and outer, that continues to re-weave fragments of identity, family, community, memory, and history.

I encountered two of my first cousins on the 1996 pilgrimage and discovered that an uncle from my mother's side and the family of my first cousin's husband had been detained in Tule Lake. These family links brought me further inside the experience of Tule Lake. By the end of the first pilgrimage, I realized that we are all affected in some way by the reality of Tule Lake, directly and indirectly. I welcomed this painful knowledge as a gift as it paradoxically brought a sense of wholeness. This new knowledge re-positioned me into the "intermediate space" about which anthropologist Ruth Behar writes:

> I think what we are seeing are efforts to map an intermediate space we
> can't quite define yet, a borderland between passion and intellect, analy-
> sis and subjectivity, ethnography and autobiography, art and life.[1]

This essay is an exploration of the layers of multiple meanings of the Tule
Lake Pilgrimage of July 4–7, 1996, which commemorated the 50th anniversary of the closing of the Tule Lake Relocation and Segregation Center for
persons of Japanese ancestry during World War II. More specifically: what is
the explicit or implicit religious motivation or goal; how is the Tule Lake
Pilgrimage a sacred journey, a phenomenon of religious experience? A Sansei
participant reflects:

> Making a pilgrimage to the site of an old prison camp was paradoxical
> in many ways for me. I had conjured up the notion that pilgrimages
> were typically religious journeys to destinations where one got closer to
> God. Stepping off the bus onto the hot, dusty floor of this dried-up
> lakebed, and guessing how my parents might have felt arriving at a sim-
> ilar camp, I immediately concluded that this was instead a God-
> forsaken place.[2]

Richard Niebuhr writes: "The boundaries of the pilgrimage category are
defined solely by the limits of the human imagination."[3] Pilgrimage involves
journey, place, seeking, intent, transformation, and renewal of life. It is a
complex process that provides a matrix composed of literary, spatial, geographical, cultural, social, ritual, and religious themes. At the same time, it is
a basic human process that is engaged in embodied spiritual planes, accessible to the hundreds of millions of people who go on pilgrimage each year.
The Latin roots of the word, "pilgrimage," *per ager*, mean "through the
fields" or *peregrinatio*, which means, "simply going abroad, to go pray at."[4]
Pilgrimage is a collective process, "human beings together on the way."[5]

There is a multiplicity of pilgrimages, from the prototypical that reveal
the root paradigms of a particular faith tradition, to the post-medieval that
contest the advancing secularization of the post-Darwinian world.[6] It is
helpful to recognize similar stages that characterize pilgrimage in general:
separation from the status quo, passage through a threshold, regeneration
and a return to social responsibility.[7] At the heart of pilgrimage is the sense of
journey, not simply in ordinary time and space but with a heightened awareness of the physical and symbolic journey in which spiritual and social transformation takes place.[8] The journey of the Tule Lake Pilgrimage is located
within the late twentieth century and responds to the historical sociopolitical
parameters and religious frameworks of its participants in the U.S. context.

Yet it is a pilgrimage back in time to a struggle fifty years in the past; it is a journey to the specific place that evokes memories of that time. Layers of meaning, memory, healing, and ongoing commitment begin to emerge. I propose that the Tule Lake Pilgrimage is a postmodern or, more accurately, a post-colonial pilgrimage.[9]

HISTORICAL CONTEXT OF THE 1996 TULE LAKE PILGRIMAGE

The Tule Lake Pilgrimage originated back in 1969 when students, community activists, and former internees organized the first pilgrimage to Newell, California, near the Oregon border.[10] This was motivated by the energies of the Civil Rights movements, the cognitive dissonance, and the desire to recover long-suppressed histories. The Tule Lake Pilgrimage is intentionally scheduled around the Fourth of July. David Mitoma of Oakland reflects: "There was a struggle here, and it was about freedom."[11] There have been thirteen subsequent pilgrimages through the year 2002. With continual interest, the pilgrimages will be organized bi-annually. These pilgrimages emphasize the significance of this ongoing movement back in time for the construction of meaning and identity for Japanese Americans and the multicultural reality of the U.S. that is part of American history. A reconnection to a pivotal time in the past, a reconnection to the lives of those who passed through barbed wire fences into a permanent sense of displacement reveals the painful liminal reality that pervades subsequent generations. The place of in-between reveals being at the margins of what may be commonly understood as Japanese and American. Yet this pilgrimage to a place of historical suffering is also a journey of honor and gratitude for the courage, perseverance, and sacrifice that made it possible for future generations of Japanese Americans to flourish. To revisit and remember is to gain a deeper "understanding and appreciation for the enduring spirit that continues far beyond the bounds of barbed wire."[12] It is to recognize the very sacredness of our lives.

To revisit and remember is to give voice to a complex silence. For the internees of Japanese ancestry, the majority of them U.S. citizens, it was a mixture of the shame of victims and of the guilt assumed for the act of the Japanese military in attacking Pearl Harbor that, in part, enveloped what happened in a cloak of silence during the post-war years.[13] As one internee explained:

> We felt we were raped by our own country—raped of our freedom, raped of our human dignity, and raped of our civil liberties. A rape victim feels guilt and shame. A victim of rape feels violated, unclean. And so it is with us.

We felt that somehow we were party to this act of defilement, that we had somehow helped to bring it on. We, innocent victims, felt guilt and shame about it all. . . . We had internalized a lot of our feelings for a long time. We had repressed these feelings.[14]

As a Segregation Camp, Tule Lake was the destination of the disloyals or the "no-no's." This was the result of the loyalty review, a process established to determine loyalty as a basis for release that became one of the most wrenching aspects of the captivity.[15] Implemented in a coercive manner, the loyalty review became a kind of wartime inquisition of Japanese Americans. Seeking personal background information, the questionnaire included the following questions: number 27: "Are you willing to serve in the armed forces of the United States whenever ordered?"—This basically asked the internees if they were willing to serve in the same army that had confined them, asking them to fight for the principles of liberty, justice and equal protection under the law, which had been denied them. Number 28: "Will you swear unqualified allegiance to the U.S.A. and faithfully defend the U.S. from any or all attack by foreign or domestic forces and foreswear any form allegiance or obedience to the Japanese emperor, to any other government, power, or organization?" To answer yes to this for the Issei, first generation, meant being left without a country as they were legally barred at that time from becoming naturalized U.S. citizens. For the Nisei, second generation, it was a trick question: to foreswear allegiance to an emperor you had never known implied some loyalty to begin with. To answer "no-no" to questions 27 and 28 destined you for Tule Lake. The Tule Lake internees were stigmatized even further as the loyalty/disloyalty issue created a fault line within the Japanese American community itself. Many, although not all, who answered "yes-yes" looked with suspicion upon the "no-no's."

The complexity of this silence also bore a respect for the painfulness of this historical disjuncture and the desire to protect the Sansei, third generation, from knowing that they were regarded as second-class citizens. Although the Nisei may have wanted to protect their children from this burden of knowledge, the silence "rather than representing the absence of something, highlighted the presence of feelings too complex and painful to discuss."[16] When interpreted in a public arena, silence can be seen as an acceptance or even passive endorsement of the injustice suffered. Eventually, for the Sansei, however, the silence of the Nisei signified the presence of a pain that could not be directly expressed. Donna Nagata aptly notes that the "silence that follows instances of massive and/or severe injustices can actually communicate the extensiveness of injustice rather than an acceptance of it."[17] The Nisei's silence underlined the displacement from their own public and personal histories, leaving them and their Sansei children without a complete sense of self-understanding. As the Sansei grew into young adulthood and began to experience this cognitive dissonance, this painfulness in part motivated the beginnings of the Days of Remembrance and pilgrimages to various relocation campsites in the 1970s. These were attempts to search out the truth of the history bound up in the silence of the Nisei and the classroom. The magnitude of the silence of the Nisei helped form the voice of the Sansei; the Nisei's absence of outward emotional response mobilized the Sansei to begin to speak out.

The connection between the pilgrimages to various internment campsites and the Redress Movement are obvious. Along with Days of Remembrance, the pilgrimages were a catalyst for the Japanese American community, enabling a space for the intergenerational community to come to terms with long buried emotions and to realize that a great injustice had been done by the U.S. government. This process garnered the emotional commitment to engage in the campaign for redress.[18] Yet in the years following the passage of the Civil Liberties Act of 1988 that granted redress to the survivors of internment, the Days of Remembrance and pilgrimages continued in response to the spiritual need for healing both persons and communities.[19] Joy Kogawa writes, "to a people for whom community was the essence of life, destruction of community was the destruction of life."[20] As it meant the termination of their communities on the West Coast, relocation and internment were attacks not merely on persons and their possessions but on their very spiritual existence.[21] The pilgrimages to internment campsites continue to renew community bonds. The diversity of racial-ethnic and geographic backgrounds among the pilgrimage participants also broadens the sense of community.

While recognizing the psychological complications of being unable to connect to the past, to reconnect to collective memory, however, does not merely remain in an individualistic therapeutic realm. To reconnect to collective memory is to regain the sense of being a community of memory, to develop practices of commitment. Robert Bellah notes that a genuine community of memory tells painful stories of shared suffering.

> The communities of memory that tie us to the past also turn us toward the future as communities of hope. They carry a context of meaning that can allow us to connect our aspirations for ourselves and those closest to us with the aspirations of a larger whole and see our own efforts as being, in part, contributions to a common good.[22]

THE PILGRIMAGE

The Tule Lake Pilgrimage is not convoked explicitly by any particular religious group. With each pilgrimage, the Tule Lake Committee, a volunteer nonprofit organization, is composed anew of volunteers who are mainly from the Japanese American community although are not limited to it. The Buena Vista United Methodist Church in Alameda, California offers supportive infrastructure and a place to meet but the religious affiliations of the committee members and pilgrimage participants are of a broad range: Buddhist, Protestant denominations, Catholic, Shinto, an interreligious combination of traditions or no particular religious affiliation. Many traditions, are implicitly involved through the diversity of the community.

At first glance, the Tule Lake Pilgrimage resembles the familiar bus tours to vacation places organized by Japanese American community groups. In fact, one of the optional activities is a tour to the nearby Lava Beds National Monument that seemingly has no direct connection to the historical experience of the internment.[23] In some sense, tourism and pilgrimage co-exist in this journey to Tule Lake. There is need for the option of psychic space during this difficult return to a historical place and time of suffering. Multiple activities are characteristic of pilgrimage, such as the marketplaces that are part of the classic pilgrimages to established sacred shrines. For authors such as MacCannell and Graburn, tourism is the pilgrimage of modern times.[24]

Nearly 300 people, some from as far away as Chicago, Detroit, Seattle and Los Angeles, boarded buses leaving from San Jose, San Francisco, Oakland, Berkeley, and Sacramento. The seven-hour bus ride was an integral part of the pilgrimage, the first of many places of encounter across generations of friends, former internees, and memories, setting the tone of the journey. People shared why they came on the pilgrimage; videos shown of the internment camps sparked stories. It was noted that for many, redress began a healing process; the supportive environment of the pilgrimage offers unique opportunities for former internees of all camps, their families, and others to share and reflect on evoked memories and experiences. The pilgrimage is open to veterans, "no-no's," former internees of all the concentration camps, different religions, generations, ages, and ethnicities. En route, origami cranes were folded for the memorial service to be held at the Klamath Falls Cemetery for those who died at Tule Lake. The First United Methodist Church of Redding provided a Japanese-style lunch; the atmosphere of food and community brought back memories of the familiar church bazaars that resembled the Obon festivals that remember and honor the dead during the summer months.

We arrived that evening at the Oregon Institute of Technology (OIT) in Klamath Falls where the participants were housed and activities and exhibits were held. Cafeteria-style meals continued to foster the community atmosphere. The Welcome Program emphasized this moment of encounter with our legacy of suffering, hope, and commitment. We make pilgrimages by accompanying each other in community to the places that evoke the memories of the past, hearing the sacredness of stories told and untold, honoring the sacrifices of the dead and the living, celebrating who we are. "Here difficult experiences are safe to explore. Together we will experience more than you could alone."[25] The evening ended with Fourth of July fireworks.

The next morning the buses departed for the twenty-minute ride to the site of the Tule Lake "camp site." Over 18,000 internees had been housed in tarpaper barracks hastily built upon a dried up lakebed encrusted with lava rock, surrounded by Abalone Mountain and Castle Rock. Not much remains today. The organizers have placed small white flags to mark remnant ruins of gardens, the Japanese-style bath tubs (*ofuro*) built with wood scraps by the internees, a few cement foundations of shower rooms. Ironically, there was a low-lying fence of barbed wire that we had to crawl through in order to roam the site. Overgrown tule grass stretched beyond where the eye could see of the 3,800 acres. As one pilgrim remarked, "The desolation caught me by surprise."[26] Others recalled the blinding dust storms and bitter cold winters. Some, while foraging through the sand to find small white seashells amidst rugged tule grass, remembered how their mothers would create beautiful jewelry, woven purses and hats. Quiet searching, taking photographs, low conversations, listening to stories, listening to the wind marked this first stop at the western end of the former camp site, originally surrounded by 32 miles of fencing, 100 miles of barbed wire, and 16 guard towers. We lingered an hour before re-boarding the buses to visit the southern end where the stockade is still standing.

The infamous stockade with eighteen-inch concrete walls was "still standing like a resolute sentinel of our confinement."[27] A prison within a prison for this Segregation Camp of "troublemakers," the tiny cells had at one point held as many as 200 men, many brutally beaten. Small windows with bent iron bars, cold cement floors, and some writings on the wall in Japanese and English evoked the memories of suffering, desperation and courage. One of the decipherable writings read: "When the golden sun has sunk beyond the desert horizon, and darkness followed, under a dim light casting my lonesome heart." Our busloads of pilgrims moved through the stockade as if in a church.

After visiting the stockade, a picnic lunch at the Newell School located on the edge of the former campsite broke the silence and heaviness as food and conversation seemed to strengthen the group, as old friends re-united and new friendships kindled. As we visited next a former barracks building now used as a storage shed for the present farmlands, the everyday stories of daily survival seemed to flow more easily. After a brief stop in the town of Newell, we returned to OIT for a panel discussion consisting of former internees and community representatives. Intergenerational discussion groups were organized for the evening. With both difficulty and release, many of the memories evoked throughout the day were shared.

The next morning, the buses departed for the Linkville Cemetery in Klamath Falls, burial place of those who died at Tule Lake, where an interfaith Memorial Service was held. For the remainder of the day, the buses departed to various destinations for the optional activities. A closing cultural ceremony was held in the evening, a celebration of movement, song, poetry and prayer. The following morning, after a lively group photo session, we began our return journey down the spine of California, using the now familiar bus-ride discussions to reflect on the changes and insights gained during the pilgrimage.

"To pilgrimage it"[28] is to enter into or embark on a sacred journey motivated by both a dis-ease and cognitive dissonance and "a quest of a place or a state that he or she believes to embody a valued ideal."[29] Erik Cohen, whose pilgrimage studies build on the Eliadean notion of a sacred center, understands pilgrimage as a movement towards the center, which is the source of the social-moral order of the cosmos. Cohen makes the distinction that the traveler in contrast with the pilgrim moves in the opposite direction towards the "Other," located beyond the boundaries of the cosmos into the surrounding chaos. Understood in this way, the Tule Lake Pilgrimage could be seen as moving away from the center as it enters into the chaos of suffering, that which has torn apart our webs of significance.

Yet it is not the direction of the movement itself that strictly distinguishes the pilgrim from the traveler, but the intent. The traveler seeks to escape, to vacate, while the pilgrim's goal is towards a renewal, a regained wholeness, a re-centering. The Tule Lake Pilgrimage as sacred journey can be understood as an attempt to regain our center as human persons and community by reconnecting to our history and each other on the periphery, on the margins. It is a sacred journey to our own otherness that brings us home to ourselves. It is not escape but a return to the center of our history, the pivotal events that have marked us as Japanese Americans. In a paradoxical way, the center of our history located on the margins recreates and revitalizes as the truth of who we are shifts into place.

More than history, it is to reconnect to memory. The Tule Lake Pilgrimage provides the space and engagement in a mnemonic landscape, the topography of collective memory.[30] To reconnect to memory is not to connect to one fixed meaning or historical event but to enter into a living process. Historical context and data are important but memory is not limited to a retelling of the facts in exact chronological order. It is concerned with the lived experience, with the internal history of subjects and not the objects of external history. Historical memory is thus apprehended from within and belongs to the destiny of persons and communities. It is concerned about values and meaning, a central ordering moment. Historical memory focuses on how explorations in the past relate to the present and the future, and on the will to remember to the point of creating memory in a context that no longer incorporates memory in daily living.[31] Re-entering into the chaos of suffering and its lack of interpretability is precisely re-engaged in order to articulate out of the silence and give voice to both the suffering and that which made the suffering bearable, resisting the challenge of emotional meaninglessness.[32]

The separation from the status quo releases the pilgrims from mundane structure. The pilgrims enter into a liminality, an in-betweenness. Van Gennep identified liminality as a transformative dimension of the social, intrinsic to the process of change. Outside of the differentiated and often hierarchical system, there is openness to "communitas," the experience of the generic human bond with others. "Community is the being no longer side by side (and, one might add, above and below) but with one another of a multitude of persons."[33] Communitas represents the *élan vital* or life force of human interrelatedness and breaks in through "the interstices of structure, in liminality."[34]

Pilgrimage is voluntary and not an obligatory social mechanism to mark the transition of an individual or group from one status to another, such as the life-cycle rituals from adolescence to adulthood. Rather than being integrated into the whole social process, pilgrimages develop along the margins; they are plural, fragmentary, and experimental in character.[35] The Tule Lake Pilgrimage is a voluntary movement that grows out of our marginal reality as Asian Americans that enables us to embrace our liminal reality. As Fumitaka Matsuoka writes:

> The search for identity as reflected in Asian American communities of faith has more to do with the question of what it means to live a life that defies any attempt for a definition than with the question of who we are socially, psychologically, or even ethnically. The search for Asian American identity is also a quest for freedom to live in a world of ambi-

guity, in the midst of the "holy insecurity" of our liminal
existence. . . . To embrace this is to receive the gift of courage to live in
the midst of an unresolved and often ambiguous state of life.[36]

The Tule Lake Pilgrimage provides the opportunity to embrace our liminal nature by connecting to the lived experience and legacy of the Issei and
Nisei generations in both their suffering and spiritual strength. It allows us
to enter into this deeper level of existence. It returns us from the pitfall of
considering the American heritage as exclusively an extension of European
tradition in contradistinction to our Asian cultural traditions, and begins to
shed light on our world of meaning as Japanese Americans.[37] Similar to
Hispanic Americans, we are in between. We find we are neither American
nor Japanese and yet we are both. And we are also something new, in an
emerging "third space."[38] This in-between life is not something to be
resolved, solved or transcended but "to be cherished and nurtured, for it is
indeed the revelation of God."[39] This engagement of our deeper level of existence is not in order to move back into a given structure that relegates us to
our "racial uniform"[40] in the midst of the alienating universalism imposed by
the dominant cultural group. Rita Nakashima Brock names the interstitial
integrity that opens ways of speaking about the construction of complex
cross-cultural identities, facing the task of making meaning out of multiple
worlds by refusing to disconnect from any of them.[41]

The Tule Lake pilgrims experienced communitas during the collective
moments of the bus rides and visiting the site together, the cultural programs, the memorial service for the dead, the meal times, and even the photo
session at the end. This nurtures the desire for the renewal of communities in
our cities and the continued organization of subsequent pilgrimages. The
challenge of communitas inspired the efforts and success of the redress
movement yet redress was concomitant to the process and struggle of
remembrance, not its only end goal. Victor Turner understands redress in
terms of structure, anti-structure, and revitalizing the structure. In light of
post-redress questions and reflections that take Japanese Americans to questions concerning more than redress, the Turnerian paradigm seems to reach a
limitation. What would redress look like for Native Americans, African
Americans, and Hispanic Americans? More than revitalizing the structure,
there is a growing sense that structural change itself is called for in a system
that has its roots in racism. It is no longer a question of modifying a structure
but envisioning another way of relating across difference that is inter-
relational and mutual. Contrasting aspects may co-exist rather than difference being only seen as oppositional.[42]

The Tule Lake Pilgrimage as a sacred journey with the dead becomes explicit particularly at the Interfaith Memorial Service. At the memorial service, Rev. Masuda, the Buddhist priest, reminded us to listen to the silence while on our pilgrimage back into time by quoting Basho:

> pond   frog jumps   the sound of water. [43]

He remarked on the usual English translation of "Splash!" for the third line. It is rather "the sound of water" for the frog that jumps is our conditional self that dives into the waters of wisdom, compassion, interconnectedness, timelessness, faith. "Rather than see the splash of water on the surface, we must listen in silence for the sound that echoes through the water's depths and also through lives."[44] In that silence, the voices, both the dead and the living, of Tule Lake are heard.

"Structural distance may be an apt symbol for death," notes Turner, a metaphoric death from the negative, alienating aspects of systems and structures.[45] He further notes that "the limen of pilgrimage is motion, the movement of travel, and that this liminalizes time; time is connected to voluntariness."[46] Voluntary election to go on pilgrimage expresses a willingness to enter the betwixt-and-between state where the dead, in a sense, inhabit timelessness. Instead of regarding the dead as "filthy and polluting," he proposes that in the interstitial realm in the pilgrimage process, the dead are conceived as transformative agencies and as mediating between what are normally classified as distinct realms. We are "in communion with the dead."[47]

Recalling Shinto and Buddhist traditions, there is a desire to console the dead as well as pay homage; consolation and gratitude are expressed in the ritual gestures of prayer and incense in the Buddhist style of *gasho*. Colorful origami cranes folded on the bus ride at the beginning of the pilgrimage are offered as expressions of homage, healing and commitment. A symbol of longevity, happiness, and prosperity in Chinese and Japanese mythology, the origami crane also became a symbol of peace after the war through the well-known story of Sadako and the Thousand Cranes. Each year, Japanese school children place thousands of colorful origami cranes on Peace Day at the Hiroshima Peace Park where a statue of Sadako holds a golden crane in outstretched hands. Visually and symbolically connecting the suffering and the dead of the two places of Hiroshima and Tule Lake, the cranes at the Linkville Cemetery honor the dead, are prayers for healing, and a commitment to be messengers of hope and reconciliation in our world.

Remembering and embracing the dead of Tule Lake, in many ways is symbolic of embracing our own otherness that is considered pollution, an impurity for a structure that has no categories where we fit. Yet "that which is rejected is ploughed back for a renewal of life," notes Mary Douglas in her image of composting religion.[48] Dirt, decay, pollution, formlessness, uncleanness is expressed ultimately by death. Confronting death and grasping it firmly says something about the nature of life. "When someone embraces freely the symbols of death, or death itself, then it is consistent with everything we have seen so far, that a real release of power for good should be expected to follow."[49] In communion with the dead, we also reconnect to the sacredness of our lives, both living and dead. This has the potential to transform the painful liminal reality of our lives into the space of interstitial integrity.[50] In the memorial service, there was a release of pain. "It was peaceful and oddly, crickets sang in broad daylight."[51] The same Sansei participant who had spoken of Tule Lake as a God-forsaken place afterwards reflected:

> As the two ministers spoke of the importance of breaking silences to honor the past and mend the future, I knew that, despite coming face to face with the horrible injustices and indignities of camp life, I had found some peace here. I looked around at the heads bowed in prayer and families holding hands, and I knew that this was an extraordinary beginning.[52]

In this space, we are faced with freedom and responsibility to continue to foster the communitas that we encounter on the pilgrimage. We renew our understanding of what it means to be human as expressed in the Japanese word for human being that means "person together with." There you find betweenness, relationship, community; fellowship with your neighbor, the nation, and nature. Time and history is "time together." Space is "room together." Remembering the forgotten dead of Tule Lake reconstitutes the living and dead as community, reminiscent of the Obon midsummer festival that marks the temporary return of the spirits of the dead.[53]

Jonathan Z. Smith states that ritual is a mode of paying attention, a process for marking interest. The role of place is understood as a fundamental component of ritual: place directs attention. A ritual object or action becomes sacred by having attention focused on it in a highly marked way. Space, place, and narrative are related as narrative is surfaced; memorialization occurs through narrative. "Sacrality is above all, a category of emplacement."[54] Sacred place is "storied place."[55] The Tule Lake Pilgrimage directs attention to our history, our lives, intergenerational connections through the past of the living and the dead, the present in community towards the future. Accompanying each other in the psychic pain of reconnecting to painful memories is the ritual process of recognizing the sacrality in this place of suffering. The process of pilgrimage to this place of Tule Lake unbounds the narratives there and new connections can be made. The Tule Lake Pilgrimage in part unbounds Tule Lake from being a Segregation Camp to being a sacred place in the midst of the circular cluster of mountains that contains our stories and offers us the opportunity to become whole by reconstructing our world of meaning. Smith values the exploration of the dimensions of incongruity in attempting to understand the complexity of such a construction. The perception of incongruity gives rise to thought (Ricoeur) and incongruity can serve as a vehicle of religious experience. Once again, the emplacement of the incongruity of our lives as Asian Americans through this pilgrimage back to a pivotal time and space of historical disjuncture neither denies nor flees from disjunction but allows, "play between the incongruities and provides an occasion for thought."[56]

The Tule Lake Pilgrimage is a ritual process of inhabiting the interstices in a collective way that reveals to ourselves and to others the past contradictions and arbitrariness of a societal structure that saw us as dangerous anomalies. In large part, this was the cause of the imprisonment of persons of Japanese ancestry based only on their ancestry. At the same time that it reveals the estrangement of Americans of Japanese ancestry, by connecting us at a deeper level, the pilgrimage also has the potential to reveal our affinity as a larger community of a multicultural America that is in the process of fully coming into being. Ritual journeys lend themselves to altruism and are a special locus of non-confrontational interaction. With the diversity of heritages of Americans who participated in the pilgrimage, in recognizing the historical injuries, the focus was not so much about who did what to whom but on the social structural inadequacies and the recognition of pain and spirit. A descendant of a white homesteader who lived in Tule Lake after the camps were closed finally connected her dreams as a child of Asian children crying with what happened at the Tule Lake Segregation Camp. Japanese American memory is part of American memory. Reclaiming Tule Lake as a sacred place also reclaims our interstitial reality as valid with a potential for good.[57]

CONCLUSION

Pilgrimage as sacred journey to sacred place is a ritual process itself. The Tule Lake Pilgrimage charts our movement to a place that also enables us to go deeper and more consciously into our liminal reality, to the place where collective memory dwells, to heal, and to enter into the transformative power of the reconstituted community of the living and the dead, a transformation towards interstitial integrity. The former "camp" sites are sacred places as storied places because they carry the topography of our lives. To journey to Tule Lake is to participate in the sheer density of meanings of suffering, spirit, earth, healing, community, silence, celebration, commitment, prayer. The pilgrimage to Tule Lake is the interiorization of the sacred story of suffering and spirit.

Redress is concomitant to the process and struggle of reconnecting to historical memory, not its only end goal. The rhetoric of civil rights instilled a grammar of empowerment that enabled a reconnection to historical memory that in turn generated the energy and commitment towards redress and an ongoing sense of solidarity and forbearance. From dissonant memories emerged a sacred journey and a convergence of hope. Yet the pilgrimages to Tule Lake and other internment campsites are only the beginning of an ongoing process. In the informal spaces of the journey, stories, realizations, emotions, and wisdom are shared—yet how will we continue to pass on this legacy when the survivors have themselves passed on? How will we continue to incorporate memory into our daily living with the larger community? How will we continue to re-imagine our social relations that are pluralistic, interconnected and life transforming? These are the questions we must continue to ask ourselves. Our point of return is our point of hopeful departure.

NOTES

1. Ruth Behar, *The Vulnerable Observer: Anthropology That Breaks Your Heart* (Boston: Beacon Press, 1996), 174.
2. Sharon Yamato Danley, "One Sansei's View of the Tule Lake Pilgrimage," *Hokubei Mainichi–North American Daily* San Francisco (August 17, 1996).
3. As cited in Alan Morinis, ed., *Sacred Journeys: The Anthropology of Pilgrimage*, with a foreword by Victor Turner (Westport, CT: Greenwood Press, 1992), 4.
4. Morinis, *Sacred Journeys*, 23; and Karen Pechilis, "To Pilgrimage It: Pilgrimage as Ritual Category in Victor Turner's Work," *Journal of Ritual Studies*, 6 (Summer 1992): 62.
5. Virgil Elizondo, "Pilgrimage: An Enduring Ritual of Humanity," *Pilgrimage/Concilium*, 4 (1996): vii–x.
6. Victor Turner and Edith Turner, *Image and Pilgrimage in Christian Culture* (New York: Columbia University Press, 1978), 17–20.
7. David Carrasco, "Those Who Go On Sacred Journey: The Shapes and Diversity of Pilgrimages," *Pilgrimage/Concilium* 4 (1996), 14.
8. Jill Dubisch, *In a Different Place: Pilgrimage, Gender and Politics at a Greek Island Shrine* (Princeton, NJ: Princeton University Press, 1995), 35.
9. I use the term post-colonial in the sense of Gloria Anzaldúa's, "We were a colonized people . . . whose ways of life were not valued in this country (U.S.)" indicating a post-

colonial consciousness. Gary A. Olson and Lynn Worsham, eds., *Race, Rhetoric and the Postcolonial* (Albany: State University of New York Press, 1999), 48.

10. Tule Lake Committee, John R. and Reiko Ross, *Second Kinenhi: Reflections on Tule Lake* (San Francisco: Tule Lake Committee, 1980, 2000), 127. The Tule Lake Committee has organized the pilgrimage since 1978; prior to this, various student groups and community organizations had organized the pilgrimages in 1969, 1974, 1975, and 1976.

11. Annie Nakao, "Painful Return to WWII Prison Camp," in *San Francisco Examiner*, July 14, 1996.

12. Quote taken from the 1996 Tule Lake Pilgrimage pamphlet.

13. "In an inexplicable spirit of atonement and with great sadness, we [Nisei] went with our parents [Issei and unable to become U.S. citizens] to concentration camps." Michi Weglyn, *Years of Infamy: The Untold Story of America's Concentration Camps* (New York: Morrow, 1976), 21.

14. From the testimony of Harry Kawahara during the Los Angeles CWRIC hearings, Aug. 4, 1981. Leslie T. Hatamiya, *Righting a Wrong: Japanese Americans and the Passage of the Civil Liberties Act of 1988* (Stanford: Stanford University Press, 1993), 133.

15. CWRIC, *Personal Justice Denied: Report of the Commission on Wartime Relocation and Internment of Civilians* (CWRIC) with a foreword by Tetsuden Kashima (Seattle: University of Washington Press; Washington D.C. & San Francisco: The Civil Liberties Public Education Fund, 1982 & 1997), 186, 191–192.

16. Donna K. Nagata, *Legacy of Injustice: Exploring the Cross-Generational Impact of the Japanese American Internment* (New York: Plenum Press, 1993), 102.

17. Ibid., 215–218.

18. Yasuko I. Takezawa, *Breaking the Silence: Redress and Japanese American Ethnicity* (Ithaca, NY: Cornell University Press, 1995), 3.

19. Please refer to CWRIC, *Personal Justice Denied* and Hatamiya, *Righting a Wrong*, 132–135.

20. Joy Kogawa, *Obasan* (Boston: David R. Godine, 1982), 311.

21. Richard Drinnon, *Keeper of Concentration Camps: Dillon S. Myer and American Racism* (Berkeley: University of California Press, 1987), xxvi, 265.

22. Robert N. Bellah, Richard Madsen, William M. Sullivan, Ann Swidler, and Steven M. Tipton, *Habits of the Heart: Individualism and Commitment in American Life* (Berkeley: University of California Press, 1985, 1996), 153–154.

23. There is a symbolic connection. The cave formed by volcanic activity includes Captain Jack's Stronghold where the Modoc Indians made their last stand, echoing the similarities between the "Indian problem" and the "Japanese problem" that motivated both the forced removal of Native Americans (Trail of Tears) and the forced relocation of Japanese Americans. See Drinnon, *Keeper of Concentration Camps*, 39, 265–267.

24. Erik Cohen, "Pilgrimage and Tourism," in *Sacred Journeys*, ed. Morinis, 48.

25. Quoted from the 1996 Tule Lake Pilgrimage pamphlet.

26. Mary Nobel, "Ex-internees Visit WWII Camp," in *Herald & News* (Klamath Falls, Oregon) July 7, 1996.

27. George Takei, "Barbed Wire Memories on the Fourth of July," *Japanese American National Museum Quarterly*, 12:2 (Fall 1997): 21–23.
28. Pechilis, "To Pilgrimage It," 59.
29. Morinis, *Sacred Journeys*, 4.
30. Maurice Halbwachs, "The Legendary Topography of the Gospels in the Holy Land," in *Maurice Halbwachs: On Collective Memory*, ed. and trans. Lewis A. Coser (Chicago: University of Chicago Press, 1992), 224.
31. Stan Yogi, "Yearning for the Past: The Dynamics of Memory in Sansei Internment Poetry," in *Memory and Cultural Politics*, ed. Armritjit Singh, Joseph T. Skerrett, Jr. and Robert E. Hogan (Boston: Northeastern University Press, 1996), 263. Yogi notes that historian Pierre Nora sharply distinguishes memory from history and contends that we live in an age of hyper historicism as opposed to an age in which memory is infused in daily life.
32. Clifford Geertz, *The Interpretation of Cultures* (New York: BasicBooks, 1973), 5, 100, 105.
33. Martin Buber, *Between Man and Man* (London: Fontana Library, 1961), 51 as cited by Victor Turner, *The Ritual Process* (New York: Aldine de Gruyter, 1969, 1995), 127.
34. Turner, *Ritual Process*, 127–128, 132.
35. Victor Turner, *Process, Performance, and Pilgrimage* (New Delhi: Concept, 1979), 53.
36. Fumitaka Matsuoka, *Out of Silence: Emerging Themes in Asian American Churches* (Cleveland, OH: United Church Press, 1995), 62–63.
37. Joseph Kitagawa, *The Christian Tradition: Beyond Its European Captivity* (Philadelphia: Trinity Press International, 1992), 110–111.
38. Refer to Edward W. Soja, *Thirdspace: Journeys to Los Angeles and Other Real-And-Imagined Places* (Cambridge, MA: Blackwell Publishers, 1996).
39. Roberto S. Goizueta, *Caminemos Con Jesus: Toward a Hispanic/Latina Theology of Accompaniment* (Maryknoll, NY: Orbis Books, 1995), 6–7.
40. Fumitaka Matsuoka, *The Color of Faith: Building Community in a Multiracial Society* (Cleveland, OH: United Church Press, 1998), 45–46. Essays by Robert Ezra Park written between 1913 and 1944 introduced the significance of racial uniforms that are associated with the way race is perceived in the United States.
41. Rita Nakashima Brock, "Interstitial Integrity: Reflections Toward an Asian American Woman's Theology," in *Introduction to Christian Theology*, ed. Roger A. Badham (Louisville, KY: Westminster John Knox Press, 1998), 187.
42. "Difference is not appreciated or embraced in the U.S. culture. Difference breeds at best a competitiveness that has to end in someone's losing. And at its worst, difference breeds a destructive contempt commonly defined as racism and ethnic prejudice..." Ada Maria Isasi-Diaz, *En La Lucha—In The Struggle* (Minneapolis: Fortress Press, 1993), 188.
43. "Old pond / Frog jumps in /—Splash!—" Stephen Mitchell, ed. *The Enlightened Heart: An Anthology of Sacred Poetry* (New York: HarperCollins, 1989), 92.
44. Christina Kei Sasaki, "Race, History, Theology: Layers of an American Identity" (M.A. thesis, Pacific School of Religion, 1997), 61.
45. Victor Turner, "Death and the Dead in the Pilgrimage Process," in *Religious Encounters*

With Death, eds. Frank E. Reynolds and Earle H. Waugh (University Park: Pennsylvania State University Press, 1977), 26.

46. Ibid., 31.
47. Ibid., 38–39.
48. Mary Douglas, *Purity and Danger: An Analysis of the Concepts of Pollution and Taboo* (London: Routledge, 1966, 1996), 162–179.
49. Ibid.
50. Nakashima Brock, "Interstitial Integrity," 189–190.
51. Annie Nakao, "Painful Return to WWII Prison Camp," *San Francisco Examiner* (July 14, 1996).
52. Sharon Yamato Danley, "One Sansei's View of the Tule Lake Pilgrimage," *Hokubei Mainichi–North American Daily,* San Francisco (August 17, 1996).
53. Catherine Bell, *Ritual: Perspective and Dimensions* (New York: Oxford University Press, 1997), 128.
54. Jonathan Z. Smith, *To Take Place: Toward Theory in Ritual* (Chicago: University of Chicago Press, 1987), 103–104.
55. Belden C. Lane, *Landscapes of the Sacred* (New York: Paulist Press, 1988).
56. Jonathan Z. Smith, *Map is Not Territory* (Chicago: University of Chicago Press, 1978), 301, 309.
57. Eade and Sallnow view pilgrimage not merely as a field of social relations but also as a realm of competing discourse; they place at center stage of the new agenda of pilgrimage studies a more diversified and discrepant theoretical discourse about pilgrimage. See John Eade and Michael J. Sallnow, eds. *Contesting the Sacred: The Anthropology of Christian Pilgrimage* (London: Routledge, 1991), 2–5.

TEXTS

PUBLIC VOICE, IDENTITY POLITICS, AND RELIGION: JAPANESE AMERICAN COMMEMORATIVE SPIRITUAL AUTOBIOGRAPHY OF THE 1970s

MADELINE DUNTLEY

Autobiographical spiritual narratives attest to religion's vital role in the political, cultural and ethnic awakening of Protestant Japanese Americans in the 1970s. Life stories reveal how ethnic congregations created supportive institutional forums for members to discover, examine, and explore the personal and communal dimensions of ethnic identity. Religion's influence in the construction of ethnic self-consciousness tends to be discounted because religious identity is often reduced to mean only a preference inspired by motivations of either assimilation or acculturation.[1] This chapter will focus on Japanese American Protestant testimonial life stories collected and publicly shared in the 1970s. The private and corporate spiritual histories produced in this decade show how Japanese Americans explored the connection between ethnic identity and religious identity, kept their ethnic history alive and relevant for each generation, articulated ethnic pride with a religious vocabulary that avoided segregationist rhetoric, and confronted and reconciled cultural and political barriers between themselves, Caucasians, and other ethnic Asian Pacific Americans. For Japanese Americans, Christianity offered a foundational experience through which they understood the meaning and purpose of ethnic identity.

Although spiritual autobiographies were a religious art form that had been cultivated in ethnic congregations for many years, the fervent grassroots interest in publicly sharing these stories was stimulated by the nationwide celebration in 1977 of the Centennial of the Establishment of Japanese Missions in North America.[2] To mark this landmark anniversary, several national and local religious groups recorded and published a wide variety of spiritual accounts from Japanese American Christians. Gathered in a much different context than oral history projects, these religious testaments helped to shape a communal memory that continuously retold and reinterpreted Japanese American historical events and experiences in light of Christian sacred narrative.

Oral and written spiritual autobiographies like the ones featured in this chapter were typical of Japanese American Christian commemoration literature.[3] Some of the selections come from the widely read non-denominational devotional magazine, *The Upper Room.* Japanese Americans from across the U.S. submitted two months (Sept/Oct 1977) of meditations for this special issue that was commissioned to celebrate the 1977 Centennial anniversary of the North American Japanese Mission.[4] Also included are autobiographical narratives published in 1972 to mark the 60th Anniversary of a five-congregation ethnic Japanese American Protestant league in Seattle, Washington called the *Domei* (also called the Seattle Christian Church Federation). Seattle currently has five historic Japanese American ethnic churches all located within two miles of one another that have been in existence for decades (Japanese Baptist founded in 1899, Blaine Memorial Methodist, 1904; Japanese Presbyterian, 1907; Japanese Congregational, 1907; and St. Peter's Episcopal, 1908). In 1912 these five ethnic churches began working cooperatively in the *Domei* federation. Before WWII, the *Domei* worked to fight unjust immigration legislation, protest urban vice (prostitution, gambling, and drinking), develop Nisei (second-generation) leadership, sponsor evangelists from Japan, launch mission programs, and bypass Caucasian denominational paternalism and control. During WWII, when Seattle's Japanese Americans were incarcerated in the camp at Minidoka, Idaho, the *Domei* combined resources to run an ecumenical interchurch federation for thousands of residents. Today the *Domei* still exists, and sponsors events aimed at both spiritual development and mission work among the urban poor of the neighborhood, especially aimed at schoolchildren, the homeless, and the elderly. In addition to utilizing *The Upper Room* and *Domei* documents, this chapter also includes representative English and Japanese-language spiritual narratives produced by two of these Japanese American churches in Seattle in celebration of congregational anniversaries (St. Peter's Episcopal 65th Anniversary in 1973 and 70th Anniversary in 1978, and Japanese Congregational's co-celebration of its 70th Anniversary and the Protestant Mission in 1977).

"Public voice" is a term used by scholars to describe two separate processes in Asian American communities. First, public voice refers to acts of preserving and sharing a group's history and heritage through local studies, video documentaries, the fine arts, historical societies, archival resources, ethnic museums, and community-based projects. Second, the term means to discover a platform or context for the public articulation of painful events. This is what is described in *Breaking the Silence*, Yasuko I. Takezawa's history of the Redress Campaign in Seattle. She attributes the emergence of Japanese Americans' public voice solely to secular movements like the Redress Campaign. Takezawa credits the Day of Remembrance rally in 1978, and the national Redress movement hearings of 1981 with launching an unprecedented cross-generational dialogue.[5] She argues that such public articulation of pain and suffering effected a profound "transformation in [Japanese American] ethnic identity, feelings about camp, intergenerational relationships, and norms and values." Takezawa argues that before these two secular events in 1978 and 1981, "the great majority of Nisei" did not talk of WWII incarceration to anyone, and "those who spoke of camp, kept the conversation superficial or dwelled on pleasant memories."[6] Yet Takezawa seems ignorant of the fact that religion also provided an institutional context for telling stories about WWII, and it provided the overarching narrative of sacred history in which people could frame these painful events and find hope in their suffering.

The role of churches in preserving history and expressing pain is important to the Japanese American community as a whole. When Sansei (third generation) activist college students began forging Pan-Asian networks, and taking Asian American studies college courses in the 1970s, it was widely presumed that public discourse about ethnic identity primarily reached only young, native-born, American-educated, and middle-class Asian Americans. Such activism, as Yen Le Espiritu noted, seemed to "barely [touch] the Asian ethnic enclaves."[7] Yet Japanese American religious communities openly discussed and ritually commemorated the experience of injustice and prejudice, and thus provided a way for some Issei and Nisei members in the so-called ethnic enclave to confront and explore these issues. Although ethnic pride, cultural preservation, pan-Asian solidarity, and minority rights were widely explored in the public sector in the late 1970s and early 1980s, these issues had been important concerns in ethnic Christian communities even earlier.

For example, in the late 1960s and early 1970s, ecumenical and denominational Asian-American ministerial associations were organized, and they served as important avenues for Japanese Americans to forge cross-Asian alliances and contribute to Pan-Asian activism. Masaru Nambu of Chicago writes about an Asian ministers' conference he attended in the early 1970s. At one point during the conference, participants split into small groups to share "spiritual pilgrimages." Here they discussed the impact of the 1930s and WWII on their lives, and the stark reality of inter-Asian historical conflict:

> A Chinese minister said he saw with his own eyes his older bother killed by a Japanese soldier. A Filipino minister confided that he almost lost his life several times while he was working underground in the Philippines. I shared my experience by relating how the Japanese went through humiliation and suffering in China after the war. We all felt how small the world is in that all three of us experienced the ugliness, misery and darkness of war at the same time; and how surprised we were to come to the same meeting to discuss the ministry for the Asian-Americans. We all felt that God can bring something constructive and creative out of our past in which we experienced hate, ugliness, suspicion and resentment. When our life is renewed though the love and sacrifice and resurrection which we discover in the life of Christ, we are indeed one in Him.[8]

Clearly, Christianity challenged Nambu to see the commonalities in all their stories. In this theological frame of reference, he understood how to make sense of his own painful experience and was able to respond in a spirit of empathy and reconciliation to other Asians whose histories might otherwise have provoked hostility and mistrust. Religious-oriented Pan-Asian reconciliation and contact such as this helped lay the groundwork for similar activism in the later 1970s.

When Japanese American Christians shared stories of pain from the war years, their stories were framed within a larger religious context. They told personal stories of suffering through incarceration and exile in such a way that it placed them in community both with Biblical ancestors and with others in the world who refused to let oppression and injustice stifle their compassion. For his published entry in the devotional magazine *The Upper Room*, Donald Toriumi of Altadena, California recalled serving as a pastor at Heart Mountain Relocation Center in Wyoming. Not only were these "fearful days" behind barbed wire, but the situation in 1942 seemed hardly one to evoke gratitude. He did not know what he could do or say to make the Thanksgiving church service meaningful. Then, the week before the holiday, his dilemma was relieved. Heart Mountain was suddenly inundated with letters, checks, money orders, and boxes of Christmas gifts from Sunday schools, youth groups, and churches all over America. But the gift he remembers most was this:

> One box came from Spanish American children in mountainous Las Truchas, New Mexico. They had no money, but they sold eggs and homegrown products. With the money, they then [walked and] bought [our] children things in town many miles away.[9]

Moved by this compassionate sacrifice of little children who knew all too well the trials of poverty and oppression, Toriumi was inspired to preach Thanksgiving Sunday from the text, I Thess. 5:16, "Rejoice always, pray without ceasing, give thanks in all circumstances."

During St. Peter's Episcopal Church's 70th Anniversary celebration in 1978, The Rev. Joseph Kitagawa was invited to share his spiritual life story for the congregation. In his poignant reminiscences about life during WWII, Kitagawa touched on Biblical passages that were emblematic for all Japanese American Protestants who suffered incarceration. Kitagawa's autobiographical testimonial told of his incarceration at Lordsburg, New Mexico:

> During my internment camp days, I often read and reread the story of Daniel in the Old Testament. According to the story . . . Daniel's enemies persuaded the king to sign a document that was designed to cast him into the den of lions. And when he learned one day that the document had been signed, we are told that Daniel went to his chamber where he had windows open toward Jerusalem, and he got down upon his knees three times and prayed. This story, too, had special significance to all of us then, because in those days we all prayed with our windows open toward home. . . . As we walked together along the barbed wire in the daytime, or as we tried to cover ourselves against the cold at night in the draughty wooden barracks, I could sense that my Issei friends were deeply troubled, not so much by the experience of physical discomfort or even the loss of their homes and property but more by the sense of uncertainty they felt concerning their own future as well as the future of their wives and children from whom they were separated. . . . I suddenly realized the emotional impact of the Hebrew Psalm: "By the waters of Babylon we sat down and wept, when we remembered thee, O Zion!" They too must have prayed with their windows open toward home. [10]

The Rev. Kitagawa's autobiographical narrative shows how stories from sacred text also became a communal Japanese American story. Biblical accounts of persecution offered Japanese American Christians an appropriate context for publicly reciting their own painful memories of the war years. Biblical examples of God's sustaining presence in the lives of those facing racial prejudice and injustice offered hope and solace for Japanese Americans who daily faced such challenges. Sacred narrative also presented a ritual mechanism for reconciliation. Caucasian members of the Japanese Americans' own denominations who were openly racist or who had been acquiescent, apathetic, or unconcerned with the wartime sufferings of Japanese Americans were later enjoined to publicly admit the injustice, and in turn Japanese Americans were asked to respond with forgiveness.[11]

As Raymond Brady Williams has discovered in his study of immigrant Asian-Indian Christians,

> the Bible acts as the template onto which the immigrants project their experiences and which brings coherence to their very different journeys. Such exposition both interprets the experience and shapes it.

Williams cites the primacy of three Bible stories that serve as "prototypical models for interpretation of migration": the Exodus/Wilderness; the Exile with Daniel being faithful in the Lion's Den; and the eternal pilgrimage to the Promised Land of Zion.[12] As we saw in Kitagawa's narrative, these stories appear in Japanese American commemorative literature. Also important are the Psalms, the stories of exile and near-genocide in Esther, the rebuilding of the Temple in Nehemiah, the New Testament stories of Pentecost and the establishment of the Early Church, and Pauline imprisonment epistles (i.e., Philippians, Ephesians, Colossians, Philemon). Like the Israelites in the Old Testament, many Japanese American Christians knew first-hand about imprisonment, oppression, and exile. By inlaying their own struggles with incarceration and exile upon those found in sacred story, Japanese Americans could identify with their spiritual ancestors, and like those forbears, find both the hope and means for redemption from bondage and pain. Religious faith, as it is depicted in Japanese American spiritual narratives, is neither lived nor perceived as an optional orientation.

Perhaps the reason why religion's connection to ethnic identity is often ignored is due to a misclassification of what religion is and does for Japanese Americans. Church members often do not think of their churches as merely social clubs or "voluntary associations."[13] In fact, individuals who claim to be a part of a religious tradition feel real value in the fact that "religious traditions have shaped and sustained them, given them communities and religious histories, and offered them language, symbols, teachings, and rituals by which to articulate their own religious ideas."[14] People have "great love for their traditions" and they express "almost visceral connections" with them, describing religion in ways such as: "It's in my bones . . . It's in my thinking; it's in my vocabulary. It's who I am."[15] Religion is so far from optional that it is entwined in one's being through "heartstrings and viscera."[16] Yet most studies of Japanese Americans fail to see the degree to which a Japanese American's connection to a religious tradition can be foundational and fundamental to his or her identity.

In his study of the semantic history of the term "identity," Philip Gleason noted that this term only entered the academic vocabulary in the 1950s, and was greatly influenced by the discussion of ethnic and religious identity in Will Herberg's landmark *Protestant-Catholic-Jew* (1955). Today, the debate between psychologists and social scientists about the meaning of "identity" centers on these questions:

> whether identity is to be understood as something internal that persists through change or as something ascribed from without that changes according to circumstance. . . . [Is identity] somehow "located" in the deep psychic structure of the individual [or] shaped and modified by the interaction between the individual and the surrounding social milieu?[17]

In terms of this debate over what aspects of identity are external and subject to change, or internal and static, one might too quickly ascribe ethnic identity to be internal and religious identity as external. Yet the question of how best to describe Japanese American religious and ethnic identity cannot be solved so easily.

Recent research in the dynamics of the construction of ethnicity focuses on the tension between personal choice and societal circumscription. Joane Nagel argues that ethnic identity consists of both "optional and mandatory" factors. Yet the existence of racial prejudice in the United States means that for Asian Americans, the contours of ethnic identity are not shaped entirely by personal choice. Thus "individual choices are circumscribed by the ethnic categories available at a particular time and place."[18] Eugeen Roosens found that ethnicity is a

> broad field for the use and manipulation of symbols...Nobody can deny that a given group of people has ancestors, that they have a past, a culture, a biological origin, a land. . . . [Yet] who exactly these ancestors were, where they lived, what type of culture they transmitted . . . and what their relationships were with other, similar ethnic groups in the past—all these are frequently open questions.[19]

Thus, according to Nagel and Roosens, ethnic identity is both static and optional: the racial condition of being a non-white minority in the U.S. is static, the symbolic manipulation and interpretation of that minority status and how one defines the ethnic dimension of one's race are in many ways optional.

If religion is one of these "optional" factors, can it be foundational to a person's core identity? Most studies of Japanese Americans would imply the answer to this is "no." [20] Too often it is presumed that Japanese Americans use religion simply to further their individual secular agendas. To many scholars, Japanese Americans' religious choice or preference has become an ethnic marker that gauges the degree of assimilation in an immigrant population. From this academic perspective, the rich concept of what might be constituted as a religious identity is rejected, and religion is distilled into a simple choice a person makes between an assimilationist or ethnic maintenance strategy. According to this interpretation, Japanese Americans would choose religion only for its culture maintenance opportunities (i.e., in either Buddhist temples or ethnic Christian churches) or for its mainstreaming advantages (i.e., in Mainline Caucasian denominational Christian churches).

Other scholars are even less kindly inclined toward the importance of religious identity for ethnic Japanese American communities because they find religion totally insignificant as any kind of ethnic marker at all. Darrell Montero's work on Japanese American ethnic affiliation cites Buddhist and Christian religion as being so flexible that it is not a good measure of either acculturation *or* ethnicity.[21] In this interpretation, religion is so insignificant to one's central and persistent core identity that it cannot reliably be considered as a factor in ethnic identity formation.

So what do spiritual narratives tell us about Japanese American religious identity? Japanese American autobiographies often deal with the issue of religious choice in terms of what I call a *resistance-acceptance* theology. For many Japanese American Protestants, faith is not a conversion based on individual's opportunistic or assimilationist decision, but was perceived as a radical encounter with and (often reluctant) acceptance of God's "will" or "providence." Thus, Japanese American autobiographical narratives commonly feature denial of a God who had long ago chosen them; of knowing about Christianity long before surrendering to its embrace. The following spiritual narrative highlights the resistance–surrender theology common in Japanese American Protestantism:

Heitaro Hikita arrived in the Northwest in the first decade of the 1900s. Professor Kumataro Takahashi and his wife, leaders of the Tacoma Japanese Baptist Church, took Hikita into their home. Although his hosts were kind, Hikita found their Christian lifestyle not at all attractive.

> Although I am very ashamed of this, I did not know anything about the religion of Christianity up to the time I was taken care of in the

Takahashi household. In the minister's home, they were in the habit of praying before eating, getting together [for prayers during the day and at bedtime] and of saying amen at the end of the prayers. For me this was something I had never seen or heard of before, and I struggled, unable to make the adjustments to this daily lifestyle. . . . [22]

Although Hikita admits he "had no particular desire to become a Christian" it was arranged that he would be baptized with five others at Easter.

Because they had been taking care of me for almost a year, I could hardly refuse. I ended up saying yes at the time, being baptized, and thinking to myself that once I left that place I would return to my Buddhist beliefs.... When I think about this now, I am truly repentant before God for my insolence. [23]

Hikita soon moved to Seattle seeking employment, and on the streets of the International District encountered a church deacon he knew from Tacoma who kindly arranged for Hikita to work at a Japanese-owned Seattle store. [24]

When I went to work at the store I came face to face with Christianity again after a short period of separation. That is to say that the employees at the Furuya Store were all devoted to the spirit of Christianity, they were filled with Christian love. . . . [We studied] a little booklet of Christian poems entitled "Our Daily Strength". Local ministers from other areas would visit, giving us a short sermon. . . . And as a result there were many employees who had been redeemed at these meetings. I am in fact one such person. As I said above, even though I was [earlier] baptized, it was a baptism born out of a sense of duty. As for God, it is written in the Bible that "you did not choose me, but I chose you." When Minister Takahashi [had] recommended to me that I be baptized [in Tacoma], God had already chosen me, a mere ignorant man. Without even being aware of my ignorance I spurned God's intentions . . . my closed mind was opened, and I came to the full realization that I had been chosen by God at some time in the past. . . . These days, I am repentant before God for my insolent attitude. I am extremely thankful that God troubled himself over me in this way, just as for one lamb. [25]

Even though Hikita became a Christian as an adult, his spiritual life story depicts a God that shaped the destiny of his entire lifespan, even at times when he was unaware of God's work. Clearly, for Hikita, religion was not his choice alone: God chose for him. It seems incredible that Japanese American religious affiliation is so often relegated to a simple decision of personal "choice" or preference when Japanese narratives like Hikita's do not describe religious commitments in that way.

In Japanese American spiritual narratives religion is expressed as a fundamental part of one's purpose or destiny, and religious commitments are merged and intermingled with ethnic loyalties. As Roosens noted, Japanese Americans have a past, a culture, a land, and ancestors. But who these ancestors were and what type of culture they transmitted are "open questions."26 Indeed, the content of Japanese American Christian commemorative histories and accompanying life stories does fill in these "open questions." They provide the following narrative of the symbolic, collective memory of Japanese American Protestants. They define the ancestors primarily in terms of religious heritage, not familial ties. They teach and transmit cultural norms through a Japanese Christian ritual culture that fixed commemoration as a central value, and finds in that definitive act the source of its survival and revitalization.

Japanese American Protestants have forged a collective memory that is retold in commemorative histories and autobiographies. As the Rev. Michael Morizono described it in *A Centennial Legacy* in 1977:

> [Here is] told the life drama of a people, the pioneer Isseis, the Niseis, and their children and grandchildren, all making up a unique people called "Japanese-American." A people with a unique experience, in which the harsh realities of prejudice and discrimination, of poverty and hardship were all transcended and overcome in a manner and style peculiarly their own. Amidst this backdrop of special people is told an even more unique story of the People of God, emerging from amongst these people, shaping and molding a history within God's plan. So every bit of the story as told in these pages of men and women and children and their church fit into the ultimate plan of God.27

From reading the way ethnicity is bound to religion in these documents, it is clear that Japanese Americans see their ethnic history as emerging from sacred story. Their Christian ancestry is as important as familial ancestry. Christian affiliation is even expressed in familial terms. The Protestant immigrant founders of 1877 are the "ancestors" in a very real sense. These Nikkei ancestors are indeed Japanese (marking a blood connection) but the significant relational tie is religion, rather than biological/familial kinship.

It is possible to reconstruct a Japanese American Protestant communal history by using commemorative anniversary documents produced by Seattle's Japanese American congregations in the 1970s. The story begins with a latter day symbolic parallel between the story of the earliest missionary church and the Bibical story in Acts and the Epistles. The core group of Japanese American immigrants in San Francisco in 1877 who formed the first assembly of Japanese Protestants were blessed by a special spiritual commission that is referred to as a kind of Japanese American "Pentecost." These faithful missionaries/apostles founded fledgling churches up and down the West Coast among the Japanese immigrant pioneers/pilgrims who journeyed far from home to farm and work the West Coast U.S. rural and urban "wildernesses." These pilgrim/pioneers planted and cultivated their own unique "Early Church": an Issei Christian community. Like the Early Church in the New Testament, the Japanese American first Christians met in homes and provisional church buildings. As these "pioneers" and their Nisei children worked to turn a wilderness into a community, they, like the first apostles in the earliest church, faced obstacles of vice, unbelief, doubt, and hostility. WWII evacuation and incarceration made them fellow-sufferers with the Biblical Jews in Exile in Babylon, and with those Persian Jews who faced betrayal and threat of annihilation in the book of Esther. Like the Jews who returned to their original homes after the Exile, the Japanese Americans returned home after WWII to face the difficult task of how best to rebuild their people and church, evoking the symbolic Biblical parallel of Nehemiah's work to restore Jewish worship and identity.

Turning to the Biblical Pentecost story again for inspiration, these congregations were able to find in the foreign language and ethnic ministry a unique calling and justification for their ongoing survival in a multicultural world. Through outreach to immigrant and refugee Asians entering the city as a result of the Vietnam War and the 1965 Immigration Act groups, they had the distinct opportunity for following Jesus' injunction to "preach to all nations." The Southeast Asian refugees, as well as other recent Chinese-speaking and Filipino immigrants, were seen by Japanese American Christians as modern-day reflections of their own pioneer ancestors. By helping these new immigrant Asian groups in refugee resettlement, and in the forming of their own immigrant ethnic congregations, Japanese Americans were able to come full circle to their own history, but this time not as the people who suffered, but as the people who reached out in compassion to those whose lives were marred by discrimination, war, and injustice. In helping these new immigrants, Japanese American Christians could replay and reenact their own communal story, only this time assuming different roles in those histories. Now they could take on the role of becoming the *givers* of domestic mission to non-Japanese Asians, by being the ones to provide language training, housing, interpretation services, friendship, and religious instruction.

Roy Y. Ishihara summarized this collective, communal story in this way:

> [We] identify with a set of pilgrims who came across the Atlantic...to work in the canefields of Hawai'i, fell trees in the Northwest...dredge the swamps of northern California. They came for varied reasons, but they had one thing in common—they were united in their hardships and in their silent sufferings. In this situation, many found one haven that encouraged their hopes and sustained their harsh lives—the Christian fellowship. Churches became places where they were welcomed. Above all, not a few discovered their purpose in coming to America—to find new life and destiny in Jesus Christ. 1977 marks the centennial of the first Japanese convert, an Issei pilgrim, in San Francisco. We are thankful for the sacrifices of our forefathers. As their heirs and heirs of Christ, we would reach out and care for the new pilgrims that are coming from Hong Kong, Thailand, Cambodia, and Vietnam.[28]

Knowing the contours of this Japanese American Protestant communal memory helps to explain the theological motivations for the aid Japanese American Christians offered to other Asian groups, especially Southeast Asian refugees who entered the country in substantial numbers in the 1970s. Because Japanese Americans knew their congregational histories through regular and consistent commemoration ceremonies, it was easy for them to see the refugees as having a similar persecution history (as victims of war), and also as akin to their pioneer ancestors (that is seeking new lives in a new land).

A congregation's self-reflection in the publication of life stories often created fertile ground for implementing mission initiatives. Soon after St. Peter's Episcopal's 1973 publication of its congregation's faith stories, the church embarked on an ambitious program to assist Vietnamese and Laotian immigrants. St. Peter's Refugee Resettlement program eventually hosted over 150 Southeast Asians.[29] That decade also marked the beginning of St. Peter's cross-cultural work with other Asian immigrants. In the late 1970s, St. Peter's helped to found the St. James of Jerusalem parish, a Chinese-language mission of the diocese, which met in its founding years in the St. Peter's chapel. This Chinese American sister parish was truly international, consisting of Chinese-language speakers from Hong Kong, Vietnam, the Philippines, Trinidad, and the United States.[30] St Peter's own Japanese American Christian history was retold in anniversaries during these years as a coming-of-age story—as a congregation that evolved from a mission-dependent parish in the archdiocese, to a mature, independent congregation capable of its own outreach programs to new immigrant groups. No doubt this impulse to emulate the pioneers also allowed them to embody the Japanese cultural concept of *on-gaeshi*, or acting in reciprocity; paying back a moral debt, to honor the missionaries who had once helped them by acting in a similar capacity for others.[31]

Many spiritual stories testify to the excitement and theological insights generated by the refugee resettlement programs in the 1970s. Arthur Tsuneishi of San Lorenzo, California wrote about a young Asian approaching him timidly as he was watering the church lawn.

> "You Chinese?" he asked in halting English. "No, I'm Japanese" I replied. Thus began a relationship that was to have a great impact upon our family as well as upon our church. For that young man was among the first Vietnamese refugees relocating in our community. The days following were filled with job hunting, searching for housing, and involving our congregation in their support.

The Vietnamese man's large family moved in with Tsuneishi's own for almost three months. Tsuneishi recalls that

> One evening when we shared with our children the words of . . . Matthew Chapter 25, they became vividly alive to us, for we had been actually experiencing them. It seemed the Lord was saying to us, "I was a stranger and you welcomed me."[32]

In *Out of Silence: Emerging Themes in Asian American Churches*, theologian Fumitaka Matsuoka explains why it was necessary for Asian American Christians to forge a communal, collective memory based on sacred text. Scripture challenges Asian Americans, Matsuoka writes, to approach "ethnicity with a prophetic eye. It calls us to recognize the signs of God's presence and activity in the whole of Asian American history, culture, and ethnicity."[33] Matsuoka argues that the celebration of ethnicity is essential to the survival of the history and culture of a particular group because religion "is a powerful cohering force for this purpose and churches are particularly well suited for this expression of ethnic assertiveness." Yet religion is more than just a mechanism for ethnic survival. It provides a goal and purpose for ethnic awareness:

> [Our] ethnicities provide the framework and perspective to enable us to see the reality of life clearly and to motivate us to engage in the civic life

in the society. The celebration of ethnicity creates a doorway into the world rather than an escape out of the world.[34]

To link an ethnic story to sacred story is "to understand the gospel anew for the sake of mutuality, reconciled diversity, and community building among the estranged." By linking ethnicity to sacred story, Japanese Americans are given the insight that "we do not remain merely ethnic peoples. We join our humanity along with other human beings."[35] Matsuoka's insight is affirmed by the spiritual narrative of Ivy Makabe Down of Loomis, California:

> As an Asian American woman who is concerned both for the ethnic minority groups and women in this society, the words of the prophet Micah [what does the Lord require of you but to do justice, and to love kindness, and to walk humbly with your God? Micah 6:8] surely have a great depth of meaning. . . . [We] need to understand that denying justice to any one group is a denial of justice to all. The struggle for recognition by the ethnic minority groups provides the potential through which all Christians may work for justice, mercy, and others' acceptance of the liberating love of God.[36]

Japanese American commemorative life stories work to create a communal memory that merges religious and ethnic identities. To study this is to learn that a spiritual life story functions in ways much more formative and far-reaching than one might at first presume. As Herbert Anderson and Edward Foley note:

> Telling stories or fashioning a narrative are not, at their root, just speech patterns but *life patterns*—[they] become the basis of our explanations and interpretations. Our stories are not so much a part of experience as they are the premise of experience. An amazing dynamic exists between our lives and our stories: each one shapes the other. Our collective life experiences are interpreted through a personal narrative framework and shaped into a master story.[37]

To study commemorative spiritual autobiography of the 1970s is to see how religion offered Japanese American Protestants a life pattern and public voice. The communal memory forged through commemorative history and life story offered more than a template for understanding the past, it offered a model for the future. Listening to words of hope, faith, and reconciliation in the autobiographical narratives of Japanese American Christians is to hear the voices of a people who, for more than a century, refused to face oppression and injustice in silence.

NOTES

1. Coverage of religion in David Yoo, *Growing Up Nisei* (Urbana: University of Illinois Press, 1999) looks only at how religious institutional contexts fostered intra-ethnic solidarity, and shows how Nisei were able to explore and solve questions about ethnicity within church/temple and parachurch settings. Brian Masaru Hayashi, *'For the Sake of Our Japanese Brethren': Assimilation, Nationalism and Protestantism Among the Japanese of Los Angeles 1895–1942* (Stanford: Stanford University Press, 1995) skirts the issue of spirituality and religious identity, but challenges the presumed correlations between religious affiliation, cultural assimilation, and Japanese nationalist loyalties. Two monographs on political activism and Asian American civil rights are Yen Le Espiritu's *Asian American Panethnicity* (Philadelphia: Temple University Press, 1992), and William Wei's *Asian American Movement* (Philadelphia: Temple University Press: 1993) but they deal only cursorily with the subject of religion.

2. While the mission movement began in 1874, 1877 marked the baptism of a core group of Japanese Americans, who founded a *Fukui Kai* (Gospel Fellowship Circle) comprised of 35 Japanese immigrants. For a brief history and chronology, see Sumio Koga (compiler), *A Centennial Legacy: History of the Japanese Christian Missions in North America 1877–1977*, Vol. 1 (Chicago: Nobard, Inc., 1977), 10ff.

3. Spiritual narratives of the kind profiled here belong to a larger class of Japanese American grassroots documents that includes biographies and autobiographies, photo essays, architectural projects, video documentaries, and narrative histories. Congregational anniversaries are typically marked at five-year intervals.

4. I am indebted to archivist Sarah Linn at the *Upper Room* headquarters in Nashville for her detective work in locating a rare copy of this commemorative edition. The audience for *The Upper Room* would have included millions of subscribers in many countries. There was also a Japanese-language edition printed.

5. Yasuko I. Takezawa, *Breaking the Silence: Redress and Japanese American Ethnicity* (Ithaca, NY: Cornell University Press 1995), 43–44, 161, 164ff. Redress was the campaign to achieve monetary restitution for Japanese Americans incarcerated during WWII. The Day of Remembrance was held in 1978 as a reenactment of the 1942 forced evacuation of Japanese Americans. The event was geared toward inter-generational unity. The Redress hearings in Seattle in 1981 were sponsored by the Commission on Wartime Relocation and Internment of Civilians.

6. Takezawa, *Breaking the Silence*, 122.

7. All the quotes are from Espiritu, *Asian American Panethnicity*, 50.

8. *Centennial Anniversary Issue, Japanese Christian Mission North America, The Upper Room*, September–October 1977 (Nashville, TN: The Upper Room, 1977); contribution quoted is by Masaru Nambu, Chicago, Sept. 10, 1977, 15.

9. *Centennial Anniversary Issue, Japanese Christian Mission North America, The Upper Room*, September–October 1977 (Nashville, TN: The Upper Room, 1977); writer was Donald Toriumi, Altadena, CA, Oct. 1977, 42.

10. *Our Issei, the Theme of the 70th Anniversary of St. Peter's Episcopal Parish, Seattle,*

1908–1978 (Seattle, WA: n.p. mimeographed booklet). The Rev. Dr. Joseph M. Kitagawa, 3–5. Courtesy of the Archives, Archidiocese of Olympia.

11. There have been various public acknowledgments of Caucasian involvement in Japanese American incarceration in Christian denominational circles in Seattle throughout the years. One recent example was the Presbytery of Seattle's 1997 resolution passed on the occasion of the retirement of a long-time pastor of an ethnic Japanese church. The resolution publicly admitted the injustice of WWII incarceration, the existence of ongoing racism, and the need for reconciliation.

12. Raymond Brady Williams, *Christian Pluralism in the United States: The Indian Immigrant Experience* (New York: Cambridge University Press, 1993). Both quotes are on p. 183.

13. See Madeline Duntley, "More than an Ethnic Club: Religion & Identity in Seattle's Historic Japanese American Churches," *Listening: Journal of Religion and Culture* 33(3) (Fall 1998): 199–210.

14. Mary Farrell Bednarowski, *The Religious Imagination of American Women* (Bloomington, IN: Indiana Univiversity Press, 1999),18.

15. Bednarowski, *Religious Imagination*, 34–35.

16. Letty Cottin Pogrebin, *Deborah, Golda and Me: Being Female and Jewish in America* (New York: Crown, 1991), 79.

17. Philip Gleason, "Identifying Identity: A Semantic History" *The Journal of American History* 69 (March 1983, 910–931): 918.

18. Joane Nagel, "Constructing Ethnicity: Creating and Recreating Ethnic Identity and Culture" *Social Problems* 14(1) (February 1994): 15

19. Eugeen E. Roosens, *Creating Ethnicity: The Process of Ethnogenesis* (London: Sage, 1989), 160.

20. Characteristic portrayals are found in the work of David J. O'Brien and Stephen S. Fugita. They mention religion rarely and only in terms of "voluntary associations." See *The Japanese American Experience* (Bloomington: Indiana University Press, 1991); and *Japanese American Ethnicity: The Persistence of Community* (Seattle: University of Washington Press, 1991). For a discussion of religion as providing a comfort zone, see Kaoru Oguri Kendis, *A Matter of Comfort: Ethnic Maintenance and Ethnic Style among Third-Generation Japanese Americans* (New York: AMS Press, 1989), 129 ff. Kendis's fieldwork was done in the late 1970s.

21. See Darrell Montero, *Japanese Americans: Changing Patterns of Ethnic Affiliation Over Three Generations* (Boulder: Westview, 1980), 62–63.

22. "The Chosen" by Heitaro Hikita (Congregational) in Juhei Kono, ed., *Shiatoru Nihonjin Kirisuto Kyokai Domei*, 299–300. Selection translated by Roger Chriss.

23. Kono, *Shiatoru Nihonjin*, 300.

24. The Furuya Company was a Japanese-owned entrepreneurial enterprise (banking, dry goods, import/export) run by Masajiro Furuya, a devout Christian who required mandatory Bible Study and Christian classes for all his immigrant employees.

25. Kono, *Shiatoru Nihonjin*, 300–304.

26. Eugeen Roosens, *Creating Ethnicity*, 160.

27. Koga, *A Centennial Legacy*, 5.

28. *Centennial Anniversary Issue, Japanese Christian Mission North America, The Upper Room,* September–October 1977 (Nashville, TN: The Upper Room, 1977); contributor is Roy Y. Ishihara, Los Angeles, October 11, 1977, 46.

29. *More than 100 Years of Ministry: The Episcopal Church in Western Washington* (Diocese of Columbia, Seattle, 1989), 101.

30. *Ever Onward with God's Love: The First Seventy-Five years of Saint Peter's Episcopal Parish, 1908–1983* (St. Peter's Episcopal Church, Seattle, WA, 1983), 35–36. This is a typed booklet photocopied and distributed to members at the Anniversary celebration. Courtesy of the Archives, Diocese of Olympia of the Episcopal Church.

31. Other scholars have found a similar model in secular Japanese American benevolent work; see Leslie A. Ito's discussion on p. 142 in Gary Y. Okihiro, *Storied Lives: Japanese American Students and World War II* (Seattle: University of Washington Press, 1999).

32. *Centennial Anniversary Issue, Japanese Christian Mission North America, The Upper Room,* September–October 1977 (Nashville, TN: The Upper Room, 1977); contributor is Arthur Tsuneishi, San Lorenzo, CA., Sept. 16, 1977, 21.

33. Fumitaka Matsuoka, *Out of Silence: Emerging Themes in Asian American Churches* (Cleveland, OH: United Church Press, 1995), 30. Matsuoka presents a theological perspective on this topic.

34. Matsuoka, *Out of Silence*, 39.

35. Matsuoka, *Out of Silence*, 138 and 91.

36. *Centennial Anniversary Issue, Japanese Christian Mission North America, The Upper Room,* September-October 1977 (Nashville: The Upper Room, 1977); contributor is Ivy Makabe Down, September 25, 1977, 30.

37. Herbert Anderson and Edward Foley, *Mighty Stories, Dangerous Rituals: Weaving Together the Human and the Divine* (San Francisco: Jossey-Bass, 1998), 11.

WITNESSING RELIGION IN MARY PAIK LEE'S
QUIET ODYSSEY

SANDRA OH

With the relatively recent explosion of published literary works by Korean
Americans, I was able to craft a book list for my Korean American literature class this past quarter that offered, what I considered "high entertainment
value." In addition to examining the myriad of complex issues relevant to
Korean Americans and the larger Asian American community, these works
contain sex, violence, mystery, and the paranormal and are written in highly
stylized prose. For this reason, I was surprised when, at the end of the quarter,
several students chose Mary Paik Lee's simply written and what one could even
call humble autobiography, *Quiet Odyssey*, as their favorite book from the class.
Published in 1990, *Quiet Odyssey* begins with the historic circumstances that
compel Lee's family to emigrate to the U.S. at the turn of the twentieth century and chronicles their experiences as they struggle to survive, offering the
reader insight into an experience about which we know very little. For this reason, Lee's text is invaluable to the field of Asian American studies and, as such,
makes her work a near constant on Asian American studies syllabi.

While my students appreciated the work's historical significance, what
they found most appealing was its first person perspective. When pressed to
elaborate, many responded by citing Lee's account of hardship and suffering
as the most moving and compelling aspect of her autobiography. This
response to the work seems appropriate given the dire conditions under
which Lee and her family lived for decades. However, I found their answer
striking because of the way it underscored the tension that exists within the
work between the subjective narrative and its editorial framing, which is as
integral and significant to the text as the subjective narrative itself.

In her introduction and preface, the work's editor, Sucheng Chan, contributes a detailed and thorough account of the historical context from which Lee's narrative arises, and argues for the work's legitimacy as an historical document in the work's appendix. Chan's substantive contribution cannot be viewed as a mere appendage or accessory, for this framework provides the reader with an interpretive lens through which to view Lee's autobiographical narrative.[1] However, a tension exists between the subjective narrative authored by Lee and the textual framing contributed by Chan. While my students viewed suffering as central to the text, a view that is also shared, as I will show, by Lee herself, Chan takes great pains to divert the reader's attentions from this element of the narrative. This conflict or tension is not merely a clash between individuals or personalities but is symptomatic of a larger dilemma within Ethnic studies.

From the work's opening pages, the conflict between authorial voices, Lee's and Chan's, is evident. Chan begins the preface by recounting the fortuitous events that brought Lee's autobiography to her attention and highlights the importance of the work as an historical document, a document that gives voice to an otherwise lost experience. When she asks Mary Paik Lee how it is that she remembers these experiences so well, Lee responds, "these things I've written down, what I'm telling you now, I remember them because they made me *suffer so.*"[2] Immediately after Lee offers this explanation, after she squarely places suffering at the center of her text, Chan takes pains to divert the reader's attention away from this element; "Suffering, however, is not her only theme. Side by side with her recollection of hard times are memories of kind gestures."[3] Chan's attempt to diminish the importance of suffering clearly conflicts with Lee's desire to position suffering at the narrative's point of genesis.

This tension can also be seen in the work's closing pages. In the appendix, Chan reveals that *Quiet Odyssey* was not the original title given to the work by Mary Paik Lee but one of her (Chan's) own choosing. We learn that Lee had originally titled her typewritten manuscript *Life Is Bittersweet*, a title that reflects the work's commingling of recollections of tragedy and hardship with memories of family triumphs and love, but that when Chan requests alternate titles, Lee responds by asking Chan to choose a title herself, which she does. Chan does not explain why she felt the need for alternative titles nor why the original title was inadequate, but in replacing *Life Is Bittersweet* with *Quiet Odyssey*, Chan, again, deflects the reader's gaze from the role that suffering plays in the narrative.

Before we can understand the reason for this conflict in the text, we must first understand the cultural "work" that Chan hopes the narrative will accomplish. In the preface, Chan characterizes Lee's text as "a unique contribution to the study of immigrants, ethnic minorities, women, and poor working people." Mary Paik Lee's work is unique in that Mary Paik Lee herself is unique; she is one of the last of seven thousand Korean immigrants who came to the United States via Hawaii between 1902 and 1905.[4] Although Chan values Lee's text for its singularity (given the scant number of Korean women and girls in the U.S. at the time) she also positions Lee's text as representative in that Lee's story offers us insight into the lives of other Asian immigrants in America at the turn of the century. Lee, as a poor, agricultural worker, is more representative of the vast majority of Asian immigrants of that era, Chan claims, than the likes of Jade Snow Wong and Monica Sone who only give us the perspective of the merchant or middle class. The claim that Lee's text is representative of those invisible to dominant history and society is crucial. By casting Lee as representative of disenfranchised and marginalized Asian immigrants, Chan establishes the expectation that Lee's text will expose the fraudulent nature of the American dream, or, at the very least, critique this privileged American myth. Chan ends the introduction to *Quiet Odyssey* by stating: "[Lee] begins and ends her tale by citing Korean history, but, in between, she shares with us what it was like to have grown up poor, Asian and female in the shadow of the American dream."[5]

Furthermore, Chan, fosters the expectation that Lee's narrative will speak against the patriarchy experienced by Korean and Korean American women by exploring, in the introduction, the "liberating" effect that Christianity had on Korean women who, prior to the introduction of Christianity, led "extremely secluded lives," and were confined to the Confucian roles of "filial daughter, the chaste woman, the obedient wife, and the devoted mother." Given the tightly circumscribed lives led by Korean women, Chan argues, Korean women found Christianity attractive because it "gave female converts a measure of freedom they had never known, and this, I think helps to account for the fervor of female converts who, in turn influenced their husbands and children."[6] Chan also goes on to argue that Christianity gave Korean women literacy and lives outside of the "household prisons" and transformed them in to "public persons."[7] This emphasis on the radical, liberating effects of Christianity on Korean women leads the reader to expect that Lee's text will work to resist, as a result of Christianity, the traditionally prescribed roles of Korean womanhood.

Given that Chan positions Lee's narrative as a refutation of the American Dream and as a critique of patriarchy, it seems counterintuitive that she should diminish the role of suffering in the work. One would expect the bleak nature of much of Lee's existence to bolster Chan's arguments and further her rhetorical objectives. However, Chan's dismissal of suffering is part of a larger obfuscation, which can be seen when we closely examine how Chan portrays the impact that Christianity had on the lives of Korean women. In the preceding passage, Chan ascribes the "fervor" demonstrated by Korean women to their new found freedom, rather than to a deeply felt spiritual experience and, as a result, constructs Christianity of the *means* through which female liberation is achieved instead of as a spiritual *end* in itself. In this way, Chan subordinates Christianity's importance to the realization of the liberated, female subject. It is this dismissal of religion as a central element of the text that leads Chan to deflect the reader's attention from the centrality of suffering, for, as I will show suffering is crucial to the religious project that Lee undertakes in her autobiography.

Chan's reluctance to address, in any significant manner, Lee's deep spiritual commitment reflects a larger silence within the field of Ethnic Studies in general about religion or spirituality.[8] Given the politically motivated origins of the field of Ethnic studies, religions, especially Christianity, are viewed, at the very least, with suspicion due to their ideological functions within dominant society, and, as I will show in the case of *Quiet Odyssey*, this suspicion is well founded. Lee employs a strategy of "witnessing," one informed by Christianity, in order to discipline the Asian American reader into conforming to dominant American ideology. Undoubtedly, this function, which is antithetical to Chan's progressive political project, compels Chan to efface its centrality to the narrative.

This is not to say, however, that Lee's narrative is completely incompatible with Chan's framing; Lee is intent on remedying the invisibility from which her people suffer in mainstream history and dominant consciousness, and does actively speak out against many of the bigots that she encounters in her life. However, it is crucial to recognize that the text is much more ambivalent and problematic than the narrative's framing might suggest.[9] The work's more outspoken moments of resistance come into conflict with its subtler, hegemonically friendly moments of witnessing. And, while I support wholeheartedly the spirit and intention behind Chan's strategy, I believe that leaving unexamined the way Christianity and dominant American ideology inform Lee's narrative in the interests of a progressive, political project is counterproductive; to leave unremarked the pernicious and powerful effects that these ideologies have on Lee's narrative is to perpetuate rather than dismantle these forces. The contradictions and ambivalence that result from the conflicting interests that inform the autobiographical account must be explored.

And finally, to avert our gaze from Christianity's centrality is to blind ourselves to the textual identity that Lee constructs for herself. While Lee's use of religion affirms ideologies oppressive to her as a poor, immigrant woman of color, it defines the very parameters and possibilities of her identity. And, as I will show, it is within the parameters of this religiously defined identity that Lee claims a measure of agency. Through the strategy of witnessing, the same strategy through which dominant ideologies are affirmed, Lee carves out a degree of agency that is fundamentally linked to and inextricable from her identity as a religious subject.

CONSTRUCTING THE DISCIPLINED SUBJECT

As the full title of Mary Paik Lee's autobiography, *Quiet Odyssey: A Pioneer Korean Woman in America,* suggests, Lee is indeed a pioneer in the sense that she, along with her family, were among the first Koreans to come to America at the beginning of the twentieth century. Lee opens her narrative with a brief account of the historical context that compelled her family to emigrate (the Japanese occupation) and goes on to chronicle their migratory existence in America: beginning in 1905, the Paik family endures near-starvation and brutal working conditions as they move first from Hawaii (their point of origin in America) to the mainland, and then to various agricultural locations in California. Despite decades of seemingly interminable hardship, the Paiks cling to their Christian faith and to their hopes for Korea's liberation from Japan.

From even a cursory reading of Lee's autobiography, one is immediately struck by her deep commitment to, or investment in, history. Lee frames her life story with two historical events; she begins with the events that enabled Japan's colonization of Korea and ends her narrative by recounting the signing of the Korean declaration of independence (which occurred when she was nineteen). This need to present the narrative as an historical, as opposed to personal, text is explained indirectly in the narrative itself. Many of the people that Lee encounters in her life demonstrate a complete ignorance of Korea and the Korean experience; her bigoted history teacher refers to Korea, in class, as a "wild, savage country that had been civilized by the 'Japs'," and even the kind principal who speaks to her employer on her behalf is completely ignorant of the country's existence.[11] This ignorance, and the text's subsequent attempt to remedy it, positions Lee's narrative as an alternative historiography, one that fills in the gaps and silences found in dominant history. Robert Holton observes in his work on historiography:

If African-American historical reality has, until recently, been a somewhat neglected field, this can be seen as an aspect of what Bourdieu has
described as the aphasia of those denied access to the instruments for
the definition of reality. As a form of historiography, historical fiction
can work against that aphasia by defamiliarising the past, by opening
access to previously marginalised perspectives on and definitions of historical experience by bearing witness.[12]

In bearing witness to a history previously silenced or erased, Lee offers her
autobiography as a textual remedy to the aphasia wrought upon marginalized peoples by dominant society, evincing a resistant political sensibility.
This stance can also be seen in Lee's decision to dedicate an entire chapter to
discrimination as well as her various "spirited"[13] confrontations with racists.

However, Lee's text must be understood as not only participating in a
resistant, historical "witnessing," it must also be understood as an example of
Christian "witnessing" as well. The Christian notion of witnessing is
informed by an evangelical spirit or mission that seeks to convert non-
believers through the dissemination of Biblical teachings or "The Word."[14]
While Lee does not quote directly from the Bible, she suffuses numerous
descriptions of nature with Biblical imagery. For example, after living in
abject poverty in Colusa, subsisting on one biscuit three times a day, the Lee
family moves to Roberts Island, a fertile environment where wild vegetables
grow in abundance and catfish practically jump out of the water and into
their boats. When they first arrive by boat, Mary notices a snake in the
branches of a tree as she disembarks and views it as a sign of "things to
come."[15] Within the narrative, the snake is an indication of things to come
in so far as the barn that they are to occupy is overrun with snakes. However,
the snake also has potent Biblical meaning, signifying that her family has
entered an Eden, a garden where all things are provided for them by God.
Lee's parents repeatedly express this faith in God's benevolence and protection throughout the book despite the seemingly unending hardships that
they endure. They maintain an unwavering belief that God "must surely [be]
leading [them] in the right direction" regardless of the fact that their trials
and hardships appear interminable.

While Mary's parents remain stalwart in their faith and gratitude throughout, Mary comes to question God and the imperative to be grateful to him.
At every meal, Mary's father would lead the family in prayer, thanking God
for his blessings despite the fact that the meals for the most part only consisted of biscuits. During their stay in Colusa, Mary, who is eleven at the

time, cannot understand her father's gratitude and confronts him.

> Once he was sitting out on the porch smoking after dinner, and I asked
> him what we had to be so thankful for. He said, "Don't you remember
> why we came here?" I had forgotten that the fate of our family in Korea
> was much worse than ours.[16]

As Mary expresses resentment and ingratitude towards God, her father counters this moment of rebellion by reminding her about their family back in Korea. The question, "Don't you remember why we came here?" seems to be alluding to a larger mission behind the family's presence in the United States, but Mary interprets her father's question as a prompt to compare her own suffering to that of her family's back in Korea. While this reflexive comparison might appear to reflect a sense of personal guilt, one unique to Mary's psychological make-up, when one takes the structure and meaning of Christian witnessing into account it becomes apparent that Mary can only respond to her father's question with this conditioned comparison of suffering. Mary's conditioned response shows the convergence of two distinct yet intimately related elements of Christian witnessing: comparison and suffering.

Christian witnessing, in addition to bearing verbal witness or testimony to one's faith, also entails "witnessing" through action or example. Jean-Pierre Jossua notes, "I do not see the witness as someone who takes the initiative in speaking to others. I see the witness, rather, as a man or woman living in such a way—and looking at the world in and everything in it in such a way —as to make other people ask themselves, and ask those who are witnesses, what gives them their unique character."[17] This evangelizing through example pertains to bearing witness to believers and nonbelievers alike. Jossua continues, "[A]ll that is left for me to say is that a great many ways of witnessing rely entirely on words. But so that we do not miss the essential point, it must also be remembered that the mutual support of believers, like their witnessing to non-believers, consists almost entirely in a certain quality of existence. It is that which others discover and which strengthens them."[18] This emphasis on witnessing through example highlights the importance of emulation in Christianity. While Christ is figured as the divine, the Son of God, Christianity collapses the distance between the divine and man in so far as his life is offered as model upon which Christians should base their own lives. The ability for man to approach divinity through emulation enables Christians to become models for each other. That is, Christians can offer their own exemplary lives as models to which others may aspire. This notion that a religious identity can be built through the emulation of exemplary lives implicitly assumes or begins with the imperative to compare; emulation is only possible after one ascertains how one's life conforms with or deviates from the given model.

Furthermore, the Christian concept of witnessing is intimately linked to suffering. Given that the crucifixion of Christ resulted from his refusal to repudiate his faith and given that Christians who lived in environments hostile to their faith were persecuted when they testified or maintained witness to their beliefs, it is not surprising that suffering has become a sign of witnessing.[19] The intimate relationship between witnessing and suffering can be seen in the fact that the English word "martyr" is derived from the Greek word *martys,* meaning "witness."

When Mary's father invokes the family's situation back in Korea, we see the convergence of the two above mentioned elements of Christian witnessing; the imperative to compare and the element of suffering for one's faith. Mary's father constructs the suffering of his family back in Korea as moments of witnessing against which Mary is compelled to compare her own suffering, which she ultimately determines to be less severe. In this we see the convergence of both elements of "witness" and, given that this call to compare is made at a moment of discontentment, we can see the deployment of witnessing as a disciplinary action.

This act of disciplining, structured on the Christian notion of witnessing, is internalized by Mary Paik Lee and erupts throughout the narrative, emerging within the very structure of the narrative itself. For example, Mary demonstrates a fervent desire to finish high school, sacrificing a great deal and working extremely hard to raise enough money to fund her education. However, during her education, she is stricken with the Spanish flu and is unconscious for most of one month. She is also stricken with temporary blindness, prompting her family to call for a doctor, who diagnoses her with severe malnutrition. As the doctor instructs Mary to eat "nourishing food, such as milk, eggs, and orange juice," Mary responds, "I laughed and said my family had never had such things in the house."[20] The doctor goes on to instruct Mary to rest her eyes completely for at least one year, ending her hopes of attaining a high school diploma. By responding with ironic laughter, Mary reveals a sense of bitterness born of disappointment and frustration. Her goal of obtaining an education, one that can be seen as an individualistic desire, is subverted.

After relating the story of her frustrated ambition and revealing a certain degree of bitterness, Mary then relates to the reader why her father takes a dangerous job in a quicksilver (mercury) mine despite the inherent risks to his health. She explains that her father took the job, which ultimately destroys his health, in order to send money back to Korea for his mother's sixtieth birthday. This tale of filial sacrifice is immediately followed by stories of national sacrifice; Mary incorporates into her personal recollections the historic events that led to the Korean uprising against the Japanese and the persecution of the Koreans who participated in the March 1, 1919 demonstration for independence. Mary then relates that her "grandparents, uncle, and relatives were all dragged off to camps where they were beaten and tortured to force them to admit that they had influenced their students to rebel and join the parade. My grandmother was blinded."[21] Because these stories of great hardship, acts of suffering and sacrifice committed for the larger familial or national good do not follow a narrative logic or chronological order, it becomes clear that these stories "discipline" Mary's own individualist desires and bitterness. That is, the sequence of the stories gives rise to the inevitable comparison of sufferings, a comparison that, again, minimizes Lee's suffering.

Thus, we see that witnessing (the act of witness provided by her father, her family, Korean nationalists) is used in the text to discipline Mary when she is critical of God and when she demonstrates an individualistic desire. However, this strategy is also invoked when she is critical of America. As her family disembarks from the boat that has brought them over from Hawaii to the mainland, the Paiks are accosted by some young white men who yell racial slurs and physically harass them. Mary questions her family's presence in a nation where they are unwanted because of their race. Again, her father responds to his daughter's rebellious questioning with the imperative to compare:

> He replied that we deserved what we got because that was the same kind of treatment that Koreans had given to the first American missionaries in Korea. . . . They showed by their action and good works that they were just as good as or even better than those who laughed at them. He said that is exactly what we must try to do here in America—study hard and learn to show Americans that we are just as good as they are. That was my first lesson in living and I have never forgotten it.[22]

The witness that Mary's father invokes here is the conduct of the American missionaries when they first arrive in Korea, a then hostile environment, which he deploys to discipline his daughter. In encouraging his daughter to model her life on the exemplary lives of the American missionaries, Mary's father conveys to his daughter the belief that through hard work, one can overcome all obstacles despite racial hatred and inequality. That is, through silent perseverance immigrants can overcome any obstacle. In this particular use of Christian witnessing, one can discern the complex intersection of a multitude of ideological forces; here Christianity, the myth of the American dream, and the model minority myth converge.[23] In this way, the structure of Christian witnessing is deployed in service of American ideology.[24] Just as the previous deployments of witnessing were used to discipline Mary during rebellious moments, this invocation of witnessing quells Mary's protests against racial oppression and compels her to comply with the demands of the dominant society.

While these tales of greater hardship are designed to silence Mary when she has resistant impulses, the effectiveness of this disciplinary strategy goes beyond the quelling of her rebelliousness. Given that the narrative repeatedly invalidates Mary Paik Lee's complaints by compelling her to compare her own situation to tales of greater hardship and persecution, it is no surprise that Lee internalizes this disciplinary impulse and discounts or diminishes her own suffering to the point of almost complete erasure. With only a few exceptions,[25] Lee demonstrates a reluctance or unwillingness to describe her own suffering; in one instance, she reduces an operation that she undergoes to one, vague sentence: "I had an operation at the St. Francis Hospital." This reticence contrasts sharply with the amount of detail she offers in the description of her husband's suffering.

> Most men recovered after the harvest, but H. M. continued to suffer and was miserable with the effects for thirty years. . . . One night the itching was so bad he felt a burning sensation. He woke up to find his body covered with a rash with big bumps. It was a frightening sight. His face and body were swollen like a balloon, and his eyes were swollen tight. . . . We went to the sulphur springs every weekend, and the swelling subsided somewhat, but the painful itching continued. When the rash was bad, a yellow pus came out all over his body. It was a very messy situation.[26]

Lee's detailed description of her husband's ailment is not the only instance where she goes into graphic detail about the physical suffering of those around her. Her son, Tony, born without muscles in his eyelids, must endure a painful operation at the age of eight. "The skin above and below the eyes had to be peeled back in order to transplant muscles to his eyelids. It was a very slow and painful ordeal that lasted for years, but he never cried or complained. . . . At the hospital, all the other children cried and screamed when their stitches were removed, but Tony always suffered in silence."[27] Like the other instances of suffering that Lee details in her narrative, the presence of these graphic descriptions can be explained, in part, by the centrality of Christianity in the narrative. In these descriptions, the theme of suffering, which is crucial to the narrative's construction of witnessing, invokes the privileged iconography of Christianity (the maimed body of Christ nailed to the crucifix), and takes as its focus the wounded body. However, the descriptions of H. M.'s skin condition and Tony's eye operation differ from the descriptions of her paternal family's persecution in Korea, her father's physical deterioration from working in the quicksilver mine, and the trials of the American missionaries in Korea in that they do not function to discipline Lee's rebelliousness. While the latter descriptions of suffering (moments of witnessing) directly or indirectly discipline Mary within the narrative for various rebellious impulses, the former cannot be said to serve the same purpose. This is not to say, however, that these moments do not function as moments of disciplinary witnessing.

Rather than disciplining Mary Paik Lee for insubordination, these graphic descriptions of physical pain target a different subject. The intended recipient of this disciplining becomes clear once we examine Lee's interaction with newer Korean immigrants in the text. In a more contemporary moment, Lee volunteers as an interpreter for a Korean Seniors' Center in the late 1970s and helps Korean immigrants new to America. Although Lee shares with these immigrants a common country of origin, she is struck by the differences between them. Lee states: "Ever since 1950, the new Korean arrivals have been from educated, high-class backgrounds. Life in America has changed so much that they don't understand the hardship we old-timers had to go through in this country. I told them: 'You have arrived in Heaven compared with the place we came to in 1906.'"[28] By characterizing modern life in America as "Heaven" relative to her own family's life of hardship, Lee employs the strategy of witnessing that her father used on her. Lee responds to the new immigrants' implied tales of hardships with her own family's experience in order to diminish or discount the magnitude of their suffering in America. Not only does Lee target newer immigrants, she also targets younger generations of Asian Americans. This can be seen in her final message to her readers. Lee states, "[s]he has written her book . . . because she wants young people to know the hardships that Asian immigrants have faced, so that they can appreciate their blessings today."[29] The tales of hardship, at the center of which is the maimed body, are intended to highlight how good the reader has it by comparison. Given that the imperative to compare is a disciplinary strategy, it becomes apparent that Mary Paik Lee aims to discipline her ungrateful, Asian American reader by invalidating or diminishing whatever protests or complaints they might have.

These graphic descriptions of physical suffering participate in the disciplinary witnessing formulated by *Quiet Odyssey* but they can also be said to bear a more traditional witness in that these "martyrs" are offered as models to be emulated. Perhaps the trait most highly praised by Lee, in addition to the ability to endure and survive physical suffering, is the ability to endure one's suffering in silence. While Lee's husband, H. M. suffered from a mysterious skin ailment for years, "he never complained, never mentioned his suffering to anyone." This stoic endurance is also praised in Lee's description of her son's eye operation: "It was a very slow and painful ordeal that lasted for years, but he never cried or complained. At the hospital, all the other children cried and screamed when their stitches were removed, but Tony always suffered in silence."[30] What is integral to the heroic quality of this suffering is the commitment to suffering in silence.

As such, the witnessing that the narrative performs imposes a "double silencing" upon the Asian American reader. Implicit in her demand that the readers "appreciate their blessings" and realize that they are in "Heaven," relative to her family's experience in America, is the assumption that such a comparison will neutralize or invalidate whatever protest the readers may wish to make. This disciplinary strategy also entails the ennobling of suffering in silence, a silence that is ultimately rewarded in the narrative. In the text's penultimate chapter, "Sons," Lee follows her tales of hardship and suffering with an account of her son Henry's extraordinary life; Henry is the first Asian American elected student body president of Georgetown, receives his Ph.D. from the Wharton School of Commerce and Finance, and eventually worked for the Federal Reserve Bank. Reflecting on his success, Lee states:

> I am always happy to see Orientals able to work almost everywhere now. America is the only place in the world where all people of all races can live in peace and harmony with one another. It is the responsibility of all persons to obey the laws of the country and do their part to maintain harmony. As my mother always said: "God is surely leading us in the right direction."[31]

Although Lee strives to expose the racism that she and her family experienced by relating numerous incidents of intolerance and racial hatred, these incidents are characterized as things of the past, giving the narrative a teleological movement whose predetermined endpoint is a more egalitarian, democratic America. The promise of the American Dream, according to Lee, is predicated upon one's obedience to American law (the unwritten as well as the written) and is figured as the reward for bearing silent witness. In this way, Lee bolsters the American Dream mythology with Christianity and disciplines her Asian American readers into silence.

THE POWER OF THE WITNESS

While Lee's strategy of Christian witnessing enacts a silencing, her strategy also enacts an "erasure" in that the spectacular display of the maimed, male body obscures the women of the narrative from view. Lee may go into graphic detail about the physical suffering of her male family members, but she only briefly mentions her own suffering, the suffering of her mother;[32] and almost completely ignores her sisters, daughters-in-law, etc. Given the privileged position enjoyed by the male body in Christian iconography, this focus is not surprising.

However, there is one exception to the invisibility of the female body. In the following passage, Lee describes the abuses suffered by her paternal family at the hands of the Japanese colonizers; "[M]y grandparents, uncle, and relatives were all dragged off to camps where they were beaten and tortured to force them to admit that they had influenced their students to rebel and join the parade. My grandmother was blinded."[33] It is striking that, out of the assumedly serious and extensive injuries suffered by her family members at the hands of the Japanese, the injury that Lee chooses to highlight in this description is her grandmother's loss of sight. As we will see, this injury is remarkable within the narrative precisely because it disenables Lee's grandmother from fulfilling the role that Lee carves out for women.

As I have already shown, the figures that are most spectacular and that are most likely to stand out in the readers' minds are the maimed bodies of the male family members; these graphic descriptions eclipse the scant, practically non-existent descriptions of the women's physical suffering. However, this is not to say that women do not serve a role within the work. As the figure of Mary's mother demonstrates, the function of women within *Quiet Odyssey* is not spectacular in nature but rather narrative. Throughout, Lee disrupts the flow of her own narrative with a very conscious and conspicuous framing of her mother as a storyteller. Lee states, "While we were living in Hawaii, Mother didn't have much housework to do in the grass hut, so she had time to talk to us about why we were the only ones in our family to have left Korea"[34] and elsewhere, "During our stay in Idria, Mother had time to talk to sit down and talk to us once in a while. We wanted to know how our grandparents and uncle were getting along in Korea. So for the first time, we learned about the tragic events that had taken place since we had left in 1905."[35] In this depiction of the mother as storyteller, we return to the more conventional understanding of the term of "witness" as one who conveys an experience or story to another through testimony. It is this function as witness that accounts for the relative invisibility of Lee's mother given that the preservation and perpetuation of these stories depends upon the transparency of the mother; Lee's mother must function like a pane of clear glass that allows us to apprehend the past without subjective distortion.

Lee's own narrative invisibility can be traced back to this concern for the truthfulness of testimony. Like her mother, Lee occupies the role of witness/storyteller and must, in the interests of believability, erase or subordinate the self in favor of the story. In this sense, Mary and her mother become vessels for the more male-defined stories of their male family members. This image of women as witnesses surrounding the spectacle of the maimed or wounded male body calls to mind the Biblical image of the four women who are gathered around the cross at Christ's crucifixion. As Robert Gordon Maccini puts it, the women at the scene of Christ's crucifixion serve a very clear purpose; "Indeed, as P. A. Kerrigan asserts, John regards the women at the cross as official witnesses who guaranteed juridically the events narrated."[36] As the use of the term "juridically" implies, central to the importance of the women in this scene is their ability to bear truthful witness. When viewed in this way, the witness is subordinate to the events being narrated, rendering the witness into a seemingly passive vessel for the story that must be told or to which they must attest.

However, as Maccini, citing J.M. Boice's *Witness and Revelation*, goes on to argue, while the witness in religious discourse serves a juridical function, his/her role exceeds the function of merely attesting to the veracity of a given event:

> Witness so considered is no mere witness in an original forensic sense but a religious witness, involving the presentation, verification, and acknowledgment of the claims of Jesus Christ.[37]

If we view Lee and her mother as witnesses within the narrative, then the above concept demonstrates that they are not passive vessels for the story but are instead active participants in a rhetorical project. While the testimony has the status of being "disinterested," within Christian witnessing, the witness him or herself is not in that they not only verify or affirm the truth of an occurrence, but interpret the meaning of that occurrence and then proceed to advocate on behalf of the resulting belief. Lee's mother, for example, does not simply relate the atrocities visited upon their family simply to verify that they happened; she relates these events to her children, and through Lee, to the reader, in order to advocate Korean independence.

As is perhaps evident by now, the work's religious nature is inextricable from its rhetorical nature. Regarding the Christian Gospels, Maccini notes; "There is disagreement regarding the literary genre(s) of the Gospels, but all are by nature rhetorical documents because they seek to persuade. Each of the Gospels has a particular strategy for addressing major rhetorical problems facing them."[38] If we regard Lee's text as an act of witnessing, then we see that the effacement of self is a strategy within a larger rhetorical project. The obfuscation of self, in this case, can thus be seen, ironically, as an act of authorial agency.[39] In fact, the ease with which her narrative can be appropriated as representative of others attests to the effectiveness of this strategy. Certainly, this is not to suggest that the erasure of self in *Quiet Odyssey* is not informed by oppressive, patriarchal structures within Korean American culture or within Christianity—but the fact that Lee's use of her authorial agency colludes with oppressive ideological structures does not negate the fact that it is an act of agency. Moreover, Lee's assumption of the authorial voice, her assumption of the power to craft a narrative and employ rhetorical strategies, can be seen as resistant to—or at the very least conflicting with— the ideologies that the novel, in part, perpetuates.

CONCLUSION

What I hope this current study has shown is that any examination of Lee's work must take into consideration her religious orientation. Religion provides her family with strength and comfort in desperate times and it informs the direction and shape of Lee's narrative. Factoring religion into our analysis gives us better insight into the complex position that Lee occupies as a Christian, Korean American woman and the powerful effect that various ideologies exert on her narrative. Located at the nexus of multiple ideologies, *Quiet Odyssey* is filled with the resulting contradictions and ambivalence; Lee's indictment of American racists and racism coexists with her belief in and propagation of the American Dream myth. While contradictions and ambivalence do characterize Lee's narrative, we must not lose sight of the rhetorical nature of the work because it is in Lee's assumption of the authorial voice, a voice that is, in this case, shaped by her religious orientation, that we can discern her exercise of agency.

NOTES

1. A quick glance at Asian American studies course syllabi available on the Internet will reveal that Chan's contributions to the text are almost always part of the reading assignment in classes teaching *Quiet Odyssey*.

2. Mary Paik Lee, *Quiet Odyssey: A Pioneer Korean Woman in America*, Sucheng Chan, ed. (Seattle: University of Washington Press, 1990), xiii.

3. Lee, *Odyssey*, xiii.

4. Ibid., xiv.

5. Ibid.,ix.

6. Ibid., xxxvi.

7. Ibid., xxxviii.

8. David K. Yoo, "Introduction: Reframing the Asian American Religious Landscape," in Yoo, ed., *New Spiritual Homes: Religion and Asian Americans,* (Honolulu: University of Hawai'i Press, 1999), 8–10.

9. In the appendix to *Quiet Odyssey*, Chan notes that she was careful not to inject the narrative with more militancy than she found in the original manuscript. It is for this reason that Lee retained some of the more "ingratiating" comments made by Lee in her narrative, reasoning that these comments were a reflection of her "contradictory postures" and should be retained because they demonstrate an ambivalence which Chan characterizes as "the hallmark of Asian American experience"(162). While Chan notes Lee's the conflicted nature of Lee's narrative, it is not explored to any great extent in Chan's framing of the work.

10. To disregard religion is to also do violence to the narrative itself in the sense that Christianity's presence is so pervasive in much of the work. Not only does Christianity inform much of the imagery that fills the narrative, it also gives the text a certain narrative continuity; throughout, regardless of the circumstances in which the family finds itself, their unwavering faith in God is expressed (or perhaps perpetuated) through the repeated utterance of the phrase, "God is surely leading us to the right place."

11. Lee, *Odyssey*, 48, 56.

12. Robert Holton, *Jarring Witnesses: Modern Fiction and the Representation of History,* (New York: Harvester Wheatsheaf, 1994), 165.

13. Sucheng Chan uses the word "spirited" to describe Lee's reaction to several incidences of bigotry in the Appendix (*Odyssey*, 161).

14. As Allison A. Trites argues in her work *New Testament Concept of Witness* (London: Cambridge University Press, 1977), the notion of witnessing in the Bible largely depends upon the juridical notion of a witness in trial. As such, the witness functions to convince both believers and nonbelievers in the validity of their faith. Robert Gordon Maccini, who also views witnessing in the Bible as a juridically informed notion, notes in *Her Testimony is True* (Sheffield, UK: Sheffield Academic Press, 1996): "Matthew, Mark, Luke and John are Evangelists not simply because they tell about Jesus Christ, but because they intend to invoke belief in him" (19).

15. Lee, *Odyssey*, 27.

16. Ibid., 23.

17. Jean-Pierre Jossua, *The Condition of the Witness*, trans. John Bowden (Paris: Les Editions du Cerf, 1985), 1.
18. Ibid, 87.
19. It is important to keep in mind that that suffering is a consequence of witnessing and that the two concepts should not be conflated. *See* Trites, *New Testament Concept of Witness*, 66.
20. Lee, *Odyssey*, 58.
21. Ibid., 61.
22. Ibid., 13–14.
23. Lee's father, in essence, invokes the myth of the model minority. This myth is one that applies to Asian Americans and paints them as hard working, successful, law-abiding, and unwilling to complain.
24. As Jung Ha Kim notes in her work, *Bridge-Makers and Cross-Bearers* (Atlanta: The American Academy of Religion, 1997), this convergence of ideologies can also be seen in the invocation of the Christian myth of God's "chosen people" to give divine meaning to the American Dream for Christian Korean Americans. Consequently, with predominantly Korean speaking immigrants as its main members, the Kyo-whe preaches a peculiar gospel of "making it" by the chosen people in the promised land, and thereby implicitly justifying oppressive systems of the dominant culture. By uplifting "the American way of life" as a "Christian" way of life, and rendering experienced oppression as the expected and "God appointed" fate for the chosen people, the Kyo-whe encourages its members to endure and "stay in their places" as prescribed both by their God and by the dominant culture (101–102).
25. "Soon after I arrived in San Francisco I became violently ill and had to call Allan to get an ambulance for me. I was freezing cold one minute and burning hot the next; I thought I had malaria. It took the hospital two weeks to find out that I had bacterial endocarditis from a germ I might have picked up in Manila. I had to have a painful penicillin treatment to clean out my veins and was in the hospital for two months" (*Odyssey*, 125).
26. Lee, *Odyssey*, 68–69.
27. Ibid., 114.
28. Ibid., 128.
29. Ibid., xvii.
30. Ibid., 114.
31. Ibid., 113.
32. Lee does mention that her mother almost died giving birth to her brother, Young Sun, on p.34 but what is different about this description is that she does not offer details about the physical suffering that her mother endures which contrasts sharply with her descriptions of her male family members.
33. Lee, *Odyssey*, 60–61.
34. Ibid., 619.
35. Ibid., 42.
36. Maccini, *Her Testimony is True*, 202.

37. Ibid., 57.
38. Ibid., 20.
39. Clearly, the conflation of "self" and "agency" is problematic but the exploration of this issue is beyond the scope of the current study. What is important here is the more common understanding that the "self" is the location or locus of "agency."

DIRECTION

ENCHANTING DIASPORAS, ASIAN AMERICANS, AND THE PASSIONATE ATTACHMENT OF RACE

DAVID KYUMAN KIM

With persistence and inevitability, the past catches the present, just as the present always looks to possible futures. Given the fluidity of memory and hope, and given the conditions of our age marked by the paradoxical movements toward increasing fragmentation and intensifying globalization, we still find value, even virtue, in collective identities. In this essay, I approach the question and the viability of the category of religious experience by examining the fruitful associations between Asian American social experience and the concept of diaspora. The argument I make is that foregrounding race and diaspora—rather than simply immigration or other New World notions—in our interrogations of Asian American religions clarifies the existential predicament of Asian Americans.[1] In an attempt to identify the animating values and norms of this cultural identity, I explore what is involved in the project of revealing the sacred in Asian and Pacific America.[2] In my discussion of the spirited contemporary interest in diaspora in Asian American studies, I argue that the discourses of diaspora and race are indications of a religious impulse. The thesis is not that diaspora and race displace the putative religious identities of Asian Americans as Hindus, Buddhists, Christians, Muslims, and so on. Rather, the hunch on which I am proceeding is that attention to the dialectic of diaspora and race will provide a deeper understanding of the cultural, political, social, and economic contexts of Asian American religious practices. In other words, the consideration of race and Asian American diasporas begins to reveal forms of agency that constitute ways of being in the world that express the psychic and spiritual effects of the racial existence of Asian Americans. The racial logic that animates Asian American lives, especially as mediated by diaspora and racism, revolves around the occupation by Asian Americans of what I call "ambiguous alterity". This is to say that Asian America represents the or *an* ambiguous other to both American *and* Asian nationalisms. I conclude the chapter with reflections on how ambiguous alterity, diaspora, religion, and the totem of race function as mediators of the suffering and hope of Asian Americans. The task is not to provide an umbrella concept for all Asian American religious practices. Instead, this interrogation of diaspora and race is an effort to lay out a theoretical—and thereby formal—framework that begins to point to ways in which we can begin to integrate the study of Asian American religions and religious practices into the broader scholarship on ethnicity and race.

The study of diasporas and the cousin-concept of transnationalism have drawn the attention of a growing number of scholars in Asian American studies. There are important reasons for this development. Among the most pressing are the difficulties that have accrued in making clear determinations about race versus ethnicity vis-à–vis Asian Americans.[3] Compounding this ambiguity is the imperative of implicating Asian American experience beyond an American nationalist perspective that has tended to ignore the past, present, and future influence of Asia.[4] This is not to say that the shift in focus to globalization and diasporas is seen as unproblematic within the intramural concerns of Asian American studies.[5] This notwithstanding, some consensus has been reached that an abiding concern with diaspora and race will continue to animate Asian American studies and Asian Americans in general for some time to come.

The interest in diaspora in Asian American studies has coincided with an incredible proliferation of commentaries on the concept of diaspora in the last decade or so.[6] We can detect a pattern in many of these reflections on diaspora.[7] Essays on the subject typically begin with an etymological account of the Greek origins of the term diaspora, particularly as "dispersion". This is followed by an excursus on the original identification of diaspora with the Jews and a reiteration of the historical narrative of diaspora and exodus. The narrative begins with the primordial flight from Palestine through the exile in Babylon and on through the destruction of the second Temple, all ending with the modern Jewish experience.[8] The historical account is usually contrasted with "modern"—read "secular"—diasporas, in contrast with some characterization of the religious character of the Jewish diaspora, for example, as a theology of exile. Once the author notes that the founding of the state of Israel has demythologized Jewish diaspora consciousness, the trajectory of the argument proceeds to a discussion of the secularization of the diaspora concept among Jews, which has corresponded to the generalization of the concept of diaspora to non-Jewish, mobile populations. In other words, diaspora is identified with peoples who are global, displaced, and cosmopolitan.[9] Among the texts that employ the trope of diaspora, perhaps the most commonly cited and presumably exemplary formulation for the new or postmodern form of diaspora is Paul Gilroy's *Black Atlantic*. Gilroy invokes the Black Atlantic as a heuristic, utopian imaginary that captures the collective experiences of the African diasporas, dispersed, largely through slavery, all over the world and throughout history. Gilroy's Black Atlantic is a good example of the narrative and cohesive power of diasporas. Furthermore, it is important to note that some contention of liberation or emancipation is the operative norm identified with most of the new versions of diaspora. For example, the appropriation of the trope of diaspora and its inflection in the allegory of the Exodus has been a central motif in liberation and political theologies.[10]

Given these theoretical considerations associated with the concept of diaspora, we should ask, what is at stake in the claims to diaspora in Asian American studies? *What is so enchanting about diaspora for Asian American intellectuals and, by extension, for Asian American consciousness?*[11] I mentioned liberation or emancipation as one of the normative concerns attached to diaspora. Other moral struggles associated with modern and postmodern diasporas include displacement, alienation, migration, cultural nationalism, dislocation, colonialism, home and homelessness, transnationalism, and, of course, hybridity. Part of the allure of diaspora derives from the increasing belief in the real and perceived permeability between Asia and Asian America, especially in consideration of structural and local influences in racial and ethnic formations. For example, it seems highly unlikely that Japanese Americans would have suffered internment during World War II if it had not been the case that their perceived allegiance was with Japan and not the United States. They were interned despite demonstrations of loyalty and patriotism to the U.S. Nonetheless, there was no attempt on the level of the federal government to distinguish Japanese Americans from the Japanese. This is permeability.

Racial and ethnic existence for Asian and Pacific Americans unfolds within the histories of oppression and resistance to oppression that have animated Asian American studies from its inception.[12] And yet the felt necessity of establishing the legitimacy of Asian American experience and Asian American studies reflects the peculiarities of academic culture as well as the larger issue of the persistent difficulty of placing and naming Asian America as an evolving phenomenon.[13] A couple of counterexamples are instructive here. Note how Sander Gilman and Steven Katz are able to establish, without much critical resistance, the claim that Jews are the "obvious other" to European modernity (evidenced by the ever evolving forms of anti-Semitism available). Note also how the sense that the legacy of white supremacy in America—at least within what some might call the mainstream American mind—is a reflection that blacks are considered the "obvious other" of American race consciousness. Within the contexts of these cultural and social imaginaries, Asian Americans remain hard to place within the American racial hierarchy.[14] For example, naming Chinese American experience as part of a larger historical narrative of the Chinese diaspora can, on the one hand, serve as a resistance to the reduction of Chinese American experience to the boundaries of the Americas. On the other hand, this move also introduces confusion as to the appropriate location of Chinese Americans in regard to nationalist loyalties (to China? to the U.S.?). The treatment of nuclear physicist Wen Ho Lee is an obvious example of this ambiguity. From the standpoint of American culture and its political landscape, foreignness continues to stick to the bodies and communities of Asian Americans. This suggests Asian Americans as the ambiguous other not only of American racial discourse but also of various Asian nationalisms. In short, these are the conditions under which diasporas enchant Asian America.

While issues of political efficacy and representation as well as cultural authenticity lie at the heart of the current debates over Asian American diasporas, it seems that the appeal to diaspora is part of a self-conscious process of the invention of traditions. This seems clear from claims such as the one made by the literary critic David Palumbo-Liu that "one can't name diaspora until *after* the fact . . . [Thus,] the concept of diaspora [can be regarded] as an enabling fiction, as a pretext for the exposition of profound notions of the national, of race, ethnicity, and history."[15] The construction of these theoretical and aesthetic articulations of diaspora vis-à-vis race is akin to Charles Taylor's notion of the articulation of constitutive goods in so far as diaspora represents the creative expression of the humanization of Asian America.[16] To name a people, a history, or a tradition is to work toward the articulation and expression of the sublime objects that facilitate our abilities to make meaning in the world. After all, would the Jews or the Armenians have survived in their cultures and in their collective psyches without a sense of inclusion and participation in a diaspora? The inculcation of these stories and narratives of collective life (call them nations, communities, diasporas) is as much a matter of forgetting as it is of memory. The cohesion of the narratives of diaspora, nation, and race makes sense only in terms of the kinds of passionate attachments that people have. Certainly, Palumbo-Liu is right when he argues that the discourse of diaspora is often used as a litmus test for conservative and conserving predilections for establishing what it means to be authentically Chinese, Indian, and so on.[17] The concern here is the formation of new ethnic identities in the diaspora within new states, as in the United States. "Under such conditions, the role of diasporic culture comes to occupy a central role, for it is in this realm of representation that the psychic displacements and spatio-temporal disjunctures we've remarked upon may be reconciled— the diasporic *imaginary*, in consolidating disparate elements of cultural life under one rubric, is looked to for a unitary moment in an otherwise fraught existence."[18] Indeed, if there is a moral to learn from a text like Hobsbawm and Ranger's *The Invention of Tradition*, it is that the practice of constructing and contriving traditions has not often been used by progressives to resist authority. Instead, it has frequently been a means of governmental control over mass societies after the dissolution of smaller forms of collective life (village, family, and so on). In other words, the construction of traditions became a necessary procedure for finding alternative means of holding these disparate groups together. This speaks to the power of common symbols and narratives, as well as to the negative (and I would add functionalist and often reductionistic) use of collective identities such as diaspora.

And yet, one might say that the kind of allegiance, solidarity, and affiliation associated with the tropes of diaspora and race involve psychic commitments that are analogous to those associated with religious life. Diaspora and race have tremendous affective power in the lives of Asian Americans. Again, this is not to argue that something like "the Indian diaspora" or "the Chinese diaspora" is an object of worship.[19] The point is not to emphasize the idolatrous potential of collective identities and the cultures associated with these identities. The dangers of this form of religious orientation—and I apply the category of religion here with severe caution—have been demonstrated again and again. On the other hand, there is plausibility to the notion that racialized and diasporic identities and histories and narratives operate along lines similar to civil religion, for example.[20] In order to gain a sense of how the collective narratives of diasporas and race remain compelling and necessary, it is necessary to understand that there must be some kind of sacralization of these identities. Presumably, this involves what Huizinga called "play," particularly in regard to the suspension of the conditions of the ordinary and the everyday.[21] And such suspensions from the everyday require forgetting and remembering, which is to say, finding new ways of living life such that it becomes possible to foresee displacing the dehumanizing forces of racist cultures and symbolic economies. In other words, the articulation of racial identities—diasporic or otherwise—requires a disruption analogous to the uncanny effects of the modernist sublime.[22]

How might this work, that is, to plausibly frame the understanding of diaspora and race as elements, indeed constitutive elements, of a religious consciousness, of a passionate attachment? The mediating factor I am identifying here is the capacity of diaspora and race to symbolize particular moral ideals, and thereby to operate as totems that provide meaning in the everyday life of Asian Americans. In other words, the retroactive and *pro*spective construction of Asian American collective identities, as well as the invention of Asian American traditions through the enabling fictions of diaspora, race, and ethnicity, reflect moral and existential commitments that speak to the religious and spiritual condition and consciousness of Asian American experience. The question here is: What would it mean to consider identity formation in light of diaspora and race as a religious and spiritual enterprise?

The impulse behind the sacralization of identity (or what Hans Mol calls "the process of becoming" or "the making sacred" of identity) is to establish order and to organize experience through the stabilization of symbol systems and meanings.[23] This process arises from the dialectics of difference and identity, and of differentiation and integration. The presupposition here is a belief "that an interpretation (*any* interpretation) of reality is necessary for the wholeness (and wholesomeness) of individual and society. The identity of either depends on a continuous fitting and consistent interpretation of features and events in one's surroundings."[24] As I have noted, foreignness is a feature of the racialization of Asian Americans, even for those of us who choose not to affirm it. Even for Asian Americans who claim citizenship, structural as well as cultural conditions require a negotiation with the perception of one's status as a foreigner. In part, the power of collective diasporic or racial identities is a question of whether there is a sacralization of the "profane" objects of racial and ethnic identities, in particular as these identities are spun out into grand narratives of diasporas. Is the reconstruction of collective memories and experience as diaspora also a transfiguring and reinterpreting of these individual and collective identities as sacred symbols? Is it not the case that the objectified concepts of the Chinese diaspora or the Indian diaspora, and so on—that is, efforts to cohere and transform fractured and destabilized peoples—are in fact products of meaning making? Can we not plausibly envision the inventions of traditions that contribute to the self-understanding and existential reality of being Asian American as, at minimum, approximate forms of religious practice? What I hope to convey here is how diaspora constructions can represent the becoming and transformation of dispersed and racialized peoples through a symbolization that marks a renewed engagement and participation within the cultural and political realities of late modernity. Or to use Taylor's expressivist idiom, the

Good of race, of diaspora, becomes manifest in its expression, in its articulation of the attendant narratives and values about what it means to be Korean, Black, and so on.

In laying claim to diaspora and race as totems of Asian American experience, I acknowledge that I am already stretching the meaning of the category of totem.[25] Diaspora and race are not technically "objects," as in tangible objects. Instead, what I am alluding to is the epistemological objectification of diaspora and race concepts, as in the Marxist sense that ideology is an object of consciousness; or, employing a Hegelian iteration, diaspora is a representation of a collective experience that symbolizes the spirit of the people. Thus, whereas more conventional or familiar forms of totems are, say, renderings of the tree of life, or the flag "Old Glory," or the crucifix, or the Star of David, or the statue of the Buddha, the construction of traditions of diaspora and race takes shape in narratives of common struggles and aspirations. For example, from the experiences of immigration and the simultaneous induction into the racial system of American life, we can find the "sacred texts" of Asian America. These are the stories and articulate silences of families and communities, of exile, immigration, discrimination, racism, and other struggles for survival. The narratives of diasporas take shape and reenforce in their capacity as psychic resources for the senses of shared histories, families, and contested definitions of "national cultures" among Asian Americans. In other words, the totemization of race and diaspora for Asian Americans can be more than merely organizing principles and concepts around which we can gather for political purposes. Race and diaspora reflect crucial psychic and existential needs and conditions. On the other hand, the task is not to romanticize immigration or to naturalize the racialization of Asian Americans to the experiences of Blacks in America. Rather, it is an interrogation of the uniqueness of the dialectic of race and diaspora, in ways that resist easy syntheses and reductions and also suggest how race and diaspora animate the spirit and souls of Asian America. Asian American diasporas and ethnicities are distinct from yet mutually constituted by the racial logic that counts Asian Americans as perpetual foreigners.

The language of totem and the use to which I am putting it derive from a reading of the classical sociologist Emile Durkheim. Most salient to this discussion is Durkheim's claim that religion is "the way of thinking characteristic of collective existence."[26] What Durkheim meant by this claim is not that all forms of society and culture are necessarily forms of religion; rather, he was referring to the ways moral and social ideals define a society or a people. These ideals are "sacred collective representations that promote moral unity and well-being. They are cherished social values, beliefs, and goals, the soul of a society."[27] Durkheim had in mind practical, concrete ideals that structure collective and individual lives as well as actions.

What is important to keep in mind in Durkheim's notions of totems and ideals, as well as the social and moral codes that define societies, is that he is attempting to identify sources of commitment and faith that mediate the relationship between individuals and societies. In contrast, I am arguing not that diaspora and race always function as forms of control over Asian Americans by societal and state apparatuses, although that is certainly a factor. (The stakes in the configuration and results of the U.S. Census reflect this ambiguity.) Instead, I am reading how the inscriptions of diaspora and race serve as forms of consciousness, that is, as totems that have an authority and power over the kinds of moral, political, and existential commitments and actions that Asian Americans will have. The complexity of these factors is present in so-called ethnic religious communities. For example, among evangelical Christian Korean Americans, there is a synthesizing and deconstructing of racial and ethnic identities as religious identities, as in "I am a Christian first, then a Korean American." While these kinds of testimonials may be true in terms of the conscious commitments of these Korean Americans, it remains an empirical fact that their Christian identities are reinforced by their worship together with other Korean Americans. In other words, the cohesion and coherence of their communities and their individual identities derive in part from their participation in ethnically and racially homogenous collectives. To wit, there is a depth to racial identity and an impulse in the articulation of diaspora that transcends individual experiences through the call to envision participation in a social imaginary.

According to Durkheim, the relationship between and among individuals and the moral ideals that societies pose for these individuals is one of respect. The upshot for Durkheim is that the religious is that which establishes a moral existence between or among individuals, in particular in the promotion of moral communities. In other words, collective representations are sacred in so far as they enable the creation and maintenance of a moral, collective existence. A Durkheimian reading of the collective representations of diaspora and race reveals the psychic power and moral authority found in expressions of migration, perceptions of foreignness, voluntary and involuntary resistance to acculturation and assimilation, and other aspects of Asian American life. While it is convenient to reduce these to the loss of tradition, it is more probing to consider these experiences in terms of the loss of moral norms and the shifts in sources of authority and legitimacy. The point here is that the Durkheimian interpretation of the relationship between individuals and empowering and moral collective representations and existence—for example, between Asian American sub-jects, race, and diaspora—is a sacred one.[28]

Nonetheless, it is crucial to recognize the limitations of this interpretation. For example, I do not want to go as far as Durkheim does when he argues that the power that society has in terms of moral authority is analogous to the relationship between the faithful and their god. However, I acknowledge that the kind of psychic hold that the elements of diaspora and race have on Asian American consciousness is certainly similar to the passionate attach-ments of religious faith. Perhaps the clearest example of this is the figuration of diaspora in the idea of home and homeland.[29] On the one hand, nostalgia for a homeland functions as a kind of repository in the invention of Asian American cultures and traditions.[30] Jon Stratton recently wrote: "perhaps the key element in the modern ideological formation of diaspora [is] the notion of having had to leave, or having left, for some reason, the place, not just of one's own origin—one's birthplace—but of the origin of one's people."[31] Or as Avtar Brah poignantly put it:

> Where is home? On the one hand, "home" is a mythic place of desire in the diasporic imagination. In this sense it is a place of no return, even if it is possible to visit geographical territory that is seen as the place of "ori-gin." On the other hand, home is also the lived experience of a locality.[32]

No doubt, there are obvious problems in this conception of home for post-immigrant generations of Asian Americans, for example in the ways the notion of home and homeland find inflections in racist discourse. This is all too clear in the baleful invective "Go back to where you came from." Nonetheless, it is hard to deny that in accounting for representations of col-lective existence of Asian Americans, some expression of home and memory is at play. For example, in the case of some Korean Americans, the reunifica-tion of Korea is in some way analogous to the imaginary of Palestine/Israel for the pre-twentieth century Jewish diaspora.[33] In the end, it seems clear that we require a dialectic that maintains the tensions between race and dias-pora for Asian Americans. Such a dialectic would mediate between what lit-erary critic Sau-ling Wong identifies as the race-imperative of "claiming America" and the diasporic imaginaries of being Chinese, being Indian, being Korean, and so on.[34] My conjecture is that such a complex of approaches and dispositions will reveal diaspora and race as psychic and spir-itual resources for Asian American experiences. Identifying and articulating common experiences through the active construction of the stories of dias-pora, for example, can give some shape to the moral commitments and reli-gious aspirations of a people. Cornel West suggests a similar reading of identity when he asks, "What is the moral content of one's cultural identity? And what are the political and existential consequences of this moral content and cultural identity?"[35] Elaborating on these, I ask: How are the moral ideals of diaspora and race—of home and homelessness, of displacement, alienation, in the final analysis, all forms of dehumanization—expressive of who we are as Asian America?

I want to be clear that the conceptual terrain I am laying out here is neither an attempt to argue that diasporic and racial identities are in fact religious identities that will replace "traditional" religious identities as Hindus, Sikhs, Buddhists, Christians, Muslims, Shamans, and so on; nor is it an effort to naturalize the sublime and the kind of transcendence associated with it. Instead, the admonition is to consider the disciplinary invocation of meta-tropes such as diaspora and race not for their domestication into so-called postmodern discourses but for the kind of social imaginaries they form. These are imaginaries of common histories, memories, the framing of particular spaces ("holy lands") and forms of sacred time.[36]

The religious and spiritual dimensions of race and diaspora point to the ways in which the construction of and identification with the moral narratives associated with diaspora and race can serve as resources of hope that provide the means for surviving in the face of the dehumanization that Asian Americans endure. The crucial issue is to determine the conditions under which we can read the creative construction of a diasporic imaginary as an articulation that empowers through clarifications of an ambiguous social existence. The ambiguity for Asian Americans lies largely in the competing commitments and demands between nationalist and cultural identities. As Charles Taylor suggests: "A formulation has power when it brings [a moral] source close, when it makes it plain and evident, in all its inherent force, its capacity to inspire our love, respect, or allegiance. An effective articulation releases this force, and this is how words have power."[37] Taylor is referring to notions of the Good that transcend yet ground ordinary experience, such as a commitment to benevolence. It may be that the passionate attachment to collective identities such as diaspora gains its power through its resonance with a commitment to resisting structures and forces that degrade and delegitimate. In this sense, the power of diaspora and race is certainly not exclusive to Asian Americans. Nonetheless, the fact that Asian Americans, like Blacks and Latinos, are consistently drawn back to a non-American identity suggests the necessary coherence of diaspora to racialized peoples.

While born in unstable conditions often marred by hatred and racism but also the focus of solidarity and hope, diaspora and race cohere ideals for racialized peoples. The creative articulation of collective life as a diaspora or as a race requires a form of practical reason; one that generates a transvaluation of racist values and traditions through the critical evaluation of the enduring narratives of living with and overcoming racism and hatred. The sublime logic in diaspora, even in race, is in the paradox of its inclusiveness, of its persistent indeterminacy, and the *real* effects it has in daily lives. As I noted, the account of diaspora I have given here is not meant as a suggestion that this kind of articulation of an existential condition is superior to or can displace the so-called "world religions." Rather, my goal is to show how the question of identity is also a question of participation in ways of being in the world that are meaningful for communities as well as individuals. In sum, through the transforming of moral visions—in the utopias and dystopias of diaspora and race—Asian Americans are striving to route their lives from the woundedness, absurdity, and despair of ambiguous alterity toward a sense of themselves that is spiritually and religiously meaningful and culturally profound.

NOTES

1. There is a tendency among academics and journalists to frame the experience of Asian Americans and Asian American religions as subjects largely defined by immigration and the associated displacements and longings for the departed homeland. While I do not deny the significance of these experiences, the narrative line in these accounts is often developed in comparison to the experiences of European immigrants to the United States. In brief, the presiding assumption, among sociologists and others, is that the European immigrant was able to assimilate into the American landscape and thus make ethnic identity largely optional. Political dispositions, cultural biases, and phenotypical differences are among the factors that deny the possibility for Asian Americans to exercise these kinds of ethnic options. For a discussion of European ethnic groups and ethnic options in America, see Mary C. Waters, *Ethnic Options: Choosing Identities in America.* (Berkeley: University of California Press, 1990).

2. An earlier version of this essay was presented at the conference "Revealing the Sacred in Asian America," held at the University of California, Santa Barbara, June 2000.

3. In part, there has been a tendency to identify or conflate the categories of ethnicity and race, especially in consideration of Asian Americans. This has been a rhetorical as well as an analytical problem. One of the central preoccupations in the study of race and ethnicity has been and continues to be categorization. For example, in regard to any ethnic or racial group, the fundamental question is who counts as a member of this group. In a similar vein, is race a category and set of experiences distinct from ethnicity? Is ethnicity a subset of a larger category of race? While most commentators do not argue that either race or ethnicity is dispensable, it is true that lines are drawn in arguing for the predominance of one category over the other. In my reading, those who favor ethnicity as a more effective organizing category than race (e.g., Spickard and Burroughs; Cornell) see a

focus on ethnicity as less preoccupied by the contingencies and oppressions of racial caste systems and thereby emphasize the constructive possibilities of ethnic cultures and articulations. Those who show a preference for the analytic of race over ethnicity (e.g., Omi and Winant) maintain that vigilance against racism requires a direct engagement with the idioms of race and racialization. Given the significance of questions of categorization and the forms of identities that follow, the constitutive role of power—broadly meaning structural, institutional, political, and moral forces of distributive dispensations—and the persistence of racism will continue to sustain these debates. In my view, it is crucial to integrate race and ethnicity as central categories for self-understanding and as sources and sites of collective and political identity for Asian Pacific Americans. Employing racial analysis, is not, as Spickard and Burroughs suggest, letting "the bad guys win," because such a move somehow implies complicity. On the contrary, it is an acknowledgment of the presiding idioms of the day, and is thus realist. Racism is fought through direct agonistic struggles, such as the engagement of dehumanizing as well as humanizing cultures. Paul Spickard and W. Jeffrey Burroughs, "We are a People," and "Ethnicity, Multiplicity, and Narrative: Problems and Possibilities," in Paul Spickard and W. Jeffrey Burroughs, eds., *We Are a People: Narrative and Multiplicity in Constructing Ethnic Identity.* (Philadelphia: Temple University Press, 2000), 1–19, 244–253; Stephen Cornell and Douglas Hartmann, *Ethnicity and Race: Making Identities in a Changing World.* (Thousand Oaks, CA: Pine Forge, 1998), 15–38; Michael Omi and Howard Winant, *Racial Formation in the United States* (New York: Routledge, 1986).

4. A number of recent writers have begun making arguments along this line. Notable in this genre are the essays in Evelyn Hu-Dehart, ed., *Transpacific Articulations: Asian Americans in the Age of Globalization* (Philadelphia: Temple University Press, 1999) and David Palumbo-Liu, *Asian/American: Historical Crossings of a Racial Frontier* (Stanford: Stanford University Press, 1999).

5. As in the case of the debate over ethnicity versus race, there is a corresponding argument among Asian American intellectuals that is largely an issue of political strategies. A distilling of this debate comes to the question of whether the emancipatory goals of Asian Americans are better served through an identification with cultural and political communities defined along panethnic or racial lines (e.g., as "Asian Pacific Americans") or along ethnic or national origins lines (e.g., as "Chinese and Chinese Americans"). As with the ethnicity versus race debate, it seems that the panethnic versus neonationalist schism is a conflict at cross-purposes. A comprehensive approach that acknowledges the hold and power of panethnic/racial identities as well as ethnic/neo-nationalist identities is not only more persuasive but also more effective and realistic. Certainly the presentation of identity is often context-determined. If the aspiration is to, on the one hand, fight racism and, on the other, determine a positive cultural content to Asian Pacific American identities, then we must seek a way of representing both sides of these debates in our rhetoric as well as cultural and political judgements and analyses. The trick is to be able to account for the distinctions *and* mutual constitution of race, ethnicity, diaspora, and traditions. See Lowe, "Heterogeneity, Hybridity, Multiplicity: Asian American

Differences," in Lisa Lowe, *Immigrant Acts: On Asian American Cultural Politics* (Durham, NC: Duke University Press, 1996), 60–83. For a critique of Lowe's position, see especially, Susan Koshy, "The Fiction of Asian American Studies," *Yale Journal of Criticism* 9:2 (1996): 315–347.

6. The founding of the journal *Diaspora* in 1990 is a convenient landmark in an effort to mark the institutionalization of diaspora studies.

7. A working model here is James Clifford's classic essay "Diasporas," in James Clifford, *Routes: Travel and Translation in the Late Twentieth Century* (Cambridge, MA: Harvard University Press, 1997), 244–278.

8. Tölölyan argues for a contrast between the modern diasporas and the three "classical" diasporas of the Jews, Greeks of Late Antiquity, and the Armenians. Khachig Tölölyan, "Rethinking Diaspora(s): Stateless Power in the Transnational Moment," *Diaspora* 5:1 (1996): 9–16. This position appears to be an attempt to suggest a historical significance to these so-called classical diasporas in opposition to the proliferation of the use of the category of diaspora to any peoples who are migrant, exilic, and so on.

9. See Tölölyan, ibid; also Martin Baumann, "Shangri-La in Exile: Portraying Tibetan Diaspora Studies and Reconsidering Diaspora(s)," *Diaspora* 6:3 (1997): 377–404.

10. For example, Michael Walzer. *Exodus and Revolution* (New York: Basic Books, 1984). See also, James H. Cone, *God of the Oppressed* (San Francisco: Harper & Row, 1975), 62–83.

11. This is not to inquire whether or not Asian American intellectuals actually lead Asian American communities. On the other hand, it is the case that Asian American intellectuals and academics are engaged in coming to determinations about the character of Asian American communities and the nature of the values and ideals that animate these communities and individuals. In other words, Asian American intellectuals, when engaged in the study of Asian Americans, are trying to understand the conditions that shape Asian American experiences.

12. "Introduction" in Omi and Winant, 1–13.

13. Rey Chow, *Writing Diaspora: Tactics of Intervention in Contemporary Cultural Studies* (Bloomington: Indiana University Press, 1993), 99–143.

14. Okihiro makes this argument pointedly in "Is Yellow Black or White?" in Gary Okihiro, *Margins and Mainstreams: Asians in American History and Culture* (Seattle: University of Washington Press, 1994), 31–63. Cf. Sander Gilman, "Introduction," in Sander Gilman and Steven T. Katz, *Anti-Semitism in Times of Crisis* (New York: New York University Press, 1991); and Cornel West, *Race Matters* (Boston: Beacon, 1993), 1–8.

15. Palumbo-Liu, *Asian/American*, 355.

16. Charles Taylor, *Sources of the Self* (Cambridge MA: Harvard University Press, 1989).

17. Palumbo-Liu, *Asian/American*, 346.

18. Ibid., 350.

19. For a counter-argument to the "quasi-sacred" character of ethnicity, see Herbert Gans, "Symbolic Ethnicity and Symbolic Religiosity: Towards a Comparison of Ethnic and Religious Acculturation," *Ethnic and Racial Studies* 17:4 (1994): 577–592.

20. See Bellah, "Religious Evolution," and "Civil Religion in America," in Robert Bellah, *Beyond Belief: Essays on Religion in a Post-Traditional World* (Berkeley: University of

California Press, 1970), 20–52, 168–192.

21. Johan Huizinga, *Homo Ludens: A Study of the Play Element in Culture* (New York: Harper & Row, 1970), 32–3.

22. The argument here runs along similar lines taken in Slavoj Zizek, *The Sublime Object of Ideology* (New York: Verso, 1989).

23. Cf. S. N. Eisenstadt and Bernard Giesen, "The Construction of Collective Identity," *European Journal of Sociology* 36 (1995): 72–102.

24. Hans Mol, *Identity and the Sacred: A Sketch for a New Social-scientific Theory of Religion* (New York: Oxford University Press, 1976), 9.

25. Emile Durkheim, *The Elementary Forms of the Religious Life,* trans. K. E. Fields, (New York: Free Press, 1995), "Book II", especially, 99–241.

26. Quoted in Mark S. Cladis, *A Communitarian Defense of Liberalism: Emile Durkheim and Contemporary Social Theory* (Stanford: Stanford University Press, 1992), 116–118.

27. Ibid.

28. Durkheim, *Elementary Forms,* 207–225, 418–448.

29. Edward W. Said, "Invention, Memory, and Place," *Critical Inquiry* 26 (2000): 175-192. Cf. Toni Morrison, "Home," in Waneema Lubiano, ed., *The House that Race Built: Black Americans, U.S. Terrain* (New York: Pantheon, 1997), 3–12.

30. See, for example, the fascinating account of nostalgia developed in Svetlana Boym, *The Future of Nostalgia* (New York: Basic Books, 2001).

31. Jon Stratton, "(Dis)placing the Jews: Historicizing the Idea of Diaspora," *Diaspora* 6:3 (1997): 301.

32. Quoted in Stratton, ibid., 316. Cf. Toni Morrison's powerful contrast between "the house that race built"—a house of hatred and discrimination and violence—and the *home* in which one does not forget the history and experiences of racism but always bears in mind the specificity of race. Morrison suggests that in a home, one asks: "How to be both free and situated; how to convert a racist house into a race-specific yet non-racist home. How to enunciate race while depriving it of its lethal cling?" Morrison, *Home*, 5.

33. Nancy Abelmann and John Lie, *Blue Dreams: Korean Americans and the Los Angeles Riots* (Cambridge, MA: Harvard University Press, 1995), 49–84.

34. Sau-ling C. Wong, "Denationalization Reconsidered: Asian American Cultural Criticism at a Theoretical Crossroads," *Amerasia Journal* 21:1 & 2 (1995): 1–28.

35. Cornel West, "The New Cultural Politics of Difference," in *Keeping Faith: Philosophy and Race in America* (New York: Routledge, 1993), 30.

36. See Said, "Invention, Memory, and Place," Also W. J. T. Mitchell, "Holy Landscapes: Israel, Palestine, and the American Wilderness," *Critical Inquiry* 26 (2000), 193–223.

37. Taylor, *Sources of the Self,* 96.

CONTRIBUTORS

Rudiger V. Busto is Assistant Professor of American Ethnic Religions at Stanford University. His interests are in Pacific Islander/Asian American and Chicano/a religious histories and cultures.

Carolyn Chen is a postdoctoral fellow at the Institute for the Advanced Study of Religion at Princeton University. She received her Ph.D. in Sociology from the University of California at Berkeley. Her current project examines religious conversion among immigrants from Taiwan in the Southern California area.

Peter Yuichi Clark is an ordained American Baptist minister and the chaplain administrator at Alta Bates Summit Medical Center in Berkeley. He has contributed articles to the *Journal of Pastoral Care, Pastoral Psychology*, and *Semeia*, and essays in *Generativity and Adult Development*, edited by Dan McAdams and Ed de St. Aubin (American Psychological Association, 1998); the *American National Biography*, edited by John A. Garraty (Oxford University Press, 1999); and *Parenthood in America*, edited by Lawrence Balter (ABC-CLIO, 2000). Peter holds a Ph.D. in religious studies from Emory University.

Joanne Doi is a Ph.D. student at the Graduate Theological Union, Berkeley. Her research areas include contextual theologies, pilgrimage and ritual studies, and Asian American historiography. Joanne is also a Maryknoll Sister, who served in the Peru/Ecuador Region (in the southern Andes) from 1983 to 1994.

Thomas J. Douglas is a Ph.D. candidate in the Department of Anthropology at the University of California, Irvine. He is currently engaged in field research among the Cambodian immigrant communities of Long Beach, California, and Seattle, Washington. He is the recipient of a Religion

341

and Immigration Dissertation Fellowship provided by the Social Science Research Council, and has also received support from the Department of Anthropology at the University of California, Irvine.

Madeline Duntley is Associate Professor of Religious Studies at the College of Wooster where she teaches and publishes in the fields of North American religions, ritual studies, and history of Christianity. She is working on a monograph on Japanese American (Protestant, Catholic, Buddhist) religion in urban Seattle, covering the period from 1899 to 2001.

Sheba George received her Ph.D. in Sociology from the University of California at Berkeley in 2001 and is currently a visiting scholar at the Institute for the Study of Social Change in Berkeley. Her dissertation project, conducted among South Asian Christians in the United States, focused on the impact of immigration on gender relations in the spheres of work, home, and church. She has published several articles on South Asian Christian social relations, and is currently working on a forthcoming monograph titled, *When Women Come First: Gender and Class in Transnational Migration among Indian Christian Immigrants.*

Himanee Gupta is studying the relationship between the Hinduizing of India's political culture and the growth of an affluent upper-caste Hindu community of Indian immigrants in the United States as part of her doctoral work in the Department of Political Science at the University of Hawai'i at Manoa. A longtime journalist, she teaches American politics and political theory courses as a lecturer in the department.

Jane Naomi Iwamura is Assistant Professor of Religion and American Studies & Ethnicity at the University of Southern California. She has published articles on Asian American religions and religious experience, as well as on the representation of Asian religions in American popular culture, in *Semeia, Amerasia Journal*, and in the volume, *Religion and Popular Culture in America* (Forbes and Mahan, eds., University of California Press, 2000). She is also the co-organizer of the Asian and Pacific American Religions Research Initiative (APARRI).

Russell Jeung is an assistant professor of sociology at San Francisco State University. A faith-based community activist, he has organized Latino and Cambodian tenants to win a landmark housing lawsuit in Oakland, California. He wrote his Ph.D. dissertation, "Emerging Asian American

Pan-Ethnic Congregations: The Religious Construction of Symbolic Racial Identity," at the University of California, Berkeley.

David Kyuman Kim is a doctoral candidate in philosophy of religion and theology at Harvard University. His dissertation is on the religious dimensions of human agency with a particular focus on the formation of norms and values at the intersection of religion, politics, and morality. In addition to teaching at Harvard, he has been Visiting Assistant Professor in the Department of Religious Studies at Brown University.

Sanjoy Mazumdar teaches in the Department of Urban and Regional Planning, School of Social Ecology, and is affiliated with the Departments of Environmental Analysis and Design, Religious Studies, and Asian American Studies, at the University of California, Irvine. He holds a B. Arch. (Honours), and M.Arch. A. S., M. C. P., and Ph.D. from M.I.T. His research interests are in the area of cultures and their physical environments, including religion and ethnicity. He is past Chair of the Environmental Design Research Association (EDRA), and co-Chair of the Cultural Aspects of Design Network (CADN). His publications appear in many journals and books.

Shampa Mazumdar has a B.A. (Honours) in History from Calcutta University, an M.A. and a Ph.D. in Sociology from Northeastern University, Boston. Her research interests are in the sociology of religion, sacred space, Asian Indian immigrant communities, religion and women, and in home environments. Her publications appear in the *Journal of Architectural and Planning Research, Journal of Environmental Psychology, Environment and Behavior, Environments, Annual Review of Women in World Religions*, and in several books and proceedings. She has taught at Northeastern University, and is currently teaching at the University of California, Irvine.

Pyong Gap Min is Professor of Sociology at Queens College and the Graduate Center of the City University of New York. He is the author of three books, including *Caught in the Middle: Korean Communities in New York and Los Angeles* (University of California Press, 1996), the winner of the 1997 National Book Award in Social Science by the Association for Asian American Studies and a co-winner of the 1998 Outstanding Book Award by the Asia and Asian America Section of the American Sociological Association. He is the editor or co-editor of five books, four of them focusing on Asian Americans, which include *Religions in Asian America: Building Faith Communities* (Altamira Press, 2002).

Sandra Oh received her Ph.D in the department of Rhetoric at the University of California at Berkeley and currently teaches Asian American literature at the University of California, Santa Barbara. She is working on a monograph, "Martyrdom in Korean American Literature" which examines the centrality of martyrs in the works of Younghill Kang, Mary Paik Lee, and Nora Okja Keller.

Jaideep Singh is a Ph.D. candidate in the Department of Comparative Ethnic Studies at the University of California at Berkeley. He is currently teaching in the History Department at Oberlin College, and serves as the Managing Director for the Sikh Mediawatch and Resource Task Force (SMART), a Sikh media watch and civil rights organization. His dissertation focuses on illuminating three disparate case studies of contemporary, grassroots political organizing by Sikh communities in the United States. In addition, he is working on a documentary film excavating the lost history of Sikhs in the Second World War, through which he hopes to recover this forgotten segment of the Sikh community's collective history.

Paul Spickard teaches history and Asian American studies at the University of California, Santa Barbara. He has written or edited eleven books and scores of articles on race and religion. His newest books are *Pacific Diaspora: Island Peoples in the United States and Across the Pacific* (University of Hawai'i Press, 2002) and *Uncompleted Independence: Racial Thinking in the United States* (University of Notre Dame Press, 2003). He is also the co-organizer of the Asian and Pacific American Religions Research Initiative (APARRI).

Sharon A. Suh is an assistant professor of World Religions in the Department of Theology and Religious Studies at Seattle University. Sharon received her Ph.D. in Buddhist Studies from Harvard University in 2000 where she completed research on the topic of Buddhism, Gender, and Subjectivity in Korean America. Her research interests include Asian American religions, gender studies, Buddhism, and religion and immigration.

Timothy Tseng is Associate Professor of American Religious History and director of the Asian American Center at the American Baptist Seminary of the West. His research interests include Asian American religious history, race and religion in North America, Asian Christianity, the Chinese Diaspora, American evangelicalism, and Baptist history and polity.

William Kauaiwiulaokalani Wallace III is Professor of History and Chair of Hawaiian Language and Cultural Studies at Brigham Young University-Hawai'i. He is also a community lawyer and activist on behalf of the culture and sovereignty of the Hawaiian people.

INDEX